# Working Papers

for use with

## Fundamental
# ACCOUNTING PRINCIPLES

Volume 1

## FIFTEENTH CANADIAN EDITION

Revised by Praise Ma
and reviewed by Michelle Young

Mc
Graw
Hill
Education

# Working Papers

for use with

# Fundamental
# ACCOUNTING PRINCIPLES

Volume 1

## FIFTEENTH CANADIAN EDITION

**Kermit D. Larson**
University of Texas—Austin

**Tilly Jensen**
Athabasca University—Alberta

**Heidi Dieckmann**
Kwantlen Polytechnic University—British Columbia

Revised by Praise Ma
and reviewed by Michelle Young

**Working Papers for use with**
**Fundamental Accounting Principles**
**Fifteenth Canadian Edition**
**Volume 1**

ISBN-13: 978-1-25-910812-9
ISBN-10: 1-25-910812-0

1 2 3 4 5 6 7 8 9 10 MP 1 9 8 7 6

Printed and bound in Canada.

Director of Product Management: Rhondda McNabb
Product Manager: Keara Emmett
Executive Marketing Manager: Joy Armitage Taylor
Product Developer: Sarah Fulton
Supervising Editor: Jessica Barnoski
Plant Production Coordinator: Scott Morrison
Manufacturing Production Coordinator: Emily Hickey
Cover Design: Michelle Losier
Cover Image: Rachel Idzerda
Page Layout: Aptara®, Inc.
Printer: Maracle Press, Ltd.

# Contents

Name:_____

## Quick Study 1-1

_____
_____
_____
_____
_____
_____
_____
_____
_____
_____
_____
_____
_____

## Quick Study 1-2

a. _____

b. _____

c. _____

d. _____

e. _____

## Quick Study 1-3

a. _____
b. _____
c. _____
d. _____
e. _____
f. _____

## Quick Study 1-4

1. _SP_        5. _C_
2. _C_         6. _C_
3. _P_         7. _P_
4. _SP_

**Quick Study 1-5**

1.    d
2.    c
3.    b
4.    a
5.    d
6.    b
7.    b
8.    c

**Quick Study 1-6**

**Quick Study 1-7**

a. Business entity principle

b. Revenue recognisition principle

c. Cost principle

**Quick Study 1-8**

1.                                  4.

2.                                  5.

3.

## Quick Study 1-9

| | | |
|---|---|---|
| | a. | Delco performed work for a client located in China and collected 8,450,000 RMB (renminbi, the Chinese currency), the equivalent of about $1,320,000 Canadian. Delco recorded it as 8,450,000. |
| | b. | Delco collected $180,000 from a customer on December 20, 2017, for work to be done in February 2018. The $180,000 was recorded as revenue during 2017. Delco's year-end is December 31. |
| | c. | Delco's December 31, 2017, balance sheet showed total assets of $840,000 and liabilities of $1,120,000. The income statements for the past six years have shown a trend of increasing losses. |
| | d. | Included in Delco's assets was land and a building purchased for $310,000 and reported on the balance sheet at $470,000. |
| | e. | Delco's owner, Tom Del, consistently buys personal supplies and charges them to the company. |

## Quick Study 1-10

| | Assets | = | Liabilities | + | Equity |
|---|---|---|---|---|---|
| a. | $ 75000 | = | $ 40500 | + | Equity |
| | ∴ Equity = $ 75000 − $ 40500 = $34,500 | | | | |
| b. | $ 300000 | = | Liabilities | + | $85,500 |
| | ∴ Liabilities = $ 300000 − $85,500 = $ 2,14,500 | | | | |
| c. | Assets = $ 187500 + $ 95,400 | | | | |
| | ∴ Assets = $ 282900 | | | | |

## Quick Study 1-11

| | Assets | = | Liabilities | + | Equity |
|---|---|---|---|---|---|
| a. | | | | | |
| b. | | | | | |
| c. | | | | | |

## Quick Study 1-12

**a.**

| Allin Servicing Income Statement For Month Ended April 30, 2017 | |
| --- | --- |
| Revenues .................................................. | $300 |
| Expenses ................................................. | ? |
| Profit (loss) ............................................. | ? |

| Allin Servicing Statement of Changes in Equity For Month Ended April 30, 2017 | | |
| --- | --- | --- |
| Tim Allin, capital, April 1 .............. | | $ 50 |
| Add: Investments by owner .......... | $ 30 | |
| Profit .................................... | ? | ? |
| Total ......................................... | | $255 |
| Less: Withdrawals by owner ......... | | ? |
| Tim Allin, capital, April 30 ............. | | ? |

| Allin Servicing Balance Sheet April 30, 2017 | | | |
| --- | --- | --- | --- |
| **Assets** | | **Liabilities** | |
| Cash ................. | $ 60 | Accounts payable .... | $ 25 |
| Equipment ......... | ? | **Equity** | |
| | | Tim Allin, capital ...... | ? |
| | | Total liabilities | |
| Total assets ....... | $265 | and equity ........... | ? |

**b.**

| Allin Servicing Income Statement For Month Ended May 31, 2017 | |
| --- | --- |
| Revenues .................................................. | ? |
| Expenses ................................................. | $ 85 |
| Profit (loss) ............................................. | ? |

| Allin Servicing Statement of Changes in Equity For Month Ended May 31, 2017 | | |
| --- | --- | --- |
| Tim Allin, capital, May 1 .............. | | ? |
| Add: Investments by owner .......... | $ 60 | |
| Profit .................................... | ? | $110 |
| Total ......................................... | | ? |
| Less: Withdrawals by owner ......... | | 75 |
| Tim Allin, capital, May 31 ............. | | ? |

| Allin Servicing Balance Sheet May 31, 2017 | | | |
| --- | --- | --- | --- |
| **Assets** | | **Liabilities** | |
| Cash ................. | $120 | Accounts payable .... | $ 45 |
| Equipment .......... | ? | **Equity** | |
| | | Tim Allin, capital ...... | ? |
| | | Total liabilities | |
| Total assets ........ | ? | and equity ........... | ? |

## Quick Study 1-13

1. _____
2. _____

_____

## Quick Study 1-14

| | Assets | = | Liabilities | + | Equity |
| --- | --- | --- | --- | --- | --- |
| a. | | | | | |
| b. | | | | | |
| c. | | | | | |
| d. | | | | | |
| e. | | | | | |

Name:_____

**Quick Study 1-15**    Profit = 105 - 77 = 28

| | | |
|---|---|---|
| c | 1. Supplies | d | 8. Utilities expense |
| d | 2. Supplies expense | c | 9. Furniture |
| c | 3. Accounts receivable | d | 10. Revenue |
| c | 4. Accounts payable | d | 11. Rent revenue |
| c | 5. Equipment | d | 12. Salaries expense |
| b | 6. Tim Roadster's withdrawals | b | 13. Tim Roadster's investments |
| c | 7. Notes payable | a+b | 14. Profit |

**Quick Study 1-16**

70 + 35 = 105        1. Total revenues
22 + 10 + 45 = 77        2. Total operating expenses
105 - 77 = 28        3. Profit
25 + 40 + 20 + 10 = 95        4. Total assets
12 + 30 = 42        5. Total liabilities
60 - 35 + 28 = 53        6. Tim Roadster, capital (April 30, 2017)
42 + 53 = 95        7. Total liabilities and equity

**Quick Study 1-17**

| | | | |
|---|---|---|---|
| _____ | 1. Loss ............................................... | $ | _____ |
| _____ | 2. Rent expense ................................. | 22 | _____ |
| _____ | 3. Rent payable ................................. | 6 | _____ |
| _____ | 4. Accounts receivable...................... | 14 | _____ |
| _____ | 5. Joan Bennish's investments in May.......... | 30 | _____ |
| _____ | 6. Interest income ............................. | 2 | _____ |
| _____ | 7. Joan Bennish, capital, May 1, 2017 .......... | 0 | _____ |
| _____ | 8. Repair supplies ............................. | 5 | _____ |
| _____ | 9. Notes payable ............................... | 25 | _____ |
| _____ | 10. Joan Bennish's withdrawals in May.......... | 5 | _____ |
| _____ | 11. Truck............................................. | 15 | _____ |
| _____ | 12. Consulting revenue....................... | 18 | _____ |
| _____ | 13. Joan Bennish, capital, May 31, 2017 ......... | | _____ |
| _____ | 14. Cash............................................. | 20 | _____ |

**Quick Study 1-18**

### Income Statement

| | | |
|---|---|---|
| | | |
| | | |
| | | |
| | | |
| | | |
| | | |
| | | |
| | | |

### Statement of Changes in Equity

| | | |
|---|---|---|
| | | |
| | | |
| | | |
| | | |
| | | |
| | | |
| | | |

### Balance Sheet

| | | | |
|---|---|---|---|
| | | | |
| | | | |
| | | | |
| | | | |
| | | | |
| | | | |
| | | | |
| | | | |
| | | | |
| | | | |
| | | | |
| | | | |

## Exercise 1-1

a.    C
b.    SP
c.    C
d.    P
e.    SP
f.    SP
g.    C

## Exercise 1-2

| External Users | Decisions |
|---|---|
| 1. | |
| 2. | |
| 3. | |
| 4. | |

| Internal Users | Decisions |
|---|---|
| 1. | |
| 2. | |
| 3. | |
| 4. | |

Name:_____

**Exercise 1-3**

| Accounting Role | Typical Day |
|---|---|
| (1) External auditor | |
| (2) Controller | |
| (3) Tax Specialist | |

**Exercise 1-4**

a.

_____
_____
_____
_____
_____
_____
_____
_____
_____
_____
_____
_____
_____
_____

b.

_____
_____
_____
_____
_____
_____
_____
_____
_____
_____
_____
_____
_____
_____

c.

_____
_____
_____
_____
_____
_____
_____
_____
_____
_____
_____

Name:_____

**Exercise 1-5**

1.   *b* _____
2.   *a* _____
3.   *d* _____
4.   *c* _____

*Fundamental Accounting Principles, 15ce, Working Papers*

Name:_____

Exercise 1-6

| Balance Sheet | | | Income Statement | | Statement of Changes in Equity |
|---|---|---|---|---|---|
| Assets | Liabilities | Owner's Equity | Revenue | Expenses | |
| | | | | | |
| | | | | | |
| | | | | | |
| | | | | | |
| | | | | | |
| | | | | | |
| | | | | | |
| | | | | | |
| | | | | | |
| | | | | | |
| | | | | | |
| | | | | | |

**Exercise 1-7**

Revenue — Expenses

a. Profit = $516000 - $492000 = $24000

b. Profit/loss = $165000 - $240000 = loss = $75000

c. Beginning equity $32000, No Invt, No withdraw
   Profit/loss = x, End of equity $86000
   ∴ $32000 + 0 - 0 + x = $86000 ∴ x profit = $54000

d. $48000 + $40000 - 0 + Profit/loss = $52000
   ∴ $88000 + profit/loss = $52000
   ∴ profit/loss = $52000 - $88000
   ∴ Loss = $36000

**Exercise 1-8**

|                                         | (a)      | (b)      | (c)      | (d)      | (e)      |
|-----------------------------------------|----------|----------|----------|----------|----------|
| Equity, January 1 ....................... | $   -0-  | $    -0- | $    -0- | $    -0- |          |
| Owner's investments during the year.    | 60,000   |          | 31,500   | 37,500   | 140,000  |
| Profit (loss) for the year.............. | 15,750   | 30,500   | (4,500)  |          | (8,000)  |
| Owner's withdrawals during the year.    |          | (27,000) | (20,000) | (15,750) | (63,000) |
| Equity, December 31...................   | 56,000   | 49,500   |          | 32,000   | 171,000  |

Name:_____

**Exercise 1-9**

| Income Statement | | |
|---|---|---|
| Revenues: | | |
| Wedding Consulting revenue | | $ 22000 |
| Operating expenses: | | |
| Rent expense | $ 2550 | |
| Salaries expense | 6000 | |
| Telephone expense | 1680 | |
| Utilities expense | 660 | |
| Total operating expenses | | $ 10890 |
| Profit | | $ 11,110 |

**Exercise 1-10**

| Statement of Changes in Equity | | |
|---|---|---|
| Jean Higgins Capital Nov 1 | | $ 0 |
| Add: Investment by Jean | $ 84000 | |
| Profit | 11,110 | $ 95,110 |
| Less: Owner's withdrawals | | $ 3360 |
| Jean Higgins Capital Nov 30 | | $ 91,750 |

*Analysis component:*
_____
_____
_____
_____
_____

Name:_____

## Balance Sheet

| Assets: | $ | Liabilities: | $ |
|---|---|---|---|
| Cash | 16000 | Ac payable | 7500 |
| Account receivable | 17000 | | |
| Office supplies | 5000 | Equity: | |
| Automobiles | 36000 | Jean Higgins | 91750 |
| Office equipment | 25250 | Capital | |
| Total Assets | $ 99250 | Total liabilities and equity | $ 99250 |

*Analysis component:*

_____

_____

_____

_____

**Exercise 1-12**

|  | | |
| --- | --- | --- |
| **Income Statement** | | |
| | | |
| | | |
| | | |
| | | |
| | | |
| | | |
| | | |
| | | |
| | | |

**Exercise 1-13**

|  | | |
| --- | --- | --- |
| **Statement of Changes in Equity** | | |
| | | |
| | | |
| | | |
| | | |
| | | |
| | | |
| | | |
| | | |
| | | |
| | | |

*Analysis component:*

_____

_____

_____

_____

**Exercise 1-14**

|  | Balance Sheet |  |  |
|---|---|---|---|
|  |  |  |  |
|  |  |  |  |
|  |  |  |  |
|  |  |  |  |
|  |  |  |  |
|  |  |  |  |
|  |  |  |  |
|  |  |  |  |
|  |  |  |  |
|  |  |  |  |
|  |  |  |  |
|  |  |  |  |
|  |  |  |  |

*Analysis component:*

_____
_____
_____
_____
_____

**Exercise 1-15**

**(a) Profit (Loss) =**      [                    ]
   **Supporting Calculations:**      _____

_____

_____

_____

_____

_____

_____


**(b) Profit (Loss) =**      [                    ]
   **Supporting Calculations:**      _____

_____

_____

_____

_____

_____


**(c) Profit (Loss) =**      [                    ]
   **Supporting Calculations:**      _____

_____

_____

_____

_____

_____


**(d) Profit (Loss) =**      [                    ]
   **Supporting Calculations:**      _____

_____

_____

_____

_____

_____

**Exercise 1-16**

**(a) Assets =** | $ 40000
**Equity =** | $ 30000

    **Supporting Calculations:** If assets decreased by $15000
then Assets = $25000 + $15000
∴ Assets = $40000
Assets = Liabilities + Equity
∴ $40000 = $10000 + Equity
∴ Equity = $30000

**(b) Liabilities =** | $19000
**Equity =** | $6000

    **Supporting Calculations:**
If liabilities increased by $9000
∴ Liabilities = $10000 + $9000
∴ Liabilities = $19000
Assets = Liabilities + Equity
∴ $25000 = $19000 + Equity
∴ Equity = $6000

**Exercise 1-17**

| | ASSETS | | | = | LIABILITIES | + | EQUITY |
|---|---|---|---|---|---|---|---|
| | | ACCOUNTS | | OFFICE | | ACCOUNTS | | MARNIE WESSON, |
| CASH | + | RECEIVABLE | + | SUPPLIES | = | PAYABLE | + | CAPITAL |
| (a) | | | | | | | |
| (b) | | | | | | | |
| (c) | | | | | | | |
| (d) | | | | | | | |
| (e) | | | | | | | |
| (f) | | | | | | | |

         *Fundamental Accounting Principles*, 15ce, Working Papers

Name:_____

**Exercise 1-18**

| | | ASSETS | | | = | LIABILITIES | + | EQUITY |
|---|---|---|---|---|---|---|---|---|
| CASH | + | ACCOUNTS RECEIVABLE | + PARTS SUPPLIES | + EQUIPMENT | = | ACCOUNTS PAYABLE | + | STACEY CROWE, CAPITAL |
| (a) $14000 | | | | | | | | $14000 |
| (b) -2500 | | | | | | | | $ -2500 |
| Bal $11500 | | | | | | | | $11500 |
| (c) | | | $800 | | | $800 | | |
| $11500 | | | $800 | | | $800 | | $11500 |
| (d) | | $3400 | | | | | | $3400 |
| $11500 | | $3400 | $800 | | | $800 | | $14900 |
| (e) $-1950 | | | | $1950 | | | | |
| $9550 | | $3400 | $800 | $1950 | | $800 | | $14900 |
| (f) NO entry | | | | | | | | |
| (g) $-800 | | | | | | $-800 | | |
| $8750 | | $3400 | $800 | $1950 | | ~ | | $14900 |
| (h) $3400 | | | | | | | | $3400 |
| $12150 | | $3400 | $800 | $1950 | | | | $18300 |
| (i) $-2700 | | | | | | | | -$2700 |
| $9450 | | $3400 | $800 | $1950 | | ~ | | $15600 |

$15,600

**Exercise 1-19**

a. _____

b. _____

c. _____

d. _____

e. _____

f. _____

g. _____

# Chapter 1

## Exercise 1-20

| | ASSETS | | | = | LIABILITIES | + | EQUITY | |
| CASH | + ACCOUNTS RECEIVABLE | + SUPPLIES | + EQUIP-MENT | = | ACCOUNTS PAYABLE | + | MAILIN MOON, CAPITAL | EXPLANATION OF EQUITY TRANSACTION |
|---|---|---|---|---|---|---|---|---|
| (a) + 3000 | | | +2500 | | | | +$5500 | Owner Invl |
| (b) +$6500 | | | | | | | +$6500 | Revenue |
| bal $9500 | | | -$2500 | | | | $12000 | |
| (c) | | +$600 | | | +$600 | | | |
| bal $9500 | | $600 | $2500 | | $600 | | $12000 | |
| (d) -$1450 | | | | | | | -$1450 | Sal Expense |
| bal 8050 | | $600 | $2500 | | $600 | | $10550 | |
| (e) No entry | | | | | | | | |
| (f) -$1400 | | | | | | | -$1400 | Rent exp |
| bal $6650 | | $600 | $2500 | | | | | |
| (g) | +$4500 | | | | | | +$4500 | Revenue |

*Fundamental Accounting Principles, 15ce, Working Papers*

**Exercise 1-21**

**Mailin Moon – Freelance Writing**
**Income Statement**
**For Month Ended March 31, 2017**

**Revenues:**
   Freelance writing revenue ............................................
**Operating expenses:**
   Salaries expense .......................................................
   Rent expense ............................................................    _____
     Total operating expenses ........................................
**Profit** ............................................................................

**Mailin Moon – Freelance Writing**
**Statement of Changes in Equity**
**For Month Ended March 31, 2017**

Mailin Moon, capital, March 1................................................
Add:  Investment by owner..................................................
Profit .................................................................................
Mailin Moon, capital, March 31..............................................

**Mailin Moon – Freelance Writing**
**Balance Sheet**
**March 31, 2017**

       **Assets**

                                 **Liabilities**

Cash ..............................            Accounts payable ..................................
Accounts receivable ....
Supplies.........................
Equipment.....................

                                      **Equity**
                          Mailin Moon, capital .............................
Total assets ...................  _____   Total liabilities and equity ...................

*Analysis component:*
_____
_____
_____
_____
_____
_____
_____

**Exercise 1-22**

| CASH | + | ACCOUNTS RECEIVABLE | + | SUPPLIES | + | EQUIP- MENT | = | ACCOUNTS PAYABLE | + | OMAR ALI, CAPITAL | EXPLANATION OF EQUITY TRANSACTION |
|---|---|---|---|---|---|---|---|---|---|---|---|
| (a) | | | | | | | | | | | |
| (b) | | | | | | | | | | | |
| (c) | | | | | | | | | | | |
| (d) | | | | | | | | | | | |
| (e) | | | | | | | | | | | |
| (f) | | | | | | | | | | | |
| (g) | | | | | | | | | | | |
| (h) | | | | | | | | | | | |
| (i) | | | | | | | | | | | |

ASSETS = LIABILITIES + EQUITY

**Exercise 1-23**

## Income Statement

|  |  |  |
|---|---|---|
|  |  |  |
|  |  |  |
|  |  |  |
|  |  |  |
|  |  |  |
|  |  |  |
|  |  |  |
|  |  |  |

## Statement of Changes in Equity

|  |  |  |
|---|---|---|
|  |  |  |
|  |  |  |
|  |  |  |
|  |  |  |
|  |  |  |

## Balance Sheet

|  |  |  |  |
|---|---|---|---|
|  |  |  |  |
|  |  |  |  |
|  |  |  |  |
|  |  |  |  |
|  |  |  |  |
|  |  |  |  |
|  |  |  |  |
|  |  |  |  |
|  |  |  |  |
|  |  |  |  |
|  |  |  |  |
|  |  |  |  |
|  |  |  |  |

**Exercise 1-23 (Continued)**

*Analysis component:*

_____

_____

_____

_____

_____

_____

_____

_____

_____

_____

**Exercise 1-24**

| | ASSETS | | | | = | LIABILITIES | + | EQUITY | |
|---|---|---|---|---|---|---|---|---|---|
| CASH | + | ACCOUNTS RECEIVABLE | + | SUPPLIES | + | EQUIP-MENT | = | ACCOUNTS PAYABLE | + | NATALIE GOLD, CAPITAL | EXPLANATION OF EQUITY TRANSACTION |
| Bal. $6,000 | | $1,200 | | $1,900 | | $6,500 | | $4,000 | | $11,600 | |
| (a) | | | | | | | | | | | |
| (b) | | | | | | | | | | | |
| (c) | | | | | | | | | | | |
| (d) | | | | | | | | | | | |
| (e) | | | | | | | | | | | |
| (f) | | | | | | | | | | | |
| (g) | | | | | | | | | | | |
| (h) | | | | | | | | | | | |

**Exercise 1-25**

### Income Statement

| | | |
|---|---|---|
| | | |
| | | |
| | | |
| | | |
| | | |
| | | |
| | | |
| | | |
| | | |
| | | |
| | | |
| | | |
| | | |
| | | |
| | | |

### Statement of Changes in Equity

| | | |
|---|---|---|
| | | |
| | | |
| | | |
| | | |
| | | |
| | | |
| | | |
| | | |

## Exercise 1-25 (Concluded)

**Balance Sheet**

| | | | |
|---|---|---|---|
| | | | |
| | | | |
| | | | |
| | | | |
| | | | |
| | | | |
| | | | |
| | | | |
| | | | |
| | | | |
| | | | |
| | | | |
| | | | |
| | | | |
| | | | |
| | | | |
| | | | |
| | | | |
| | | | |

*Analysis component:*

_____

_____

_____

_____

_____

Name:_____

## Problem 1-1A

| Characteristic | Type of Business Organization | | |
|---|---|---|---|
| | Sole Proprietorship | Partnership | Corporation |
| Limited liability | | | |
| Unlimited liability | | | |
| Owners are shareholders | | | |
| Owners are partners | | | |
| Taxed as a separate legal entity | | | |

## Problem 1-2A

### EMAIL

| | |
|---|---|
| **To:** | |
| **From:** | |
| **Subject:** | |

_____
_____
_____
_____
_____
_____
_____
_____
_____
_____
_____
_____
_____
_____
_____
_____
_____
_____
_____
_____
_____
_____
_____
_____
_____
_____
_____
_____
_____

Name:_____

**Problem 1-3A**

**2016 Profit (Loss) =** [_____]
    **Supporting Calculations:**

_____
_____
_____
_____
_____
_____
_____
_____
_____

**Problem 1-4A**

_____
**Income Statement**
_____

| | | |
|---|---|---|
| | | |
| | | |
| | | |
| | | |
| | | |
| | | |
| | | |
| | | |
| | | |
| | | |
| | | |
| | | |
| | | |
| | | |
| | | |

Name:_____

**Problem 1-4A (Continued)**

### Statement of Changes in Equity

| | | |
|---|---|---|
| | | |
| | | |
| | | |
| | | |
| | | |
| | | |
| | | |

### Balance Sheet

| | | | |
|---|---|---|---|
| | | | |
| | | | |
| | | | |
| | | | |
| | | | |
| | | | |
| | | | |
| | | | |
| | | | |
| | | | |

*Analysis component:*

_____
_____
_____
_____
_____

Name:_____

**Problem 1-5A**

**Part 1**

## Balance Sheet

| | | | |
|---|---|---|---|
| | | | |
| | | | |
| | | | |
| | | | |
| | | | |
| | | | |
| | | | |
| | | | |
| | | | |
| | | | |
| | | | |

## Balance Sheet

| | | | |
|---|---|---|---|
| | | | |
| | | | |
| | | | |
| | | | |
| | | | |
| | | | |
| | | | |
| | | | |
| | | | |
| | | | |
| | | | |

Name:_____

**Problem 1-5A (Concluded) Part 2**

**Profit (Loss) Calculation:** _____

_____

_____

_____

_____

_____

_____

_____

_____

_____

_____

_____

_____

*Analysis component:*

_____

_____

_____

_____

_____

_____

_____

_____

Name:_____

**Problem 1-6A**

**Part 1: Company A**

(a)

_____
_____
_____
_____
_____

(b)

_____
_____
_____
_____
_____
_____
_____
_____

(c)

_____
_____
_____
_____
_____
_____

**Part 2: Company B**

(a)

_____
_____
_____

(b)

_____
_____
_____
_____
_____

(c)

_____
_____
_____
_____
_____

Name:_____

## Problem 1-6A (Continued)

### Part 3: Company C

_____
_____
_____
_____
_____
_____
_____
_____
_____
_____
_____
_____
_____
_____

### Part 4: Company D

_____
_____
_____
_____
_____
_____
_____
_____
_____
_____
_____
_____
_____
_____
_____
_____

**Problem 1-6A (Concluded)**

**Part 5: Company E**

_____
_____
_____
_____
_____
_____
_____

_____
_____
_____
_____
_____
_____
_____
_____

Name:_____

| | CASH + | ACCOUNTS RECEIVABLE + | OFFICE SUPPLIES + | OFFICE EQUIPMENT + | BUILDING = | ACCOUNTS PAYABLE + | NOTES PAYABLE + | GEORGE LITTLECHILD, CAPITAL | EXPLANATION OF EQUITY TRANSACTION |
|---|---|---|---|---|---|---|---|---|---|
| (a) | +16000 | | | +20000 | | | | +18000 | Invt by owner |
| (b) | -100000 | | | | +600000 | | | +500000 | |
| Bal. | | | | | | | | | |
| (c) | -3000 | | +3000 | | | | | | |
| Bal. | | | | | | | | | |
| (d) | | | | +72000 | | +72000 | | | |
| Bal. | | | | | | | | | |
| (e) | No entry | | | | | | | | |
| Bal. | | | | | | | | | |
| (f) | | +5200 | | | | | | +5200 | Service revenue |
| Bal. | | | | | | | | | |
| (g) | -3500 | | | | | | | -3500 | Advertising exp |
| Bal. | | | | | | | | | |
| (h) | +4000 | | | | | | | +4000 | service rev |
| Bal. | | | | | | | | | |
| (i) | -4000 | | | | | -4000 | | | |
| Bal. | | | | | | | | | |
| (j) | +2500 | -2500 | | | | | | | |
| Bal. | | | | | | | | | |
| (k) | -7000 | | | | | | | -7000 | Wages exp |
| Bal. | | | | | | | | | |
| (l) | -3600 | | | | | | | -3600 | Withdrew by owner |
| Bal. | | | | | | | | | |

ASSETS = LIABILITIES + EQUITY

**Problem 1-7A (Concluded)**

**Part 3**

**Littlechild Enterprises**
**Income Statement**
**For Month Ended March 31, 2017**

Revenues :
    Service revenue................................................................
Operating expenses:
    Wages expense ...........................................................
    Advertising expense .....................................................   _____
        Total operating expenses .........................................
Loss ...................................................................................

**Littlechild Enterprises**
**Statement of Changes in Equity**
**For Month Ended March 31, 2017**

George Littlechild, capital, March 1
Add:  Investment by owner
   Total
Less:  Withdrawal by owner
Loss
George Littlechild, capital, March 31

**Littlechild Enterprises**
**Balance Sheet**
**March 31, 2017**

      **Assets**

                                **Liabilities**

Cash                           Accounts payable
Accounts receivable          Notes payable
Office supplies                  Total liabilities
Office equipment
Building

                                     **Equity**
                        George Littlechild, capital

Total assets       _____      Total liabilities and equity

*Analysis component:*

_____
_____
_____
_____
_____
_____
_____
_____

**Problem 1-8A (Part 1)**

| DATE | CASH | + | ACCOUNTS RECEIVABLE | + | OFFICE SUPPLIES | + | OFFICE EQUIPMENT | + ELECTRICAL EQUIPMENT | = | = | ACCOUNTS PAYABLE | + | + | LARRY POWER, CAPITAL | EXPLANATION OF EQUITY TRANSACTION |
|---|---|---|---|---|---|---|---|---|---|---|---|---|---|---|---|
| Oct 31 | 30000 | | 7000 | | 1900 | | 25000 | 14000 | | | 15000 | | | 62900 | |
| Nov 1 | -7200 | | | | | | | | | | | | | -7200 | Rent exp |
| 3 | +10000 | | | | | | | | | | +8000 | | | +10000 | trust by ou |
| 3 | -10000 | | | | | | +18000 | | | | | | | | |
| 5 | -1800 | | | | +1800 | | | | | | | | | | |
| 6 | 7200 | | | | | | | | | | | | | | |
| 8 | | | | | | | +5200 | | | | +5200 | | | +2000 | Electrical ren |
| 31 | | | | | | | | | | | | | | | |

**Problem 1-8A (Concluded)**

*Analysis component:*

_____
_____
_____
_____
_____
_____

**Problem 1-9A**

### Income Statement

| | | |
|---|---|---|
| | | |
| | | |
| | | |
| | | |
| | | |
| | | |
| | | |
| | | |
| | | |
| | | |
| | | |
| | | |
| | | |
| | | |

### Statement of Changes in Equity

| | | |
|---|---|---|
| | | |
| | | |
| | | |
| | | |
| | | |
| | | |
| | | |
| | | |
| | | |

Name:_____

**Problem 1-9A (Concluded)**

| | Balance Sheet | | |
|---|---|---|---|

**Balance Sheet**

| | | | |
|---|---|---|---|
| | | | |
| | | | |
| | | | |
| | | | |
| | | | |
| | | | |
| | | | |
| | | | |
| | | | |
| | | | |
| | | | |
| | | | |
| | | | |
| | | | |
| | | | |
| | | | |
| | | | |
| | | | |

*Analysis component:*

_____
_____
_____
_____
_____
_____
_____

**Problem 1-10A**

| | TRANSACTION | BALANCE SHEET | | | INCOME STATEMENT |
|---|---|---|---|---|---|
| | | TOTAL ASSETS | TOTAL LIABILITIES | EQUITY | PROFIT |
| 1. | Owner invests cash | | | | |
| 2. | Sell services for cash | | | | |
| 3. | Acquire services on credit | | | | |
| 4. | Pay wages with cash | | | | |
| 5. | Owner withdraws cash | | | | |
| 6. | Borrow cash with note payable | | | | |
| 7. | Sell services on credit | | | | |
| 8. | Buy office equipment for cash | | | | |
| 9. | Collect receivable from (7) | | | | |
| 10. | Buy asset with note payable | | | | |

Name:_____

**Problem 1-1B**

a. _____
_____
_____

b. _____
_____

**Problem 1-2B**

**EMAIL**

To: _____
From: _____
Subject: _____
_____
_____
_____
_____
_____
_____
_____
_____
_____
_____
_____
_____
_____
_____
_____
_____
_____
_____
_____
_____
_____
_____
_____
_____
_____
_____
_____
_____

Name:_____

**Problem 1-3B**

**2016 Profit (Loss) =**
    **Supporting Calculations:**

_____

_____

_____

_____

_____

_____

_____

_____

_____

_____

**Problem 1-4B**

_____

### Income Statement

| | | |
|---|---|---|
| | | |
| | | |
| | | |
| | | |
| | | |
| | | |
| | | |
| | | |
| | | |
| | | |
| | | |
| | | |
| | | |
| | | |
| | | |
| | | |
| | | |

Name:_____

**Problem 1-4B (Concluded)**

## Statement of Changes in Equity

| | | |
|---|---|---|
| | | |
| | | |
| | | |
| | | |
| | | |
| | | |
| | | |
| | | |
| | | |

## Balance Sheet

| | | | |
|---|---|---|---|
| | | | |
| | | | |
| | | | |
| | | | |
| | | | |
| | | | |
| | | | |
| | | | |
| | | | |
| | | | |
| | | | |

*Analysis component:*

_____

_____

_____

_____

_____

_____

**Chapter 1**

Name:_____

**Problem 1-5B    Part 1**

### Balance Sheet

| | | | |
|---|---|---|---|
| | | | |
| | | | |
| | | | |
| | | | |
| | | | |
| | | | |
| | | | |
| | | | |
| | | | |

### Balance Sheet

| | | | |
|---|---|---|---|
| | | | |
| | | | |
| | | | |
| | | | |
| | | | |
| | | | |
| | | | |
| | | | |
| | | | |
| | | | |

*Fundamental Accounting Principles, 15ce, Working Papers*

**Problem 1-5B (Concluded)**

**Part 2**

**Profit (Loss) Calculation:** _____

_____
_____
_____
_____
_____
_____
_____
_____
_____
_____
_____

*Analysis component:*

_____
_____
_____
_____
_____

**Problem 1-6B**

**Part 1:  Company V**

**(a)** _____

_____
_____
_____

**(b)** _____

_____
_____
_____

**(c)** _____

_____
_____
_____
_____
_____
_____

**Problem 1-6B (Continued)**

**Part 2: Company W**

**(a)** _____

_____

_____

_____

_____

**(b)** _____

_____

_____

_____

_____

_____

_____

**(c)** _____

_____

_____

_____

_____

_____

_____

**Part 3: Company X**

_____

_____

_____

_____

_____

_____

_____

_____

_____

_____

_____

_____

_____

_____

Name:_____

**Problem 1-6B (Concluded)**

**Part 4: Company Y**

_____
_____
_____
_____
_____
_____
_____
_____
_____
_____
_____
_____
_____
_____
_____
_____
_____
_____
_____
_____

**Part 5: Company Z**

_____
_____
_____
_____
_____
_____
_____
_____
_____
_____
_____
_____
_____
_____
_____
_____
_____
_____

Name:_____

## Problem 1-7B (Parts 1 and 2)

| CASH | + ACCOUNTS RECEIVABLE | + OFFICE SUPPLIES | + OFFICE EQUIPMENT | + BUILDING | = ACCOUNTS PAYABLE | + NOTES PAYABLE | + LILY ZHANG, CAPITAL | EXPLANATION OF EQUITY TRANSACTION |
|---|---|---|---|---|---|---|---|---|
| (a) | | | | | | | | |
| (b) | | | | | | | | |
| Bal. | | | | | | | | |
| (c) | | | | | | | | |
| Bal. | | | | | | | | |
| (d) | | | | | | | | |
| Bal. | | | | | | | | |
| (e) | | | | | | | | |
| Bal. | | | | | | | | |
| (f) | | | | | | | | |
| Bal. | | | | | | | | |
| (g) | | | | | | | | |
| Bal. | | | | | | | | |
| (h) | | | | | | | | |
| Bal. | | | | | | | | |
| (i) | | | | | | | | |
| Bal. | | | | | | | | |
| (j) | | | | | | | | |
| Bal. | | | | | | | | |
| (k) | | | | | | | | |
| Bal. | | | | | | | | |
| (l) | | | | | | | | |
| Bal. | | | | | | | | |

**ASSETS** = **LIABILITIES** + **EQUITY**

**Problem 1-8B (Concluded)**

**Part 3**

**Zhang Consulting**
**Income Statement**
**For Year Ended December 31, 2017**

Revenues:
    Consulting services revenue .......................................
Operating expenses:
    Wages expense ................................................................
    Advertising expense ......................................................
        Total operating expenses .......................................
Profit ..........................................................................................

**Zhang Consulting**
**Statement of Changes in Equity**
**For Year Ended December 31, 2017**

Lily Zhang, capital, January 1
Add:  Investment by owner
Profit
    Total
Less:  Withdrawals by owner
Lily Zhang, capital, December 31

**Zhang Consulting**
**Balance Sheet**
**December 31, 2017**

| Assets | Liabilities |
|---|---|
| Cash | Accounts payable |
| Accounts receivable | Notes payable |
| Office supplies | Total liabilities |
| Office equipment | |
| Building | |
| | Equity |
| | Lily Zhang, capital |
| Total assets | Total liabilities and equity |

*Analysis component:*

_____
_____
_____
_____
_____
_____
_____

Name:_____

**Problem 1-8B (Part 1)**

| DATE | ASSETS | | | | | LIABILITIES | EQUITY | |
| | CASH | + ACCOUNTS RECEIVABLE | + OFFICE SUPPLIES | + OFFICE EQUIPMENT | + EXCAVATING EQUIPMENT | = ACCOUNTS PAYABLE | + MICHAEL CANTU, CAPITAL | EXPLANATION OF EQUITY TRANSACTION |
|---|---|---|---|---|---|---|---|---|
| | | | | | | | | |

Name:_____

**Problem 1-8B (Concluded)**

*Analysis component:*

_____
_____
_____
_____
_____
_____
_____
_____

**Problem 1-9B**

### Income Statement

| | | |
|---|---|---|
| | | |
| | | |
| | | |
| | | |
| | | |
| | | |
| | | |
| | | |
| | | |
| | | |
| | | |
| | | |
| | | |

### Statement of Changes in Equity

| | | |
|---|---|---|
| | | |
| | | |
| | | |
| | | |
| | | |
| | | |
| | | |
| | | |
| | | |

## Problem 1-9B (Concluded)

| | Balance Sheet | | |
|---|---|---|---|
| | | | |
| | | | |
| | | | |
| | | | |
| | | | |
| | | | |
| | | | |
| | | | |
| | | | |
| | | | |
| | | | |

*Analysis component:*

_____
_____
_____
_____
_____
_____
_____
_____

## Problem 1-10B

| | TRANSACTION | BALANCE SHEET | | | INCOME STATEMENT |
|---|---|---|---|---|---|
| | | TOTAL ASSETS | TOTAL LIABILITIES | EQUITY | PROFIT |
| 1. | Owner invests cash | | | | |
| 2. | Pay wages with cash | | | | |
| 3. | Acquire services on credit | | | | |
| 4. | Buy store equipment for cash | | | | |
| 5. | Borrow cash with note payable | | | | |
| 6. | Sell services for cash | | | | |
| 7. | Sell services on credit | | | | |
| 8. | Pay rent with cash | | | | |
| 9. | Owner withdraws cash | | | | |
| 10. | Collect receivable from (7) | | | | |

## Quick Study 2-1

| | | | | | | |
|---|---|---|---|---|---|---|
| 1. | A | Buildings | 16. | L | Unearned Subscription Revenue |
| 2. | E | Building Repair Expense | 17. | A | Prepaid Subscription Fees |
| 3. | E | Wages Expense | 18. | A | Supplies |
| 4. | L | Wages Payable | 19. | E | Supplies Expense |
| 5. | A | Notes Receivable | 20. | R | Rent Revenue |
| 6. | L | Notes Payable | 21. | L | Unearned Rent Revenue |
| 7. | A | Prepaid Advertising | 22. | A | Prepaid Rent |
| 8. | E | Advertising Expense | 23. | L | Rent Payable |
| 9. | L | Advertising Payable | 24. | R | Service Revenue |
| 10. | L | Unearned Advertising | 25. | OW | Jessica Vuong, Withdrawals |
| 11. | R | Advertising Revenue | 26. | OC | Jessica Vuong, Capital |
| 12. | R | Interest Income | 27. | E | Salaries Expense |
| 13. | E | Interest Expense | 28. | L | Salaries Payable |
| 14. | L | Interest Payable | 29. | A | Furniture |
| 15. | R | Subscription Revenue | 30. | A | Equipment |

# Chapter 2

## Quick Study 2-2

a. *Debit* Equipment
b. *Debit* Land
c. *Debit* Amrit Sandhu, Withdrawals
d. *Debit* Rent Expense
e. *Credit* Interest Income
f. *Debit* Prepaid Rent
g. *Ac Recei* Accounts Receivable
h. *Debit* Office Supplies

i. *Debit* Notes Receivable
j. *Credit* Notes Payable
k. *Credit* Amrit Sandhu, Capital
l. *Credit* Rent Revenue
m. *Credit* Rent Payable
n. *Debit* Interest Expense
o. *Credit* Interest Payable

## Quick Study 2-3

a. *Credit* To increase Notes Payable
b. *Credit* To decrease Accounts Rec'ble.
c. *Credit* To increase Owner, Capital
d. *Debit* To decrease Unearned Fees
e. *Credit* To decrease Prepaid Insurance
f. *Credit* To decrease Cash
g. *Debit* To increase Utilities Expense
h. *Credit* To increase Revenue

i. *Debit* *Credit* To increase Store Equip.
j. *Debit* To increase Owner, With.
k. *Debit* To decrease Rent Payable
l. *Credit* To decrease Prepaid Rent
m. *Debit* To increase Supplies
n. *Debit* To increase Supplies Exp.
o. *Debit* To decrease Accts. Payable

## Quick Study 2-4

a. _____ Buildings
b. _____ Interest Income
c. _____ Bob Norton, Withdrawals
d. _____ Bob Norton, Capital
e. _____ Prepaid Insurance
f. _____ Interest Payable
g. _____ Accounts Receivable
h. _____ Salaries Expense

i. _____ Office Supplies
j. _____ Repair Services Revenue
k. _____ Interest Expense
l. _____ Unearned Revenue
m. _____ Salaries Payable
n. _____ Furniture
o. _____ Interest Receivable

## Quick Study 2-5

a. _____ Buildings
b. _____ Interest Income
c. _____ Matthew Lee, Withdrawals
d. _____ Matthew Lee, Capital
e. _____ Prepaid Insurance
f. _____ Interest Payable
g. _____ Accounts Receivable
h. _____ Salaries Expense

i. _____ Office Supplies
j. _____ Repair Services Revenue
k. _____ Interest Expense
l. _____ Unearned Revenue
m. _____ Salaries Payable
n. _____ Furniture
o. _____ Interest Receivable

Name:_____

**Quick Study 2-6**

| a. | **Analysis** | Assets increase, Assets decrease |
|---|---|---|
| | **Journal entry analysis** | Debit the furniture account for $400. Credit the cash account for $400. |
| b. | **Analysis** | No transaction required. |
| | **Journal entry analysis** | |
| c. | **Analysis** | Assets increase, Equity increases |
| | **Journal entry analysis** | Debit the a/c receivable for $600. Credit the revenue account for $600 |
| d. | **Analysis** | Liabilities increase, Equity decrease |
| | **Journal entry analysis** | Debit the cleaning exp a/c for $300. Credit the A/c payable a/c for $300 |
| e. | **Analysis** | Assets increase, Equity increases. |
| | **Journal entry analysis** | Debit the cash account for $25000. Credit the Douglas Malone capital a/c for $25000 |
| | | |

**Quick Study 2-7**

|  | Date | Account Titles | Debit | Credit |
|---|---|---|---|---|
| a. | Aug 1 | Furniture ................................ | 400 | |
| | | Cash ........................... | | 400 |
| | | Purchase of furniture | | |
| | | for cash. | | |
| b. | Aug 7 | No transaction required. | | |
| | | | | |
| | | | | |
| c. | Aug 13 | Accounts Receivable ........ | 600 | |
| | | Revenue ................. | | 600 |
| | | Provided services on credit | | |
| d. | Aug 14 | Cleaning Expense ......... | 300 | |
| | | Accounts payable ...... | | 300 |
| | | Purchased cleaning services | | |
| | | on credit. | | |
| e. | Aug 31 | Cash ............................ | 25000 | |
| | | Douglas Malone, Capital... | | 25000 |
| | | Investment by owner | | |
| | | | | |

Name:_____

## Quick Study 2-8

### Part 1 and 2

|              Cash              |   |            Accounts Receivable            |   |
| ----------------------------- | - | ----------------------------------------- | - |
| Jul 31   25,000               |   | Apr. 30   3,200                           |   |

|           Furniture           |   |             Accounts Payable              |   |
| ----------------------------- | - | ----------------------------------------- | - |
| Jul 31   5,000                |   |                         500     Jul 31    |   |

|      Douglas Malone, Capital      |   |                Revenue                |   |
| --------------------------------- | - | ------------------------------------- | - |
|           28,000     Jul. 31      |   |           4,500     Jul. 31           |   |

|        Cleaning Expense       |   |
| ----------------------------- | - |
| Jul. 31 1,500                 |   |

### Part 3

_____

_____

_____

_____

Name:_____

**Quick Study 2-9**

| May 2 | Analysis | | | |
|---|---|---|---|---|
| | Journal entry analysis | | | |
| | Journal Entry | | | |
| | Date | Account Titles and Explanation | Debit | Credit |
| | | | | |
| | | | | |
| | | | | |

| May 10 | Analysis | | | |
|---|---|---|---|---|
| | Journal entry analysis | | | |
| | Journal Entry | | | |
| | Date | Account Titles and Explanation | Debit | Credit |
| | | | | |
| | | | | |
| | | | | |

| May 12 | Analysis | | | |
|---|---|---|---|---|
| | Journal entry analysis | | | |
| | Journal Entry | | | |
| | Date | Account Titles and Explanation | Debit | Credit |
| | | | | |
| | | | | |
| | | | | |
| | | | | |

## Quick Study 2-9 (Continued)

| May 15 | Analysis | | | |
|---|---|---|---|---|
| | Journal entry analysis | | | |
| | Journal Entry | | | |
| | Date | Account Titles and Explanation | Debit | Credit |
| | | | | |
| | | | | |
| | | | | |

| May 16 | Analysis | | | |
|---|---|---|---|---|
| | Journal entry analysis | | | |
| | Journal Entry | | | |
| | Date | Account Titles and Explanation | Debit | Credit |
| | | | | |
| | | | | |
| | | | | |

| May 22 | Analysis | | | |
|---|---|---|---|---|
| | Journal entry analysis | | | |
| | Journal Entry | | | |
| | Date | Account Titles and Explanation | Debit | Credit |
| | | | | |
| | | | | |
| | | | | |

Name:_____

## Quick Study 2-10

### Parts 1&2

| Cash | |
|---|---|
| Apr. 30    15,000 | |

| Accounts Receivable | |
|---|---|
| Apr. 30    3,200 | |

| Car | |
|---|---|
| | |

| Accounts Payable | |
|---|---|
| | 6,000    Apr. 30 |

| Unearned Revenue | |
|---|---|
| | 1,800    Apr. 30 |

| Dee Bell, Capital | |
|---|---|
| | 8,900    Apr. 30 |

| Revenue | 410 |
|---|---|
| | 3,000    Apr. 30 |

| Wages Expense | 650 |
|---|---|
| Apr. 30    1,500 | |

### Part 3

_____
_____
_____
_____

*Fundamental Accounting Principles*, 15ce, Working Papers

**Quick Study 2-11**

| Accounts Receivable | |
|---:|---:|
| 1,000 | 650 |
| 400 | 920 |
| 920 | 1,500 |
| 3,000 | |

| Accounts Payable | |
|---:|---:|
| 250 | 250 |
| 900 | 1,800 |
| 650 | 1,400 |
| | 650 |

| Service Revenue | |
|---:|---:|
| | 13,000 |
| | 2,500 |
| | 810 |
| | 3,500 |

| Utilities Expense | |
|---:|---:|
| 610 | |
| 520 | |
| 390 | |
| 275 | |

| Cash | |
|---:|---:|
| 3,900 | 2,400 |
| 17,800 | 3,900 |
| 14,500 | 21,800 |
| 340 | |

| Notes Payable | |
|---:|---:|
| 4,000 | 50,000 |
| 8,000 | |

**Quick Study 2-12**

## GENERAL JOURNAL                              Page ____

| Date | Account Titles and Explanation | PR | Debit | Credit |
|------|-------------------------------|-----|-------|--------|
| 2017 | | | | |
| May 1 | Equipment ---------- | | 500 | |
| |    Accounts payable--- | | | 500 |
| | Purchased equipment | | | |
| | on account. | | | |
| 2 | Accounts payable ----- | | 500 | |
| |    Cash --------- | | | 500 |
| | Paid for the equipment | | | |
| | purchased May 1. | | | |
| 3 | Supplies --------- | | 100 | |
| |    Cash -------- | | | 100 |
| | Purchased supplies for | | | |
| | Cash | | | |
| 4 | Wages Expense ------ | | 2000 | |
| |    Cash -------- | | | 2000 |
| | Paid wages to employee | | | |
| 5 | Cash --------- | | 750 | |
| |    Service Revenue --- | | | 750 |
| | Performed services | | | |
| | for a client for cash. | | | |
| 6 | Accounts Receivable---- | | 2500 | |
| |    Service Revenue--- | | | 2500 |
| | Did work for a | | | |
| | customer on credit. | | | |
| 7 | Cash --------- | | 2500 | |
| |    Accounts Receivable- | | | 2500 |
| | Collected May 6 | | | |
| | customer account. | | | |
| | | | | |
| | | | | |
| | | | | |
| | | | | |
| | | | | |

## GENERAL JOURNAL

Page _____

| Date | Account Titles and Explanation | PR | Debit | Credit |
|------|-------------------------------|----|----|----|
|  |  |  |  |  |
|  |  |  |  |  |
|  |  |  |  |  |
|  |  |  |  |  |
|  |  |  |  |  |
|  |  |  |  |  |
|  |  |  |  |  |
|  |  |  |  |  |
|  |  |  |  |  |
|  |  |  |  |  |
|  |  |  |  |  |
|  |  |  |  |  |
|  |  |  |  |  |
|  |  |  |  |  |
|  |  |  |  |  |
|  |  |  |  |  |
|  |  |  |  |  |
|  |  |  |  |  |
|  |  |  |  |  |
|  |  |  |  |  |
|  |  |  |  |  |
|  |  |  |  |  |
|  |  |  |  |  |
|  |  |  |  |  |
|  |  |  |  |  |
|  |  |  |  |  |
|  |  |  |  |  |
|  |  |  |  |  |
|  |  |  |  |  |
|  |  |  |  |  |
|  |  |  |  |  |
|  |  |  |  |  |
|  |  |  |  |  |
|  |  |  |  |  |
|  |  |  |  |  |
|  |  |  |  |  |
|  |  |  |  |  |
|  |  |  |  |  |

Name:_____

**Quick Study 2-14**

**Cash**                                                                    ACCOUNT NO. _____

| DATE | EXPLANATION | PR | DEBIT | CREDIT | BALANCE |
|---|---|---|---|---|---|
|  |  |  |  |  |  |
|  |  |  |  |  |  |
|  |  |  |  |  |  |
|  |  |  |  |  |  |
|  |  |  |  |  |  |

**Office Supplies**                                                     ACCOUNT NO. _____

| DATE | EXPLANATION | PR | DEBIT | CREDIT | BALANCE |
|---|---|---|---|---|---|
|  |  |  |  |  |  |
|  |  |  |  |  |  |
|  |  |  |  |  |  |

**Equipment**                                                          ACCOUNT NO. _____

| DATE | EXPLANATION | PR | DEBIT | CREDIT | BALANCE |
|---|---|---|---|---|---|
|  |  |  |  |  |  |
|  |  |  |  |  |  |
|  |  |  |  |  |  |

**Accounts Payable**                                                 ACCOUNT NO. _____

| DATE | EXPLANATION | PR | DEBIT | CREDIT | BALANCE |
|---|---|---|---|---|---|
|  |  |  |  |  |  |
|  |  |  |  |  |  |
|  |  |  |  |  |  |
|  |  |  |  |  |  |
|  |  |  |  |  |  |
|  |  |  |  |  |  |

**Stan Adams, Capital**                                             ACCOUNT NO. _____

| DATE | EXPLANATION | PR | DEBIT | CREDIT | BALANCE |
|---|---|---|---|---|---|
|  |  |  |  |  |  |
|  |  |  |  |  |  |
|  |  |  |  |  |  |

**Landscaping Services Revenue**                              ACCOUNT NO. _____

| DATE | EXPLANATION | PR | DEBIT | CREDIT | BALANCE |
|---|---|---|---|---|---|
|  |  |  |  |  |  |
|  |  |  |  |  |  |

*Fundamental Accounting Principles*, 15ce, Working Papers

**Quick Study 2-15**

Vahn Landscaping
Trial Balance
January 31, 2017

| ct No. | Account | Debit $ | Credit $ |
|---|---|---|---|
| 01 | Cash | 7000 | |
| 63 | Equipment | 9000 | |
| 233 | Unearned revenue | | 2000 |
| 301 | Bred Vahn, capital | | 14000 |
| 302 | Bred Vahn, withdrawals | 1000 | |
| 101 | Revenue | | 11000 |
| 40 | Rent expense | 6000 | |
| 590 | Utilities expense | 4000 | |
| | Totals | $ 27000 | $ 27000 |

**Quick Study 2-16**

**Quick Study 2-17**

**Quick Study 2-18**

Name:_____

Exercise 2-1

| | | (a) Basic Account | (b) Financial Statement | (c) Normal Balance | (d) Effect of a Debit | (e) Effect of a Credit |
|---|---|---|---|---|---|---|
| a. | Cash | | | | | |
| b. | Supplies | | | | | |
| c. | Accounts Payable | | | | | |
| d. | Yoojin Chang, Capital Account | | | | | |
| e. | Yoojin Chang, Withdrawals | | | | | |
| f. | Design Revenue | | | | | |
| g. | Salaries Expense | | | | | |
| h. | Accounts Receivable | | | | | |
| i. | Notes Payable | | | | | |
| j. | Prepaid insurance | | | | | |

*Fundamental Accounting Principles*, 15ce, Working Papers

**Exercise 2-2**

| a. | Analysis | Assets increase, Equity increases |
|----|----------|-----------------------------------|
| | Journal entry analysis | Debit the cash account for $15000 Credit the Christina Reis Capital ac in equity for $15000 |
| b. | Analysis | Assets increase, Liabilities increase |
| | Journal entry analysis | Debit the Equipment account for $2000 Credit the Accounts payable ac for $2000 |
| c. | Analysis | Assets increase, Assets decrease |
| | Journal entry analysis | Debit the Equipment account for $500 Credit the cash account for $500. |
| d. | Analysis | Assets increase, Equity increases form Revenue. |
| | Journal entry analysis | Debit the cash account for $1000. Credit the Revenue account for $1000. |
| e. | Analysis | Assets increase, Equity increases from Revenue |
| | Journal entry analysis | Debit the account Receivable ac for $700 Credit the Revenue account for $700. |
| f. | Analysis | Assets decrease, Liabilities decrease |
| | Journal entry analysis | Debit the Acount payable ac for $1000 credit the cash account for $1000. |
| g. | Analysis | Assets increase, Assets decrease |
| | Journal entry analysis | Debit the cash account for $300 Credit the Acount Receivable ac for $300 |

| | Date | Account Titles and Explanation | | Debit | Credit |
|---|---|---|---|---|---|
| a. | Sept 1 | Cash | | 15000 | |
| | | Christina Reis, Capital | | | 15000 |
| | | Investment by owner | | | |
| | | | | | |
| b. | Sept 12 | Equipment | | 2000 | |
| | | Accounts payable | | | 2000 |
| | | Purchased equipment on credit | | | |
| | | | | | |
| c. | Sept 13 | Equipment | | 500 | |
| | | Cash | | | 500 |
| | | Purchased equipment with cash | | | |
| | | | | | |
| d. | Sept 18 | Cash | | 1000 | |
| | | Revenue | | | 1000 |
| | | Provided service for cash | | | |
| | | | | | |
| e. | Sept 21 | Accounts Receivable | | 700 | |
| | | Revenue | | | 700 |
| | | Provided service on account | | | |
| | | | | | |
| f. | Sept 26 | Accounts payable | | 1000 | |
| | | Cash | | | 1000 |
| | | Payment for equipment | | | |
| | | | | | |
| g. | Sept 29 | Cash | | 300 | |
| | | Accounts Receivable | | | 300 |
| | | Collection of cash from | | | |
| | | Customer | | | |

**Chapter 2**

Name:_____

**Exercise 2-4**

**Part 1 and 2**

| Cash | 101 |
|---|---|
| a) 15000 | 500 e |
| d) 1000 | 1000 (f |
| g) 300 | |
| Bal 14,800 | |

| Accounts Receivable | 106 |
|---|---|
| (e) 700 | 300 (g) |
| Bal 400 | |

| Equipment | 161 |
|---|---|
| (b) 2000 | |
| (c) 500 | |
| Bal 2500 | |

| Accounts Payable | 201 |
|---|---|
| f) 1000 | 2000 (b) |
| | Bal 1000 |

| Christina Reis, Capital | 301 |
|---|---|
| | 15000 (a) |
| | Bal 15000 |

| Revenue | 403 |
|---|---|
| | 1000 (a) |
| | 700 (e) |
| | Bal 1700 |

3.

The account balance for each T-account is shown above. The accounting equation (Assets = liabilities + equity) is proved as follows:
$17,700 = $1000 + $16,700

Name:_____

**Exercise 2-5**

| a. | Analysis | | | |
|---|---|---|---|---|
| | Journal entry analysis | | | |
| | Journal Entry | | | |
| | Date | Account Titles and Explanation | Debit | Credit |
| | | | | |
| | | | | |
| | | | | |

| b. | Analysis | | | |
|---|---|---|---|---|
| | Journal entry analysis | | | |
| | Journal Entry | | | |
| | Date | Account Titles and Explanation | Debit | Credit |
| | | | | |
| | | | | |
| | | | | |
| | | | | |

| c. | Analysis | | | |
|---|---|---|---|---|
| | Journal entry analysis | | | |
| | Journal Entry | | | |
| | Date | Account Titles and Explanation | Debit | Credit |
| | | | | |
| | | | | |
| | | | | |

*Fundamental Accounting Principles*, 15ce, Working Papers

**Exercise 2-5 (Continued)**

| d. | Analysis | |
|---|---|---|
| | Journal entry analysis | |
| | Journal Entry | |

| Date | Account Titles and Explanation | Debit | Credit |
|---|---|---|---|
| | | | |
| | | | |
| | | | |

| e. | Analysis | |
|---|---|---|
| | Journal entry analysis | |
| | Journal Entry | |

| Date | Account Titles and Explanation | Debit | Credit |
|---|---|---|---|
| | | | |
| | | | |
| | | | |

| f. | Analysis | |
|---|---|---|
| | Journal entry analysis | |
| | Journal Entry | |

| Date | Account Titles and Explanation | Debit | Credit |
|---|---|---|---|
| | | | |
| | | | |
| | | | |

**Exercise 2-5 (Concluded)**

| g. | Analysis | | | |
|----|----------|---|---|---|
| | Journal entry analysis | | | |
| | Journal Entry | | | |
| | Date | Account Titles and Explanation | Debit | Credit |
| | | | | |
| | | | | |
| | | | | |

| h. | Analysis | | | |
|----|----------|---|---|---|
| | Journal entry analysis | | | |
| | Journal Entry | | | |
| | Date | Account Titles and Explanation | Debit | Credit |
| | | | | |
| | | | | |
| | | | | |

| i. | Analysis | | | |
|----|----------|---|---|---|
| | Journal entry analysis | | | |
| | Journal Entry | | | |
| | Date | Account Titles and Explanation | Debit | Credit |
| | | | | |
| | | | | |
| | | | | |

Name:_____

**Exercise 2-6**

|                          |                          |
|--------------------------|--------------------------|
| **Cash**                 | **Accounts Payable**     |
|                          | **William Curtis, Capital** |
| **Accounts Receivable**  | **William Curtis, Withdrawals** |
| **Office Supplies**      | **Revenue**              |
| **Office Equipment**     | **Rent Expense**         |

**Chapter 2**

Name:_____

**Exercise 2-7**

### GENERAL JOURNAL

Page _____

| Date | | Account Titles and Explanation | PR | Debit | Credit |
|------|---|---|----|-------|--------|
| | | | | | |
| | | | | | |
| | | | | | |
| | | | | | |
| | | | | | |
| | | | | | |
| | | | | | |
| | | | | | |

**Transactions not creating revenue and the reasons:**

_____
_____
_____
_____
_____
_____
_____
_____
_____
_____
_____
_____
_____
_____
_____
_____
_____

**Exercise 2-8**

### GENERAL JOURNAL

Page _____

| Date | | Account Titles and Explanation | PR | Debit | Credit |
|------|---|---|----|-------|--------|
| | | | | | |
| | | | | | |
| | | | | | |
| | | | | | |
| | | | | | |
| | | | | | |
| | | | | | |
| | | | | | |
| | | | | | |
| | | | | | |

*Fundamental Accounting Principles, 15ce, Working Papers*

**Chapter 2**

Name:_____

**Exercise 2-8 (Continued)**

Transactions not creating revenue and the reasons:
_____
_____
_____
_____
_____
_____
_____
_____
_____
_____
_____
_____
_____

**Exercise 2-9**

**Parts 1 and 3**

*Note: T-accounts may be used or the balance column format; both are provided for in Parts 1 and 3 of this exercise.*

| | Cash | 101 |
|---|---|---|
| July 1  5000 | 3500 | July 14 |
| 12  10000 | 250 | 31 |
| Bal  11,250 | | |

| | Accounts Receivable | 106 |
|---|---|---|
| July 15  1500 | | |

| | Equipment | 150 |
|---|---|---|
| July 10  2500 | | |

| | Accounts Payable | 201 |
|---|---|---|
| | 2500 | July 10 |

| | Manny Gill, Capital | 301 |
|---|---|---|
| | 5000 | July 1 |

| | Manny Gill, Withdrawals | 302 |
|---|---|---|
| July 31  250 | | |

| | Revenue | 401 |
|---|---|---|
| | 10000 | July 12 |
| | 1500 | 15 |
| | 11,500 | Bal |

| | Expenses | 501 |
|---|---|---|
| July 14  3500 | | |

Exercise 2-9

*Continued*

*Note: T-accounts may be used or the balance column format; both are provided for in Parts 1 and 3 of this exercise.*

### GENERAL LEDGER

#### Cash — ACCOUNT NO. 101

| DATE | | EXPLANATION | PR | DEBIT | CREDIT | BALANCE |
|------|------|-------------|----|-------|--------|---------|
| 2017 | 1 | | GI | 5000 | | 5000 |
| July | 12 | | GI | 10000 | | 15000 |
| | 14 | | | | 3500 | 11500 |
| | 31 | | | | 250 | 11250 |
| | | | | | | |
| | | | | | | |

#### Accounts Receivable — ACCOUNT NO. 106

| DATE | | EXPLANATION | PR | DEBIT | CREDIT | BALANCE |
|------|------|-------------|----|-------|--------|---------|
| 2017 | 15 | | GI | 1500 | | 1500 |
| July | | | | | | |
| | | | | | | |

#### Equipment — ACCOUNT NO. 150

| DATE | | EXPLANATION | PR | DEBIT | CREDIT | BALANCE |
|------|------|-------------|----|-------|--------|---------|
| 2017 | 10 | | GI | 2500 | | 2500 |
| July | | | | | | |
| | | | | | | |

#### Accounts Payable — ACCOUNT NO. 201

| DATE | | EXPLANATION | PR | DEBIT | CREDIT | BALANCE |
|------|------|-------------|----|-------|--------|---------|
| 2017 | 10 | | GI | | 2500 | 2500 |
| July | | | | | | |
| | | | | | | |

#### Manny Gill, Capital — ACCOUNT NO. 301

| DATE | | EXPLANATION | PR | DEBIT | CREDIT | BALANCE |
|------|------|-------------|----|-------|--------|---------|
| 2017 | 1 | | GI | | 5000 | 5000 |
| July | | | | | | |

#### Manny Gill, Withdrawals — ACCOUNT NO. 302

| DATE | | EXPLANATION | PR | DEBIT | CREDIT | BALANCE |
|------|------|-------------|----|-------|--------|---------|
| 2017 | 31 | | GI | 250 | | 250 |
| July | | | | | | |

**Exercise 2-9**

|  | Revenue |  |  | ACCOUNT NO. 401 |  |
|---|---|---|---|---|---|
| **DATE** | **EXPLANATION** | **PR** | **DEBIT** | **CREDIT** | **BALANCE** |
| 2017 12 |  | G1 |  | 10000 | 10000 |
| July 15 |  | G1 |  | 1500 | 11500 |
|  |  |  |  |  |  |

|  | Expenses |  |  | ACCOUNT NO. 501 |  |
|---|---|---|---|---|---|
| **DATE** | **EXPLANATION** | **PR** | **DEBIT** | **CREDIT** | **BALANCE** |
| 2017 14 |  | G1 | 3500 |  | 3500 |
| July |  |  |  |  |  |

**Part 2**

**GENERAL JOURNAL**                    Page ____

| Date | Account Titles and Explanation | PR | Debit | Credit |
|---|---|---|---|---|
| 2017 1 | Cash | 101 | 5000 |  |
| July | Munny Grill, Capital | 301 |  | 5000 |
|  | To record investment |  |  |  |
|  | by owner. |  |  |  |
|  |  |  |  |  |
|  | 10 Equipment | 150 | 2500 |  |
|  | Accounts payable | 201 |  | 2500 |
|  | Purchased equipment |  |  |  |
|  | on credit. |  |  |  |
|  |  |  |  |  |
|  | 12 Cash | 101 | 10000 |  |
|  | Revenue | 401 |  | 10000 |
|  | Performed services |  |  |  |
|  | for cash. |  |  |  |
|  |  |  |  |  |
|  | 14 Expense | 501 | 3500 |  |
|  | Cash | 101 |  | 3500 |
|  | Paid expenses. |  |  |  |

Exercise 2-9 (cont'd.)

## GENERAL JOURNAL

Page ____

| Date | Account Titles and Explanation | PR | Debit | Credit |
|------|-------------------------------|-----|-------|--------|
| 15 | Accounts Receivable | 106 | 1500 | |
| | Revenue | 401 | | 1500 |
| | Completed services | | | |
| | on account | | | |
| | | | | |
| 31 | Manny Grill, withdrawals | 302 | 250 | |
| | Cash | 101 | | 250 |
| | Owner withdrew | | | |
| | cash. | | | |
| | | | | |

**Part 4**

**Wild West Secure**

**Trial Balance**

**July 31, 2017**

| Acct. No. | Account Title | Debit $ | Credit $ |
|-----------|---------------|---------|----------|
| 101 | Cash | 11250 | |
| 106 | Accounts Receivable | 1500 | |
| 150 | Equipment | 2500 | |
| 201 | Accounts payable | | 2500 |
| 301 | Manny Grill, Capital | | 5000 |
| 302 | Manny Grill, withdrawals | 250 | |
| 401 | Revenue | | 11500 |
| 501 | Expenses | 3500 | |
| | | $ 19000 | $ 19000 |
| | | | |

**Part 5**

**Wild West Secure**

**Income Statement**

**For Month Ended July 31, 2017**

| | | |
|---|---|---|
| Revenue | | |
| Expenses | | |
| Profit | | |
| | | |

Name:_____

Exercise 2-9 (concl'd.)

**Wild West Secure**
**Statement of Changes in Equity**
**For Month Ended July 31, 2017**

| | | |
|---|---|---|
| Manny Gill, capital, July 1 | | |
| Add:　Investments by owner | | |
| Profit | | |
| 　　Total | | |
| Less: Withdrawals by owner | | |
| Manny Gill, capital, July 31 | | |
| | | |

**Wild West Secure**
**Balance Sheet**
**July 31, 2017**

| Assets | | Liabilities | |
|---|---|---|---|
| Cash | | Accounts payable | |
| Accounts receivable | | Equity | |
| Equipment | | Manny Gill, capital | |
| Total assets | | Total liabilities and equity | |
| | | | |
| | | | |

*Analysis component:*

_____
_____
_____
_____
_____
_____
_____
_____
_____
_____
_____

Name:_____

## Exercise 2-10

| Account Number | Account Name | Account Number | Account Name |
|---|---|---|---|
| _____ | Cash | _____ | Aaron Paquette, Withdrawals |
| _____ | Accounts Receivable | _____ | Consulting Revenues |
| _____ | Office Equipment | _____ | Salaries Expense |
| _____ | Accounts Payable | _____ | Rent Expense |
| _____ | Unearned Revenue | _____ | Utilities Expense |
| _____ | Aaron Paquette, Capital | | |

## Exercise 2-11  Part 1

**GENERAL JOURNAL**                    Page _____

| Date | Account Titles and Explanation | PR | Debit | Credit |
|---|---|---|---|---|
| | | | | |
| | | | | |
| | | | | |
| | | | | |
| | | | | |
| | | | | |
| | | | | |
| | | | | |
| | | | | |
| | | | | |
| | | | | |
| | | | | |
| | | | | |
| | | | | |
| | | | | |
| | | | | |
| | | | | |
| | | | | |
| | | | | |
| | | | | |
| | | | | |
| | | | | |
| | | | | |
| | | | | |
| | | | | |

Name:_____

**Exercise 2-11 (cont'd.)**

**Part 2**

| Cash | 101 |
|---|---|
| Bal. 15,000 | |

| Accounts Receivable | 115 |
|---|---|
| Bal. 3,800 | |

| Office Equipment | 160 |
|---|---|
| Bal. 22,500 | |

| Accounts Payable | 210 |
|---|---|
| | 8,000 Bal. |

| Unearned Revenue | 215 |
|---|---|
| | 2,600 Bal. |

| Aaron Paquette, Capital | 310 |
|---|---|
| | 9,500 Bal. |

| Aaron Paquette, Withdrawals | 320 |
|---|---|
| Bal. 2,000 | |

| Consulting Revenues | 410 |
|---|---|
| | 41,700 Bal. |

| Salaries Expense | 510 |
|---|---|
| Bal. 10,000 | |

| Rent Expense | 520 |
|---|---|
| Bal. 7,500 | |

| Utilities Expense | 530 |
|---|---|
| Bal. 1,000 | |

**Exercise 2-11 (cont'd.)**

**Part 3**

| Trial Balance | | |
|---|---|---|
| | | |
| | | |
| | | |
| | | |
| | | |
| | | |
| | | |
| | | |
| | | |
| | | |
| | | |
| | | |
| | | |
| | | |

**Part 4**

| Income Statement | | |
|---|---|---|
| | | |
| | | |
| | | |
| | | |
| | | |
| | | |
| | | |
| | | |
| | | |
| | | |

*Fundamental Accounting Principles,* **15ce, Working Papers**

**Exercise 2-11 (cont'd.)**

**Part 5**

## Statement of Changes in Equity

| | | |
|---|---|---|
| | | |
| | | |
| | | |
| | | |
| | | |
| | | |
| | | |
| | | |
| | | |

**Part 6**

## Balance Sheet

| | | | |
|---|---|---|---|
| | | | |
| | | | |
| | | | |
| | | | |
| | | | |
| | | | |
| | | | |
| | | | |
| | | | |
| | | | |
| | | | |

*Analysis component:*

## GENERAL JOURNAL

Page ____

| Date | | Account Titles and Explanation | PR | Debit | Credit |
|------|---|---|---|---|---|
| **a.** | | | | | |
| | | | | | |
| | | | | | |
| | | | | | |
| | | | | | |
| | | | | | |
| **b.** | | | | | |
| | | | | | |
| | | | | | |
| | | | | | |
| **c.** | | | | | |
| | | | | | |
| | | | | | |
| | | | | | |
| | | | | | |
| **d.** | | | | | |
| | | | | | |
| | | | | | |
| | | | | | |
| **e.** | | | | | |
| | | | | | |
| | | | | | |
| **f.** | | | | | |
| | | | | | |
| | | | | | |
| **g.** | | | | | |
| | | | | | |
| | | | | | |

Exercise 2-13

### GENERAL JOURNAL

Page ____

| Date | Account Titles and Explanation | PR | Debit | Credit |
|---|---|---|---|---|
| | | | | |
| | | | | |
| | | | | |
| | | | | |
| | | | | |
| | | | | |
| | | | | |
| | | | | |
| | | | | |
| | | | | |
| | | | | |
| | | | | |
| | | | | |
| | | | | |
| | | | | |
| | | | | |
| | | | | |
| | | | | |
| | | | | |
| | | | | |
| | | | | |
| | | | | |
| | | | | |
| | | | | |
| | | | | |
| | | | | |
| | | | | |
| | | | | |
| | | | | |
| | | | | |
| | | | | |
| | | | | |
| | | | | |

Name:_____

**Exercise 2-14**

## GENERAL LEDGER

### Cash     ACCOUNT NO. 101

| DATE | EXPLANATION | PR | DEBIT | CREDIT | BALANCE |
|------|-------------|----|-------|--------|---------|
| 2016 | | | | | |
| Dec. 31 | Beginning balance | | | | 850 |
| | | | | | |
| | | | | | |
| | | | | | |
| | | | | | |
| | | | | | |
| | | | | | |

### Accounts Receivable     ACCOUNT NO. 106

| DATE | EXPLANATION | PR | DEBIT | CREDIT | BALANCE |
|------|-------------|----|-------|--------|---------|
| 2016 | | | | | |
| Dec. 31 | Beginning balance | | | | 300 |
| | | | | | |
| | | | | | |
| | | | | | |
| | | | | | |

### Equipment     ACCOUNT NO. 167

| DATE | EXPLANATION | PR | DEBIT | CREDIT | BALANCE |
|------|-------------|----|-------|--------|---------|
| 2016 | | | | | |
| Dec. 31 | Beginning balance | | | | 1,500 |
| | | | | | |
| | | | | | |

### Accounts Payable     ACCOUNT NO. 201

| DATE | EXPLANATION | PR | DEBIT | CREDIT | BALANCE |
|------|-------------|----|-------|--------|---------|
| 2016 | | | | | |
| Dec. 31 | Beginning balance | | | | 325 |
| | | | | | |
| | | | | | |

### Toshi Sato, Capital     ACCOUNT NO. 301

| DATE | EXPLANATION | PR | DEBIT | CREDIT | BALANCE |
|------|-------------|----|-------|--------|---------|
| 2016 | | | | | |
| Dec. 31 | Beginning balance | | | | 2,325 |
| | | | | | |
| | | | | | |

**Exercise 2-14 (concl'd.)**

### Toshi Sato, Withdrawals                     ACCOUNT NO. 302

| DATE | EXPLANATION | PR | DEBIT | CREDIT | BALANCE |
|------|-------------|----|-------|--------|---------|
| 2016 | | | | | |
| Dec.31 | Beginning balance | | | | 300 |
| | | | | | |
| | | | | | |

### Revenue                                    ACCOUNT NO. 401

| DATE | EXPLANATION | PR | DEBIT | CREDIT | BALANCE |
|------|-------------|----|-------|--------|---------|
| 2016 | | | | | |
| Dec.31 | Beginning balance | | | | 1,800 |
| | | | | | |
| | | | | | |

### Salaries Expense                           ACCOUNT NO. 622

| DATE | EXPLANATION | PR | DEBIT | CREDIT | BALANCE |
|------|-------------|----|-------|--------|---------|
| 2016 | | | | | |
| Dec.31 | Beginning balance | | | | 1,500 |
| | | | | | |
| | | | | | |

*Analysis component:*

_____
_____
_____
_____
_____
_____
_____
_____
_____
_____
_____
_____

**GENERAL JOURNAL**                                    Page ____

| Date | Account Titles and Explanation | PR | Debit | Credit |
|------|-------------------------------|-----|-------|--------|
|      |                               |     |       |        |
|      |                               |     |       |        |
|      |                               |     |       |        |
|      |                               |     |       |        |
|      |                               |     |       |        |
|      |                               |     |       |        |
|      |                               |     |       |        |
|      |                               |     |       |        |
|      |                               |     |       |        |
|      |                               |     |       |        |
|      |                               |     |       |        |
|      |                               |     |       |        |
|      |                               |     |       |        |
|      |                               |     |       |        |
|      |                               |     |       |        |
|      |                               |     |       |        |
|      |                               |     |       |        |
|      |                               |     |       |        |
|      |                               |     |       |        |
|      |                               |     |       |        |
|      |                               |     |       |        |
|      |                               |     |       |        |
|      |                               |     |       |        |
|      |                               |     |       |        |

**Exercise 2-16**

### Cash                                                    ACCOUNT NO. 101

| DATE | EXPLANATION | PR | DEBIT | CREDIT | BALANCE |
|------|-------------|-----|-------|--------|---------|
|      |             |     |       |        |         |
|      |             |     |       |        |         |
|      |             |     |       |        |         |
|      |             |     |       |        |         |
|      |             |     |       |        |         |

### Office Supplies                                         ACCOUNT NO. 124

| DATE | EXPLANATION | PR | DEBIT | CREDIT | BALANCE |
|------|-------------|-----|-------|--------|---------|
|      |             |     |       |        |         |
|      |             |     |       |        |         |

### Prepaid Rent                                            ACCOUNT NO. 131

| DATE | EXPLANATION | PR | DEBIT | CREDIT | BALANCE |
|------|-------------|-----|-------|--------|---------|
|      |             |     |       |        |         |
|      |             |     |       |        |         |

### Photography Equipment                                   ACCOUNT NO. 167

| DATE | EXPLANATION | PR | DEBIT | CREDIT | BALANCE |
|------|-------------|-----|-------|--------|---------|
|      |             |     |       |        |         |
|      |             |     |       |        |         |

### Joseph Eetok, Capital                                   ACCOUNT NO. 301

| DATE | EXPLANATION | PR | DEBIT | CREDIT | BALANCE |
|------|-------------|-----|-------|--------|---------|
|      |             |     |       |        |         |
|      |             |     |       |        |         |

### Photography Revenue                                     ACCOUNT NO. 401

| DATE | EXPLANATION | PR | DEBIT | CREDIT | BALANCE |
|------|-------------|-----|-------|--------|---------|
|      |             |     |       |        |         |
|      |             |     |       |        |         |

### Utilities Expense                                       ACCOUNT NO. 690

| DATE | EXPLANATION | PR | DEBIT | CREDIT | BALANCE |
|------|-------------|-----|-------|--------|---------|
|      |             |     |       |        |         |
|      |             |     |       |        |         |

**Exercise 2-16 (concl'd.)**

| Trial Balance | Debit | Credit |
|---|---|---|
| | | |
| | | |
| | | |
| | | |
| | | |
| | | |
| | | |
| | | |
| | | |

*Analysis component:*

_____
_____
_____
_____
_____
_____
_____
_____
_____
_____

Name:_____

**Exercise 2-17**

|  Cash | 101 | | Office Supplies | 124 |

|  Photography Equipment | 167 |

|  Prepaid Rent | 131 | | Photography Revenue | 401 |

|  Joseph Eetok, Capital | 301 | | Utilities Expense | 690 |

### Trial Balance

|  | Debit | Credit |
|---|---|---|
|  |  |  |
|  |  |  |
|  |  |  |
|  |  |  |
|  |  |  |
|  |  |  |
|  |  |  |
|  |  |  |
|  |  |  |

*Analysis component:*

_____
_____
_____
_____
_____
_____
_____
_____
_____

**Exercise 2-18**

## Income Statement

| | | |
|---|---|---|
| | | |
| | | |
| | | |
| | | |
| | | |
| | | |

## Statement of Changes in Equity

| | | |
|---|---|---|
| | | |
| | | |
| | | |
| | | |
| | | |

## Balance Sheet

| | | | |
|---|---|---|---|
| | | | |
| | | | |
| | | | |
| | | | |
| | | | |
| | | | |

*Analysis component:*

**Exercise 2-19**

## Income Statement

| | | |
|---|---|---|
| | | |
| | | |
| | | |
| | | |
| | | |
| | | |
| | | |
| | | |
| | | |
| | | |

## Statement of Changes in Equity

| | | |
|---|---|---|
| | | |
| | | |
| | | |
| | | |
| | | |
| | | |
| | | |
| | | |
| | | |
| | | |
| | | |

## Balance Sheet

| | | | |
|---|---|---|---|
| | | | |
| | | | |
| | | | |
| | | | |
| | | | |
| | | | |
| | | | |
| | | | |
| | | | |
| | | | |

**Exercise 2-20**

## Income Statement

| | | |
|---|---|---|
| | | |
| | | |
| | | |
| | | |
| | | |
| | | |
| | | |
| | | |
| | | |
| | | |

## Statement of Changes in Equity

| | | |
|---|---|---|
| | | |
| | | |
| | | |
| | | |
| | | |
| | | |
| | | |
| | | |
| | | |
| | | |

## Balance Sheet

| | | | |
|---|---|---|---|
| | | | |
| | | | |
| | | | |
| | | | |
| | | | |
| | | | |
| | | | |
| | | | |
| | | | |
| | | | |
| | | | |
| | | | |

Name:_____

## Exercise 2-21

| | Description | (1) Difference Between Debit and Credit Column | (2) Column With the Larger Total | (3) Identify Account(s) Incorrectly Stated | (4) Amount That Account(s) is Overstated or Understated |
|---|---|---|---|---|---|
| a. | A $2,400 debit to Rent Expense was posted as a $1,590 debit. | $810 | Credit | Rent Expense | Rent Expense is understated by $810 |
| b. | A $42,000 debit to Machinery was posted as a debit to Accounts Payable. | | | | |
| c. | A $4,950 credit to Services Revenue was posted as a $495 credit. | | | | |
| d. | A $1,440 debit to Store Supplies was not posted at all. | | | | |
| e. | A $2,250 debit to Prepaid Insurance was posted as a debit to Insurance Expense. | | | | |
| f. | A $4,050 credit to Cash was posted twice as two credits to the Cash account. | | | | |
| g. | A $9,900 debit to the owner's withdrawals account was debited to the owner's capital account. | | | | |

## Exercise 2-22

a. _____
_____

b. _____
_____
_____

c. _____
_____

d. _____
_____

e. _____
_____
_____

Name:_____

**Exercise 2-23**

**Case A:**

_____
_____
_____
_____
_____
_____
_____
_____
_____
_____
_____
_____

**Case B:**

_____
_____
_____
_____
_____
_____
_____
_____
_____
_____

**Case C:**

_____
_____
_____
_____
_____
_____
_____
_____
_____
_____
_____
_____
_____

*Fundamental Accounting Principles*, 15ce, Working Papers

**Problem 2-1A**

| Nov 1 | Analysis | Assets increase, Equity increases. | | |
|---|---|---|---|---|
| | Journal entry analysis | Debit the Cash account for $200000 Debit the Aircraft Equipment ac for $50000. Credit the Tobias Eaden Capital ac for $250000. | | |
| | Journal Entry | | | |
| | **Date** | **Account Titles and Explanation** | **Debit** | **Credit** |
| | Nov 1 | Cash | 200,000 | |
| | | Aircraft Equipment | 50,000 | |
| | | Tobias Eaden, capital | | 250,000 |
| | | Owner investment of | | |
| | | Cash and equipment. | | |

| Nov 3 | Analysis | Assets increase and assets decrease. Liabilities increase. | | |
|---|---|---|---|---|
| | Journal entry analysis | Debit the land account for $400,000 Debit the Building account for $100,000. Credit the cash account for $125,000. Credit the Long term Notes payable ac for $375,000. | | |
| | Journal Entry | | | |
| | **Date** | **Account Titles and Explanation** | **Debit** | **Credit** |
| | Nov 3 | Land | 400,000 | |
| | | Building | 100,000 | |
| | | Cash | | 125,000 |
| | | Long term Notes payable | | 375,000 |
| | | Purchased Land & building | | |
| | | with cash and a long term | | |
| | | notes payable. | | |

**Problem 2-1A (Cont'd.)**

| Nov 7 | Analysis | Assets increase, Equity increase. | | |
|---|---|---|---|---|
| | Journal entry analysis | Debit the Airplane account for $200,000 Credit the Tobias Eaden account for $200,000 | | |
| | Journal Entry | | | |
| | Date | Account Titles and Explanation | Debit | Credit |
| | Nov 7 | Airplane | 200,000 | |
| | |    Tobias Eaden, Capital | | 200,000 |
| | | Owner investment if asset | | |

| Nov 9 | Analysis | Assets increase, liabilities increase. | | |
|---|---|---|---|---|
| | Journal entry analysis | Debit the Supplies account for $5000 Credit the Ac payable ac for $5000 | | |
| | Journal Entry | | | |
| | Date | Account Titles and Explanation | Debit | Credit |
| | Nov 9 | Supplies | 5000 | |
| | |    Accounts payable | | 5000 |
| | | Purchased supplies on credit | | |

| Nov 13 | Analysis | Assets increase, Equity increases | | |
|---|---|---|---|---|
| | Journal entry analysis | Debit the Ac receivable ac for $16000 Credit the Revenue account for $16000 | | |
| | Journal Entry | | | |
| | Date | Account Titles and Explanation | Debit | Credit |
| | Nov 13 | Accounts Receivable | 16,000 | |
| | |    Revenue | | 16,000 |
| | | Billed customer for services provided. | | |

Name:_____

**Problem 2-1A (Cont'd.)**

| Nov 17 | Analysis | Assets decrease, Equity decreases. | | |
|---|---|---|---|---|
| | Journal entry analysis | Debit the Wages Expense ac for $3000. Credit the Cash account for $3000. | | |
| | Journal Entry | | | |
| | Date | Account Titles and Explanation | Debit | Credit |
| | Nov 17 | Wages Expense | 3,000 | |
| | | Cash | | 3,000 |
| | | Paid wages. | | |

| Nov 21 | Analysis | No Transaction required. | | |
|---|---|---|---|---|
| | Journal entry analysis | | | |
| | Journal Entry | | | |
| | Date | Account Titles and Explanation | Debit | Credit |
| | | | | |
| | | | | |
| | | | | |

| Nov 23 | Analysis | Assets decrease. Liabilities decrease. | | |
|---|---|---|---|---|
| | Journal entry analysis | Debit the liabilities ac for $2500. Credit the Cash account for $2500. | | |
| | Journal Entry | | | |
| | Date | Account Titles and Explanation | Debit | Credit |
| | Nov 23 | Accounts Payable | 2,500 | |
| | | Cash | | 2,500 |
| | | Paid accounts payable | | |

**Problem 2-1A (Cont'd.)**

| Nov 27 | Analysis | Assets increase, Assets decrease | | |
|---|---|---|---|---|
| | Journal entry analysis | Debit the Aircraft equipment (new) ac for $2000 Credit the Cash ac for $15000 Credit the Aircraft equipment (old) ac for $5000 | | |
| | Journal Entry | | | |
| | **Date** | **Account Titles and Explanation** | **Debit** | **Credit** |
| | Nov 27 | Aircraft equipment (new) | 20,000 | |
| | | Cash | | 15,000 |
| | | Aircraft equipment (old) | | 5000 |
| | | Purchase of Aircraft equipment | | |
| Nov 30 | Analysis | Assets decrease, Equity decreases | | |
| | Journal entry analysis | Debit the Tobias Eaden. withdrawal ac for $3200 Credit the cash account for $3200 | | |
| | Journal Entry | | | |
| | **Date** | **Account Titles and Explanation** | **Debit** | **Credit** |
| | Nov 30 | Tobias Eaden, withdrawals | 3200 | |
| | | Cash | | 3200 |
| | | Withdrawal of cash by owner. | | |

**Problem 2-2A Parts 1 and 2**

Cash
Nov 1 200,000 | 125,000 Nov 3
3000 Nov 17
2500 Nov 23
15000 Nov 27
3200 Nov 30
Bal 51300

Land
Nov 3 400,000

Accounts Payable
Nov 23 2500 | 5000 Nov 9
2500 Bal

Long-Term Notes Payable
375,000 Nov 3

**Problem 2-2A (cont'd.)**

Name:_____

**Accounts Receivable**

Nov 13   16,000

Bal  16,000

**Tobias Eaden, Capital**

250,000  Nov 1
200,000  Nov 7
450,000  Bal

**Supplies**

Nov 9   5000

**Tobias Eaden, Withdrawals**

Nov 30   3200

**Airplane**

Nov 7  200,000

**Revenue**

16000   Nov 13
16,000   Bal

**Aircraft Equipment**

Nov 1   50000    5000  Nov 27
Nov 27  20000

Bal   65,000

**Wages Expense**

Nov 17   3000

Bal  3000

**Building**

Nov 3   100,000

**Part 3**

Assets = Liabilities + Equity
$ 837300 = $ 377500 + $ 459,800

Problem 2-3A

## GENERAL JOURNAL

Page ____

| Date | Account Titles and Explanation | PR | Debit | Credit |
|------|-------------------------------|----|-------|--------|
| 2017 | 1. Equipment | | 46,000 | |
| May | Cash | | | 14,000 |
| | Notes payable | | | 32,000 |
| | Purchased new equipment | | | |
| | paying cash and signing | | | |
| | a 90 day note payable. | | | |
| | | | | |
| · | 2 Prepaid Insurance | | 24,000 | |
| | Cash | | | 24,000 |
| | Purchased 12 months of | | | |
| | insurance to begin May 2. | | | |
| | | | | |
| | 3 Cash | | 6000 | |
| | Design Revenue | | | 6000 |
| | Completed a fitness contract | | | |
| | for a group of customers | | | |
| | and collected cash | | | |
| | | | | |
| | 4 Office supplies | | 3750 | |
| | Accounts payable | | | 3750 |
| | Purchased office supplies | | | |
| | on account. | | | |
| | | | | |
| | 6 Accounts payable | | 750 | |
| | Office supplies | | | 750 |
| | Returned defective supplies to supplier. | | | |
| | | | | |
| | 10. Accounts Receivable | | 11,500 | |
| | Fitness contract revenue | | | 11,500 |
| | Did work for a client today on account. | | | |
| | | | | |
| | 15 Accounts payable | | 3000 | |
| | Cash | | | 3000 |
| | Paid for the May 4 | | | |
| | Purchase less the return of May 6 | | | |
| | $ 3750 - $750 return= $3000 | | | |
| | | | | |
| | 20 Cash | | 11,500 | |
| | Accounts Receivable | | | 11,500 |
| | Received payment from client | | | |
| | of May 10 | | | |

**Problem 2-3A (concl'd.)**

## GENERAL JOURNAL                                    Page ____

| Date | Account Titles and Explanation | PR | Debit | Credit |
|------|-------------------------------|----|-------|--------|
| 25 | Cash | | 2500 | |
| | Unearned Revenue | | | 2500 |
| | Received cash for work to be done in June | | | |
| 31 | Salaries Expense | | 47000 | |
| | Cash | | | 47000 |
| 31 | Telephone Expense | | 2250 | |
| | Cash | | | 2250 |
| 31 | Utilities Expense | | 3100 | |
| | Ac Payable (Utilities payable) | | | 3100 |

**Problem 2-4A**

## GENERAL JOURNAL                                    Page ____

| Date | Account Titles and Explanation | PR | Debit | Credit |
|------|-------------------------------|-----|-------|--------|
| 2017 1 | Cash | 101 | 50000 | |
| Mar | Office Equipment | 163 | 12000 | |
| | Abe fractor, capital | 301 | | 62000 |
| | Invested cash & equipment | | | |
| | to start the business. | | | |
| 1 | Prepaid Rent | 131 | 9000 | |
| | Cash | 101 | | 9000 |
| | Prepaid three months rent | | | |
| 3 | Office equipment | 163 | 6000 | |
| | Office supplies | 124 | 1200 | |
| | Accounts payable | 201 | | 7200 |
| | Purchased equipment & | | | |
| | supplies on credit | | | |
| 5 | Cash | 101 | 6200 | |
| | Accounting Revenue | 401 | | 6200 |
| | Received cash from client | | | |
| | for completed work. | | | |
| 9 | Accounts Receivable | 106 | 4000 | |
| | Accounting Revenue | 401 | | 4000 |
| | Billed client for | | | |
| | completed work | | | |

## GENERAL JOURNAL

Page ____

| Date | Account Titles and Explanation | PR | Debit | Credit |
|---|---|---|---|---|
| 11 | Accounts payable | 201 | 7200 | |
| | Cash | 101 | | 7200 |
| | Paid balance due on accounts payable. | | | |
| 15 | Prepaid Insurance | 128 | 3000 | |
| | Cash | 101 | | 3000 |
| | Paid annual prem for insu. | | | |
| 20 | Cash | 101 | 1500 | |
| | Accounts Receivable | 106 | | 1500 |
| | Collected part of amt owed by client | | | |
| 22 | No entry | | | |
| 23 | Accounts Receivable | 106 | 2850 | |
| | Accounting Revenue | 401 | | 2850 |
| | Billed client for completed work | | | |
| 27 | Abe Factor, Withdrawals | 302 | 3600 | |
| | Cash | 101 | | 3600 |
| 30 | office supplies | 124 | 650 | |
| | Ac payable | 201 | | 650 |
| 31 | Utilities Expense | 690 | 860 | |
| | cash | 101 | | 860 |

**Problem 2-5A    Parts 1 and 2**

### GENERAL LEDGER

Cash                                    ACCOUNT NO. 101

| DATE | EXPLANATION | PR | DEBIT | CREDIT | BALANCE |
|---|---|---|---|---|---|
| 2017 1 | | G1 | 50000 | | 50000 |
| Mar 1 | | G1 | | 9000 | 41000 |
| 5 | | G1 | 6200 | | 47200 |
| 11 | | G1 | | 7200 | 40000 |
| 15 | | G1 | | 3000 | 37000 |
| 20 | | G1 | 1500 | | 38500 |
| 27 | | G1 | | 3600 | 34900 |
| 31 | | G1 | | 860 | 34040 |

## Problem 2-5A (cont'd.)

### Accounts Receivable · ACCOUNT NO. 106

| DATE | EXPLANATION | PR | DEBIT | CREDIT | BALANCE |
|---|---|---|---|---|---|
| 2017 9 | | G1 | 4000 | | 4000 |
| Mar 20 | | G1 | | 1500 | 2500 |
| 23 | | G1 | 2850 | | 5350 |

### Office Supplies · ACCOUNT NO. 124

| DATE | EXPLANATION | PR | DEBIT | CREDIT | BALANCE |
|---|---|---|---|---|---|
| 2017 3 | | G1 | 1200 | | 1200 |
| Mar 30 | | G1 | 650 | | 1850 |

### Prepaid Insurance · ACCOUNT NO. 128

| DATE | EXPLANATION | PR | DEBIT | CREDIT | BALANCE |
|---|---|---|---|---|---|
| 2017 15 Mar | | G1 | 3000 | | 3000 |

### Prepaid Rent · ACCOUNT NO. 131

| DATE | EXPLANATION | PR | DEBIT | CREDIT | BALANCE |
|---|---|---|---|---|---|
| 2017 1 Mar | | G1 | 9000 | | 9000 |

### Office Equipment · ACCOUNT NO. 163

| DATE | EXPLANATION | PR | DEBIT | CREDIT | BALANCE |
|---|---|---|---|---|---|
| 2017 1 | | G1 | 12000 | | 12000 |
| Mar 3 | | G1 | 6000 | | 18000 |

### Accounts Payable · ACCOUNT NO. 201

| DATE | EXPLANATION | PR | DEBIT | CREDIT | BALANCE |
|---|---|---|---|---|---|
| 2017 3 | | G1 | | 7200 | 7200 |
| Mar 11 | | G1 | 7200 | | 0 |
| 30 | | G1 | | 650 | 650 |

### Abe Factor, Capital · ACCOUNT NO. 301

| DATE | EXPLANATION | PR | DEBIT | CREDIT | BALANCE |
|---|---|---|---|---|---|
| 2017 1 Mar | | G1 | | 62000 | 62000 |

### Abe Factor, Withdrawals · ACCOUNT NO. 302

| DATE | EXPLANATION | PR | DEBIT | CREDIT | BALANCE |
|---|---|---|---|---|---|
| 2017 27 Mar | | G1 | 3600 | | 3600 |

**Problem 2-5A (concl'd.)**

**Accounting Fees Earned**
ACCOUNT NO. 401

| DATE | | EXPLANATION | PR | DEBIT | CREDIT | BALANCE |
|---|---|---|---|---|---|---|
| 2017 | 5 | | G1 | | 6200 | 6200 |
| Mar | 9 | | G1 | | 4000 | 10200 |
| | 23 | | G1 | | 2850 | 13050 |
| | | | | | | |

**Utilities Expense**
ACCOUNT NO. 690

| DATE | | EXPLANATION | PR | DEBIT | CREDIT | BALANCE |
|---|---|---|---|---|---|---|
| 2017 | 31 | | G1 | 860 | | 860 |
| Mar | | | | | | |

**Part 3**

X-Factor Accounting
**Trial Balance**
March 31, 2017

| Acct No. | Account Title | Debit $ | Credit $ |
|---|---|---|---|
| 101 | Cash | 34040 | |
| 106 | Accounts Receivable | 5350 | |
| 124 | Office supplies | 1850 | |
| 128 | Prepaid Insurance | 3000 | |
| 131 | Prepaid rent | 9000 | |
| 163 | Office equipment | 18000 | |
| 201 | Accounts payable | | 650 |
| 301 | Abe Factor, Capital | | 62000 |
| 302 | Abe Factor, withdrawals | 3600 | |
| 401 | Accounting revenue | | 13050 |
| 690 | Utilities expense | 860 | |
| | Totals | $ 75700 | $ 75700 |

Name:_____

**Problem 2-6A**

## Income Statement

| | | | |
|---|---|---|---|
| | | | |
| | | | |
| | | | |
| | | | |
| | | | |
| | | | |
| | | | |
| | | | |

## Statement of Changes in Equity

| | | | |
|---|---|---|---|
| | | | |
| | | | |
| | | | |
| | | | |
| | | | |
| | | | |
| | | | |
| | | | |

## Balance Sheet

| | | | | |
|---|---|---|---|---|
| | | | | |
| | | | | |
| | | | | |
| | | | | |
| | | | | |
| | | | | |
| | | | | |
| | | | | |
| | | | | |
| | | | | |
| | | | | |

**Chapter 2**

Name:_____

Problem 2-7A

## GENERAL JOURNAL

Page ____

| Date | Account Titles and Explanation | PR | Debit | Credit |
|------|-------------------------------|-----|-------|--------|
| 2017 | 1 Cash | 101 | 75000 | |
| May | Office Equipment | 163 | 48000 | |
| | Elizabeth Wong, Capital | 301 | | 123000 |
| | Invested cash & equipment | | | |
| | to start the business. | | | |
| | | | | |
| | 1 Prepaid rent | 131 | 14400 | |
| | Cash | 101 | | 14400 |
| | Prepaid 3 months rent. | | | |
| | | | | |
| | 2 Office Equipment | 163 | 24000 | |
| | Office supplies | 124 | 4800 | |
| | Accounts payable | 201 | | 28800 |
| | Pur equip & supplies on credit | | | |
| | | | | |
| | 6 Cash | 101 | 8000 | |
| | Services Revenue | 403 | | 8000 |
| | Received cash from client for | | | |
| | services performed. | | | |
| | | | | |
| | 9 Accounts Receivable | 106 | 16000 | |
| | Services Revenue | 403 | | 16000 |
| | Billed client for completed work | | | |
| | | | | |
| | 10 Accounts payable | 201 | 14400 | |
| | Cash | 101 | | 14400 |
| | Paid one-half of bal due on ac payable | | | |
| | | | | |
| | 19 Prepaid Insurance | 128 | 7500 | |
| | Cash | 101 | | 7500 |
| | Paid annual prem for Insurance | | | |
| | | | | |
| | 22 Cash | 101 | 12800 | |
| | Accounts Receivable | 106 | | 12800 |
| | Collected part of amt owed by client | | | |
| | | | | |
| | 25 Accounts Receivable | 106 | 5280 | |
| | Services Revenue | 403 | | 5280 |
| | Billed client for completed work | | | |
| | 25. Wages exp | 623 | 34000 | |
| | Cash | 101 | | 34000 |
| | 31 Elizabeth wong withdrawals | 302 | 5000 | |
| | Cash | 101 | | 5000 |

| | 31. Office supplies | 124 | 1600 | |
| | Ac payable | 201 | | 1600 |
| | 31. Utilities exp | 690 | 1900 | |
| | Cash | 101 | | 1900 |

Name:_____

**Problem 2-7A (cont'd.)**

## GENERAL JOURNAL

Page _____

| Date | | Account Titles and Explanation | PR | Debit | Credit |
|---|---|---|---|---|---|
| | | | | | |
| | | | | | |
| | | | | | |
| | | | | | |
| | | | | | |
| | | | | | |
| | | | | | |
| | | | | | |
| | | | | | |
| | | | | | |
| | | | | | |
| | | | | | |
| | | | | | |
| | | | | | |
| | | | | | |
| | | | | | |
| | | | | | |
| | | | | | |
| | | | | | |
| | | | | | |
| | | | | | |
| | | | | | |
| | | | | | |
| | | | | | |
| | | | | | |
| | | | | | |
| | | | | | |

Name:_____

Problem 2-7A (concl'd.)

Parts 2 and 3

## GENERAL LEDGER

### Cash — ACCOUNT NO. 101

| DATE | | EXPLANATION | PR | DEBIT | CREDIT | BALANCE |
|---|---|---|---|---|---|---|
| 2017 May | 1 | | G1 | 75000 | | 75000 |
| | 1 | | G1 | | 14400 | 60600 |
| | 6 | | G1 | 8000 | | 68600 |
| | 10 | | G1 | | 14400 | 54200 |
| | 19 | | G1 | | 7500 | 46700 |
| | 22 | | G1 | 12800 | | 59500 |
| | 25 | | G1 | | 34000 | 25500 |
| | 31 | | G1 | | 5000 | 20500 |
| | 31 | | G1 | | 1400 | 19100 |

### Accounts Receivable — ACCOUNT NO. 106

| DATE | | EXPLANATION | PR | DEBIT | CREDIT | BALANCE |
|---|---|---|---|---|---|---|
| 2017 May | 9 | | G1 | 16000 | | 16000 |
| | 22 | | G1 | | 12800 | 3200 |
| | 25 | | G1 | 5280 | | 8480 |

### Office Supplies — ACCOUNT NO. 124

| DATE | | EXPLANATION | PR | DEBIT | CREDIT | BALANCE |
|---|---|---|---|---|---|---|
| 2017 May | 2 | | G1 | 4800 | | 4800 |
| | 31 | | G1 | 1600 | | 6400 |

### Prepaid Insurance — ACCOUNT NO. 128

| DATE | | EXPLANATION | PR | DEBIT | CREDIT | BALANCE |
|---|---|---|---|---|---|---|
| 2017 May | 19 | | G1 | 7500 | | 7500 |

### Prepaid Rent — ACCOUNT NO. 131

| DATE | | EXPLANATION | PR | DEBIT | CREDIT | BALANCE |
|---|---|---|---|---|---|---|
| 2017 May | 1 | | G1 | 14400 | | 14400 |

### Office Equipment — ACCOUNT NO. 163

| DATE | | EXPLANATION | PR | DEBIT | CREDIT | BALANCE |
|---|---|---|---|---|---|---|
| 2017 May | 1 | | G1 | 48000 | | 48000 |
| | 2 | | G1 | 24000 | | 72000 |

**Problem 2-7A (cont'd.)**

**Accounts Payable**                                    ACCOUNT NO. 201

| DATE | | EXPLANATION | PR | DEBIT | CREDIT | BALANCE |
|---|---|---|---|---|---|---|
| 2017 | 2 | | G1 | | 28800 | 28800 |
| May | 10 | | G1 | 14400 | | 14400 |
| | 31 | | G1 | | 1600 | 16000 |

**Elizabeth Wong, Capital**                              ACCOUNT NO. 301

| DATE | | EXPLANATION | PR | DEBIT | CREDIT | BALANCE |
|---|---|---|---|---|---|---|
| 2017 | 1 | | G1 | | 123000 | 123000 |
| May | | | | | | |

**Elizabeth Wong, Withdrawals**                          ACCOUNT NO. 302

| DATE | | EXPLANATION | PR | DEBIT | CREDIT | BALANCE |
|---|---|---|---|---|---|---|
| 2017 | 31 | | G1 | 5000 | | 5000 |
| May | | | | | | |

**Services Revenue**                                     ACCOUNT NO. 403

| DATE | | EXPLANATION | PR | DEBIT | CREDIT | BALANCE |
|---|---|---|---|---|---|---|
| 2017 | 6 | | G1 | | 8000 | 8000 |
| May | 9 | | G1 | | 16000 | 24000 |
| | 25 | | G1 | | 5280 | 29280 |

**Wages Expense**                                        ACCOUNT NO. 623

| DATE | | EXPLANATION | PR | DEBIT | CREDIT | BALANCE |
|---|---|---|---|---|---|---|
| 2017 | 25 | | G1 | 34000 | | 34000 |
| May | | | | | | |
| | | | | | | |

**Utilities Expense**                                    ACCOUNT NO. 690

| DATE | | EXPLANATION | PR | DEBIT | CREDIT | BALANCE |
|---|---|---|---|---|---|---|
| 2017 | 31 | | G1 | 1400 | | 1400 |
| May | | | | | | |
| | | | | | | |
| | | | | | | |

**Problem 2-7A (concl'd.)**

**Part 4**

HR Solutions
Trial Balance
May 31, 2017

| Acct No. | Account Title | Debit $ | Credit $ |
|---|---|---|---|
| 101 | Cash | 19100 | |
| 106 | Accounts Receivable | 8480 | |
| 124 | Office Supplies | 6400 | |
| 128 | Prepaid Insurance | 7500 | |
| 131 | Prepaid rent | 14400 | |
| 163 | Office equipment | 72000 | |
| 201 | Accounts payable | | 16000 |
| 301 | Elizabeth Wong, Capital | | 123000 |
| 302 | Elizabeth Wong, Withdrawals | 5000 | |
| 403 | Services revenue | | 29280 |
| 623 | Wages expense | 34000 | |
| 690 | Utilities expense | 1400 | |
| | Totals | $168280 | $168280 |

*Analysis component:*

_____

_____

_____

_____

_____

_____

_____

_____

_____

_____

_____

_____

_____

**Problem 2-8A**

### Income Statement

| | | |
|---|---|---|
| | | |
| | | |
| | | |
| | | |
| | | |
| | | |
| | | |
| | | |
| | | |
| | | |

### Statement of Changes in Equity

| | | |
|---|---|---|
| | | |
| | | |
| | | |
| | | |
| | | |
| | | |
| | | |
| | | |
| | | |
| | | |
| | | |
| | | |

### Balance Sheet

| | | | |
|---|---|---|---|
| | | | |
| | | | |
| | | | |
| | | | |
| | | | |
| | | | |
| | | | |
| | | | |
| | | | |
| | | | |
| | | | |
| | | | |

Name:_____

**Problem 2-9A**

## Income Statement

| | | |
|---|---|---|
| | | |
| | | |
| | | |
| | | |
| | | |
| | | |
| | | |
| | | |
| | | |
| | | |
| | | |

## Statement of Changes in Equity

| | | |
|---|---|---|
| | | |
| | | |
| | | |
| | | |
| | | |
| | | |
| | | |
| | | |
| | | |
| | | |

## Balance Sheet

| | | | |
|---|---|---|---|
| | | | |
| | | | |
| | | | |
| | | | |
| | | | |
| | | | |
| | | | |
| | | | |
| | | | |
| | | | |
| | | | |
| | | | |

Name:_____

**Problem 2-9A (concl'd.)**

*Analysis component:*    **GENERAL JOURNAL**    Page_____

| Date | Account Titles and Explanation | PR | Debit | Credit |
|------|-------------------------------|-----|-------|--------|
|      |                               |     |       |        |
|      |                               |     |       |        |
|      |                               |     |       |        |
|      |                               |     |       |        |
|      |                               |     |       |        |
|      |                               |     |       |        |
|      |                               |     |       |        |
|      |                               |     |       |        |
|      |                               |     |       |        |
|      |                               |     |       |        |

**Problem 2-10A**

**Part 1**

**GENERAL JOURNAL**    Page_____

| Date | Account Titles and Explanation | PR | Debit | Credit |
|------|-------------------------------|-----|-------|--------|
| 2017 1 July | Cash | 101 | 300000 | |
|      | Office Equipment | 163 | 12000 | |
|      | Drafting equipment | 167 | 90000 | |
|      | Bishr Binbentti, capital | 301 | | 402000 |
|      | Investment by owner | | | |
|      |                               |     |       |        |
| 2 | Land | 183 | 108000 | |
|      | Cash | 101 | | 10800 |
|      | Long term notes payable | 251 | | 97200 |
|      | Purchased land. | | | |
|      |                               |     |       |        |
| 3 | Building | 173 | 150000 | |
|      | Cash | 101 | | 150000 |
|      | Purchased a building | | | |
|      |                               |     |       |        |
| 5 | Prepaid Insurance | 128 | 12000 | |
|      | Cash | 101 | | 12000 |
|      | Pur two one year Insu policies | | | |
|      |                               |     |       |        |
| 7 | Cash | 101 | 1400 | |
|      | Engineering revenue | 401 | | 1400 |
|      | Completed servecies | | | |
|      | Por cash | | | |

## GENERAL JOURNAL

Page____

| Date | Account Titles and Explanation | PR | Debit | Credit |
|------|-------------------------------|-----|-------|--------|
| 9 | Drafting Equipment | 167 | 45000 | |
| | Cash | 101 | | 21000 |
| | Long term notes payable | 251 | | 24000 |
| | Purchased drafting equipment. | | | |
| | | | | |
| 10 | Accounts Receivable | 106 | 4000 | |
| | Engineering Revenue | 401 | | 4000 |
| | Completed services on credit | | | |
| | | | | |
| 12 | Office Equipment | 163 | 4500 | |
| | Accounts payable | 201 | | 4500 |
| | Pur office equip on credit | | | |
| | | | | |
| 15 | Accounts Receivable | 106 | 7000 | |
| | Engineering Revenue | 401 | | 7000 |
| | Completed services on credit. | | | |
| | | | | |
| 16 | Equipment Rental exp | 645 | 13800 | |
| | Accounts payable | 201 | | 13800 |
| | Equip rental to be paid in 30 days | | | |
| | | | | |
| 17 | Cash | 101 | 400 | |
| | Accounts Receivable | 106 | | 400 |
| | Collection from credit customers | | | |
| | | | | |
| 19 | Wages Expense | 623 | 12000 | |
| | Cash | 601 | | 12000 |
| | Paid drafting assistants | | | |
| | | | | |
| 22 | Accounts payable | 201 | 4500 | |
| | Cash | 101 | | 4500 |
| | Paid July 12 transaction | | | |
| | | | | |
| 25 | Repairs Expense | 684 | 1350 | |
| | Cash | 101 | | 1350 |
| | Paid for repairs on | | | |
| | drafting equipment. | | | |
| | | | | |

Problem 2-10A (cont'd.)

## GENERAL JOURNAL

Page_____

| Date | Account Titles and Explanation | PR | Debit | Credit |
|------|--------------------------------|-----|-------|--------|
| 26 | Bishr Binbutti, withdrawals | 302 | 800 | |
| | Cash | 101 | | 800 |
| | Owner withdrawals. | | | |
| | | | | |
| 30 | Wages expense | 623 | 12000 | |
| | Cash | 101 | | 12000 |
| | Paid drafting assistants | | | |
| | | | | |
| 31 | Advertising expense | 655 | 6000 | |
| | Cash | 101 | | 6000 |
| | Paid for advertising | | | |
| | in local newspaper. | | | |
| | | | | |
| | | | | |
| | | | | |
| | | | | |

### Parts 2 and 3

## GENERAL LEDGER

Cash                                                  ACCOUNT NO. 101

| DATE | EXPLANATION | PR | DEBIT | CREDIT | BALANCE |
|------|-------------|-----|-------|--------|---------|
| 2017 | | | | | |
| Jun. 30 | Beginning balance | | | | 26,000 |
| July 1 | | G1 | 300000 | | 326000 |
| 2 | | G1 | | 10800 | 315200 |
| 3 | | G1 | | 150000 | 165200 |
| 5 | | G1 | | 12000 | 153200 |
| 7 | | G1 | 1400 | | 154600 |
| 9 | | G1 | | 21000 | 133600 |
| 17 | | G1 | 400 | | 134000 |
| 19 | | G1 | | 12000 | 122000 |
| 22 | | G1 | | 4500 | 117500 |
| 25 | | G1 | | 1350 | 116150 |
| 26 | | G1 | | 800 | 115350 |
| 30 | | G1 | | 12000 | 103350 |
| 31 | | G1 | | 6000 | 97350 |
| | | | | | |

**Problem 2-10A (cont'd.)**

### Accounts Receivable                    ACCOUNT NO. 106

| DATE | EXPLANATION | PR | DEBIT | CREDIT | BALANCE |
|------|-------------|-----|-------|--------|---------|
| 2017 | | | | | |
| Jun. 30 | Beginning balance | | | | 3,000 |
| July 10 | | GI | 4000 | | 7000 |
| 15 | | GI | 7000 | | 14000 |
| 17 | | GI | | 400 | 13600 |

### Prepaid Insurance                    ACCOUNT NO. 128

| DATE | EXPLANATION | PR | DEBIT | CREDIT | BALANCE |
|------|-------------|-----|-------|--------|---------|
| 2017 | | | | | |
| Jun. 30 | Beginning balance | | | | 500 |
| July 5 | | GI | 12000 | | 12500 |

### Office Equipment                    ACCOUNT NO. 163

| DATE | EXPLANATION | PR | DEBIT | CREDIT | BALANCE |
|------|-------------|-----|-------|--------|---------|
| 2017 | | | | | |
| Jun. 30 | Beginning balance | | | | 1,700 |
| July 1 | | GI | 12000 | | 13700 |
| 12 | | GI | 4500 | | 18200 |

### Drafting Equipment                    ACCOUNT NO. 167

| DATE | EXPLANATION | PR | DEBIT | CREDIT | BALANCE |
|------|-------------|-----|-------|--------|---------|
| 2017 | | | | | |
| Jun. 30 | Beginning balance | | | | 1,200 |
| July 1 | | GI | 90000 | | 91200 |
| 9 | | GI | 45000 | | 136200 |

### Building                    ACCOUNT NO. 173

| DATE | EXPLANATION | PR | DEBIT | CREDIT | BALANCE |
|------|-------------|-----|-------|--------|---------|
| 2017 | | | | | |
| Jun. 30 | Beginning balance | | | | 42,000 |
| July 3 | | GI | 150000 | | 192000 |

### Land                    ACCOUNT NO. 183

| DATE | EXPLANATION | PR | DEBIT | CREDIT | BALANCE |
|------|-------------|-----|-------|--------|---------|
| 2017 | | | | | |
| Jun. 30 | Beginning balance | | | | 28,000 |
| July 2 | | GI | 108000 | | 136000 |

Name:_____

**Problem 2-10A (cont'd.)**

### Accounts Payable           ACCOUNT NO. 201

| DATE | EXPLANATION | PR | DEBIT | CREDIT | BALANCE |
|------|-------------|----|-------|--------|---------|
| 2017 | | | | | |
| Jun. 30 | Beginning balance | | | | 1,740 |
| July 12 | | G1 | | 4500 | 6240 |
| 16 | | G1 | | 13800 | 20040 |
| 22 | | G1 | 4500 | | 15540 |

### Long-Term Notes Payable          ACCOUNT NO. 251

| DATE | EXPLANATION | PR | DEBIT | CREDIT | BALANCE |
|------|-------------|----|-------|--------|---------|
| 2017 | | | | | |
| Jun. 30 | Beginning balance | | | | 24,000 |
| July 2 | | G1 | | 97200 | 121200 |
| 9 | | G1 | | 24000 | 145200 |

### Bishr Binbutti, Capital           ACCOUNT NO. 301

| DATE | EXPLANATION | PR | DEBIT | CREDIT | BALANCE |
|------|-------------|----|-------|--------|---------|
| 2017 | | | | | |
| Jun. 30 | Beginning balance | | | | 54,000 |
| July 1 | | G1 | | 402000 | 456000 |

### Bishr Binbutti, Withdrawals        ACCOUNT NO. 302

| DATE | EXPLANATION | PR | DEBIT | CREDIT | BALANCE |
|------|-------------|----|-------|--------|---------|
| 2017 | | | | | |
| Jun. 30 | Beginning balance | | | | 1,000 |
| July 26 | | G1 | 800 | | 1800 |

### Engineering Revenue           ACCOUNT NO. 401

| DATE | EXPLANATION | PR | DEBIT | CREDIT | BALANCE |
|------|-------------|----|-------|--------|---------|
| 2017 | | | | | |
| Jun. 30 | Beginning balance | | | | 29,600 |
| July 7 | | G1 | | 1400 | 31000 |
| 10 | | G1 | | 4000 | 35000 |
| 15 | | G1 | | 7000 | 42000 |

### Wages Expense               ACCOUNT NO. 623

| DATE | EXPLANATION | PR | DEBIT | CREDIT | BALANCE |
|------|-------------|----|-------|--------|---------|
| 2017 | | | | | |
| Jun. 30 | Beginning balance | | | | 4,000 |
| July 19 | | G1 | 12000 | | 16000 |
| 30 | | G1 | 12000 | | 28000 |

**Problem 2-10A (concl'd.)**

### Equipment Rental Expense　　　　　　　ACCOUNT NO. 645

| DATE | EXPLANATION | PR | DEBIT | CREDIT | BALANCE |
|------|-------------|-----|-------|--------|---------|
| 2017 | | | | | |
| Jun. 30 | Beginning balance | | | | 1,000 |
| July 16 | | G1 | 13800 | | 14800 |

### Advertising Expense　　　　　　　　　ACCOUNT NO. 655

| DATE | EXPLANATION | PR | DEBIT | CREDIT | BALANCE |
|------|-------------|-----|-------|--------|---------|
| 2017 | | | | | |
| Jun. 30 | Beginning balance | | | | 640 |
| July 31 | | G1 | 6000 | | 6640 |

### Repairs Expense　　　　　　　　　　　ACCOUNT NO. 684

| DATE | EXPLANATION | PR | DEBIT | CREDIT | BALANCE |
|------|-------------|-----|-------|--------|---------|
| 2017 | | | | | |
| Jun. 30 | Beginning balance | | | | 300 |
| July 25 | | G1 | 1350 | | 1650 |

**Parts 4**

**Binbutti Engineering**
**Trial Balance**
**July 31, 2017**

| Acct No. | Account Title | Debit $ | Credit $ |
|----------|---------------|---------|----------|
| 101 | Cash | 97350 | |
| 106 | Accounts Receivable | 13600 | |
| 128 | Prepaid Insurance | 12500 | |
| 163 | Office Equipment | 18200 | |
| 167 | Drafting Equipment | 136200 | |
| 173 | Building | 192000 | |
| 183 | Land | 136000 | |
| 201 | Accounts Payable | | 15540 |
| 251 | Long term Notes Payable | | 145200 |
| 301 | Bishr Binbutti, Capital | | 456000 |
| 302 | Engineering Revenue | | 42000 |
| 401 | Wages Expense | 28000 | |
| 623 | Equipment rental Expense | 14800 | |
| 645 | Advertising Expense | 6640 | |
| 655 | Repairs Expense | 1650 | |
| 684 | Bishr Binbutti withdrawals | 1800 | |
| | Totals | $ 658,740 | $ 658740 |

Name:_____

**Problem 2-11A**

## Income Statement

|  |  |  |
|---|---|---|
|  |  |  |
|  |  |  |
|  |  |  |
|  |  |  |
|  |  |  |
|  |  |  |
|  |  |  |
|  |  |  |
|  |  |  |

## Statement of Changes in Equity

|  |  |  |
|---|---|---|
|  |  |  |
|  |  |  |
|  |  |  |
|  |  |  |
|  |  |  |
|  |  |  |
|  |  |  |
|  |  |  |
|  |  |  |
|  |  |  |

## Balance Sheet

|  |  |  |  |
|---|---|---|---|
|  |  |  |  |
|  |  |  |  |
|  |  |  |  |
|  |  |  |  |
|  |  |  |  |
|  |  |  |  |
|  |  |  |  |
|  |  |  |  |
|  |  |  |  |
|  |  |  |  |
|  |  |  |  |
|  |  |  |  |
|  |  |  |  |

**Problem 2-12A Part 1**

GENERAL JOURNAL      Page____

| Date | Account Titles and Explanation | PR | Debit | Credit |
|---|---|---|---|---|
|  |  |  |  |  |
|  |  |  |  |  |
|  |  |  |  |  |
|  |  |  |  |  |
|  |  |  |  |  |
|  |  |  |  |  |
|  |  |  |  |  |
|  |  |  |  |  |
|  |  |  |  |  |
|  |  |  |  |  |
|  |  |  |  |  |
|  |  |  |  |  |
|  |  |  |  |  |
|  |  |  |  |  |
|  |  |  |  |  |
|  |  |  |  |  |
|  |  |  |  |  |
|  |  |  |  |  |
|  |  |  |  |  |
|  |  |  |  |  |

**Problem 2-12A (cont'd.)**

Name:_____

**Parts 2 and 3**

|  | Cash | | 101 |
|---|---|---|---|
| Bal. | 6,000 | | |

|  | Supplies | | 126 |
|---|---|---|---|
| Bal. | | 950 | |

|  | Equipment | | 161 |
|---|---|---|---|
| Bal. | | 8,000 | |

|  | Accounts Payable | | 201 |
|---|---|---|---|
| | | 1,500 | Bal. |

|  | Unearned Teaching Revenue | | 233 |
|---|---|---|---|
| | | 9,800 | Bal. |

|  | Teaching Revenue | | 401 |
|---|---|---|---|
| | | 46,000 | Bal. |

|  | Taylor Smith, Capital | | 301 |
|---|---|---|---|
| | | 3,000 | Bal. |

|  | Wages Expense | | 623 |
|---|---|---|---|
| Bal. | 26,350 | | |

|  | Rent Expense | | 640 |
|---|---|---|---|
| Bal. | 6,000 | | |

|  | Taylor Smith, Withdrawals | | 302 |
|---|---|---|---|
| Bal. | 13,000 | | |

**Chapter 2**

Name:_____

**Problem 2-12A (cont'd)**

**Part 4**

| Trial Balance | | |
|---|---|---|
| | | |
| | | |
| | | |
| | | |
| | | |
| | | |
| | | |
| | | |
| | | |
| | | |
| | | |
| | | |
| | | |
| | | |
| | | |
| | | |
| | | |
| | | |
| | | |

*Fundamental Accounting Principles,* **15ce, Working Papers**

Name:_____

**Problem 2-12A (concl'd.)**

**Part 5**

## Income Statement

| | | |
|---|---|---|
| | | |
| | | |
| | | |
| | | |
| | | |
| | | |
| | | |
| | | |
| | | |
| | | |

## Statement of Changes in Equity

| | | |
|---|---|---|
| | | |
| | | |
| | | |
| | | |
| | | |
| | | |
| | | |
| | | |
| | | |

## Balance Sheet

| | | | |
|---|---|---|---|
| | | | |
| | | | |
| | | | |
| | | | |
| | | | |
| | | | |
| | | | |
| | | | |
| | | | |
| | | | |
| | | | |
| | | | |

**Problem 2-13A**

## Income Statement

| | | |
|---|---|---|
| | | |
| | | |
| | | |
| | | |
| | | |
| | | |
| | | |
| | | |

## Statement of Changes in Equity

| | | |
|---|---|---|
| | | |
| | | |
| | | |
| | | |
| | | |
| | | |
| | | |
| | | |

## Balance Sheet

| | | | |
|---|---|---|---|
| | | | |
| | | | |
| | | | |
| | | | |
| | | | |
| | | | |
| | | | |
| | | | |
| | | | |
| | | | |

Name:_____

## Problem 2-13A (concl'd)

*Analysis component:*

### GENERAL JOURNAL

Page_____

| Date | Account Titles and Explanation | PR | Debit | Credit |
|------|-------------------------------|----|-------|--------|
|      |                               |    |       |        |
|      |                               |    |       |        |
|      |                               |    |       |        |
|      |                               |    |       |        |
|      |                               |    |       |        |
|      |                               |    |       |        |
|      |                               |    |       |        |
|      |                               |    |       |        |

## Problem 2-14A

### Trial Balance

|  |  |  |
|--|--|--|
|  |  |  |
|  |  |  |
|  |  |  |
|  |  |  |
|  |  |  |
|  |  |  |
|  |  |  |
|  |  |  |
|  |  |  |
|  |  |  |
|  |  |  |
|  |  |  |
|  |  |  |
|  |  |  |
|  |  |  |
|  |  |  |

**Calculations:**

_____
_____
_____
_____
_____
_____
_____
_____

**Problem 2-1B**

| June 2 | Analysis | | | |
|---|---|---|---|---|
| | Journal entry analysis | | | |
| | Journal Entry | | | |
| | **Date** | **Account Titles and Explanation** | **Debit** | **Credit** |
| | | | | |
| | | | | |
| | | | | |
| | | | | |

| Jun 4 | Analysis | | | |
|---|---|---|---|---|
| | Journal entry analysis | | | |
| | Journal Entry | | | |
| | **Date** | **Account Titles and Explanation** | **Debit** | **Credit** |
| | | | | |
| | | | | |
| | | | | |
| | | | | |
| | | | | |

| Jun 8 | Analysis | | | |
|---|---|---|---|---|
| | Journal entry analysis | | | |
| | Journal Entry | | | |
| | **Date** | **Account Titles and Explanation** | **Debit** | **Credit** |
| | | | | |
| | | | | |
| | | | | |

Name:_____

## Problem 2-1B (cont'd.)

| Jun 10 | Analysis | | | |
|---|---|---|---|---|
| | Journal entry analysis | | | |
| | Journal Entry | | | |
| | Date | Account Titles and Explanation | Debit | Credit |
| | | | | |
| | | | | |
| | | | | |

| Jun 14 | Analysis | | | |
|---|---|---|---|---|
| | Journal entry analysis | | | |
| | Journal Entry | | | |
| | Date | Account Titles and Explanation | Debit | Credit |
| | | | | |
| | | | | |
| | | | | |

| Jun 18 | Analysis | | | |
|---|---|---|---|---|
| | Journal entry analysis | | | |
| | Journal Entry | | | |
| | Date | Account Titles and Explanation | Debit | Credit |
| | | | | |
| | | | | |
| | | | | |

Name:_____

## Problem 2-1B (cont'd.)

| Jun 22 | Analysis | | | |
|---|---|---|---|---|
| | Journal entry analysis | | | |
| | Journal Entry | | | |
| | Date | Account Titles and Explanations | Debit | Credit |
| | | | | |
| | | | | |
| | | | | |

| Jun 24 | Analysis | | | |
|---|---|---|---|---|
| | Journal entry analysis | | | |
| | Journal Entry | | | |
| | Date | Account Titles and Explanations | Debit | Credit |
| | | | | |
| | | | | |
| | | | | |
| | | | | |

| Jun 28 | Analysis | | | |
|---|---|---|---|---|
| | Journal entry analysis | | | |
| | Journal Entry | | | |
| | Date | Account Titles and Explanations | Debit | Credit |
| | | | | |
| | | | | |
| | | | | |

Name:_____

Problem 2-1B (concl'd.)

| Jun 30 | Analysis | | | | |
|--------|----------|---|---|---|---|
| | Journal entry analysis | | | | |
| | Journal Entry | | | | |
| | Date | Account Titles and Explanations | | Debit | Credit |
| | | | | | |
| | | | | | |
| | | | | | |

**Problem 2-2B Part 1&2**

| Cash | | Land |
|---|---|---|

**Accounts Payable**

**Long-Term Notes Payable**

**Accounts Receivable**

**Trevor Peeters, Capital**

**Office Supplies**

**Trevor Peeters, Withdrawals**

**Automobiles**

**Revenue**

**Office Equipment**

**Salaries Expense**

**Utilities Expense**

**Building**

Name:_____

**Problem 2-2B Part 3**

_____
_____
_____
_____

**Problem 2-3B**

## GENERAL JOURNAL

| Date | Account Titles and Explanation | PR | Debit | Credit |
|------|-------------------------------|----|-------|--------|
|  |  |  |  |  |
|  |  |  |  |  |
|  |  |  |  |  |
|  |  |  |  |  |
|  |  |  |  |  |
|  |  |  |  |  |
|  |  |  |  |  |
|  |  |  |  |  |
|  |  |  |  |  |
|  |  |  |  |  |
|  |  |  |  |  |
|  |  |  |  |  |
|  |  |  |  |  |
|  |  |  |  |  |
|  |  |  |  |  |
|  |  |  |  |  |
|  |  |  |  |  |
|  |  |  |  |  |
|  |  |  |  |  |
|  |  |  |  |  |
|  |  |  |  |  |
|  |  |  |  |  |
|  |  |  |  |  |
|  |  |  |  |  |
|  |  |  |  |  |
|  |  |  |  |  |
|  |  |  |  |  |
|  |  |  |  |  |
|  |  |  |  |  |
|  |  |  |  |  |
|  |  |  |  |  |
|  |  |  |  |  |
|  |  |  |  |  |
|  |  |  |  |  |
|  |  |  |  |  |
|  |  |  |  |  |
|  |  |  |  |  |
|  |  |  |  |  |
|  |  |  |  |  |
|  |  |  |  |  |

Name:_____

## Problem 2-3B (concl'd.)

### GENERAL JOURNAL                                    Page ____

| Date | Account Titles and Explanation | PR | Debit | Credit |
|------|-------------------------------|----|-------|--------|
|      |                               |    |       |        |
|      |                               |    |       |        |
|      |                               |    |       |        |
|      |                               |    |       |        |
|      |                               |    |       |        |
|      |                               |    |       |        |
|      |                               |    |       |        |
|      |                               |    |       |        |
|      |                               |    |       |        |

## Problem 2-4B

### GENERAL JOURNAL                                    Page ____

| Date | Account Titles and Explanation | PR | Debit | Credit |
|------|-------------------------------|----|-------|--------|
|      |                               |    |       |        |
|      |                               |    |       |        |
|      |                               |    |       |        |
|      |                               |    |       |        |
|      |                               |    |       |        |
|      |                               |    |       |        |
|      |                               |    |       |        |
|      |                               |    |       |        |
|      |                               |    |       |        |
|      |                               |    |       |        |
|      |                               |    |       |        |
|      |                               |    |       |        |
|      |                               |    |       |        |
|      |                               |    |       |        |
|      |                               |    |       |        |
|      |                               |    |       |        |
|      |                               |    |       |        |
|      |                               |    |       |        |
|      |                               |    |       |        |
|      |                               |    |       |        |
|      |                               |    |       |        |
|      |                               |    |       |        |

Name:_____

## Problem 2-4B (concl'd.)

### GENERAL JOURNAL

Page ____

| Date | Account Titles and Explanation | PR | Debit | Credit |
|---|---|---|---|---|
|  |  |  |  |  |
|  |  |  |  |  |
|  |  |  |  |  |
|  |  |  |  |  |
|  |  |  |  |  |
|  |  |  |  |  |
|  |  |  |  |  |
|  |  |  |  |  |
|  |  |  |  |  |
|  |  |  |  |  |
|  |  |  |  |  |
|  |  |  |  |  |
|  |  |  |  |  |
|  |  |  |  |  |
|  |  |  |  |  |
|  |  |  |  |  |
|  |  |  |  |  |
|  |  |  |  |  |
|  |  |  |  |  |
|  |  |  |  |  |
|  |  |  |  |  |
|  |  |  |  |  |
|  |  |  |  |  |
|  |  |  |  |  |
|  |  |  |  |  |
|  |  |  |  |  |
|  |  |  |  |  |
|  |  |  |  |  |
|  |  |  |  |  |
|  |  |  |  |  |
|  |  |  |  |  |
|  |  |  |  |  |
|  |  |  |  |  |
|  |  |  |  |  |
|  |  |  |  |  |
|  |  |  |  |  |
|  |  |  |  |  |
|  |  |  |  |  |
|  |  |  |  |  |

*Fundamental Accounting Principles*, 15ce, Working Papers

Name:_____

**Problem 2-5B**
**Parts 1 and 2**

## GENERAL LEDGER

### Cash                                                                ACCOUNT NO. 101

| DATE | EXPLANATION | PR | DEBIT | CREDIT | BALANCE |
|------|-------------|-----|-------|--------|---------|
|      |             |     |       |        |         |
|      |             |     |       |        |         |
|      |             |     |       |        |         |
|      |             |     |       |        |         |
|      |             |     |       |        |         |
|      |             |     |       |        |         |
|      |             |     |       |        |         |
|      |             |     |       |        |         |
|      |             |     |       |        |         |

### Accounts Receivable                                      ACCOUNT NO. 106

| DATE | EXPLANATION | PR | DEBIT | CREDIT | BALANCE |
|------|-------------|-----|-------|--------|---------|
|      |             |     |       |        |         |
|      |             |     |       |        |         |
|      |             |     |       |        |         |
|      |             |     |       |        |         |

### Office Supplies                                               ACCOUNT NO. 124

| DATE | EXPLANATION | PR | DEBIT | CREDIT | BALANCE |
|------|-------------|-----|-------|--------|---------|
|      |             |     |       |        |         |
|      |             |     |       |        |         |
|      |             |     |       |        |         |

### Prepaid Insurance                                          ACCOUNT NO. 128

| DATE | EXPLANATION | PR | DEBIT | CREDIT | BALANCE |
|------|-------------|-----|-------|--------|---------|
|      |             |     |       |        |         |
|      |             |     |       |        |         |

### Prepaid Rent                                                   ACCOUNT NO. 131

| DATE | EXPLANATION | PR | DEBIT | CREDIT | BALANCE |
|------|-------------|-----|-------|--------|---------|
|      |             |     |       |        |         |
|      |             |     |       |        |         |

### Office Equipment                                            ACCOUNT NO. 163

| DATE | EXPLANATION | PR | DEBIT | CREDIT | BALANCE |
|------|-------------|-----|-------|--------|---------|
|      |             |     |       |        |         |
|      |             |     |       |        |         |
|      |             |     |       |        |         |

## Problem 2-5B (cont'd.)

### Accounts Payable                                      ACCOUNT NO. 201

| DATE | EXPLANATION | PR | DEBIT | CREDIT | BALANCE |
|------|-------------|-----|-------|--------|---------|
|      |             |     |       |        |         |
|      |             |     |       |        |         |
|      |             |     |       |        |         |
|      |             |     |       |        |         |

### Susan Hurley, Capital                                  ACCOUNT NO. 301

| DATE | EXPLANATION | PR | DEBIT | CREDIT | BALANCE |
|------|-------------|-----|-------|--------|---------|
|      |             |     |       |        |         |
|      |             |     |       |        |         |

### Susan Hurley, Withdrawals                              ACCOUNT NO. 302

| DATE | EXPLANATION | PR | DEBIT | CREDIT | BALANCE |
|------|-------------|-----|-------|--------|---------|
|      |             |     |       |        |         |
|      |             |     |       |        |         |

### Accounting Fees Revenue                                ACCOUNT NO. 401

| DATE | EXPLANATION | PR | DEBIT | CREDIT | BALANCE |
|------|-------------|-----|-------|--------|---------|
|      |             |     |       |        |         |
|      |             |     |       |        |         |
|      |             |     |       |        |         |
|      |             |     |       |        |         |

### Professional Development Expense                       ACCOUNT NO. 680

| DATE | EXPLANATION | PR | DEBIT | CREDIT | BALANCE |
|------|-------------|-----|-------|--------|---------|
|      |             |     |       |        |         |
|      |             |     |       |        |         |

### Utilities Expense                                      ACCOUNT NO. 690

| DATE | EXPLANATION | PR | DEBIT | CREDIT | BALANCE |
|------|-------------|-----|-------|--------|---------|
|      |             |     |       |        |         |
|      |             |     |       |        |         |

Name:_____

**Problem 2-5B (concl'd.)**

**Part 3**

|  | Trial Balance | | |
|---|---|---|---|
|  |  |  |  |
|  |  |  |  |
|  |  |  |  |
|  |  |  |  |
|  |  |  |  |
|  |  |  |  |
|  |  |  |  |
|  |  |  |  |
|  |  |  |  |
|  |  |  |  |
|  |  |  |  |
|  |  |  |  |
|  |  |  |  |
|  |  |  |  |
|  |  |  |  |
|  |  |  |  |
|  |  |  |  |
|  |  |  |  |
|  |  |  |  |
|  |  |  |  |
|  |  |  |  |

**Problem 2-6B**

## Income Statement

| | | |
|---|---|---|
| | | |
| | | |
| | | |
| | | |
| | | |
| | | |
| | | |
| | | |
| | | |
| | | |

## Statement of Changes in Equity

| | | |
|---|---|---|
| | | |
| | | |
| | | |
| | | |
| | | |
| | | |
| | | |
| | | |
| | | |

## Balance Sheet

| | | | |
|---|---|---|---|
| | | | |
| | | | |
| | | | |
| | | | |
| | | | |
| | | | |
| | | | |
| | | | |
| | | | |
| | | | |
| | | | |
| | | | |

Name:_____

**Problem 2-7B**

**Part 1**

**GENERAL JOURNAL**          Page____

| Date | Account Titles and Explanation | PR | Debit | Credit |
|------|-------------------------------|-----|-------|--------|
|      |                               |     |       |        |
|      |                               |     |       |        |
|      |                               |     |       |        |
|      |                               |     |       |        |
|      |                               |     |       |        |
|      |                               |     |       |        |
|      |                               |     |       |        |
|      |                               |     |       |        |
|      |                               |     |       |        |
|      |                               |     |       |        |
|      |                               |     |       |        |
|      |                               |     |       |        |
|      |                               |     |       |        |
|      |                               |     |       |        |
|      |                               |     |       |        |
|      |                               |     |       |        |
|      |                               |     |       |        |
|      |                               |     |       |        |
|      |                               |     |       |        |
|      |                               |     |       |        |
|      |                               |     |       |        |
|      |                               |     |       |        |
|      |                               |     |       |        |
|      |                               |     |       |        |
|      |                               |     |       |        |
|      |                               |     |       |        |
|      |                               |     |       |        |
|      |                               |     |       |        |
|      |                               |     |       |        |
|      |                               |     |       |        |
|      |                               |     |       |        |
|      |                               |     |       |        |
|      |                               |     |       |        |
|      |                               |     |       |        |
|      |                               |     |       |        |
|      |                               |     |       |        |
|      |                               |     |       |        |
|      |                               |     |       |        |
|      |                               |     |       |        |
|      |                               |     |       |        |

Name:_____

**Problem 2-7B (cont'd.)**

## GENERAL JOURNAL

Page_____

| Date | Account Titles and Explanation | PR | Debit | Credit |
|------|-------------------------------|----|----|----|
| | | | | |
| | | | | |
| | | | | |
| | | | | |
| | | | | |
| | | | | |
| | | | | |
| | | | | |
| | | | | |
| | | | | |
| | | | | |
| | | | | |
| | | | | |
| | | | | |
| | | | | |
| | | | | |
| | | | | |
| | | | | |
| | | | | |

**Parts 2 and 3**

## GENERAL LEDGER

Cash                                                    ACCOUNT NO. 101

| DATE | EXPLANATION | PR | DEBIT | CREDIT | BALANCE |
|------|-------------|----|----|----|----|
| | | | | | |
| | | | | | |
| | | | | | |
| | | | | | |
| | | | | | |
| | | | | | |
| | | | | | |
| | | | | | |
| | | | | | |
| | | | | | |
| | | | | | |
| | | | | | |

Accounts Receivable                                      ACCOUNT NO. 106

| DATE | EXPLANATION | PR | DEBIT | CREDIT | BALANCE |
|------|-------------|----|----|----|----|
| | | | | | |
| | | | | | |
| | | | | | |
| | | | | | |

## Problem 2-7B (cont'd.)

**Office Supplies**      ACCOUNT NO. 124

| DATE | EXPLANATION | PR | DEBIT | CREDIT | BALANCE |
|------|-------------|----|-------|--------|---------|
|      |             |    |       |        |         |
|      |             |    |       |        |         |
|      |             |    |       |        |         |

**Prepaid Insurance**      ACCOUNT NO. 128

| DATE | EXPLANATION | PR | DEBIT | CREDIT | BALANCE |
|------|-------------|----|-------|--------|---------|
|      |             |    |       |        |         |
|      |             |    |       |        |         |

**Prepaid Rent**      ACCOUNT NO. 131

| DATE | EXPLANATION | PR | DEBIT | CREDIT | BALANCE |
|------|-------------|----|-------|--------|---------|
|      |             |    |       |        |         |
|      |             |    |       |        |         |

**Office Equipment**      ACCOUNT NO. 163

| DATE | EXPLANATION | PR | DEBIT | CREDIT | BALANCE |
|------|-------------|----|-------|--------|---------|
|      |             |    |       |        |         |
|      |             |    |       |        |         |
|      |             |    |       |        |         |

**Accounts Payable**      ACCOUNT NO. 201

| DATE | EXPLANATION | PR | DEBIT | CREDIT | BALANCE |
|------|-------------|----|-------|--------|---------|
|      |             |    |       |        |         |
|      |             |    |       |        |         |
|      |             |    |       |        |         |
|      |             |    |       |        |         |

**Tait Unger, Capital**      ACCOUNT NO. 301

| DATE | EXPLANATION | PR | DEBIT | CREDIT | BALANCE |
|------|-------------|----|-------|--------|---------|
|      |             |    |       |        |         |
|      |             |    |       |        |         |

**Tait Unger, Withdrawals**      ACCOUNT NO. 302

| DATE | EXPLANATION | PR | DEBIT | CREDIT | BALANCE |
|------|-------------|----|-------|--------|---------|
|      |             |    |       |        |         |
|      |             |    |       |        |         |

Name:_____

## Problem 2-7B (concl'd.)

### Service Fees Earned                                          ACCOUNT NO. 401

| DATE | EXPLANATION | PR | DEBIT | CREDIT | BALANCE |
|------|-------------|----|-------|--------|---------|
|      |             |    |       |        |         |
|      |             |    |       |        |         |
|      |             |    |       |        |         |
|      |             |    |       |        |         |

### Wages Expense                                          ACCOUNT NO. 680

| DATE | EXPLANATION | PR | DEBIT | CREDIT | BALANCE |
|------|-------------|----|-------|--------|---------|
|      |             |    |       |        |         |
|      |             |    |       |        |         |

### Utilities Expense                                          ACCOUNT NO. 690

| DATE | EXPLANATION | PR | DEBIT | CREDIT | BALANCE |
|------|-------------|----|-------|--------|---------|
|      |             |    |       |        |         |
|      |             |    |       |        |         |

## Part 4

### Trial Balance

|  |  |  |
|--|--|--|
|  |  |  |
|  |  |  |
|  |  |  |
|  |  |  |
|  |  |  |
|  |  |  |
|  |  |  |
|  |  |  |
|  |  |  |
|  |  |  |
|  |  |  |
|  |  |  |
|  |  |  |
|  |  |  |
|  |  |  |
|  |  |  |

*Analysis component:*

_____

_____

_____

_____

_____

**Problem 2-8B**

## Income Statement

|  |  |  |
|---|---|---|
|  |  |  |
|  |  |  |
|  |  |  |
|  |  |  |
|  |  |  |
|  |  |  |
|  |  |  |
|  |  |  |
|  |  |  |

## Statement of Changes in Equity

|  |  |  |
|---|---|---|
|  |  |  |
|  |  |  |
|  |  |  |
|  |  |  |
|  |  |  |
|  |  |  |
|  |  |  |
|  |  |  |

## Balance Sheet

|  |  |  |  |
|---|---|---|---|
|  |  |  |  |
|  |  |  |  |
|  |  |  |  |
|  |  |  |  |
|  |  |  |  |
|  |  |  |  |
|  |  |  |  |
|  |  |  |  |
|  |  |  |  |
|  |  |  |  |
|  |  |  |  |

Name:_____

**Problem 2-9B**

## Income Statement

| | | |
|---|---|---|
| | | |
| | | |
| | | |
| | | |
| | | |
| | | |
| | | |
| | | |
| | | |
| | | |
| | | |

## Statement of Changes in Equity

| | | |
|---|---|---|
| | | |
| | | |
| | | |
| | | |
| | | |
| | | |
| | | |

## Balance Sheet

| | | | |
|---|---|---|---|
| | | | |
| | | | |
| | | | |
| | | | |
| | | | |
| | | | |
| | | | |
| | | | |
| | | | |
| | | | |
| | | | |
| | | | |
| | | | |

*Fundamental Accounting Principles,* 15ce, Working Papers

Name:_____

**Problem 2-9B (concl'd.)**

*Analysis Component:*

## GENERAL JOURNAL

Page _____

| Date | Account Titles and Explanation | PR | Debit | Credit |
|---|---|---|---|---|
|  |  |  |  |  |
|  |  |  |  |  |
|  |  |  |  |  |
|  |  |  |  |  |
|  |  |  |  |  |
|  |  |  |  |  |
|  |  |  |  |  |
|  |  |  |  |  |
|  |  |  |  |  |
|  |  |  |  |  |

**Problem 2-10B    Part 1**

## GENERAL JOURNAL

Page _____

| Date | Account Titles and Explanation | PR | Debit | Credit |
|---|---|---|---|---|
|  |  |  |  |  |
|  |  |  |  |  |
|  |  |  |  |  |
|  |  |  |  |  |
|  |  |  |  |  |
|  |  |  |  |  |
|  |  |  |  |  |
|  |  |  |  |  |
|  |  |  |  |  |
|  |  |  |  |  |
|  |  |  |  |  |
|  |  |  |  |  |
|  |  |  |  |  |
|  |  |  |  |  |
|  |  |  |  |  |
|  |  |  |  |  |
|  |  |  |  |  |
|  |  |  |  |  |
|  |  |  |  |  |
|  |  |  |  |  |
|  |  |  |  |  |
|  |  |  |  |  |
|  |  |  |  |  |
|  |  |  |  |  |

Name:_____

**Problem 2-10B (cont'd.)**

## GENERAL JOURNAL

Page _____

| Date | Account Titles and Explanation | PR | Debit | Credit |
|------|-------------------------------|----|-------|--------|
|      |                               |    |       |        |
|      |                               |    |       |        |
|      |                               |    |       |        |
|      |                               |    |       |        |
|      |                               |    |       |        |
|      |                               |    |       |        |
|      |                               |    |       |        |
|      |                               |    |       |        |
|      |                               |    |       |        |
|      |                               |    |       |        |
|      |                               |    |       |        |
|      |                               |    |       |        |
|      |                               |    |       |        |
|      |                               |    |       |        |
|      |                               |    |       |        |
|      |                               |    |       |        |
|      |                               |    |       |        |
|      |                               |    |       |        |
|      |                               |    |       |        |
|      |                               |    |       |        |
|      |                               |    |       |        |
|      |                               |    |       |        |
|      |                               |    |       |        |
|      |                               |    |       |        |
|      |                               |    |       |        |
|      |                               |    |       |        |
|      |                               |    |       |        |
|      |                               |    |       |        |
|      |                               |    |       |        |
|      |                               |    |       |        |
|      |                               |    |       |        |
|      |                               |    |       |        |
|      |                               |    |       |        |
|      |                               |    |       |        |
|      |                               |    |       |        |
|      |                               |    |       |        |
|      |                               |    |       |        |
|      |                               |    |       |        |

**Problem 2-10B (cont'd.)**

**Parts 2 and 3**

## GENERAL LEDGER

### Cash                                                    ACCOUNT NO. 101

| DATE | EXPLANATION | PR | DEBIT | CREDIT | BALANCE |
|------|-------------|----|-------|--------|---------|
| 2017 | | | | | |
| Jun. 30 | Beginning balance | | | | 75,000 |
| | | | | | |
| | | | | | |
| | | | | | |
| | | | | | |
| | | | | | |
| | | | | | |
| | | | | | |
| | | | | | |
| | | | | | |
| | | | | | |
| | | | | | |
| | | | | | |
| | | | | | |
| | | | | | |
| | | | | | |
| | | | | | |

### Accounts Receivable                                     ACCOUNT NO. 106

| DATE | EXPLANATION | PR | DEBIT | CREDIT | BALANCE |
|------|-------------|----|-------|--------|---------|
| 2017 | | | | | |
| Jun. 30 | Beginning balance | | | | 950 |
| | | | | | |
| | | | | | |
| | | | | | |

### Prepaid Insurance                                       ACCOUNT NO. 128

| DATE | EXPLANATION | PR | DEBIT | CREDIT | BALANCE |
|------|-------------|----|-------|--------|---------|
| 2017 | | | | | |
| Jun. 30 | Beginning balance | | | | 275 |
| | | | | | |

### Trucks                                                   ACCOUNT NO. 153

| DATE | EXPLANATION | PR | DEBIT | CREDIT | BALANCE |
|------|-------------|----|-------|--------|---------|
| 2017 | | | | | |
| Jun. 30 | Beginning balance | | | | 20,800 |
| | | | | | |
| | | | | | |

## Problem 2-10B (cont'd.)

### Office Equipment                                ACCOUNT NO. 163

| DATE | EXPLANATION | PR | DEBIT | CREDIT | BALANCE |
|------|-------------|-----|-------|--------|---------|
| 2017 | | | | | |
| Jun. 30 | Beginning balance | | | | 1,200 |
| | | | | | |
| | | | | | |

### Building                                ACCOUNT NO. 173

| DATE | EXPLANATION | PR | DEBIT | CREDIT | BALANCE |
|------|-------------|-----|-------|--------|---------|
| 2017 | | | | | |
| Jun. 30 | Beginning balance | | | | 0 |
| | | | | | |

### Land                                ACCOUNT NO. 183

| DATE | EXPLANATION | PR | DEBIT | CREDIT | BALANCE |
|------|-------------|-----|-------|--------|---------|
| 2017 | | | | | |
| Jun. 30 | Beginning balance | | | | 0 |
| | | | | | |

### Accounts Payable                                ACCOUNT NO. 201

| DATE | EXPLANATION | PR | DEBIT | CREDIT | BALANCE |
|------|-------------|-----|-------|--------|---------|
| 2017 | | | | | |
| Jun. 30 | Beginning balance | | | | 725 |
| | | | | | |
| | | | | | |

### Unearned Revenue                                ACCOUNT NO. 233

| DATE | EXPLANATION | PR | DEBIT | CREDIT | BALANCE |
|------|-------------|-----|-------|--------|---------|
| 2017 | | | | | |
| Jun. 30 | Beginning balance | | | | 0 |
| | | | | | |

### Long-Term Notes Payable                                ACCOUNT NO. 251

| DATE | EXPLANATION | PR | DEBIT | CREDIT | BALANCE |
|------|-------------|-----|-------|--------|---------|
| 2017 | | | | | |
| Jun. 30 | Beginning balance | | | | 7,000 |
| | | | | | |
| | | | | | |
| | | | | | |

## Problem 2-10B (cont'd.)

### Brett Wilson, Capital ACCOUNT NO. 301

| DATE | EXPLANATION | PR | DEBIT | CREDIT | BALANCE |
|------|-------------|----|----|-----|------|
| 2017 | | | | | |
| Jun. 30 | Beginning balance | | | | 83,825 |
| | | | | | |

### Brett Wilson, Withdrawals ACCOUNT NO. 302

| DATE | EXPLANATION | PR | DEBIT | CREDIT | BALANCE |
|------|-------------|----|----|-----|------|
| 2017 | | | | | |
| Jun. 30 | Beginning balance | | | | 600 |
| | | | | | |

### Revenue ACCOUNT NO. 401

| DATE | EXPLANATION | PR | DEBIT | CREDIT | BALANCE |
|------|-------------|----|----|-----|------|
| 2017 | | | | | |
| Jun. 30 | Beginning balance | | | | 8,400 |
| | | | | | |
| | | | | | |
| | | | | | |

### Wages Expense ACCOUNT NO. 623

| DATE | EXPLANATION | PR | DEBIT | CREDIT | BALANCE |
|------|-------------|----|----|-----|------|
| 2017 | | | | | |
| Jun. 30 | Beginning balance | | | | 780 |
| | | | | | |
| | | | | | |

### Truck Rental Expense ACCOUNT NO. 645

| DATE | EXPLANATION | PR | DEBIT | CREDIT | BALANCE |
|------|-------------|----|----|-----|------|
| 2017 | | | | | |
| Jun. 30 | Beginning balance | | | | 230 |
| | | | | | |

### Advertising Expense ACCOUNT NO. 655

| DATE | EXPLANATION | PR | DEBIT | CREDIT | BALANCE |
|------|-------------|----|----|-----|------|
| 2017 | | | | | |
| Jun. 30 | Beginning balance | | | | 75 |
| | | | | | |

### Repairs Expense ACCOUNT NO. 684

| DATE | EXPLANATION | PR | DEBIT | CREDIT | BALANCE |
|------|-------------|----|----|-----|------|
| 2017 | | | | | |
| Jun. 30 | Beginning balance | | | | 40 |
| | | | | | |

**Problem 2-10B (concl'd.)**

**Part 4**

| Trial Balance | | |
|---|---|---|
| | | |
| | | |
| | | |
| | | |
| | | |
| | | |
| | | |
| | | |
| | | |
| | | |
| | | |
| | | |
| | | |
| | | |
| | | |
| | | |
| | | |
| | | |
| | | |
| | | |
| | | |
| | | |
| | | |

## Income Statement

| | | |
|---|---|---|
| | | |
| | | |
| | | |
| | | |
| | | |
| | | |
| | | |
| | | |
| | | |
| | | |

## Statement of Changes in Equity

| | | |
|---|---|---|
| | | |
| | | |
| | | |
| | | |
| | | |
| | | |

## Balance Sheet

| | | | |
|---|---|---|---|
| | | | |
| | | | |
| | | | |
| | | | |
| | | | |
| | | | |
| | | | |
| | | | |
| | | | |
| | | | |

Chapter 2                          Name:_____

**Problem 2-12B Part 1**

GENERAL JOURNAL                          Page_____

| Date | Account Titles and Explanation | PR | Debit | Credit |
|------|-------------------------------|----|-------|--------|
|      |                               |    |       |        |
|      |                               |    |       |        |
|      |                               |    |       |        |
|      |                               |    |       |        |
|      |                               |    |       |        |
|      |                               |    |       |        |
|      |                               |    |       |        |
|      |                               |    |       |        |
|      |                               |    |       |        |
|      |                               |    |       |        |
|      |                               |    |       |        |
|      |                               |    |       |        |
|      |                               |    |       |        |
|      |                               |    |       |        |
|      |                               |    |       |        |
|      |                               |    |       |        |
|      |                               |    |       |        |
|      |                               |    |       |        |
|      |                               |    |       |        |
|      |                               |    |       |        |
|      |                               |    |       |        |
|      |                               |    |       |        |
|      |                               |    |       |        |
|      |                               |    |       |        |
|      |                               |    |       |        |
|      |                               |    |       |        |
|      |                               |    |       |        |
|      |                               |    |       |        |
|      |                               |    |       |        |
|      |                               |    |       |        |
|      |                               |    |       |        |
|      |                               |    |       |        |
|      |                               |    |       |        |
|      |                               |    |       |        |
|      |                               |    |       |        |
|      |                               |    |       |        |
|      |                               |    |       |        |
|      |                               |    |       |        |

*Fundamental Accounting Principles*, 15ce, Working Papers

Name:_____

Problem 2-12B (cont'd.)

Parts 2 and 3

| Cash | 101 |
|---|---|
| Bal. 26,000 | |

| Office Supplies | 124 |
|---|---|
| Bal. 900 | |

| Office Equipment | 163 |
|---|---|
| Bal. 36,000 | |

| Accounts Payable | 201 |
|---|---|
| | 43,000 Bal. |

| Notes Payable | 205 |
|---|---|
| | 20,000 Bal. |

| Travel Revenue | 401 |
|---|---|
| | 34,000 Bal. |

| Wages Expense | 623 |
|---|---|
| Bal. 38,000 | |

| Ike Petrov, Capital | 301 |
|---|---|
| | 8,000 Bal. |

| Interest Expense | 633 |
|---|---|
| Bal. 100 | |

| Ike Petrov, Withdrawals | 302 |
|---|---|
| Bal. 4,000 | |

Name:_____

**Problem 2-12B (cont'd.)**

**Part 4**

| | Trial Balance | | |
|---|---|---|---|
| | | | |
| | | | |
| | | | |
| | | | |
| | | | |
| | | | |
| | | | |
| | | | |
| | | | |
| | | | |
| | | | |
| | | | |
| | | | |
| | | | |
| | | | |
| | | | |

**Problem 2-12B (cont'd.)**

**Part 5**

### Income Statement

| | | |
|---|---|---|
| | | |
| | | |
| | | |
| | | |
| | | |
| | | |
| | | |
| | | |
| | | |

### Statement of Changes in Equity

| | | |
|---|---|---|
| | | |
| | | |
| | | |
| | | |
| | | |
| | | |
| | | |
| | | |

### Balance Sheet

| | | | |
|---|---|---|---|
| | | | |
| | | | |
| | | | |
| | | | |
| | | | |
| | | | |
| | | | |
| | | | |
| | | | |

Name:_____

**Problem 2-12B (concl'd.)**

*Analysis component:*

_____

_____

_____

_____

_____

_____

_____

_____

_____

**Problem 2-13B**

_____

| | Income Statement | | |
|---|---|---|---|
| | | | |
| | | | |
| | | | |
| | | | |
| | | | |
| | | | |
| | | | |
| | | | |
| | | | |
| | | | |
| | | | |
| | | | |
| | | | |
| | | | |
| | | | |
| | | | |
| | | | |
| | | | |

*Fundamental Accounting Principles*, 15ce, Working Papers

## Statement of Changes in Equity

| | | |
|---|---|---|
| | | |
| | | |
| | | |
| | | |
| | | |
| | | |
| | | |
| | | |
| | | |
| | | |
| | | |
| | | |

## Balance Sheet

| | | | |
|---|---|---|---|
| | | | |
| | | | |
| | | | |
| | | | |
| | | | |
| | | | |
| | | | |
| | | | |
| | | | |
| | | | |
| | | | |
| | | | |
| | | | |
| | | | |
| | | | |
| | | | |
| | | | |
| | | | |
| | | | |
| | | | |

Name:_____

**Problem 2-14B**

| Trial Balance | | |
|---|---|---|
| | | |
| | | |
| | | |
| | | |
| | | |
| | | |
| | | |
| | | |
| | | |
| | | |
| | | |
| | | |
| | | |
| | | |
| | | |
| | | |
| | | |

**Calculations:**

Name:_____

**Cumulative Problem**

**Echo Systems**

**Parts 2 and 6:  October/November Transactions**

### GENERAL JOURNAL

| Date | Account Titles and Explanation | PR | Debit | Credit |
|------|-------------------------------|----|----|----|
| | | | | |
| | | | | |
| | | | | |
| | | | | |
| | | | | |
| | | | | |
| | | | | |
| | | | | |
| | | | | |
| | | | | |
| | | | | |
| | | | | |
| | | | | |
| | | | | |
| | | | | |
| | | | | |
| | | | | |
| | | | | |
| | | | | |
| | | | | |
| | | | | |
| | | | | |
| | | | | |
| | | | | |
| | | | | |
| | | | | |
| | | | | |
| | | | | |
| | | | | |
| | | | | |
| | | | | |
| | | | | |
| | | | | |
| | | | | |
| | | | | |
| | | | | |
| | | | | |
| | | | | |

**Cumulative Problem**

Echo Systems (Cont'd.)

| Date | Account Titles and Explanation | PR | Debit | Credit |
|------|-------------------------------|-----|-------|--------|
|      |                               |     |       |        |
|      |                               |     |       |        |
|      |                               |     |       |        |
|      |                               |     |       |        |
|      |                               |     |       |        |
|      |                               |     |       |        |
|      |                               |     |       |        |
|      |                               |     |       |        |
|      |                               |     |       |        |
|      |                               |     |       |        |
|      |                               |     |       |        |
|      |                               |     |       |        |
|      |                               |     |       |        |
|      |                               |     |       |        |
|      |                               |     |       |        |
|      |                               |     |       |        |
|      |                               |     |       |        |
|      |                               |     |       |        |
|      |                               |     |       |        |
|      |                               |     |       |        |
|      |                               |     |       |        |
|      |                               |     |       |        |
|      |                               |     |       |        |
|      |                               |     |       |        |
|      |                               |     |       |        |
|      |                               |     |       |        |
|      |                               |     |       |        |
|      |                               |     |       |        |
|      |                               |     |       |        |
|      |                               |     |       |        |
|      |                               |     |       |        |
|      |                               |     |       |        |
|      |                               |     |       |        |
|      |                               |     |       |        |
|      |                               |     |       |        |
|      |                               |     |       |        |
|      |                               |     |       |        |
|      |                               |     |       |        |

Cumulative Problem

### Echo Systems (Cont'd.)

| Date | Account Titles and Explanation | PR | Debit | Credit |
|------|-------------------------------|----|----|----|
|  |  |  |  |  |
|  |  |  |  |  |
|  |  |  |  |  |
|  |  |  |  |  |
|  |  |  |  |  |
|  |  |  |  |  |
|  |  |  |  |  |
|  |  |  |  |  |
|  |  |  |  |  |
|  |  |  |  |  |
|  |  |  |  |  |
|  |  |  |  |  |
|  |  |  |  |  |
|  |  |  |  |  |
|  |  |  |  |  |
|  |  |  |  |  |
|  |  |  |  |  |
|  |  |  |  |  |
|  |  |  |  |  |
|  |  |  |  |  |
|  |  |  |  |  |
|  |  |  |  |  |
|  |  |  |  |  |
|  |  |  |  |  |
|  |  |  |  |  |
|  |  |  |  |  |
|  |  |  |  |  |
|  |  |  |  |  |
|  |  |  |  |  |
|  |  |  |  |  |
|  |  |  |  |  |
|  |  |  |  |  |
|  |  |  |  |  |
|  |  |  |  |  |
|  |  |  |  |  |
|  |  |  |  |  |
|  |  |  |  |  |
|  |  |  |  |  |
|  |  |  |  |  |
|  |  |  |  |  |

**Cumulative Problem (cont.)**

**Parts 1, 3, and 7**          **GENERAL LEDGER**

Cash                                                                ACCOUNT NO. 101

| DATE | EXPLANATION | PR | DEBIT | CREDIT | BALANCE |
|------|-------------|-----|-------|--------|---------|
|      |             |     |       |        |         |
|      |             |     |       |        |         |
|      |             |     |       |        |         |
|      |             |     |       |        |         |
|      |             |     |       |        |         |
|      |             |     |       |        |         |
|      |             |     |       |        |         |
|      |             |     |       |        |         |
|      |             |     |       |        |         |
|      |             |     |       |        |         |
|      |             |     |       |        |         |
|      |             |     |       |        |         |
|      |             |     |       |        |         |
|      |             |     |       |        |         |
|      |             |     |       |        |         |
|      |             |     |       |        |         |
|      |             |     |       |        |         |
|      |             |     |       |        |         |
|      |             |     |       |        |         |
|      |             |     |       |        |         |
|      |             |     |       |        |         |

Accounts Receivable                                        ACCOUNT NO. 106

| DATE | EXPLANATION | PR | DEBIT | CREDIT | BALANCE |
|------|-------------|-----|-------|--------|---------|
|      |             |     |       |        |         |
|      |             |     |       |        |         |
|      |             |     |       |        |         |
|      |             |     |       |        |         |
|      |             |     |       |        |         |
|      |             |     |       |        |         |
|      |             |     |       |        |         |
|      |             |     |       |        |         |
|      |             |     |       |        |         |

Computer Supplies                                          ACCOUNT NO. 126

| DATE | EXPLANATION | PR | DEBIT | CREDIT | BALANCE |
|------|-------------|-----|-------|--------|---------|
|      |             |     |       |        |         |
|      |             |     |       |        |         |
|      |             |     |       |        |         |

**Cumulative Problem (cont'd.)**

### Prepaid Insurance ACCOUNT NO. 128

| DATE | EXPLANATION | PR | DEBIT | CREDIT | BALANCE |
|------|-------------|----|-------|--------|---------|
|      |             |    |       |        |         |
|      |             |    |       |        |         |

### Prepaid Rent ACCOUNT NO. 131

| DATE | EXPLANATION | PR | DEBIT | CREDIT | BALANCE |
|------|-------------|----|-------|--------|---------|
|      |             |    |       |        |         |
|      |             |    |       |        |         |

### Office Equipment ACCOUNT NO. 163

| DATE | EXPLANATION | PR | DEBIT | CREDIT | BALANCE |
|------|-------------|----|-------|--------|---------|
|      |             |    |       |        |         |
|      |             |    |       |        |         |

### Computer Equipment ACCOUNT NO. 167

| DATE | EXPLANATION | PR | DEBIT | CREDIT | BALANCE |
|------|-------------|----|-------|--------|---------|
|      |             |    |       |        |         |
|      |             |    |       |        |         |

### Accounts Payable ACCOUNT NO. 201

| DATE | EXPLANATION | PR | DEBIT | CREDIT | BALANCE |
|------|-------------|----|-------|--------|---------|
|      |             |    |       |        |         |
|      |             |    |       |        |         |
|      |             |    |       |        |         |

### Mary Graham, Capital ACCOUNT NO. 301

| DATE | EXPLANATION | PR | DEBIT | CREDIT | BALANCE |
|------|-------------|----|-------|--------|---------|
|      |             |    |       |        |         |
|      |             |    |       |        |         |

### Mary Graham, Withdrawals ACCOUNT NO. 302

| DATE | EXPLANATION | PR | DEBIT | CREDIT | BALANCE |
|------|-------------|----|-------|--------|---------|
|      |             |    |       |        |         |
|      |             |    |       |        |         |

## Cumulative Problem (cont'd.)

### Computer Services Revenue     ACCOUNT NO. 403

| DATE | EXPLANATION | PR | DEBIT | CREDIT | BALANCE |
|------|-------------|----|-------|--------|---------|
|      |             |    |       |        |         |
|      |             |    |       |        |         |
|      |             |    |       |        |         |
|      |             |    |       |        |         |
|      |             |    |       |        |         |
|      |             |    |       |        |         |
|      |             |    |       |        |         |

### Wages Expense     ACCOUNT NO. 623

| DATE | EXPLANATION | PR | DEBIT | CREDIT | BALANCE |
|------|-------------|----|-------|--------|---------|
|      |             |    |       |        |         |
|      |             |    |       |        |         |
|      |             |    |       |        |         |

### Advertising Expense     ACCOUNT NO. 655

| DATE | EXPLANATION | PR | DEBIT | CREDIT | BALANCE |
|------|-------------|----|-------|--------|---------|
|      |             |    |       |        |         |
|      |             |    |       |        |         |

### Mileage Expense     ACCOUNT NO. 676

| DATE | EXPLANATION | PR | DEBIT | CREDIT | BALANCE |
|------|-------------|----|-------|--------|---------|
|      |             |    |       |        |         |
|      |             |    |       |        |         |
|      |             |    |       |        |         |

### Repairs Expense, Computer     ACCOUNT NO. 684

| DATE | EXPLANATION | PR | DEBIT | CREDIT | BALANCE |
|------|-------------|----|-------|--------|---------|
|      |             |    |       |        |         |
|      |             |    |       |        |         |

### Charitable Donations Expense     ACCOUNT NO. 699

| DATE | EXPLANATION | PR | DEBIT | CREDIT | BALANCE |
|------|-------------|----|-------|--------|---------|
|      |             |    |       |        |         |
|      |             |    |       |        |         |

Cumulative Problem (cont'd.)

**Part 4**

### ECHO SYSTMES
### Trial Balance
### October 31, 2017

|  | Debit | Credit |
|---|---|---|
|  |  |  |
|  |  |  |
|  |  |  |
|  |  |  |
|  |  |  |
|  |  |  |
|  |  |  |
|  |  |  |
|  |  |  |
|  |  |  |
|  |  |  |
|  |  |  |
|  |  |  |
|  |  |  |
|  |  |  |
|  |  |  |
|  |  |  |
|  |  |  |
|  |  |  |
|  |  |  |
|  |  |  |
|  |  |  |

**Part 5**

### ECHO SYSTEMS
### Income Statement
### Month Ended October 31, 2017

|  |  |  |
|---|---|---|
|  |  |  |
|  |  |  |
|  |  |  |
|  |  |  |
|  |  |  |
|  |  |  |
|  |  |  |
|  |  |  |
|  |  |  |
|  |  |  |
|  |  |  |
|  |  |  |

**Cumulative Problem (cont'd.)**

|  | | |
| --- | --- | --- |
| **ECHO SYSTEMS** | | |
| **Statement of Changes in Equity** | | |
| **Month Ended October 31, 2017** | | |
|  |  |  |
|  |  |  |
|  |  |  |
|  |  |  |
|  |  |  |
|  |  |  |
|  |  |  |
|  |  |  |

|  | | | |
| --- | --- | --- | --- |
| **ECHO SYSTEMS** | | | |
| **Balance Sheet** | | | |
| **October 31, 2017** | | | |
|  |  |  |  |
|  |  |  |  |
|  |  |  |  |
|  |  |  |  |
|  |  |  |  |
|  |  |  |  |
|  |  |  |  |
|  |  |  |  |
|  |  |  |  |
|  |  |  |  |
|  |  |  |  |
|  |  |  |  |
|  |  |  |  |
|  |  |  |  |
|  |  |  |  |

Name:_____

**Cumulative Problem (cont.)**

**Part 8**

### ECHO SYSTEMS
### Trial Balance
### November 30, 2017

| | Debit | Credit |
|---|---|---|
| | | |
| | | |
| | | |
| | | |
| | | |
| | | |
| | | |
| | | |
| | | |
| | | |
| | | |
| | | |
| | | |
| | | |
| | | |
| | | |
| | | |
| | | |
| | | |
| | | |
| | | |
| | | |

**Part 9**

### ECHO SYSTEMS
### Income Statement
### For Two Months Ended November 30, 2017

| | | |
|---|---|---|
| | | |
| | | |
| | | |
| | | |
| | | |
| | | |
| | | |
| | | |
| | | |
| | | |
| | | |
| | | |

**Cumulative Problem (concl'd.)**

## ECHO SYSTEMS
### Statement of Changes in Equity
### For Two Months Ended November 30, 2017

|  |  |  |
|---|---|---|
|  |  |  |
|  |  |  |
|  |  |  |
|  |  |  |
|  |  |  |
|  |  |  |
|  |  |  |
|  |  |  |
|  |  |  |

## ECHO SYSTEMS
### Balance Sheet
### November 30, 2017

|  |  |  |  |
|---|---|---|---|
|  |  |  |  |
|  |  |  |  |
|  |  |  |  |
|  |  |  |  |
|  |  |  |  |
|  |  |  |  |
|  |  |  |  |
|  |  |  |  |
|  |  |  |  |
|  |  |  |  |
|  |  |  |  |
|  |  |  |  |
|  |  |  |  |
|  |  |  |  |
|  |  |  |  |
|  |  |  |  |
|  |  |  |  |
|  |  |  |  |
|  |  |  |  |

Name:_____

## Quick Study 3-1

1. _____
_____
_____

2. _____
_____
_____

3. _____
_____

4. _____
_____

## Quick Study 3-2

1. _____
_____
_____
_____

2. _____
_____
_____
_____

## Quick Study 3-3

1. **Cash Basis:** _____
_____
_____
_____

2. **Accrual Basis:** _____
_____
_____
_____

3. **Difference:** _____
_____
_____
_____

### Quick Study 3-4

**a.** One year Insurance policy for $12000.
∴ $12000/12 months = $1000.
∴ The Insurance policy cost per month $1000.

**b.**
There are 6 months between July 1,2017
and December 31, 2017.

### GENERAL JOURNAL                                  Page____

| Date | | Account Titles and Explanation | $ Debit | $ Credit |
|---|---|---|---|---|
| | | | | |
| **c.** Jul 1 | | Prepaid Insurance | 12000 | |
| | |     Cash | | 12000 |
| | | To record purchase of prepaid | | |
| | | Insurance for one year. | | |
| | | | | |
| **d.** Dec 31 | | Insurance expense | 6000 | |
| | |     Prepaid Insurance | | 6000 |
| | | To record expired Insurance | | |
| | | $12000 x6months = $6000. | | |
| | | 12 months | | |

### Quick Study 3-5
### GENERAL JOURNAL                                  Page____

| Date | | Account Titles and Explanation | Debit | Credit |
|---|---|---|---|---|
| | | | | |
| **a.** 2017 Jul | 1 | Supplies | 12000 | |
| | |     Cash | | 12000 |
| | | To record purchases of | | |
| | | supplies. | | |
| | | | | |
| **b.** Dec 31 | | Supplies expense | 7000 | |
| | |     Supplies | | 7000 |
| | | To record supplies used. | | |
| | | | | |

**c.**
On January 1, 2018 Organic Market
has $5000 of supplies.

**Quick Study 3-6**

## GENERAL JOURNAL

Page____

| Date | Account Titles and Explanation | Debit | Credit |
|------|-------------------------------|-------|--------|
| a. | | | |
| | | | |
| | | | |
| | | | |

b. _____

_____

_____

_____

## GENERAL JOURNAL

Page____

| Date | Account Titles and Explanation | Debit | Credit |
|------|-------------------------------|-------|--------|
| | | | |
| | | | |
| | | | |
| | | | |
| | | | |

c. _____

_____

_____

## GENERAL JOURNAL

Page____

| Date | Account Titles and Explanation | Debit | Credit |
|------|-------------------------------|-------|--------|
| | | | |
| | | | |
| | | | |
| | | | |
| | | | |

d. _____

_____

_____

_____

_____

**Chapter 3**

Name:_____

**Quick Study 3-7**

GENERAL JOURNAL                                    Page____

| Date | | | Account Titles and Explanation | Debit | Credit |
|---|---|---|---|---|---|
| a. 2017 Jan | 1 | | Equipment | 12000 | |
| | | | Cash | | 12000 |
| | | | To record the purchase | | |
| | | | of equipment. | | |

b. Straight-line depreciation:
<u>Cost of assets - Estimated value at the end of estimated useful l</u>
       Estimated useful life

c. Annual depreciation for 2017 (Jan 1 to Dec 31 2017):
= <u>Cost of assets - Estimated value</u>
    Estimated useful life
= <u>$12000 - $2000</u> = $2000 annual depreciation
    5 years

GENERAL JOURNAL                                    Page____

| Date | | | Account Titles and Explanation | Debit | Credit |
|---|---|---|---|---|---|
| d. 2017 Dec | 31 | | Depreciation expense, Equipment | 2000 | |
| | | | Accumulated dep, Equipment | | 2000 |
| | | | To record annual depreciation | | |
| | | | on equipment. | | |

**Quick Study 3-8**

GENERAL JOURNAL                                    Page____

| Date | | | Account Titles and Explanation | Debit | Credit |
|---|---|---|---|---|---|
| a. 2017 Mar | 1 | | Vehicle | 32000 | |
| | | | Cash | | 32000 |
| | | | To record purchase of | | |
| | | | vehicle. | | |

**Quick Study 3-8 (concl'd.)**

b. $32000 - 8000 = 24000$; $24000/4$ yrs $= 6000$ yr.
$\frac{6000}{12} = 500$; $500 \times 10$ months $= 5000$

**GENERAL JOURNAL**                              Page____

| Date | | Account Titles and Explanation | Debit | Credit |
|------|---|-------------------------------|-------|--------|
| c. Dec | 31 | Depreciation Expense, vehicle | 5000 | |
| | | Accumulated Dep, vehicle | | 5000 |
| | | $32000 - 8000 = 24000/4$ yrs $= 6000$ | | |
| | | $\frac{6000}{12} \times 10$ months $= \$5000$ | | |

d. Depreciation for Jan 1 to Dec 31, 2018.
$= \frac{32000 - 8000}{4 \text{ yrs}} = \$6000$

**GENERAL JOURNAL**                              Page____

| Date | | Account Titles and Explanation | Debit | Credit |
|------|---|-------------------------------|-------|--------|
| e. 2018 Dec | 31 | Depreciation Expense, vehicle | 6000 | |
| | | Accumulated Dep, vehicle | | 6000 |
| | | $\frac{32000 - 8000}{4 \text{ yrs}} = \$6000$ | | |

**Quick Study 3-9**

**GENERAL JOURNAL**                              Page____

| Date | | Account Titles and Explanation | Debit | Credit |
|------|---|-------------------------------|-------|--------|
| 2017 | 1 | Cash | 300 | |
| a. Oct | | Unearned Revenue | | 300 |
| | | To record collection of | | |
| | | cash for future | | |
| | | services. | | |

b.
$\frac{\$300}{12 \text{ months}} = \$25$

**Quick Study 3-9 (cont'd.)**

**c.**

_3 Months_

## GENERAL JOURNAL

Page____

| Date | | Account Titles and Explanation | PR | Debit | Credit |
|---|---|---|---|---|---|
| 2017 | 31 | Unearned Revenue | | 75 | |
| d. Dec | | Revenue | | | 75 |
| | | To record the earned | | | |
| | | Position of revenue | | | |
| | | received in advance | | | |
| | | $25 x 3 Months = $75 | | | |

**Quick Study 3-10**

## GENERAL JOURNAL

Page____

| Date | | Account Titles and Explanation | PR | Debit | Credit |
|---|---|---|---|---|---|
| 2017 | 1 | Cash | | 12000 | |
| a. Nov | | Unearned Revenue | | | 12000 |
| | | To record cash | | | |
| | | received for services | | | |
| | | to be performed in | | | |
| | | the future. | | | |

**b.**

$12000 - $3000 (unearned) = $9000 (earned)

## GENERAL JOURNAL

Page____

| Date | | Account Titles and Explanation | PR | Debit | Credit |
|---|---|---|---|---|---|
| c. Dec | 31 | Unearned Revenue | | 9000 | |
| | | Revenue | | | 9000 |
| | | To record earned | | | |
| | | portion of revenue | | | |
| | | received in advance. | | | |

**Quick Study 3-11**

a. Interest expense =

Principal × interest rate × number of months
                                    12 months

b.

10 Months

**GENERAL JOURNAL**                                        Page____

| Date | Account Titles and Explanation | PR | Debit | Credit |
|------|-------------------------------|----|-------|--------|
| 2017 31 | Interest Expense | | 800 | |
| c. Dec |     Interest payable | | | 800 |
| | To record accrued | | | |
| | interest expense. | | | |
| | $12000 × 8% × 10 = $800 | | | |
| |         12 | | | |

**Quick Study 3-12**

a.

$400   ($5600/14 days)

b.

1 day

**GENERAL JOURNAL**                                        Page____

| Date | Account Titles and Explanation | PR | Debit | Credit |
|------|-------------------------------|----|-------|--------|
| c. 2017 31 | Wages Expense | | 400 | |
| Dec |     wages payable | | | 400 |
| | To record one day's | | | |
| | accrued wages. | | | |
| d. 2018 15 | Wages payable | | 400 | |
| Jan | wages expense | | 5200 | |
| |     Cash | | | 5600 |
| | To record payment of two weeks | | | |
| | wages including 1 day accrued in Dec | | | |
| | (1 day $400; 13 days at $5200 = $5600) | | | |

# Chapter 3

Name:_____

## Quick Study 3-13

### GENERAL JOURNAL

Page_____

| Date | Account Titles and Explanation | PR | Debit | Credit |
|------|-------------------------------|----|-------|--------|
| a. | | | | |
| | | | | |
| | | | | |
| | | | | |
| b. | | | | |
| | | | | |
| | | | | |
| | | | | |
| | | | | |

## Quick Study 3-14

a.

Tigrsoft has earned the $17000 of revenue bcz the company has provided the service to their customer. Based on the accrual basic of accounting revenue is recorded when it is earned and not when the customer is billed or when the cash is received.

### GENERAL JOURNAL

Page_____

| Date | Account Titles and Explanation | PR | Debit | Credit |
|------|-------------------------------|----|-------|--------|
| b. 2017/31 Mar | Accounts Receivable | | 17000 | |
| | Revenues | | | 17000 |
| | To record accrued | | | |
| | revenues. | | | |
| c. Apr 16 | Cash | | 12000 | |
| | Accounts Receivable | | | 12000 |
| | To record collection | | | |
| | of receivable. | | | |

### Quick Study 3-15

| Debit | Credit | |
|-------|--------|--|
| a. _____ | _____ | Accrual of unpaid and unrecorded advertising that was used by Stark Company. |
| b. _____ | _____ | Adjustment of Unearned Services Revenue to recognize earned revenue. |
| c. _____ | _____ | Recorded revenue for work completed this accounting period; the cash will be received in the next period. |
| d. _____ | _____ | The cost of Equipment was matched to the time periods benefited. |
| e. _____ | _____ | Adjustment of Prepaid Advertising to recognize the portion used. |

### Quick Study 3-16

|     | Dr./Cr. | Account Titles | Statement |
|-----|---------|----------------|-----------|
| (a) | Debit   |                |           |
|     | Credit  |                |           |
| (b) | Debit   |                |           |
|     | Credit  |                |           |
| (c) | Debit   |                |           |
|     | Credit  |                |           |
| (d) | Debit   |                |           |
|     | Credit  |                |           |
| (e) | Debit   |                |           |
|     | Credit  |                |           |

### Quick Study 3-17

| | If adjustment is not recorded: | | | |
|---|---|---|---|---|
| Type of Adjustment | Profit will be overstated, understated, or no effect | Assets will be overstated, understated, or no effect | Liabilities will be overstated, understated, or no effect | Equity will be overstated, understated, or no effect |
| a. Prepaid Expenses | | | | |
| b. Depreciation | | | | |
| c. Unearned Revenues | | | | |
| d. Accrued Expenses | | | | |
| e. Accrued Revenues | | | | |

Chapter 3

Name:_____

**Quick Study 3-18**

## GENERAL JOURNAL

Page____

| Date | Account Titles and Explanation | PR | Debit | Credit |
|------|-------------------------------|----|-------|--------|
|      |                               |    |       |        |
|      |                               |    |       |        |
|      |                               |    |       |        |
|      |                               |    |       |        |
|      |                               |    |       |        |
|      |                               |    |       |        |
|      |                               |    |       |        |
|      |                               |    |       |        |
|      |                               |    |       |        |
|      |                               |    |       |        |
|      |                               |    |       |        |

*Quick Study 3-19

## GENERAL JOURNAL

Page____

| Date | Account Titles and Explanation | PR | Debit | Credit |
|------|-------------------------------|----|-------|--------|
|      |                               |    |       |        |
|      |                               |    |       |        |
|      |                               |    |       |        |
|      |                               |    |       |        |
|      |                               |    |       |        |
|      |                               |    |       |        |
|      |                               |    |       |        |
|      |                               |    |       |        |
|      |                               |    |       |        |
|      |                               |    |       |        |
|      |                               |    |       |        |

Name:_____

*Quick Study 3-20

**GENERAL JOURNAL**                                    Page_____

| Date | Account Titles and Explanation | PR | Debit | Credit |
|---|---|---|---|---|
|  |  |  |  |  |
|  |  |  |  |  |
|  |  |  |  |  |
|  |  |  |  |  |
|  |  |  |  |  |
|  |  |  |  |  |
|  |  |  |  |  |
|  |  |  |  |  |
|  |  |  |  |  |
|  |  |  |  |  |

*Quick Study 3-21

**GENERAL JOURNAL**                                    Page_____

| Date | Account Titles and Explanation | PR | Debit | Credit |
|---|---|---|---|---|
| a. |  |  |  |  |
|  |  |  |  |  |
|  |  |  |  |  |
| b. |  |  |  |  |
|  |  |  |  |  |
|  |  |  |  |  |
| c. |  |  |  |  |
|  |  |  |  |  |
|  |  |  |  |  |
| d. |  |  |  |  |
|  |  |  |  |  |
|  |  |  |  |  |
|  |  |  |  |  |

Name:_____

**Exercise 3-1**

a. _____
_____
_____
_____
_____

b. _____
_____
_____
_____
_____

c. _____
_____
_____
_____
_____

**Exercise 3-2**

| | | | |
|---|---|---|---|
| 1. | | 7. | |
| 2. | | 8. | |
| 3. | | 9. | |
| 4. | | 10. | |
| 5. | | 11. | |
| 6. | | 12. | |

**Exercise 3-3**

**GENERAL JOURNAL**                                    Page_____

| Date | | Account Titles and Explanation | PR | Debit | Credit |
|---|---|---|---|---|---|
| a. | | | | | |
| | | | | | |
| | | | | | |
| | | | | | |
| | | | | | |
| | | | | | |
| | | | | | |
| | | | | | |
| | | | | | |

## Exercise 3-3 (concl'd.)

| Date | | Account Titles and Explanation | PR | Debit | Credit |
|---|---|---|---|---|---|
| **b.** | | | | | |
| | | | | | |
| | | | | | |
| | | | | | |
| | | | | | |
| | | | | | |
| | | | | | |
| | | | | | |
| | | | | | |
| **c.** | | | | | |
| | | | | | |
| | | | | | |
| | | | | | |
| | | | | | |
| | | | | | |
| | | | | | |
| | | | | | |

## Exercise 3-4

### Part 1: Calculations

a. _____
_____
_____
_____

b. _____
_____
_____
_____

c. _____
_____
_____
_____
_____
_____

Name:_____

Exercise 3-4 (concl'd.)

**Part 1: Adjusting entries**

GENERAL JOURNAL                                    Page_____

| Date | Account Titles and Explanation | PR | Debit | Credit |
|---|---|---|---|---|
| a. | | | | |
| | | | | |
| | | | | |
| | | | | |
| b. | | | | |
| | | | | |
| | | | | |
| | | | | |
| c. | | | | |
| | | | | |
| | | | | |
| | | | | |
| | | | | |

**2.** _____

_____

_____

_____

**3.** _____

_____

_____

_____

**Exercise 3-5**

## GENERAL JOURNAL

Page____

| Date | Account Titles and Explanation | PR | Debit | Credit |
|---|---|---|---|---|
| a. | | | | |
| | | | | |
| | | | | |
| | | | | |
| | | | | |
| | | | | |
| | | | | |
| b. | | | | |
| | | | | |
| | | | | |
| | | | | |
| | | | | |
| | | | | |
| | | | | |
| | | | | |
| c. | | | | |
| | | | | |
| | | | | |
| | | | | |
| | | | | |
| | | | | |
| | | | | |

Name:_____

**Exercise 3-6**

## GENERAL JOURNAL                                    Page____

| Date | Account Titles and Explanation | PR | Debit | Credit |
|------|-------------------------------|----|-------|--------|
| a. | | | | |
| | | | | |
| | | | | |
| | | | | |
| b. | | | | |
| | | | | |
| | | | | |
| | | | | |
| c. | | | | |
| | | | | |
| | | | | |
| | | | | |

**Exercise 3-7**

**1.**

## GENERAL JOURNAL                                    Page____

| Date | Account Titles and Explanation | PR | Debit | Credit |
|------|-------------------------------|----|-------|--------|
| a. | | | | |
| | | | | |
| | | | | |
| | | | | |
| b. | | | | |
| | | | | |
| | | | | |
| | | | | |
| c. | | | | |
| | | | | |
| | | | | |
| | | | | |

Name:_____

## Exercise 3-7 (concl'd.)

| Date | | Account Titles and Explanation | PR | Debit | Credit |
|---|---|---|---|---|---|
| d. | | | | | |
| | | | | | |
| | | | | | |
| | | | | | |
| | | | | | |

## Part 2

### GENERAL JOURNAL

Page_____

| Date | | Account Titles and Explanation | PR | Debit | Credit |
|---|---|---|---|---|---|
| a. | | | | | |
| | | | | | |
| | | | | | |
| | | | | | |
| b. | | | | | |
| | | | | | |
| | | | | | |
| | | | | | |
| c. | | | | | |
| | | | | | |
| | | | | | |
| | | | | | |
| d. | | | | | |
| | | | | | |
| | | | | | |
| | | | | | |
| e. | | | | | |
| | | | | | |
| | | | | | |
| | | | | | |
| f. | | | | | |
| | | | | | |
| | | | | | |
| | | | | | |

Name:_____

**Exercise 3-8**

## GENERAL JOURNAL

Page____

| Date | Account Titles and Explanation | PR | Debit | Credit |
|------|-------------------------------|-----|-------|--------|
| a.   |                               |     |       |        |
|      |                               |     |       |        |
|      |                               |     |       |        |
|      |                               |     |       |        |
| b.   |                               |     |       |        |
|      |                               |     |       |        |
|      |                               |     |       |        |
|      |                               |     |       |        |
| c.   |                               |     |       |        |
|      |                               |     |       |        |
|      |                               |     |       |        |
|      |                               |     |       |        |
| d.   |                               |     |       |        |
|      |                               |     |       |        |
|      |                               |     |       |        |
|      |                               |     |       |        |
| e.   |                               |     |       |        |
|      |                               |     |       |        |
|      |                               |     |       |        |
|      |                               |     |       |        |

**Exercise 3-8 (cont'd.)**

| Date | | Account Titles and Explanation | PR | Debit | Credit |
|---|---|---|---|---|---|
| f. | | | | | |
| | | | | | |
| | | | | | |
| | | | | | |
| g. | | | | | |
| | | | | | |
| | | | | | |
| | | | | | |

**Exercise 3-9**

**GENERAL JOURNAL**  Page____

| Date | | Account Titles and Explanation | PR | Debit | Credit |
|---|---|---|---|---|---|
| 1. | | | | | |
| | | | | | |
| | | | | | |
| | | | | | |
| 2. | | | | | |
| a. | | | | | |
| | | | | | |
| | | | | | |
| | | | | | |
| b. | | | | | |
| | | | | | |
| | | | | | |
| c. | | | | | |
| | | | | | |
| | | | | | |
| d. | | | | | |
| | | | | | |
| | | | | | |
| | | | | | |

Name:_____

**Exercise 3-10**

GENERAL JOURNAL

| Date | Account Titles and Explanation | PR | Debit | Credit |
|------|-------------------------------|----|-------|--------|
| a. | | | | |
| | | | | |
| | | | | |
| | | | | |
| b. | | | | |
| | | | | |
| | | | | |
| | | | | |
| c. | | | | |
| | | | | |
| | | | | |
| | | | | |
| d. | | | | |
| | | | | |
| | | | | |
| | | | | |
| e. | | | | |
| | | | | |
| | | | | |
| | | | | |
| f. | | | | |
| | | | | |
| | | | | |
| | | | | |

**Exercise 3-11**

GENERAL JOURNAL                                    Page____

| Date | Account Titles and Explanation | PR | Debit | Credit |
|------|-------------------------------|----|-------|--------|
| a. | | | | |
| | | | | |
| | | | | |
| | | | | |
| b. | | | | |
| | | | | |
| | | | | |
| | | | | |
| c. | | | | |
| | | | | |
| | | | | |
| | | | | |

**Exercise 3-12**
**GENERAL JOURNAL**                                    Page____

| Date | Account Titles and Explanation | PR | Debit | Credit |
|------|-------------------------------|----|-------|--------|
| a. | | | | |
| | | | | |
| | | | | |
| b. | | | | |
| | | | | |
| | | | | |
| c. | | | | |
| | | | | |
| | | | | |
| d. | | | | |
| | | | | |
| | | | | |
| e. | | | | |
| | | | | |
| | | | | |

Name:_____

**Exercise 3-13**

a. _____

_____

_____

_____

b. _____

_____

_____

_____

c. _____

_____

_____

_____

d. _____

_____

_____

_____

**Exercise 3-14**

**Adjusting Entry:**

**GENERAL JOURNAL**                                              Page____

| Date | Account Titles and Explanation | PR | Debit | Credit |
|------|-------------------------------|----|-------|--------|
|      |                               |    |       |        |
|      |                               |    |       |        |
|      |                               |    |       |        |
|      |                               |    |       |        |
|      |                               |    |       |        |

**Payday Entry:**

**GENERAL JOURNAL**                                              Page____

| Date | Account Titles and Explanation | PR | Debit | Credit |
|------|-------------------------------|----|-------|--------|
|      |                               |    |       |        |
|      |                               |    |       |        |
|      |                               |    |       |        |
|      |                               |    |       |        |
|      |                               |    |       |        |

*Fundamental Accounting Principles*, 15ce, Working Papers

Name:_____

**Exercise 3-15**

**(a)**

**Adjusting Entry:**

GENERAL JOURNAL

Page____

| Date | Account Titles and Explanation | PR | Debit | Credit |
|------|-------------------------------|----|-------|--------|
|      |                               |    |       |        |
|      |                               |    |       |        |
|      |                               |    |       |        |
|      |                               |    |       |        |
|      |                               |    |       |        |

**Journal Entry (Next Period):**

GENERAL JOURNAL

Page____

| Date | Account Titles and Explanation | PR | Debit | Credit |
|------|-------------------------------|----|-------|--------|
|      |                               |    |       |        |
|      |                               |    |       |        |
|      |                               |    |       |        |
|      |                               |    |       |        |
|      |                               |    |       |        |

**(b)**

**Adjusting Entry:**

**GENERAL JOURNAL**           Page____

| Date | Account Titles and Explanation | PR | Debit | Credit |
|------|-------------------------------|----|-------|--------|
|      |                               |    |       |        |
|      |                               |    |       |        |
|      |                               |    |       |        |
|      |                               |    |       |        |
|      |                               |    |       |        |

**Journal Entry (Next Period):**

GENERAL JOURNAL

Page____

| Date | Account Titles and Explanation | PR | Debit | Credit |
|------|-------------------------------|----|-------|--------|
|      |                               |    |       |        |
|      |                               |    |       |        |
|      |                               |    |       |        |
|      |                               |    |       |        |
|      |                               |    |       |        |

Name:_____

**Exercise 3-15 (concl'd.)**

**(c)**
**Adjusting Entry:**

GENERAL JOURNAL                                          Page_____

| Date | Account Titles and Explanation | PR | Debit | Credit |
|------|-------------------------------|----|-------|--------|
|      |                               |    |       |        |
|      |                               |    |       |        |
|      |                               |    |       |        |
|      |                               |    |       |        |
|      |                               |    |       |        |

**Journal Entry (Next Period):**

GENERAL JOURNAL                                          Page_____

| Date | Account Titles and Explanation | PR | Debit | Credit |
|------|-------------------------------|----|-------|--------|
|      |                               |    |       |        |
|      |                               |    |       |        |
|      |                               |    |       |        |
|      |                               |    |       |        |
|      |                               |    |       |        |

**Exercise 3-16**

GENERAL JOURNAL                                          Page_____

| Date | Account Titles and Explanation | PR | Debit | Credit |
|------|-------------------------------|----|-------|--------|
|      |                               |    |       |        |
|      |                               |    |       |        |
|      |                               |    |       |        |
|      |                               |    |       |        |
|      |                               |    |       |        |
|      |                               |    |       |        |
|      |                               |    |       |        |
|      |                               |    |       |        |
|      |                               |    |       |        |
|      |                               |    |       |        |
|      |                               |    |       |        |
|      |                               |    |       |        |
|      |                               |    |       |        |
|      |                               |    |       |        |
|      |                               |    |       |        |
|      |                               |    |       |        |

Name:_____

**Exercise 3-16 (concl'd.)**

### GENERAL JOURNAL

Page____

| Date | | Account Titles and Explanation | PR | Debit | Credit |
|---|---|---|---|---|---|
| | | | | | |
| | | | | | |
| | | | | | |
| | | | | | |
| | | | | | |
| | | | | | |
| | | | | | |
| | | | | | |
| | | | | | |
| | | | | | |
| | | | | | |
| | | | | | |
| | | | | | |
| | | | | | |
| | | | | | |
| | | | | | |
| | | | | | |
| | | | | | |
| | | | | | |
| | | | | | |
| | | | | | |
| | | | | | |

*Analysis component:*

_____
_____
_____
_____
_____
_____
_____

**Exercise 3-17**

| ACCOUNT | UNADJUSTED TRIAL BALANCE | | ADJUSTMENTS | | ADJUSTED TRIAL BALANCE | |
|---|---|---|---|---|---|---|
| | Debit | Credit | Debit | Credit | Debit | Credit |
| Cash | $ 14,000 | | | | | |
| Accounts receivable | 32,000 | | | | | |
| Prepaid insurance | 16,800 | | | | | |
| Equipment | 102,000 | | | | | |
| Accum. deprec., equipment | | $ 23,000 | | | | |
| Accounts payable | | 19,000 | | | | |
| Abraham Nuna, capital | | 213,000 | | | | |
| Abraham Nuna, withdrawals | 102,000 | | | | | |
| Revenues | | 214,000 | | | | |
| Deprec. exp., equipment | -0- | | | | | |
| Salaries expense | 187,700 | | | | | |
| Insurance expense | 14,500 | | | | | |
| Totals | $469,000 | $469,000 | | | | |
| | | | | | | |

**Exercise 3-18**

| Income Statement | | |
|---|---|---|
| | | |
| | | |
| | | |
| | | |
| | | |
| | | |
| | | |
| | | |

| Statement of Changes in Equity | | |
|---|---|---|
| | | |
| | | |
| | | |
| | | |
| | | |
| | | |
| | | |

**Exercise 3-18 (concl'd.)**

| Balance Sheet | | |
|---|---|---|
| | | |
| | | |
| | | |
| | | |
| | | |
| | | |
| | | |
| | | |
| | | |

*Analysis component:*

_____

_____

_____

_____

_____

**\*Exercise 3-19**

**GENERAL JOURNAL**                    Page_____

| Date | Account Titles and Explanation | PR | Debit | Credit |
|---|---|---|---|---|
| **a.** | | | | |
| | | | | |
| | | | | |
| | | | | |
| | | | | |
| | | | | |
| | | | | |
| **b.** | | | | |
| | | | | |
| | | | | |
| | | | | |
| | | | | |
| | | | | |
| | | | | |
| | | | | |

*Exercise 3-19 (concl'd.)

| | GENERAL JOURNAL | | | Page____ |
|---|---|---|---|---|

| Date | Account Titles and Explanation | PR | Debit | Credit |
|---|---|---|---|---|
| c. | | | | |
| | | | | |
| | | | | |
| | | | | |
| | | | | |
| | | | | |
| | | | | |
| | | | | |
| | | | | |
| d. | | | | |
| | | | | |
| | | | | |
| | | | | |
| | | | | |
| | | | | |
| | | | | |
| | | | | |
| | | | | |
| | | | | |

*Analysis component:*

_____

_____

_____

_____

_____

_____

_____

Name:_____

*Exercise 3-20

### GENERAL JOURNAL

Page____

| Date | Account Titles and Explanation | PR | Debit | Credit |
|---|---|---|---|---|
| a. | | | | |
| | | | | |
| | | | | |
| | | | | |
| | | | | |
| | | | | |
| | | | | |
| b. | | | | |
| | | | | |
| | | | | |
| | | | | |
| | | | | |
| | | | | |
| c. | | | | |
| | | | | |
| | | | | |
| | | | | |
| | | | | |
| | | | | |
| d. | | | | |
| | | | | |
| | | | | |
| | | | | |
| | | | | |
| | | | | |
| e. | | | | |
| | | | | |
| | | | | |
| | | | | |
| | | | | |
| | | | | |
| f. | | | | |
| | | | | |
| | | | | |
| | | | | |
| | | | | |
| | | | | |

Name:_____

*Exercise 3-21

a. Initial credit recorded in Unearned Revenue account:

GENERAL JOURNAL                     Page____

| Date | Account Titles and Explanation | PR | Debit | Credit |
|------|-------------------------------|----|-------|--------|
|      |                               |    |       |        |
|      |                               |    |       |        |
|      |                               |    |       |        |
|      |                               |    |       |        |
|      |                               |    |       |        |
|      |                               |    |       |        |
|      |                               |    |       |        |
|      |                               |    |       |        |
|      |                               |    |       |        |
|      |                               |    |       |        |
|      |                               |    |       |        |
|      |                               |    |       |        |
|      |                               |    |       |        |
|      |                               |    |       |        |
|      |                               |    |       |        |
|      |                               |    |       |        |
|      |                               |    |       |        |
|      |                               |    |       |        |
|      |                               |    |       |        |
|      |                               |    |       |        |
|      |                               |    |       |        |
|      |                               |    |       |        |
|      |                               |    |       |        |
|      |                               |    |       |        |
|      |                               |    |       |        |
|      |                               |    |       |        |
|      |                               |    |       |        |
|      |                               |    |       |        |
|      |                               |    |       |        |
|      |                               |    |       |        |
|      |                               |    |       |        |
|      |                               |    |       |        |
|      |                               |    |       |        |
|      |                               |    |       |        |
|      |                               |    |       |        |
|      |                               |    |       |        |
|      |                               |    |       |        |

Name:_____

**\*Exercise 3-21 (concl'd.)**

**b. Initial credit recorded in Revenue account:**

GENERAL JOURNAL

Page____

| Date | Account Titles and Explanation | PR | Debit | Credit |
|------|-------------------------------|----|-------|--------|
|      |                               |    |       |        |
|      |                               |    |       |        |
|      |                               |    |       |        |
|      |                               |    |       |        |
|      |                               |    |       |        |
|      |                               |    |       |        |
|      |                               |    |       |        |
|      |                               |    |       |        |
|      |                               |    |       |        |
|      |                               |    |       |        |
|      |                               |    |       |        |
|      |                               |    |       |        |
|      |                               |    |       |        |
|      |                               |    |       |        |
|      |                               |    |       |        |
|      |                               |    |       |        |
|      |                               |    |       |        |
|      |                               |    |       |        |
|      |                               |    |       |        |
|      |                               |    |       |        |
|      |                               |    |       |        |
|      |                               |    |       |        |
|      |                               |    |       |        |
|      |                               |    |       |        |
|      |                               |    |       |        |
|      |                               |    |       |        |

**c.**

_____
_____
_____
_____
_____
_____
_____
_____

Problem 3-1A

**GENERAL JOURNAL**                                    Page____

| Date | Account Titles and Explanation | PR | Debit | Credit |
|------|-------------------------------|----|----|----|
| 2017 31 | Insurance Expense | | 1200 | |
| a. Dec | Prepaid Insurance | | | 1200 |
| | To record expired Insurance | | | |
| | 7200 / 6 months = 1200 | | | |
| | | | | |
| b. | 31 Office Rent Expense | | 16200 | |
| | Prepaid office rent | | | 16200 |
| | 21000 - 4800 = 16200 | | | |
| | | | | |
| c. | 31 Subscription Expense | | 1100 | |
| | Prepaid Subscriptions | | | 1100 |
| | Used $1100 of prepaid subscriptions. | | | |
| | | | | |
| d. | 31 Equipment rent expense | | 900 | |
| | Prepaid equipment Rental | | | 900 |
| | To record rent expense | | | |
| | 32400 / 3yrs = 10800 / 12 = 900 | | | |

*Analysis component:* _____
_____
_____
_____

Problem 3-2A

**GENERAL JOURNAL**                                    Page____

| Date | Account Titles and Explanation | PR | Debit | Credit |
|------|-------------------------------|----|----|----|
| 2017 31 | Depr Exp, Machine A | | 20400 | |
| a. Dec | Accumulated Dep, Machine A | | | 20400 |
| | To record dep on machine A. | | | |
| | 102000 - 0 = $20400 | | | |
| | 5 yrs | | | |
| | | | | |
| b. | 31 Dep Exp, Machine B | | 10800 | |
| | Accumulated dep, Machine B | | | 10800 |
| | 61000 - 3400 = 57600 / 4 yrs = 14400 | | | |
| | 14400 × 9/12 = 10800 | | | |
| | | | | |
| c. | 31 Depr Expense, Machine C | | 2300 | |
| | Accumulated dep, Machine C | | | 2300 |
| | 30500 - 2900 = 27600 / 2 yrs = | | | |
| | 13800 × 2/12 = 2300 | | | |

**Problem 3-2A (concl'd.)**

*Analysis component:*

_____
_____
_____
_____
_____
_____
_____
_____
_____

**Problem 3-3A**

**GENERAL JOURNAL**                                    Page_____

| Date | Account Titles and Explanation | PR | Debit | Credit |
|------|-------------------------------|-----|-------|--------|
| 2017 30 | Unearned lawn services |  | 16000 |  |
| a. Nov |    lawn services earned |  |  | 16000 |
|  | To record lawn services |  |  |  |
|  |   earned. |  |  |  |
|  | 102000 − 86000 = 16000 earned. |  |  |  |
| b. | 30 Unearned Garden services |  | 31950 |  |
|  |    Garden Services earned. |  |  | 31950 |
|  | Garden services earned |  |  |  |
| c. | 30 Unearned snow removal services |  | 2600 |  |
|  |    Snow Removal services earned |  |  | 2600 |
|  | To record lawn services earned |  |  |  |
|  | 11800 − 9200 = 2600 earned |  |  |  |
| d. | 30 No entry required on |  |  |  |
|  | November 30, 2017. |  |  |  |

*Analysis component:*

_____
_____
_____
_____
_____
_____
_____

**Adjusting Entries:**           **GENERAL JOURNAL**                    Page____

| Date | | Account Titles and Explanation | PR | Debit | Credit |
|---|---|---|---|---|---|
| **a.** Mar 31 | | Interest expense | | 1050 | |
| | | Interest payable | | | 1050 |
| | | To record accrued | | | |
| | | interest. | | | |
| | | | | | |
| **b.** Mar 31 | | Salaries Expense | | 32850 | |
| | | Salaries payable | | | 32850 |
| | | To record accrued | | | |
| | | salaries expense. | | | |
| **c.** Mar 31 | | Telephone expense | | 440 | |
| | | Accounts payable | | | 440 |
| | | To record telephone | | | |
| | | bill. | | | |
| **d.** Mar 31 | | Rent Expense | | 4200 | |
| | | Rent payable | | | 4200 |
| | | To record accrued | | | |
| | | rent for March. | | | |
| | | | | | |
| **e.** Mar 31 | | Commission Expense | | 16400 | |
| | | Commission payable | | | 16400 |
| | | To record accrued commissions. | | | |
| | | 410000 X 4% = 16400 | | | |

Name:_____

**Problem 3-4A (concl'd.)**

Subsequent Entries:          **GENERAL JOURNAL**                    Page____

| Date | | | Account Titles and Explanation | PR | Debit | Credit |
|---|---|---|---|---|---|---|
| a. Apr | 2 | | Interest payable | | 1050 | |
| | | | Cash | | | 1050 |
| | | | To record payment of | | | |
| | | | accrued interest. | | | |
| | | | | | | |
| b. Apr | 3 | | Salaries payable | | 32850 | |
| | | | Salaries expense | | 21900 | |
| | | | Cash | | | 54750 |
| | | | To record payment of salaries. | | | |
| | | | | | | |
| c. Apr | 15 | | Accounts payable | | 440 | |
| | | | Cash | | | 440 |
| | | | To record payment of | | | |
| | | | telephone bill. | | | |
| | | | | | | |
| d. Apr | 26 | | Rent payable | | 8400 | |
| | | | Rent expense | | 4200 | |
| | | | Prepaid Rent | | 12600 | |
| | | | Cash | | | 25200 |
| | | | To record pay of rent for 6 month. | | | |
| | | | | | | |
| e. Apr | 15 | | Commissions payable | | 16400 | |
| | | | Cash | | | 16400 |
| | | | To record payment | | | |
| | | | of accrued commissions | | | |

**Problem 3-5A**

**Adjusting Entries:**                **GENERAL JOURNAL**                Page____

| Date | Account Titles and Explanation | PR | Debit | Credit |
|---|---|---|---|---|
| **a.** Mar 31 | Rent Receivable | | 4150 | |
| |     Rent Revenue | | | 4150 |
| | To record accrued revenue. | | | |
| **b.** Mar 31 | Accounts Receivable | | 8400 | |
| |     Service Revenue | | | 8400 |
| | To record accrued revenue. | | | |
| **c.** Mar 31 | Interest Receivable | | 640 | |
| |     Interest Income | | | 640 |
| | To record accrued revenue. | | | |
| **d.** Mar 31 | Accounts Receivable | | 11500 | |
| |     Service Revenue | | | 11500 |
| | To record accrued Ser Rev. for feb & mar. | | | |
| | $34500/6 = 5750 \times 2 = 11500$ | | | |

**Subsequent Entries:**              **GENERAL JOURNAL**                Page____

| Date | Account Titles and Explanation | PR | Debit | Credit |
|---|---|---|---|---|
| Apr 3 | Cash | | 4150 | |
| **a.** |     Rent Receivable | | | 4150 |
| | To record collection | | | |
| | of accrued revenue. | | | |
| **b.** Apr 7 | Cash | | 8400 | |
| |     Accounts Receivable | | | 8400 |
| | To record collection of accrued rev. | | | |
| **c.** Apr 1 | Cash | | 640 | |
| |     Interest Receivable | | | 640 |
| | To record collection of accrued Rev. | | | |
| **d.** Apr 2 | Cash | | 11500 | |
| |     Accounts Receivable | | | 11500 |
| | To record collection | | | |
| | of accrued revenue. | | | |

Name:_____

**Problem 3-6A**

### GENERAL JOURNAL

Page_____

| Date | | Account Titles and Explanation | PR | Debit | Credit |
|---|---|---|---|---|---|
| a. | | | | | |
| | | | | | |
| | | | | | |
| b. | | | | | |
| | | | | | |
| | | | | | |
| c. | | | | | |
| | | | | | |
| | | | | | |
| d. | | | | | |
| | | | | | |
| | | | | | |
| e. | | | | | |
| | | | | | |
| | | | | | |
| f. | | | | | |
| | | | | | |
| | | | | | |
| g. | | | | | |
| | | | | | |
| | | | | | |
| h. | | | | | |
| | | | | | |
| | | | | | |

**Part 2:** *See next page for Part 2 working paper.*

**Part 3:** _____

_____

_____

**Part 4:** _____

_____

_____

_____

## Problem 3-6A (concl'd.)

### Part 2

| ACCOUNT | UNADJUSTED TRIAL BALANCE | | ADJUSTMENTS | | ADJUSTED TRIAL BALANCE | |
|---|---|---|---|---|---|---|
| | Debit | Credit | Debit | Credit | Debit | Credit |
| Cash | $ 18,000 | | | | | |
| Accounts receivable | -0- | | | | | |
| Teaching supplies | 6,500 | | | | | |
| Prepaid insurance | 1,400 | | | | | |
| Prepaid rent | 7,200 | | | | | |
| Professional library | 60,000 | | | | | |
| Accum. deprec., library | | 18,000 | | | | |
| Equipment | 96,000 | | | | | |
| Accum. deprec., equipment | | 32,000 | | | | |
| Accounts payable | | 2,500 | | | | |
| Salaries payable | | -0- | | | | |
| Unearned extension revenue | | 6,300 | | | | |
| Karoo Ashevak, capital | | 229,000 | | | | |
| Karoo Ashevak, withdrwls | 92,000 | | | | | |
| Tuition revenue | | 196,000 | | | | |
| Extension revenue | | 72,500 | | | | |
| Deprec. exp., equipment | -0- | | | | | |
| Deprec. exp., library | -0- | | | | | |
| Salaries expense | 206,000 | | | | | |
| Insurance expense | -0- | | | | | |
| Rent expense | 44,000 | | | | | |
| Teaching supplies expense | -0- | | | | | |
| Advertising expense | 14,000 | | | | | |
| Utilities expense | 11,200 | | | | | |
| Totals | $556,300 | $556,300 | | | | |

### Problem 3-7A

#### GENERAL JOURNAL                                                                Page____

| Date | Account Titles and Explanation | PR | Debit | Credit |
|---|---|---|---|---|
| 2017 a. Jan 31 | Dep Exp, Equipment | | 600 | |
| |    Accumulated Dep, Equipment | | | 600 |
| | To record depreciation, | | | |
| | 21600/3 yrs = 7200 x 1/12 = 600 | | | |
| | | | | |
| b. 31 | Unearned Consulting Revenue | | 8700 | |
| |    Consulting Revenue | | | 8700 |
| | To record revenue. | | | |
| | | | | |

**Problem 3-7A (concl'd.)**

## GENERAL JOURNAL　　　　　　　　　Page____

| Date | Account Titles and Explanation | PR | Debit | Credit |
|---|---|---|---|---|
| c. | 31 Rent Expense | | 2250 | |
| | Prepaid Rent | | | 2250 |
| | To record expired rent, | | | |
| | 13500 = 2250 | | | |
| | 6 | | | |
| | | | | |
| d. | 31 Wages Expense | | 18500 | |
| | Wages payable | | | 18500 |
| | To record accrued | | | |
| | wages. | | | |
| e. | 31 Interest Expense | | 140 | |
| | Interest payable | | | 140 |
| | To record accrued interest | | | |
| | 42000 × 4% = 1680 × 1/12 = 140 | | | |
| f. | 31 Accounts Receivable | | 6150 | |
| | Consulting Revenue | | | 6150 |
| | To record accrued | | | |
| | revenue. | | | |
| g. | 31 Insurance Expense | | 195 | |
| | Prepaid Insurance | | | 195 |
| | To record expired Insurance | | | |
| | 3510/18 months = 195/month | | | |
| h. | 31 Dep Exp, office furniture | | 625 | |
| | Accumulated Dep, office furnit | | | 625 |
| | To record depreciation | | | |
| | of office furniture | | | |
| i. | 31 Accounts Receivable | | 3400 | |
| | Repair Revenue earned | | | 3400 |
| | To record accrued | | | |
| | repair revenues. | | | |
| j. | 31 Store supplies Expense | | 1930 | |
| | Store supplies | | | 1930 |
| | To record store | | | |
| | supplies used, | | | |
| | 800 + 1780 − 650 = 1930 | | | |

**Problem 3-8A**
**Part 1**                    **GENERAL JOURNAL**                    Page____

| Date | Account Titles and Explanation | PR | Debit | Credit |
|---|---|---|---|---|
| a. 2017 30 Nov | Office supplies expense | | 23300 | |
| | office supplies | | | 23300 |
| | To record the cost of | | | |
| | supplies used during | | | |
| | the year. | | | |
| | $4800 + $24800 - $6300 | | | |
| | | | | |
| b. | 30 Insurance Expense | | 10035 | |
| | Prepaid Insurance | | | 10035 |
| | Policy CPM No of month 2017 Cost | | | |
| | 1    240    12    2880 | | | |
| | 2    620    9     5580 | | | |
| | 3    315    5     1575 | | | |
| | Total              $10,035 | | | |
| c. | 30 Salaries Expense | | 24000 | |
| | Salaries payable | | | 24000 |
| | To record accrued | | | |
| | but unpaid wages. | | | |
| | 4800 x 5 days | | | |
| | | | | |
| | | | | |
| d. | 30 Dep Expense, Building | | 3903 | |
| | Accumulated Dep, Building | | | 3903 |
| | Annual dep = 306000 - 25000/30 | | | |
| | = 9367. dep for five months | | | |
| | $9367 x 5/12 = 3903 | | | |
| | To record dep expense. | | | |
| | | | | |
| e. | 30 Rent Receivable | | 3100 | |
| | Rent Revenue | | | 3100 |
| | To record earned | | | |
| | but unpaid rent. | | | |
| | | | | |
| | | | | |
| f. | 30 Unearned Rent | | 7300 | |
| | Rent Revenue | | | 7300 |
| | To record the amt of | | | |
| | rent revenue: 3650 x 2 | | | |

## Problem 3-8A (concl'd.)

Part 2                          **GENERAL JOURNAL**                          Page____

| Date | Account Titles and Explanation | PR | Debit | Credit |
|---|---|---|---|---|
| C2017 Dec | 1 Salaries Payable | | 24000 | |
| |     Cash | | | 24000 |
| | To record payment of accrued salaries. | | | |
| e | 15 Cash | | 6200 | |
| |     Rent Receivable | | | 3100 |
| |     Rent Revenue. | | | 3100 |
| | To record past due rent for two Months. | | | |

## Problem 3-9A

**GENERAL JOURNAL**                          Page____

| Date | Account Titles and Explanation | PR | Debit | Credit |
|---|---|---|---|---|
| 2017 a. Oct | 31 Unearned Consulting Rev | | 14000 | |
| |     Consulting Revenue | | | 14000 |
| | To record unearned consulting revenue, 26000 - 12000 = 14000 earned. | | | |
| b. | 31 Consulting Revenue | | 14000 | |
| |     Unearned Consulting Rev | | | 14000 |
| | To record as unearned on amt incorrectly recorded as earned. | | | |
| c. | 31 Rent Expense | | 18000 | |
| |     Prepaid Rent | | | 18000 |
| | To record expired rent. 27000/3 = 9000/Month × 2 Month = 18000 used | | | |
| d. | 31 Wages Expense | | 6800 | |
| |     Wages payable | | | 6800 |
| | To record accrued wages. | | | |

Name:_____

**Problem 3-9A (concl'd.)**

GENERAL JOURNAL                                    Page____

| Date | | Account Titles and Explanation | PR | Debit | Credit |
|------|---|-------------------------------|----|-------|--------|
| e. | 31 | Dep Exp, office furniture | | 42000 | |
| | | Accumulated Dep, office fur | | | 42000 |
| | | To record dep Exp. | | | |
| | | 84000/2 yrs = 42000/year. | | | |
| f. | 31 | Accounts Receivable | | 4200 | |
| | | Consulting Revenue. | | | 4200 |
| | | To record accrued Rev. | | | |
| g. | 31 | Interest receivable | | 85 | |
| | | Interest Income | | | 85 |
| | | To record accrued | | | |
| | | Interest Income. | | | |
| h. | 31 | Insurance Expense | | 2400 | |
| | | Prepaid Insurance | | | 2400 |
| | | To record expired prepaid insl. | | | |
| | | 3400 ÷ 17 month = 200/month X 12 months = 2400 | | | |
| i. | 31 | Supplies Expense | | 4680 | |
| | | Supplies | | | 4680 |
| | | To record the use of supplies. | | | |
| | | 5300 - 620 = 4680 used. | | | |

Name:_____

**Problem 3-10A**

**Parts 1 and 2 (in balance column account format)**

**Note: The T-account template is provided at the end of this question.**

### GENERAL LEDGER

**Cash**                 **ACCOUNT NO. 101**

| DATE | EXPLANATION | PR | DEBIT | CREDIT | BALANCE |
|------|-------------|----|-------|--------|---------|
| 2017 | | | | | |
| Oct. 31 | Balance | | | | 26,000 |

**Accounts Receivable**       **ACCOUNT NO. 106**

| DATE | EXPLANATION | PR | DEBIT | CREDIT | BALANCE |
|------|-------------|----|-------|--------|---------|
| 2017 | | | | | |
| Oct. 31 | Balance | | | | 61,000 |
| | | | | | |

**Interest Receivable**       **ACCOUNT NO. 109**

| DATE | EXPLANATION | PR | DEBIT | CREDIT | BALANCE |
|------|-------------|----|-------|--------|---------|
| 2017 | | | | | |
| | | | | | |

**Notes Receivable**       **ACCOUNT NO. 111**

| DATE | EXPLANATION | PR | DEBIT | CREDIT | BALANCE |
|------|-------------|----|-------|--------|---------|
| 2017 | | | | | |
| Oct. 31 | Balance | | | | 50,000 |

**Supplies**       **ACCOUNT NO. 126**

| DATE | EXPLANATION | PR | DEBIT | CREDIT | BALANCE |
|------|-------------|----|-------|--------|---------|
| 2017 | | | | | |
| Oct. 31 | Balance | | | | 5,300 |
| | | | | | |

**Prepaid Insurance**       **ACCOUNT NO. 128**

| DATE | EXPLANATION | PR | DEBIT | CREDIT | BALANCE |
|------|-------------|----|-------|--------|---------|
| 2017 | | | | | |
| Oct. 31 | Balance | | | | 3,400 |
| | | | | | |

# Chapter 3

Name:_____

## Problem 3-10A (cont'd.)

### Prepaid Rent            ACCOUNT NO. 131

| DATE | EXPLANATION | PR | DEBIT | CREDIT | BALANCE |
|------|-------------|----|-------|--------|---------|
| 2017 | | | | | |
| Oct. 31 | Balance | | | | 27,000 |
| | | | | | |

### Office Furniture          ACCOUNT NO. 161

| DATE | EXPLANATION | PR | DEBIT | CREDIT | BALANCE |
|------|-------------|----|-------|--------|---------|
| 2017 | | | | | |
| Oct. 31 | Balance | | | | 84,000 |

### Accumulated Depreciation, Office Furniture     ACCOUNT NO. 162

| DATE | EXPLANATION | PR | DEBIT | CREDIT | BALANCE |
|------|-------------|----|-------|--------|---------|
| 2017 | | | | | |
| Oct. 31 | Balance | | | | 28,000 |
| | | | | | |

### Accounts Payable         ACCOUNT NO. 201

| DATE | EXPLANATION | PR | DEBIT | CREDIT | BALANCE |
|------|-------------|----|-------|--------|---------|
| 2017 | | | | | |
| Oct. 31 | Balance | | | | 18,000 |

### Wages Payable          ACCOUNT NO. 210

| DATE | EXPLANATION | PR | DEBIT | CREDIT | BALANCE |
|------|-------------|----|-------|--------|---------|
| 2017 | | | | | |
| | | | | | |

### Unearned Consulting Revenue      ACCOUNT NO. 233

| DATE | EXPLANATION | PR | DEBIT | CREDIT | BALANCE |
|------|-------------|----|-------|--------|---------|
| 2017 | | | | | |
| Oct. 31 | Balance | | | | 26,000 |
| | | | | | |
| | | | | | |

### Jeff Moore, Capital         ACCOUNT NO. 301

| DATE | EXPLANATION | PR | DEBIT | CREDIT | BALANCE |
|------|-------------|----|-------|--------|---------|
| 2017 | | | | | |
| Oct. 31 | Balance | | | | 223,000 |

## Problem 3-10A (cont'd.)

### Jeff Moore, Withdrawals — ACCOUNT NO. 302

| DATE | EXPLANATION | PR | DEBIT | CREDIT | BALANCE |
|------|-------------|----|-------|--------|---------|
| 2017 | | | | | |
| Oct. 31 | Balance | | | | 28,000 |

### Consulting Revenue — ACCOUNT NO. 401

| DATE | EXPLANATION | PR | DEBIT | CREDIT | BALANCE |
|------|-------------|----|-------|--------|---------|
| 2017 | | | | | |
| Oct. 31 | Balance | | | | 232,020 |
| | | | | | |
| | | | | | |
| | | | | | |

### Interest Income — ACCOUNT NO. 409

| DATE | EXPLANATION | PR | DEBIT | CREDIT | BALANCE |
|------|-------------|----|-------|--------|---------|
| 2017 | | | | | |
| Oct. 31 | Balance | | | | 480 |
| | | | | | |

### Depreciation Expense, Office Furniture — ACCOUNT NO. 601

| DATE | EXPLANATION | PR | DEBIT | CREDIT | BALANCE |
|------|-------------|----|-------|--------|---------|
| 2017 | | | | | |
| | | | | | |

### Wages Expense — ACCOUNT NO. 622

| DATE | EXPLANATION | PR | DEBIT | CREDIT | BALANCE |
|------|-------------|----|-------|--------|---------|
| 2017 | | | | | |
| Oct. 31 | Balance | | | | 192,000 |
| | | | | | |

### Insurance Expense — ACCOUNT NO. 637

| DATE | EXPLANATION | PR | DEBIT | CREDIT | BALANCE |
|------|-------------|----|-------|--------|---------|
| 2017 | | | | | |
| | | | | | |

## Problem 3-10A (cont'd.)

**Rent Expense**                                         ACCOUNT NO. 640

| DATE | EXPLANATION | PR | DEBIT | CREDIT | BALANCE |
|------|-------------|----|-------|--------|---------|
| 2017 | | | | | |
| Oct. 31 | Balance | | | | 44,000 |
| | | | | | |

**Supplies Expense**                                     ACCOUNT NO. 650

| DATE | EXPLANATION | PR | DEBIT | CREDIT | BALANCE |
|------|-------------|----|-------|--------|---------|
| 2017 | | | | | |
| Oct. 31 | Balance | | | | 6,800 |
| | | | | | |

Name:_____

**Problem 3-10A (cont'd.)  Part 3**

## Adjusted Trial Balance

| | | | |
|---|---|---|---|
| | | | |
| | | | |
| | | | |
| | | | |
| | | | |
| | | | |
| | | | |
| | | | |
| | | | |
| | | | |
| | | | |
| | | | |
| | | | |
| | | | |
| | | | |
| | | | |
| | | | |
| | | | |
| | | | |
| | | | |
| | | | |
| | | | |

**Part 4**

## Income Statement

| | | | |
|---|---|---|---|
| | | | |
| | | | |
| | | | |
| | | | |
| | | | |
| | | | |
| | | | |
| | | | |
| | | | |
| | | | |
| | | | |

Name:_____

**Problem 3-10A (cont'd.)**

## Statement of Changes in Equity

| | | |
|---|---|---|
| | | |
| | | |
| | | |
| | | |
| | | |
| | | |
| | | |

## Balance Sheet

| | | |
|---|---|---|
| | | |
| | | |
| | | |
| | | |
| | | |
| | | |
| | | |
| | | |
| | | |
| | | |
| | | |
| | | |
| | | |
| | | |
| | | |
| | | |
| | | |
| | | |
| | | |
| | | |

*Analysis component:*

Problem 3-10A (cont'd.)

Part 1 and 2 (in T-account format)

| Cash | 101 | | Accounts Receivable | 106 | | Interest Receivable | 109 |
|------|-----|--|---------------------|-----|--|--------------------|-----|
| Unadj Bal | | | Unadj Bal | | | | |
| Oct 31  26,000 | | | Oct 31  61,000 | | | | |

| Notes Receivable | 111 | | Supplies | 126 | | Prepaid Insurance | 128 |
|------------------|-----|--|----------|-----|--|-------------------|-----|
| Unadj Bal | | | Unadj Bal | | | Unadj Bal | |
| Oct 31  50,000 | | | Oct 31  5,300 | | | Oct 31  3,400 | |

| Prepaid Rent | 131 | | Office Furniture | 161 | | Accum. Deprec., Office Furniture | 162 |
|--------------|-----|--|------------------|-----|--|----------------------------------|-----|
| Unadj Bal | | | Unadj Bal | | | | Unadj Bal |
| Oct 31  27,000 | | | Oct 31  84,000 | | | | 28,000  Oct 31 |

| Accounts Payable | 201 | | Wages Payable | 210 | | Unearned Consulting Revenue | 233 |
|------------------|-----|--|---------------|-----|--|-----------------------------|-----|
| | Unadj Bal | | | | | | Unadj Bal |
| | 18,000  Oct 31 | | | | | | 26,000  Oct 31 |

Problem 3-10A (concl'd.)

**Jeff Moore, Capital**   301

|  |  |
|---|---|
|  | Unadj Bal   Oct 31   223,000 |

**Jeff Moore, Withdrawals**   302

|  |  |
|---|---|
| Unadj Bal   Oct 31   28,000 |  |

**Consulting Revenue**   401

|  |  |
|---|---|
|  | Unadj Bal   Oct 31   232,020 |

**Interest Income**   409

|  |  |
|---|---|
|  | Unadj Bal   Oct 31   480 |

**Deprec. Expense, Office Furniture**   601

**Wages Expense**   622

|  |  |
|---|---|
| Unadj Bal   Oct 31   192,000 |  |

**Insurance Expense**   637

**Rent Expense**   640

|  |  |
|---|---|
| Unadj Bal   Oct 31   44,000 |  |

**Supplies Expense**   650

|  |  |
|---|---|
| Unadj Bal   Oct 31   6,800 |  |

**Problem 3-11A**

### GENERAL JOURNAL

| Date | Account Titles and Explanation | PR | Debit | Credit |
|------|-------------------------------|----|-------|--------|
| a.   |                               |    |       |        |
|      |                               |    |       |        |
|      |                               |    |       |        |
|      |                               |    |       |        |
| b.   |                               |    |       |        |
|      |                               |    |       |        |
|      |                               |    |       |        |
|      |                               |    |       |        |
| c.   |                               |    |       |        |
|      |                               |    |       |        |
|      |                               |    |       |        |
|      |                               |    |       |        |
| d.   |                               |    |       |        |
|      |                               |    |       |        |
|      |                               |    |       |        |
|      |                               |    |       |        |
| e.   |                               |    |       |        |
|      |                               |    |       |        |
|      |                               |    |       |        |
|      |                               |    |       |        |
| f.   |                               |    |       |        |
|      |                               |    |       |        |
|      |                               |    |       |        |
|      |                               |    |       |        |
| g.   |                               |    |       |        |
|      |                               |    |       |        |
|      |                               |    |       |        |
|      |                               |    |       |        |
|      |                               |    |       |        |

**Problem 3-12A    Part 1**

| ACCOUNT | UNADJUSTED TRIAL BALANCE | | ADJUSTMENTS | | ADJUSTED TRIAL BALANCE | |
|---|---|---|---|---|---|---|
| | Debit | Credit | Debit | Credit | Debit | Credit |
| Cash | $ 6,000 | | | | | |
| Accounts receivable | 11,200 | | | | | |
| Repair supplies | 2,200 | | | | | |
| Prepaid rent | 14,000 | | | | | |
| Office furniture | 26,000 | | | | | |
| Accounts payable | | $ 8,000 | | | | |
| Notes payable | | 21,600 | | | | |
| Eli Arrow, capital | | 67,758 | | | | |
| Eli Arrow, withdrawals | 5,000 | | | | | |
| Hospitality revenues | | 128,000 | | | | |
| Salaries expense | 144,000 | | | | | |
| Wages expense | 16,958 | | | | | |
| Totals | $225,358 | $225,358 | | | | |
| | | | | | | |
| | | | | | | |
| | | | | | | |
| | | | | | | |
| | | | | | | |
| | | | | | | |
| | | | | | | |
| | | | | | | |
| | | | | | | |

**Part 2**

## Income Statement

| | | |
|---|---|---|
| | | |
| | | |
| | | |
| | | |
| | | |
| | | |
| | | |
| | | |
| | | |
| | | |
| | | |

**Problem 3-12A (concl'd.)**

### Statement of Changes in Equity

| | | |
|---|---|---|
| | | |
| | | |
| | | |
| | | |
| | | |
| | | |
| | | |
| | | |

### Balance Sheet

| | | |
|---|---|---|
| | | |
| | | |
| | | |
| | | |
| | | |
| | | |
| | | |
| | | |
| | | |
| | | |
| | | |
| | | |
| | | |
| | | |
| | | |
| | | |
| | | |
| | | |
| | | |

*Analysis component:*

_____
_____
_____
_____
_____
_____
_____
_____
_____

**Problem 3-13A**

**Part a.**

GALAVU ENTERTAINMENT

**Income Statement**

For year ended December 31, 2017

| | $ | $ |
|---|---|---|
| Revenues: | | |
| Revenue | 240000 | |
| Interest income | 150 | |
| Total revenues | | 240150 |
| Operating expenses: | | |
| Salaries expense | 76225 | |
| Wages expense | 27800 | |
| Dep. expense, automobiles | 13200 | |
| Office supplies expense | 13000 | |
| Advertising expense | 9000 | |
| Repairs expense, automobiles | 8400 | |
| Dep exp, equipment | 4100 | |
| Interest expense | 3500 | |
| Total operating expenses | | 155225 |
| Profit | | $84925 |
| | | |
| | | |

**Part b.**

GALAVU ENTERTAINMENT

**Statement of Changes in Equity**

For year Ended December 31, 2017

| | | |
|---|---|---|
| John Conroe, capital January 1 | | $8000 |
| Add: Investment by owner | 15000 | |
| Profit | 84925 | 99925 |
| Total | | $107925 |
| Less: withdrawal by owner | | 19000 |
| John Conroe capital, December 31 | | $88925 |

**Problem 3-13A (concl'd.)**

Part c.

# GALAVU ENTERTAINMENT
**Balance Sheet**

## December 31, 2017

| Assets | $ | $ |
|---|---|---|
| Cash | | 11000 |
| Accounts Receivable | | 18700 |
| Interest Receivable | | 300 |
| Notes Receivable (due in 90 days) | | 80000 |
| Office supplies | | 4000 |
| Automobiles | 140000 | |
| Less: Accumulated depreciation | 69000 | 71000 |
| Equipment | 65000 | |
| Less: Accumulated depreciation | 20500 | 44500 |
| Land | | 35000 |
| Total Assets | | $264500 |
| | | |
| Liabilities | | |
| Accounts payable | | 44000 |
| Interest payable | | 75 |
| Salaries payable | | 5500 |
| Unearned Revenue | | 11000 |
| Long term notes payable | | 115000 |
| Total liabilities | | $175,575 |
| | | |
| Equity | | |
| John Conroe, capital | | 88925 |
| Total liabilities and equity | | $264500 |

**Analysis component:**

_____
_____
_____
_____
_____
_____
_____
_____
_____
_____

Name:_____

**Problem 3-14A     Part 1**

## GENERAL JOURNAL

Page____

| Date | Account Titles and Explanation | PR | Debit | Credit |
|---|---|---|---|---|
|  |  |  |  |  |
|  |  |  |  |  |
|  |  |  |  |  |
|  |  |  |  |  |
|  |  |  |  |  |
|  |  |  |  |  |
|  |  |  |  |  |
|  |  |  |  |  |
|  |  |  |  |  |
|  |  |  |  |  |
|  |  |  |  |  |
|  |  |  |  |  |
|  |  |  |  |  |
|  |  |  |  |  |
|  |  |  |  |  |
|  |  |  |  |  |
|  |  |  |  |  |
|  |  |  |  |  |
|  |  |  |  |  |
|  |  |  |  |  |
|  |  |  |  |  |
|  |  |  |  |  |
|  |  |  |  |  |
|  |  |  |  |  |
|  |  |  |  |  |
|  |  |  |  |  |
|  |  |  |  |  |
|  |  |  |  |  |
|  |  |  |  |  |
|  |  |  |  |  |
|  |  |  |  |  |
|  |  |  |  |  |
|  |  |  |  |  |
|  |  |  |  |  |
|  |  |  |  |  |
|  |  |  |  |  |
|  |  |  |  |  |
|  |  |  |  |  |
|  |  |  |  |  |
|  |  |  |  |  |
|  |  |  |  |  |

Name:_____

## Problem 3-14A (cont'd.)

### Parts 2, 3 and 5

| Cash | 101 | | Prepaid Rent | 131 |
|---|---|---|---|---|

| Office Furniture | 161 | | Accum. Deprec., Office Furn. | 162 |
|---|---|---|---|---|

| Accounts Payable | 201 | | Unearned Revenue | 233 |
|---|---|---|---|---|

| Delanie Tugut, Capital | 301 | | Delanie Tugut, Withdrawals | 302 |
|---|---|---|---|---|

| Revenue 401 | | | Deprec. Exp., Office Furniture | 602 |
|---|---|---|---|---|

| Wages Expense | 623 | | Rent Expense | 640 |
|---|---|---|---|---|

| Telephone Expense | 688 | | Hotel Expenses | 696 |
|---|---|---|---|---|

**Problem 3-14A (cont'd.)**

**Part 4**

| Trial Balance | | |
|---|---|---|
| | Debit | Credit |
| | | |
| | | |
| | | |
| | | |
| | | |
| | | |
| | | |
| | | |
| | | |
| | | |
| | | |
| | | |
| | | |

**Part 5 – Adjusting entries**

GENERAL JOURNAL

Page_____

| Date | | Account Titles and Explanation | PR | Debit | Credit |
|---|---|---|---|---|---|
| | | | | | |
| | | | | | |
| | | | | | |
| | | | | | |
| | | | | | |
| | | | | | |
| | | | | | |
| | | | | | |
| | | | | | |
| | | | | | |
| | | | | | |
| | | | | | |
| | | | | | |
| | | | | | |
| | | | | | |
| | | | | | |
| | | | | | |
| | | | | | |
| | | | | | |
| | | | | | |

**Problem 3-14A (cont'd.)**

**Part 6**

| | Debit | Credit |
|---|---|---|
| **Trial Balance** | | |
| | | |
| | | |
| | | |
| | | |
| | | |
| | | |
| | | |
| | | |
| | | |
| | | |
| | | |
| | | |
| | | |
| | | |
| | | |
| | | |
| | | |
| | | |
| | | |
| | | |

**Part 7**

| | | |
|---|---|---|
| **Income Statement** | | |
| | | |
| | | |
| | | |
| | | |
| | | |
| | | |
| | | |
| | | |
| | | |
| | | |
| | | |
| | | |
| | | |
| | | |

Name:_____

**Problem 3-14A (concl'd.)**

**Part 7 (concl'd.)**

### Statement of Changes in Equity

|  |  |  |
|---|---|---|
|  |  |  |
|  |  |  |
|  |  |  |
|  |  |  |
|  |  |  |
|  |  |  |
|  |  |  |

### Balance Sheet

|  |  |  |
|---|---|---|
|  |  |  |
|  |  |  |
|  |  |  |
|  |  |  |
|  |  |  |
|  |  |  |
|  |  |  |
|  |  |  |
|  |  |  |
|  |  |  |
|  |  |  |
|  |  |  |
|  |  |  |
|  |  |  |
|  |  |  |
|  |  |  |
|  |  |  |
|  |  |  |

*Analysis component:*

Name:_____

**\*Problem 3-15A**

**GENERAL JOURNAL**

Page_____

| Date | | Account Titles and Explanation | PR | Debit | Credit |
|---|---|---|---|---|---|
| **a.** | | | | | |
| | | | | | |
| | | | | | |
| | | | | | |
| | | | | | |
| **b.** | | | | | |
| | | | | | |
| | | | | | |
| **c.** | | | | | |
| | | | | | |
| | | | | | |
| **d.** | | | | | |
| | | | | | |
| | | | | | |
| | | | | | |
| | | | | | |
| | | | | | |
| | | | | | |
| **e.** | | | | | |
| | | | | | |
| | | | | | |
| | | | | | |
| | | | | | |
| | | | | | |

*Analysis component:*

_____
_____
_____
_____
_____
_____
_____

**\*Problem 3-16A**

| ACCOUNT | UNADJUSTED TRIAL BALANCE | | ADJUSTMENTS | | ADJUSTED TRIAL BALANCE | |
|---|---|---|---|---|---|---|
| | Debit | Credit | Debit | Credit | Debit | Credit |
| Cash | $ 32,000 | | | | | |
| Accounts receivable | 63,000 | | | | | |
| Prepaid rent | -0- | | | | | |
| Prepaid insurance | -0- | | | | | |
| Accounts payable | | $ 16,000 | | | | |
| Unearned consulting revenue | | -0- | | | | |
| Bruce Willis, capital | | 38,400 | | | | |
| Consulting revenue | | 82,000 | | | | |
| Rent expense | 38,990 | | | | | |
| Insurance expense | 2,410 | | | | | |
| Totals | $136,400 | $136,400 | | | | |

**\*Problem 3-17A**

Part 1 - Entries that initially recognize assets and liabilities:

GENERAL JOURNAL                                Page_____

| Date | Account Titles and Explanation | PR | Debit | Credit |
|---|---|---|---|---|
| | | | | |
| | | | | |
| | | | | |
| | | | | |
| | | | | |
| | | | | |
| | | | | |
| | | | | |
| | | | | |
| | | | | |
| | | | | |
| | | | | |
| | | | | |
| | | | | |
| | | | | |
| | | | | |
| | | | | |
| | | | | |
| | | | | |
| | | | | |
| | | | | |
| | | | | |
| | | | | |

Name:_____

**\*Problem 3-17A (cont'd.)**

### GENERAL JOURNAL

Page____

| Date | Account Titles and Explanation | PR | Debit | Credit |
|------|-------------------------------|----|-------|--------|
|  |  |  |  |  |
|  |  |  |  |  |
|  |  |  |  |  |
|  |  |  |  |  |
|  |  |  |  |  |
|  |  |  |  |  |
|  |  |  |  |  |
|  |  |  |  |  |
|  |  |  |  |  |
|  |  |  |  |  |
|  |  |  |  |  |
|  |  |  |  |  |
|  |  |  |  |  |
|  |  |  |  |  |
|  |  |  |  |  |
|  |  |  |  |  |
|  |  |  |  |  |
|  |  |  |  |  |

**Part 2 – Entries that initially recognize expenses and revenues:**

### GENERAL JOURNAL

Page____

| Date | Account Titles and Explanation | PR | Debit | Credit |
|------|-------------------------------|----|-------|--------|
|  |  |  |  |  |
|  |  |  |  |  |
|  |  |  |  |  |
|  |  |  |  |  |
|  |  |  |  |  |
|  |  |  |  |  |
|  |  |  |  |  |
|  |  |  |  |  |
|  |  |  |  |  |
|  |  |  |  |  |
|  |  |  |  |  |
|  |  |  |  |  |
|  |  |  |  |  |
|  |  |  |  |  |
|  |  |  |  |  |
|  |  |  |  |  |
|  |  |  |  |  |
|  |  |  |  |  |
|  |  |  |  |  |

Name:_____

**\*Problem 3-17A (concl'd.)**
**Part 2 (concluded)**

## GENERAL JOURNAL

Page_____

| Date | Account Titles and Explanation | PR | Debit | Credit |
|---|---|---|---|---|
|  |  |  |  |  |
|  |  |  |  |  |
|  |  |  |  |  |
|  |  |  |  |  |
|  |  |  |  |  |
|  |  |  |  |  |
|  |  |  |  |  |
|  |  |  |  |  |
|  |  |  |  |  |
|  |  |  |  |  |
|  |  |  |  |  |
|  |  |  |  |  |
|  |  |  |  |  |
|  |  |  |  |  |
|  |  |  |  |  |
|  |  |  |  |  |
|  |  |  |  |  |
|  |  |  |  |  |
|  |  |  |  |  |
|  |  |  |  |  |
|  |  |  |  |  |
|  |  |  |  |  |
|  |  |  |  |  |

*Analysis component:*

_____
_____
_____
_____
_____
_____
_____
_____
_____
_____
_____
_____
_____
_____
_____
_____
_____

## Problem 3-1B

### GENERAL JOURNAL            Page____

| Date | Account Titles and Explanation | PR | Debit $ | Credit $ |
|------|--------------------------------|----|---------|----------|
| a. 2017 Apr | 30 Equipment Rental Expense | | 6875 | |
| |      Prepaid Equipment Rental | | | 6875 |
| | 24750 = 1375 x 5 months | | | |
| | 18 months | | | |
| b. | 30 Warehouse Rental expense | | 6000 | |
| |      Prepaid Warehouse rental | | | 6000 |
| | To record expired rent. | | | |
| c. | 30 Insurance Expense | | 4080 | |
| |      Prepaid Insurance | | | 4080 |
| | To record use of Insu $8160 × 3/6 | | | |
| d. | 30 Cleaning Supplies Expense | | 2400 | |
| |      Cleaning Supplies | | | 2400 |
| | To record the use of | | | |
| | cleaning supplies. | | | |

**Analysis component:**

_____

_____

_____

_____

## Problem 3-2B

### GENERAL JOURNAL            Page____

| Date | Account Titles and Explanation | PR | Debit | Credit |
|------|--------------------------------|----|-------|--------|
| 2017 a. Nov | 30 Depr Expense, furniture | | 750 | |
| |      Accumulated Depr, furniture | | | 750 |
| | To record depr on furniture | | | |
| | 27000 - 0 = 9000 = $750 | | | |
| | 3 yrs    12 | | | |
| b. | 30 Depr Exp, Equipment | | 1230 | |
| |      Accumulated depr, Equipment | | | 1230 |
| | 171600 - 24000 = 14760 = 1230$ | | | |
| | 10 yrs    12 | | | |
| c. | 30 Depr Exp, Building | | 1950 | |
| |      Accumulated Depr, Building | | | 1950 |
| | 491000 - 140000 = 23400 = 1950 | | | |
| | 15 yrs    12 | | | |

**Problem 3-2B  (concl'd.)**

*Analysis component:*

_____
_____
_____
_____
_____
_____
_____
_____
_____
_____

**Problem 3-3B**

## GENERAL JOURNAL

Page____

| Date | Account Titles and Explanation | PR | Debit | Credit |
|------|-------------------------------|----|-------|--------|
| a. 2017 31<br>Jan | No entry required<br>on January 31, 2017. | | | |
| b. 31 | Unearned Tour pckg Revenue<br>  Tour Package Revenue<br>To record tour revenue earned.<br>¾ × 652000 = 489000 | | 489000 | 489000 |
| c. 31 | Unearned scuba Diving Revenue<br>  scuba Diving Revenue<br>To record scuba diving revenue.<br>290000 − 72000 = 218000 | | 218000 | 218000 |
| d. 31 | Unearned Kayaking Tour Revenue<br>  Kayaking Tour Revenue<br>To record Kayaking tour revenue earned<br>116000 − 15500 = 100500 earned | | 100500 | 100500 |

*Analysis component:*

_____
_____
_____
_____
_____
_____
_____

**Problem 3-4B**

**Adjusting Entries:**                    **GENERAL JOURNAL**                        Page____

| Date | | Account Titles and Explanation | PR | Debit | Credit |
|---|---|---|---|---|---|
| a. Sept | 30 | Interest Expense | | 1500 | |
| | | Interest payable | | | 1500 |
| | | To record accrued | | | |
| | | interest. | | | |
| | | | | | |
| b. Sept | 30 | Wages Expense | | 80500 | |
| | | Wages payable | | | 80500 |
| | | To record accrued | | | |
| | | wages expense. | | | |
| | | | | | |
| c. Sept | 30 | Cell phone expense | | 215 | |
| | | Accounts payable | | | 215 |
| | | To record accrued | | | |
| | | cell phone expense. | | | |
| | | | | | |
| d. Sept | 30 | Cable Expense | | 1150 | |
| | | Accounts payable | | | 1150 |
| | | To record accrued | | | |
| | | expense. | | | |
| | | | | | |
| e. Sept | 30 | Property tax Expense | | 1140 | |
| | | Property tax payable | | | 1140 |
| | | To record accrued | | | |
| | | expense. | | | |

**Problem 3-4B (concl'd.)**

**Subsequent Entries:**      **GENERAL JOURNAL**      Page____

| Date | | Account Titles and Explanation | PR | Debit | Credit |
|---|---|---|---|---|---|
| **a.** Oct | 2 | Interest payable | | 1500 | |
| | | Cash | | | 1500 |
| | | To record payment of | | | |
| | | accrued interest. | | | |
| **b.** Oct | 4 | Wages payable | | 80500 | |
| | | Wages Expense | | 34500 | |
| | | Cash | | | 115000 |
| | | To record pay of wages. | | | |
| **c.** Oct | 5 | Accounts Payable | | 215 | |
| | | Cash | | | 215 |
| | | To record payment | | | |
| | | of accrual. | | | |
| **d.** Oct | 2 | Accounts payable | | 1150 | |
| | | Cash | | | 1150 |
| | | To record payment | | | |
| | | of accrual. | | | |
| **e.** Oct | 15 | Property tax payable | | 1140 | |
| | | Cash | | | 1140 |
| | | To record payment | | | |
| | | of accrual. | | | |

Chapter 3                                    Name:_____

Problem 3-5B

| Date | | Account Titles and Explanation | PR | Debit | Credit |
|---|---|---|---|---|---|
| a. Mar | 31 | Interest Receivable | | 450 | |
| | |     Interest Income | | | 450 |
| | | To record accrued int income. | | | |
| b. Mar | 31 | Accounts Receivable | | 5600 | |
| | |     Consulting Revenue | | | 5600 |
| | | To record accrued Revenue. | | | |
| c. Mar | 31 | Accounts Receivable | | 8750 | |
| | |     Web design Revenue | | | 8750 |
| | | To record accrued Revenue. | | | |
| d. Mar | 31 | Rent Receivable | | 950 | |
| | |     Rent Revenue | | | 950 |
| | | To record accrued rent for March. | | | |

Subsequent Entries:          GENERAL JOURNAL                    Page____

| Date | | Account Titles and Explanation | PR | Debit | Credit |
|---|---|---|---|---|---|
| | | Cash | | 540 | |
| a. Apr | 5 |     Interest Receivable | | | 450 |
| | |     Interest Income | | | 90 |
| | | To record collection of int. | | | |
| | | 450/25 = 18 day x5days=90 | | | |
| b. Apr | 6 | Cash | | 5600 | |
| | |     Accounts Receivable | | | 5600 |
| | | To record collection of accrued Revenue. | | | |
| c. Apr | 13 | Cash | | 8750 | |
| | |     Accounts Receivable | | | 8750 |
| | | To rec collection of accrued Rev. | | | |
| d. Apr | 27 | Cash | | 1900 | |
| | |     Rent Receivable | | | 950 |
| | |     Rent Revenue | | | 950 |
| | | To record collection of March and April rent. | | | |

**Problem 3-6B**

**GENERAL JOURNAL**                                                  Page____

| Date | Account Titles and Explanation | PR | Debit | Credit |
|------|-------------------------------|-----|-------|--------|
| a. | | | | |
| | | | | |
| | | | | |
| b. | | | | |
| | | | | |
| | | | | |
| c. | | | | |
| | | | | |
| | | | | |
| d. | | | | |
| | | | | |
| | | | | |
| e. | | | | |
| | | | | |
| | | | | |
| f. | | | | |
| | | | | |
| | | | | |
| g. | | | | |
| | | | | |
| | | | | |
| h. | | | | |
| | | | | |
| | | | | |

**Part 2:**  *See next page for Part 2 working paper.*

**Part 3:**  _____

_____

_____

**Part 4:**  _____

_____

_____

_____

## Problem 3-6B (concl'd.)

### Part 2

| ACCOUNT | UNADJUSTED TRIAL BALANCE | | ADJUSTMENTS | | ADJUSTED TRIAL BALANCE | |
|---|---|---|---|---|---|---|
| | Debit | Credit | Debit | Credit | Debit | Credit |
| Cash | $ 25,000 | | | | | |
| Accounts receivable | -0- | | | | | |
| Teaching supplies | 107,200 | | | | | |
| Prepaid insurance | 36,000 | | | | | |
| Prepaid rent | 11,600 | | | | | |
| Professional library | 20,000 | | | | | |
| Accum. deprec., library | | 3,000 | | | | |
| Equipment | 141,400 | | | | | |
| Accum. deprec., equipment | | 32,000 | | | | |
| Accounts payable | | 24,400 | | | | |
| Salaries payable | | -0- | | | | |
| Unearned extension revenue | | 55,200 | | | | |
| Jay Fawcett, capital | | 62,000 | | | | |
| Jay Fawcett, withdrawals | 40,000 | | | | | |
| Tuition revenue | | 285,000 | | | | |
| Extension revenue | | 124,000 | | | | |
| Deprec. exp., equipment | -0- | | | | | |
| Deprec. exp., library | -0- | | | | | |
| Salaries expense | 143,600 | | | | | |
| Insurance expense | -0- | | | | | |
| Rent expense | -0- | | | | | |
| Teaching supplies expense | -0- | | | | | |
| Advertising expense | 36,000 | | | | | |
| Utilities expense | 24,800 | | | | | |
| Totals | $585,600 | $585,600 | | | | |

## Problem 3-7B

Subsequent Entries:      **GENERAL JOURNAL**      Page____

| Date | | Account Titles and Explanation | PR | Debit | Credit |
|---|---|---|---|---|---|
| a. | | | | | |
| | | | | | |
| | | | | | |
| | | | | | |
| b. | | | | | |
| | | | | | |
| | | | | | |
| | | | | | |

**Problem 3-7B (concl'd.)**

## GENERAL JOURNAL                                              Page____

| Date | Account Titles and Explanation | PR | Debit | Credit |
|------|-------------------------------|----|-------|--------|
| c. | | | | |
| | | | | |
| | | | | |
| | | | | |
| d. | | | | |
| | | | | |
| | | | | |
| | | | | |
| e. | | | | |
| | | | | |
| | | | | |
| | | | | |
| f. | | | | |
| | | | | |
| | | | | |
| | | | | |
| g. | | | | |
| | | | | |
| | | | | |
| | | | | |
| h. | | | | |
| | | | | |
| | | | | |
| | | | | |
| i. | | | | |
| | | | | |
| | | | | |
| | | | | |
| j. | | | | |
| | | | | |
| | | | | |
| | | | | |
| | | | | |

Name:_____

Problem 3-8B

Part 1            GENERAL JOURNAL           Page____

| Date | Account Titles and Explanation | PR | Debit | Credit |
|---|---|---|---|---|
| a. | | | | |
| | | | | |
| | | | | |
| | | | | |
| b. | | | | |
| | | | | |
| | | | | |
| | | | | |
| | | | | |
| | | | | |
| c. | | | | |
| | | | | |
| | | | | |
| d. | | | | |
| | | | | |
| | | | | |
| | | | | |
| e. | | | | |
| | | | | |
| | | | | |
| | | | | |
| f. | | | | |
| | | | | |
| | | | | |
| | | | | |
| | | | | |
| | | | | |

Name:_____

**Problem 3-8B (concl'd.)**

Part 2                     GENERAL JOURNAL                     Page____

| Date | Account Titles and Explanation | PR | Debit | Credit |
|------|-------------------------------|----|----|----|
|  |  |  |  |  |
|  |  |  |  |  |
|  |  |  |  |  |
|  |  |  |  |  |
|  |  |  |  |  |
|  |  |  |  |  |
|  |  |  |  |  |
|  |  |  |  |  |
|  |  |  |  |  |
|  |  |  |  |  |
|  |  |  |  |  |
|  |  |  |  |  |

**Problem 3-9B**

GENERAL JOURNAL                     Page____

| Date | Account Titles and Explanation | PR | Debit | Credit |
|------|-------------------------------|----|----|----|
| a. |  |  |  |  |
|  |  |  |  |  |
|  |  |  |  |  |
|  |  |  |  |  |
| b. |  |  |  |  |
|  |  |  |  |  |
|  |  |  |  |  |
|  |  |  |  |  |
| c. |  |  |  |  |
|  |  |  |  |  |
|  |  |  |  |  |
|  |  |  |  |  |
| d. |  |  |  |  |
|  |  |  |  |  |
|  |  |  |  |  |
|  |  |  |  |  |
|  |  |  |  |  |

**Name:** _____

**Problem 3-9B (concl'd.)**

## GENERAL JOURNAL

Page_____

| Date | Account Titles and Explanation | PR | Debit | Credit |
|------|-------------------------------|----|-------|--------|
| e. | | | | |
| | | | | |
| | | | | |
| f. | | | | |
| | | | | |
| | | | | |
| g. | | | | |
| | | | | |
| | | | | |
| h. | | | | |
| | | | | |
| | | | | |
| i. | | | | |
| | | | | |
| | | | | |
| | | | | |

*Analysis component:*

_____
_____
_____
_____
_____
_____
_____
_____

**Problem 3-10B**

**Parts 1 and 2**

### Cash ACCOUNT NO. 101

| DATE | EXPLANATION | PR | DEBIT | CREDIT | BALANCE |
|------|-------------|-----|-------|--------|---------|
| 2017 | | | | | |
| Dec. 31 | Balance | | | | 15,600 |

### Accounts Receivable ACCOUNT NO. 106

| DATE | EXPLANATION | PR | DEBIT | CREDIT | BALANCE |
|------|-------------|-----|-------|--------|---------|
| 2017 | | | | | |
| Dec. 31 | Balance | | | | 29,200 |
| | | | | | |

### Supplies ACCOUNT NO. 126

| DATE | EXPLANATION | PR | DEBIT | CREDIT | BALANCE |
|------|-------------|-----|-------|--------|---------|
| 2017 | | | | | |
| Dec. 31 | Balance | | | | 1,640 |
| | | | | | |

### Prepaid Advertising ACCOUNT NO. 128

| DATE | EXPLANATION | PR | DEBIT | CREDIT | BALANCE |
|------|-------------|-----|-------|--------|---------|
| 2017 | | | | | |
| Dec. 31 | Balance | | | | 1,280 |
| | | | | | |

### Prepaid Rent ACCOUNT NO. 131

| DATE | EXPLANATION | PR | DEBIT | CREDIT | BALANCE |
|------|-------------|-----|-------|--------|---------|
| 2017 | | | | | |
| Dec. 31 | Balance | | | | 17,880 |
| | | | | | |

### Surveying Equipment ACCOUNT NO. 167

| DATE | EXPLANATION | PR | DEBIT | CREDIT | BALANCE |
|------|-------------|-----|-------|--------|---------|
| 2017 | | | | | |
| Dec. 31 | Balance | | | | 58,000 |
| | | | | | |

### Accum. Deprec. – Surveying Equipment ACCOUNT NO. 168

| DATE | EXPLANATION | PR | DEBIT | CREDIT | BALANCE |
|------|-------------|-----|-------|--------|---------|
| 2017 | | | | | |
| Dec. 31 | Balance | | | | 7,348 |
| | | | | | |

### Accounts Payable          ACCOUNT NO. 201

| DATE | EXPLANATION | PR | DEBIT | CREDIT | BALANCE |
|------|-------------|----|-------|--------|---------|
| 2017 | | | | | |
| Dec. 31 | Balance | | | | 13,800 |
| | | | | | |

### Interest Payable          ACCOUNT NO. 203

| DATE | EXPLANATION | PR | DEBIT | CREDIT | BALANCE |
|------|-------------|----|-------|--------|---------|
| 2017 | | | | | |
| | | | | | |

### Wages Payable          ACCOUNT NO. 210

| DATE | EXPLANATION | PR | DEBIT | CREDIT | BALANCE |
|------|-------------|----|-------|--------|---------|
| 2017 | | | | | |
| | | | | | |

### Unearned Surveying Revenue          ACCOUNT NO. 233

| DATE | EXPLANATION | PR | DEBIT | CREDIT | BALANCE |
|------|-------------|----|-------|--------|---------|
| 2017 | | | | | |
| Dec. 31 | Balance | | | | 14,800 |
| | | | | | |

### Notes Payable          ACCOUNT NO. 251

| DATE | EXPLANATION | PR | DEBIT | CREDIT | BALANCE |
|------|-------------|----|-------|--------|---------|
| 2017 | | | | | |
| Dec. 31 | Balance | | | | 36,000 |

### Ben Hallmark, Capital          ACCOUNT NO. 301

| DATE | EXPLANATION | PR | DEBIT | CREDIT | BALANCE |
|------|-------------|----|-------|--------|---------|
| 2017 | | | | | |
| Dec. 31 | Balance | | | | 28,652 |

### Ben Hallmark, Withdrawals          ACCOUNT NO. 302

| DATE | EXPLANATION | PR | DEBIT | CREDIT | BALANCE |
|------|-------------|----|-------|--------|---------|
| 2017 | | | | | |
| Dec. 31 | Balance | | | | 24,300 |

## Problem 3-10B (cont'd.)

**Surveying Revenue**           ACCOUNT NO. 401

| DATE | EXPLANATION | PR | DEBIT | CREDIT | BALANCE |
|------|-------------|----|-------|--------|---------|
| 2017 | | | | | |
| Dec. 31 | Balance | | | | 170,948 |
| | | | | | |
| | | | | | |

**Depreciation Expense, Surveying Equipment**      ACCOUNT NO. 601

| DATE | EXPLANATION | PR | DEBIT | CREDIT | BALANCE |
|------|-------------|----|-------|--------|---------|
| 2017 | | | | | |
| | | | | | |
| | | | | | |

**Salaries Expense**           ACCOUNT NO. 622

| DATE | EXPLANATION | PR | DEBIT | CREDIT | BALANCE |
|------|-------------|----|-------|--------|---------|
| 2017 | | | | | |
| Dec. 31 | Balance | | | | 56,000 |
| | | | | | |

**Wages Expense**           ACCOUNT NO. 623

| DATE | EXPLANATION | PR | DEBIT | CREDIT | BALANCE |
|------|-------------|----|-------|--------|---------|
| 2017 | | | | | |
| Dec. 31 | Balance | | | | 39,726 |
| | | | | | |

**Interest Expense**           ACCOUNT NO. 633

| DATE | EXPLANATION | PR | DEBIT | CREDIT | BALANCE |
|------|-------------|----|-------|--------|---------|
| 2017 | | | | | |
| | | | | | |
| | | | | | |

**Insurance Expense**           ACCOUNT NO. 637

| DATE | EXPLANATION | PR | DEBIT | CREDIT | BALANCE |
|------|-------------|----|-------|--------|---------|
| 2017 | | | | | |
| Dec. 31 | Balance | | | | 6,000 |
| | | | | | |

**Rent Expense**           ACCOUNT NO. 640

| DATE | EXPLANATION | PR | DEBIT | CREDIT | BALANCE |
|------|-------------|----|-------|--------|---------|
| 2017 | | | | | |
| | | | | | |
| | | | | | |

**Problem 3-10B (cont'd.)**

## Supplies Expense                                              ACCOUNT NO. 650

| DATE | EXPLANATION | PR | DEBIT | CREDIT | BALANCE |
|------|-------------|----|-------|--------|---------|
| 2017 | | | | | |
| Dec. 31 | Balance | | | | 2,958 |
| | | | | | |
| | | | | | |

## Advertising Expense                                          ACCOUNT NO. 655

| DATE | EXPLANATION | PR | DEBIT | CREDIT | BALANCE |
|------|-------------|----|-------|--------|---------|
| 2017 | | | | | |
| | | | | | |
| | | | | | |

## Gas and Oil Expense                                          ACCOUNT NO. 671

| DATE | EXPLANATION | PR | DEBIT | CREDIT | BALANCE |
|------|-------------|----|-------|--------|---------|
| 2017 | | | | | |
| Dec. 31 | Balance | | | | 6,564 |
| | | | | | |

## Repairs Expense                                              ACCOUNT NO. 684

| DATE | EXPLANATION | PR | DEBIT | CREDIT | BALANCE |
|------|-------------|----|-------|--------|---------|
| 2017 | | | | | |
| Dec. 31 | Balance | | | | 12,400 |
| | | | | | |

## Utilities Expense                                            ACCOUNT NO. 690

| DATE | EXPLANATION | PR | DEBIT | CREDIT | BALANCE |
|------|-------------|----|-------|--------|---------|
| 2017 | | | | | |
| | | | | | |
| | | | | | |

**Problem 3-10B (cont'd.) Part 3**

---

### Adjusted Trial Balance

| | | | |
|---|---|---|---|
| | | | |
| | | | |
| | | | |
| | | | |
| | | | |
| | | | |
| | | | |
| | | | |
| | | | |
| | | | |
| | | | |
| | | | |
| | | | |
| | | | |
| | | | |
| | | | |
| | | | |
| | | | |
| | | | |
| | | | |
| | | | |
| | | | |
| | | | |
| | | | |
| | | | |
| | | | |
| | | | |
| | | | |
| | | | |
| | | | |
| | | | |

Name:_____

**Problem 3-10B (cont'd.) Part 4**

## Income Statement

| | | |
|---|---|---|
| | | |
| | | |
| | | |
| | | |
| | | |
| | | |
| | | |
| | | |
| | | |
| | | |
| | | |
| | | |
| | | |
| | | |
| | | |
| | | |
| | | |
| | | |

## Statement of Changes in Equity

| | | |
|---|---|---|
| | | |
| | | |
| | | |
| | | |
| | | |
| | | |

**Problem 3-10B (concl'd.)**

| | Balance Sheet | | |
|---|---|---|---|
| | | | |
| | | | |
| | | | |
| | | | |
| | | | |
| | | | |
| | | | |
| | | | |
| | | | |
| | | | |
| | | | |
| | | | |
| | | | |
| | | | |
| | | | |
| | | | |
| | | | |
| | | | |
| | | | |
| | | | |
| | | | |
| | | | |
| | | | |

*Analysis component:*

_____
_____
_____
_____
_____
_____
_____
_____
_____
_____

## GENERAL JOURNAL
Page_____

| Date | Account Titles and Explanation | PR | Debit | Credit |
|------|-------------------------------|-----|-------|--------|
| a. | | | | |
| | | | | |
| | | | | |
| | | | | |
| b. | | | | |
| | | | | |
| | | | | |
| | | | | |
| c. | | | | |
| | | | | |
| | | | | |
| | | | | |
| d. | | | | |
| | | | | |
| | | | | |
| | | | | |
| e. | | | | |
| | | | | |
| | | | | |
| | | | | |
| f. | | | | |
| | | | | |
| | | | | |
| | | | | |
| g. | | | | |
| | | | | |
| | | | | |
| | | | | |
| | | | | |

## Problem 3-12B  Part 1

| ACCOUNT | UNADJUSTED TRIAL BALANCE | | ADJUSTMENTS | | ADJUSTED TRIAL BALANCE | |
|---|---|---|---|---|---|---|
| | Debit | Credit | Debit | Credit | Debit | Credit |
| Cash | $ 112,000 | | | | | |
| Accounts receivable | 28,000 | | | | | |
| Repair supplies | 2,800 | | | | | |
| Prepaid arena rental | 182,000 | | | | | |
| Skate equipment | 428,000 | | | | | |
| Accum. deprec., skate eq. | | $ 164,000 | | | | |
| Accounts payable | | 5,400 | | | | |
| Unearned training revenue | | 19,600 | | | | |
| Notes payable | | 160,000 | | | | |
| Ben Gibson, capital | | 451,400 | | | | |
| Ben Gibson, withdrawals | 72,000 | | | | | |
| Training revenue | | 550,000 | | | | |
| Salaries expense | 350,000 | | | | | |
| Arena rental expense | 168,000 | | | | | |
| Other expenses | 7,600 | | | | | |
| Totals | $1,350,400 | $1,350,400 | | | | |
| | | | | | | |
| | | | | | | |
| | | | | | | |
| | | | | | | |
| | | | | | | |
| | | | | | | |
| | | | | | | |

## Part 2

### Income Statement

| | | |
|---|---|---|
| | | |
| | | |
| | | |
| | | |
| | | |
| | | |
| | | |
| | | |
| | | |
| | | |
| | | |
| | | |
| | | |

Name:_____

## Problem 3-12B (concl'd.)

### Statement of Changes in Equity

| | | |
|---|---|---|
| | | |
| | | |
| | | |
| | | |
| | | |
| | | |
| | | |

### Balance Sheet

| | | |
|---|---|---|
| | | |
| | | |
| | | |
| | | |
| | | |
| | | |
| | | |
| | | |
| | | |
| | | |
| | | |
| | | |
| | | |
| | | |
| | | |
| | | |
| | | |
| | | |
| | | |

*Analysis component:*

_____
_____
_____
_____
_____
_____
_____
_____

**Problem 3-13B**

## Income Statement

| | | |
|---|---|---|
| | | |
| | | |
| | | |
| | | |
| | | |
| | | |
| | | |
| | | |
| | | |
| | | |
| | | |
| | | |
| | | |
| | | |
| | | |
| | | |
| | | |

## Statement of Changes in Equity

| | | |
|---|---|---|
| | | |
| | | |
| | | |
| | | |
| | | |
| | | |
| | | |

**Problem 3-13B (concl'd.)**

## Balance Sheet

| | | |
|---|---|---|
| | | |
| | | |
| | | |
| | | |
| | | |
| | | |
| | | |
| | | |
| | | |
| | | |
| | | |
| | | |
| | | |
| | | |
| | | |
| | | |
| | | |
| | | |
| | | |
| | | |
| | | |
| | | |
| | | |
| | | |
| | | |
| | | |
| | | |
| | | |
| | | |
| | | |
| | | |
| | | |
| | | |
| | | |
| | | |
| | | |
| | | |

Name:_____

**Problem 3-14B    Part 1**

**GENERAL JOURNAL**                                    Page_____

| Date | Account Titles and Explanation | PR | Debit | Credit |
|------|-------------------------------|----|-------|--------|
|      |                               |    |       |        |
|      |                               |    |       |        |
|      |                               |    |       |        |
|      |                               |    |       |        |
|      |                               |    |       |        |
|      |                               |    |       |        |
|      |                               |    |       |        |
|      |                               |    |       |        |
|      |                               |    |       |        |
|      |                               |    |       |        |
|      |                               |    |       |        |
|      |                               |    |       |        |
|      |                               |    |       |        |
|      |                               |    |       |        |
|      |                               |    |       |        |
|      |                               |    |       |        |
|      |                               |    |       |        |
|      |                               |    |       |        |
|      |                               |    |       |        |
|      |                               |    |       |        |
|      |                               |    |       |        |
|      |                               |    |       |        |
|      |                               |    |       |        |
|      |                               |    |       |        |
|      |                               |    |       |        |
|      |                               |    |       |        |
|      |                               |    |       |        |
|      |                               |    |       |        |
|      |                               |    |       |        |
|      |                               |    |       |        |
|      |                               |    |       |        |
|      |                               |    |       |        |
|      |                               |    |       |        |
|      |                               |    |       |        |
|      |                               |    |       |        |
|      |                               |    |       |        |
|      |                               |    |       |        |
|      |                               |    |       |        |
|      |                               |    |       |        |
|      |                               |    |       |        |

Name:_____

## Problem 3-14B (cont'd.)

### Parts 2, 3, and 5

| Cash | 101 |
|---|---|
| Bal. 6,400 | |

| Repair Supplies | 131 |
|---|---|
| Bal. 3,000 | |

| Accum. Deprec., Tools | 162 |
|---|---|
| | 560 Bal. |

| Tools | 161 |
|---|---|
| Bal. 16,800 | |

| Unearned Revenue | 233 |
|---|---|
| | 700 Bal. |

| Accounts Payable | 201 |
|---|---|
| | 3,200 Bal. |

| Melanie Thornhill, Capital | 301 |
|---|---|
| | Bal. |

| Melanie Thornhill, Withdrawals | 302 |
|---|---|
| Bal. -0- | |

| Revenue 401 | |
|---|---|
| | 25,800 Bal. |

| Deprec. Exp., Tools | 602 |
|---|---|
| Bal. 560 | |

| Wages Expense | 623 |
|---|---|
| Bal. 1,960 | |

| Rent Expense | 640 |
|---|---|
| Bal. 8,000 | |

| Repairs Supplies Expense | 696 |
|---|---|
| Bal. 2,700 | |

**Problem 3-14B (cont'd.)**
  **Part 4**

## Trial Balance

|                                                    | Debit | Credit |
|----------------------------------------------------|-------|--------|
|                                                    |       |        |
|                                                    |       |        |
|                                                    |       |        |
|                                                    |       |        |
|                                                    |       |        |
|                                                    |       |        |
|                                                    |       |        |
|                                                    |       |        |
|                                                    |       |        |
|                                                    |       |        |
|                                                    |       |        |
|                                                    |       |        |
|                                                    |       |        |
|                                                    |       |        |

**Part 5 – Adjusting entries**

### GENERAL JOURNAL                                   Page_____

| Date | Account Titles and Explanation | PR | Debit | Credit |
|------|-------------------------------|----|-------|--------|
|      |                               |    |       |        |
|      |                               |    |       |        |
|      |                               |    |       |        |
|      |                               |    |       |        |
|      |                               |    |       |        |
|      |                               |    |       |        |
|      |                               |    |       |        |
|      |                               |    |       |        |
|      |                               |    |       |        |
|      |                               |    |       |        |
|      |                               |    |       |        |
|      |                               |    |       |        |
|      |                               |    |       |        |
|      |                               |    |       |        |
|      |                               |    |       |        |
|      |                               |    |       |        |
|      |                               |    |       |        |
|      |                               |    |       |        |
|      |                               |    |       |        |
|      |                               |    |       |        |
|      |                               |    |       |        |

**Problem 3-14B (cont'd.)**

Part 6

## Trial Balance

|  | Debit | Credit |
|---|---|---|
|  |  |  |
|  |  |  |
|  |  |  |
|  |  |  |
|  |  |  |
|  |  |  |
|  |  |  |
|  |  |  |
|  |  |  |
|  |  |  |
|  |  |  |
|  |  |  |
|  |  |  |
|  |  |  |
|  |  |  |
|  |  |  |
|  |  |  |
|  |  |  |

Part 7

## Income Statement

|  |  |  |
|---|---|---|
|  |  |  |
|  |  |  |
|  |  |  |
|  |  |  |
|  |  |  |
|  |  |  |
|  |  |  |
|  |  |  |
|  |  |  |
|  |  |  |
|  |  |  |
|  |  |  |
|  |  |  |

**Problem 3-14B (concl'd.)**

**Part 6 (concl'd.)**

### Statement of Changes in Equity

| | | |
|---|---|---|
| | | |
| | | |
| | | |
| | | |
| | | |
| | | |

### Balance Sheet

| | | |
|---|---|---|
| | | |
| | | |
| | | |
| | | |
| | | |
| | | |
| | | |
| | | |
| | | |
| | | |
| | | |
| | | |
| | | |
| | | |
| | | |
| | | |
| | | |

*Analysis component:*

_____
_____
_____
_____
_____
_____
_____
_____

*Problem 3-15B

**GENERAL JOURNAL**                     Page_____

| Date | Account Titles and Explanation | PR | Debit | Credit |
|------|-------------------------------|----|-------|--------|
| a. | | | | |
| | | | | |
| | | | | |
| | | | | |
| | | | | |
| | | | | |
| b. | | | | |
| | | | | |
| | | | | |
| | | | | |
| | | | | |
| | | | | |
| c. | | | | |
| | | | | |
| | | | | |
| | | | | |
| | | | | |
| | | | | |
| d. | | | | |
| | | | | |
| | | | | |
| | | | | |
| e. | | | | |
| | | | | |
| | | | | |
| | | | | |

*Analysis component:*

_____

_____

_____

_____

_____

_____

_____

*Problem 3-16B

| ACCOUNT | UNADJUSTED TRIAL BALANCE | | ADJUSTMENTS | | ADJUSTED TRIAL BALANCE | |
|---|---|---|---|---|---|---|
| | Debit | Credit | Debit | Credit | Debit | Credit |
| Cash | $  3,500 | | | | | |
| Accounts receivable | 7,200 | | | | | |
| Prepaid advertising | -0- | | | | | |
| Cleaning supplies | -0- | | | | | |
| Equipment | 29,000 | | | | | |
| Accum. deprec., equipment | | $  3,200 | | | | |
| Unearned window washing revenue | | -0- | | | | |
| Unearned office cleaning revenue | | -0- | | | | |
| William Nahanee, capital | | 9,150 | | | | |
| Window washing revenue | | 23,800 | | | | |
| Office cleaning revenue | | 71,500 | | | | |
| Advertising expense | 2,900 | | | | | |
| Salaries expense | 56,900 | | | | | |
| Depreciation expense, equip. | -0- | | | | | |
| Cleaning supplies expense | 8,150 | | | | | |
| Totals | $107,650 | $107,650 | | | | |

*Problem 3-17B

Part 1 - Entries that initially recognize assets and liabilities:

## GENERAL JOURNAL                                    Page_____

| Date | Account Titles and Explanation | PR | Debit | Credit |
|---|---|---|---|---|
| | | | | |
| | | | | |
| | | | | |
| | | | | |
| | | | | |
| | | | | |
| | | | | |
| | | | | |
| | | | | |
| | | | | |
| | | | | |
| | | | | |
| | | | | |
| | | | | |
| | | | | |
| | | | | |
| | | | | |
| | | | | |
| | | | | |

Name:_____

**\*Problem 3-17B (cont'd.)**

**GENERAL JOURNAL**                    Page_____

| Date | Account Titles and Explanation | PR | Debit | Credit |
|------|-------------------------------|----|-------|--------|
|      |                               |    |       |        |
|      |                               |    |       |        |
|      |                               |    |       |        |
|      |                               |    |       |        |
|      |                               |    |       |        |
|      |                               |    |       |        |
|      |                               |    |       |        |
|      |                               |    |       |        |
|      |                               |    |       |        |
|      |                               |    |       |        |
|      |                               |    |       |        |
|      |                               |    |       |        |
|      |                               |    |       |        |
|      |                               |    |       |        |
|      |                               |    |       |        |
|      |                               |    |       |        |
|      |                               |    |       |        |
|      |                               |    |       |        |
|      |                               |    |       |        |
|      |                               |    |       |        |
|      |                               |    |       |        |
|      |                               |    |       |        |
|      |                               |    |       |        |
|      |                               |    |       |        |
|      |                               |    |       |        |

**Part 2 – Entries that initially recognize expenses and revenues:**

**GENERAL JOURNAL**                    Page_____

| Date | Account Titles and Explanation | PR | Debit | Credit |
|------|-------------------------------|----|-------|--------|
|      |                               |    |       |        |
|      |                               |    |       |        |
|      |                               |    |       |        |
|      |                               |    |       |        |
|      |                               |    |       |        |
|      |                               |    |       |        |
|      |                               |    |       |        |
|      |                               |    |       |        |
|      |                               |    |       |        |
|      |                               |    |       |        |
|      |                               |    |       |        |
|      |                               |    |       |        |
|      |                               |    |       |        |
|      |                               |    |       |        |
|      |                               |    |       |        |

Name:_____

*Problem 3-17B (concl'd.)

Part 2 (concl'd)

## GENERAL JOURNAL

Page_____

| Date | Account Titles and Explanation | PR | Debit | Credit |
|---|---|---|---|---|
| | | | | |
| | | | | |
| | | | | |
| | | | | |
| | | | | |
| | | | | |
| | | | | |
| | | | | |
| | | | | |
| | | | | |
| | | | | |
| | | | | |
| | | | | |
| | | | | |
| | | | | |
| | | | | |
| | | | | |
| | | | | |
| | | | | |
| | | | | |
| | | | | |
| | | | | |

*Analysis component:*

_____
_____
_____
_____
_____
_____
_____
_____
_____
_____
_____
_____
_____
_____
_____
_____

Name:_____

**Cumulative Problem**

Part 1          **Echo Systems**
                **Journal Entries**

### GENERAL JOURNAL

Page _____

| Date | Account Titles and Explanation | PR | Debit | Credit |
|------|-------------------------------|----|-------|--------|
|      |                               |    |       |        |
|      |                               |    |       |        |
|      |                               |    |       |        |
|      |                               |    |       |        |
|      |                               |    |       |        |
|      |                               |    |       |        |
|      |                               |    |       |        |
|      |                               |    |       |        |
|      |                               |    |       |        |
|      |                               |    |       |        |
|      |                               |    |       |        |
|      |                               |    |       |        |
|      |                               |    |       |        |
|      |                               |    |       |        |
|      |                               |    |       |        |
|      |                               |    |       |        |
|      |                               |    |       |        |
|      |                               |    |       |        |
|      |                               |    |       |        |
|      |                               |    |       |        |
|      |                               |    |       |        |
|      |                               |    |       |        |
|      |                               |    |       |        |
|      |                               |    |       |        |
|      |                               |    |       |        |
|      |                               |    |       |        |
|      |                               |    |       |        |
|      |                               |    |       |        |
|      |                               |    |       |        |
|      |                               |    |       |        |
|      |                               |    |       |        |
|      |                               |    |       |        |
|      |                               |    |       |        |
|      |                               |    |       |        |
|      |                               |    |       |        |
|      |                               |    |       |        |
|      |                               |    |       |        |
|      |                               |    |       |        |
|      |                               |    |       |        |
|      |                               |    |       |        |

**Cumulative Problem**

**Part 2**     **Echo Systems**
              **Adjusting Entries**

### GENERAL JOURNAL

| Date | Account Titles and Explanation | PR | Debit | Credit |
|------|-------------------------------|----|-------|--------|
|      |                               |    |       |        |
|      |                               |    |       |        |
|      |                               |    |       |        |
|      |                               |    |       |        |
|      |                               |    |       |        |
|      |                               |    |       |        |
|      |                               |    |       |        |
|      |                               |    |       |        |
|      |                               |    |       |        |
|      |                               |    |       |        |
|      |                               |    |       |        |
|      |                               |    |       |        |
|      |                               |    |       |        |
|      |                               |    |       |        |
|      |                               |    |       |        |
|      |                               |    |       |        |
|      |                               |    |       |        |
|      |                               |    |       |        |
|      |                               |    |       |        |
|      |                               |    |       |        |
|      |                               |    |       |        |
|      |                               |    |       |        |
|      |                               |    |       |        |
|      |                               |    |       |        |
|      |                               |    |       |        |
|      |                               |    |       |        |
|      |                               |    |       |        |
|      |                               |    |       |        |
|      |                               |    |       |        |
|      |                               |    |       |        |
|      |                               |    |       |        |
|      |                               |    |       |        |
|      |                               |    |       |        |
|      |                               |    |       |        |
|      |                               |    |       |        |
|      |                               |    |       |        |
|      |                               |    |       |        |
|      |                               |    |       |        |

Name:_____

Cumulative Problem

Part 2            Echo Systems  (Cont'd.)

## GENERAL LEDGER

### Cash                                                              ACCOUNT NO. 101

| DATE | EXPLANATION | PR | DEBIT | CREDIT | BALANCE |
|------|-------------|----|-------|--------|---------|
| 2017 Nov. 30 | Balance | | | | 70,340 |
| | | | | | |
| | | | | | |
| | | | | | |
| | | | | | |
| | | | | | |
| | | | | | |
| | | | | | |
| | | | | | |
| | | | | | |

### Accounts Receivable                                              ACCOUNT NO. 106

| DATE | EXPLANATION | PR | DEBIT | CREDIT | BALANCE |
|------|-------------|----|-------|--------|---------|
| 2017 Nov. 30 | Balance | | | | 18,900 |
| | | | | | |
| | | | | | |
| | | | | | |

### Computer Supplies                                                ACCOUNT NO. 126

| DATE | EXPLANATION | PR | DEBIT | CREDIT | BALANCE |
|------|-------------|----|-------|--------|---------|
| 2017 Nov. 30 | Balance | | | | 4,560 |
| | | | | | |
| | | | | | |
| | | | | | |

### Prepaid Insurance                                                ACCOUNT NO. 128

| DATE | EXPLANATION | PR | DEBIT | CREDIT | BALANCE |
|------|-------------|----|-------|--------|---------|
| 2017 Nov. 30 | Balance | | | | 4,320 |
| | | | | | |

### Prepaid Rent                                                     ACCOUNT NO. 131

| DATE | EXPLANATION | PR | DEBIT | CREDIT | BALANCE |
|------|-------------|----|-------|--------|---------|
| 2017 Nov. 30 | Balance | | | | 9,000 |
| | | | | | |

**Cumulative Problem**

**Part 2**          **Echo Systems  (Cont'd.)**

### Office Equipment                                      ACCOUNT NO. 163

| DATE | EXPLANATION | PR | DEBIT | CREDIT | BALANCE |
|------|-------------|----|-------|--------|---------|
| 2017 Nov. 30 | Balance | | | | 18,000 |
| | | | | | |

### Accumulated Depreciation, Office Equipment          ACCOUNT NO. 164

| DATE | EXPLANATION | PR | DEBIT | CREDIT | BALANCE |
|------|-------------|----|-------|--------|---------|
| 2017 Nov. 30 | Balance | | | | -0- |
| | | | | | |

### Computer Equipment                                   ACCOUNT NO. 167

| DATE | EXPLANATION | PR | DEBIT | CREDIT | BALANCE |
|------|-------------|----|-------|--------|---------|
| 2017 Nov. 30 | Balance | | | | 36,000 |
| | | | | | |

### Accumulated Depreciation, Computer Equipment         ACCOUNT NO. 168

| DATE | EXPLANATION | PR | DEBIT | CREDIT | BALANCE |
|------|-------------|----|-------|--------|---------|
| 2017 Nov. 30 | Balance | | | | -0- |
| | | | | | |

### Accounts Payable                                     ACCOUNT NO. 201

| DATE | EXPLANATION | PR | DEBIT | CREDIT | BALANCE |
|------|-------------|----|-------|--------|---------|
| 2017 Nov. 30 | Balance | | | | -0- |
| | | | | | |

### Wages Payable                                        ACCOUNT NO. 210

| DATE | EXPLANATION | PR | DEBIT | CREDIT | BALANCE |
|------|-------------|----|-------|--------|---------|
| 2017 Nov. 30 | Balance | | | | -0- |
| | | | | | |

### Unearned Computer Services Revenue                   ACCOUNT NO. 236

| DATE | EXPLANATION | PR | DEBIT | CREDIT | BALANCE |
|------|-------------|----|-------|--------|---------|
| 2017 Nov. 30 | Balance | | | | -0- |
| | | | | | |

### Mary Graham, Capital                                 ACCOUNT NO. 301

| DATE | EXPLANATION | PR | DEBIT | CREDIT | BALANCE |
|------|-------------|----|-------|--------|---------|
| 2017 Nov. 30 | Balance | | | | 144,000 |

**Cumulative Problem**

**Part 2          Echo Systems  (Cont'd.)**

### Mary Graham, Withdrawals                    ACCOUNT NO. 302

| DATE | EXPLANATION | PR | DEBIT | CREDIT | BALANCE |
|------|-------------|----|----|------|------|
| 2017 Nov. 30 | Balance | | | | 10,800 |
| | | | | | |

### Computer Services Revenue                    ACCOUNT NO. 403

| DATE | EXPLANATION | PR | DEBIT | CREDIT | BALANCE |
|------|-------------|----|----|------|------|
| 2017 Nov. 30 | Balance | | | | 40,950 |
| | | | | | |

### Depreciation Expense, Office Equipment          ACCOUNT NO. 612

| DATE | EXPLANATION | PR | DEBIT | CREDIT | BALANCE |
|------|-------------|----|----|------|------|
| 2017 Nov. 30 | Balance | | | | -0- |
| | | | | | |

### Depreciation Expense, Computer Equipment          ACCOUNT NO. 613

| DATE | EXPLANATION | PR | DEBIT | CREDIT | BALANCE |
|------|-------------|----|----|------|------|
| 2017 Nov. 30 | Balance | | | | -0- |
| | | | | | |

### Wages Expense                    ACCOUNT NO. 623

| DATE | EXPLANATION | PR | DEBIT | CREDIT | BALANCE |
|------|-------------|----|----|------|------|
| 2017 Nov. 30 | Balance | | | | 4,200 |
| | | | | | |
| | | | | | |
| | | | | | |

### Insurance Expense                    ACCOUNT NO. 637

| DATE | EXPLANATION | PR | DEBIT | CREDIT | BALANCE |
|------|-------------|----|----|------|------|
| 2017 Nov. 30 | Balance | | | | -0- |
| | | | | | |

### Rent Expense                    ACCOUNT NO. 640

| DATE | EXPLANATION | PR | DEBIT | CREDIT | BALANCE |
|------|-------------|----|----|------|------|
| 2017 Nov. 30 | Balance | | | | -0- |
| | | | | | |

**Cumulative Problem**

**Part 2**        **Echo Systems (Cont'd.)**

### Computer Supplies Expense     ACCOUNT NO. 652

| DATE | EXPLANATION | PR | DEBIT | CREDIT | BALANCE |
|------|-------------|----|-------|--------|---------|
| 2017 Nov. 30 | Balance | | | | -0- |
| | | | | | |

### Advertising Expense     ACCOUNT NO. 655

| DATE | EXPLANATION | PR | DEBIT | CREDIT | BALANCE |
|------|-------------|----|-------|--------|---------|
| 2017 Nov. 30 | Balance | | | | 3,720 |
| | | | | | |

### Mileage Expense     ACCOUNT NO. 676

| DATE | EXPLANATION | PR | DEBIT | CREDIT | BALANCE |
|------|-------------|----|-------|--------|---------|
| 2017 Nov. 30 | Balance | | | | 2,200 |
| | | | | | |

### Repairs Expense, Computer     ACCOUNT NO. 684

| DATE | EXPLANATION | PR | DEBIT | CREDIT | BALANCE |
|------|-------------|----|-------|--------|---------|
| 2017 Nov. 30 | Balance | | | | 1,410 |
| | | | | | |

### Charitable Donations Expense     ACCOUNT NO. 699

| DATE | EXPLANATION | PR | DEBIT | CREDIT | BALANCE |
|------|-------------|----|-------|--------|---------|
| 2017 Nov. 30 | Balance | | | | 1,500 |

**Cumulative Problem**

Part 3          Echo Systems  (Cont'd.)

### ECHO SYSTEMS
#### Adjusted Trial Balance
#### December 31, 2017

| | Debit | Credit |
|---|---|---|
| | | |
| | | |
| | | |
| | | |
| | | |
| | | |
| | | |
| | | |
| | | |
| | | |
| | | |
| | | |
| | | |
| | | |
| | | |
| | | |
| | | |
| | | |
| | | |
| | | |
| | | |
| | | |
| | | |
| | | |
| | | |
| | | |
| | | |
| | | |
| | | |
| | | |
| | | |

Name:_____

**Cumulative Problem**

Part 4          Echo Systems (Cont'd.)

## ECHO SYSTEMS
### Income Statement
### For Three Months Ended December 31, 2017

| | | |
|---|---|---|
| | | |
| | | |
| | | |
| | | |
| | | |
| | | |
| | | |
| | | |
| | | |
| | | |
| | | |
| | | |
| | | |
| | | |
| | | |
| | | |
| | | |
| | | |
| | | |
| | | |
| | | |
| | | |
| | | |
| | | |
| | | |

## ECHO SYSTEMS
### Statement of Changes in Equity
### For Three Months Ended December 31, 2017

| | | |
|---|---|---|
| | | |
| | | |
| | | |
| | | |
| | | |
| | | |
| | | |
| | | |

Name:_____

**Cumulative Problem**

**Part 5**        **Echo Systems (Concl'd.)**

| ECHO SYSTEMS | | |
|---|---|---|
| Balance Sheet | | |
| December 31, 2017 | | |
|  |  |  |
|  |  |  |
|  |  |  |
|  |  |  |
|  |  |  |
|  |  |  |
|  |  |  |
|  |  |  |
|  |  |  |
|  |  |  |
|  |  |  |
|  |  |  |
|  |  |  |
|  |  |  |
|  |  |  |
|  |  |  |
|  |  |  |
|  |  |  |
|  |  |  |
|  |  |  |
|  |  |  |
|  |  |  |
|  |  |  |
|  |  |  |
|  |  |  |
|  |  |  |
|  |  |  |
|  |  |  |
|  |  |  |
|  |  |  |
|  |  |  |
|  |  |  |
|  |  |  |
|  |  |  |
|  |  |  |
|  |  |  |

Name:_____

## Quick Study 4-1

1. _____Equipment
2. _____Owner, withdrawals
3. _____Insurance expense

4. _____Prepaid insurance
5. _____Accounts receivable
6. _____Depreciation expense, equipment

## Quick Study 4-2

- see next page for QS 4-2 working paper

## Quick Study 4-3

_____
_____
_____
_____
_____
_____
_____
_____
_____
_____

## Quick Study 4-4

_____
_____
_____
_____
_____
_____
_____
_____
_____
_____
_____
_____
_____
_____
_____
_____
_____
_____
_____
_____
_____
_____

## Quick Study 4-2

| Account Title | Unadjusted Trial Balance Debit | Unadjusted Trial Balance Credit | Adjustments Debit | Adjustments Credit | Adjusted Trial Balance Debit | Adjusted Trial Balance Credit | Income Statement Debit | Income Statement Credit | Balance Sheet & Statement of Changes in Equity Debit | Balance Sheet & Statement of Changes in Equity Credit |
|---|---|---|---|---|---|---|---|---|---|---|
| Cash | 15 | | | | | | | | | |
| Accounts receivable | 22 | | | | | | | | | |
| Supplies | 25 | | | 8 | | | | | | |
| Ed Wolt, capital | | 40 | | | | | | | | |
| Ed Wolt, withdrawals | 12 | | | | | | | | | |
| Service Revenue | | 48 | | | | | | | | |
| Supplies expense | 14 | — | 8 | | | | | | | |
| Totals | 88 | 88 | 8 | 8 | | | | | | |
| | | | | | | | | | | |
| | | | | | | | | | | |
| | | | | | | | | | | |
| | | | | | | | | | | |

**Quick Study 4-5**

| Account | (1) Temporary? | (1) Permanent? | (2) Financial Statement? |
|---|---|---|---|
| a.  Accounts Payable | | | Balance Sheet |
| b.  Insurance Expense | | | Income Statement |
| c.  Delivery Vehicle | | | Balance Sheet |
| d.  Interest income | | | Income Statement |
| e.  Unearned Revenue | | | Balance Sheet |
| f.  Accumulated depreciation | | | Balance Sheet |
| g.  Stephos Petridis, Capital | | | Balance Sheet and Statement of Changes in Equity |
| h.  Depreciation Expense | | | Income Statement |
| i.  Stephos Petridis, withdrawals | | | Statement of Changes in Equity |
| j.  Wages Payable | | | Balance Sheet |
| k.  Prepaid Insurance | | | Balance Sheet |
| l.  Utility Expense | | | Income Statement |
| m. Building | | | Balance Sheet |
| n.  Supplies Expense | | | Income Statement |

**Quick Study 4-6**

_____
_____
_____
_____
_____
_____
_____
_____
_____
_____
_____
_____
_____
_____
_____
_____

**Quick Study 4-7**

**GENERAL JOURNAL**         Page_____

| Date | Account Titles and Explanation | PR | Debit | Credit |
|------|-------------------------------|----|-------|--------|
|  |  |  |  |  |
|  |  |  |  |  |
|  |  |  |  |  |
|  |  |  |  |  |
|  |  |  |  |  |
|  |  |  |  |  |
|  |  |  |  |  |
|  |  |  |  |  |
|  |  |  |  |  |
|  |  |  |  |  |
|  |  |  |  |  |
|  |  |  |  |  |
|  |  |  |  |  |
|  |  |  |  |  |
|  |  |  |  |  |
|  |  |  |  |  |
|  |  |  |  |  |
|  |  |  |  |  |
|  |  |  |  |  |

**Assets**
250

**Liabilities**
30

**Capital**
200

**Withdrawals**
20

**Revenue**
100

**Expenses**
60

**Income Summary**

Name:_____

**Quick Study 4-8**

### GENERAL JOURNAL

Page____

| Date | Account Titles and Explanation | PR | Debit | Credit |
|---|---|---|---|---|
|  |  |  |  |  |
|  |  |  |  |  |
|  |  |  |  |  |
|  |  |  |  |  |
|  |  |  |  |  |
|  |  |  |  |  |
|  |  |  |  |  |
|  |  |  |  |  |
|  |  |  |  |  |
|  |  |  |  |  |
|  |  |  |  |  |
|  |  |  |  |  |
|  |  |  |  |  |
|  |  |  |  |  |
|  |  |  |  |  |
|  |  |  |  |  |
|  |  |  |  |  |
|  |  |  |  |  |
|  |  |  |  |  |

| Assets | Liabilities |
|---|---|
| 250 | 110 |

| Capital | Withdrawals |
|---|---|
| 200 | 20 |

| Revenue | Expenses |
|---|---|
| 100 | 140 |

| | Income Summary |
|---|---|

Name:_____

**Quick Study 4-9**

| Post-Closing Trial Balance | | |
|---|---|---|
| | **Debit** | **Credit** |
| | | |
| | | |
| | | |
| | | |
| | | |
| | | |
| | | |
| | | |
| | | |

**Quick Study 4-10**

a. _____ Preparing the unadjusted trial balance.
b. _____ Preparing the post-closing trial balance.
c. _____ Journalizing and posting adjusting entries.
d. _____ Journalizing and posting closing entries.
e. _____ Preparing the financial statements.
f. _____ Journalizing transactions.
g. _____ Posting the transaction entries.
h. _____ Completing the work sheet.

**Quick Study 4-11**

1. *Property, Plant, equipment* Store equipment
2. *Current liabilities* Wages payable
3. *Current assets* Cash
4. *Non current liabilities* Notes payable (due in three years)
5. *Non Current investments* Land not currently used in business operations
6. *Current assets* Accounts receivable
7. *Intangible assets* Trademarks

## Quick Study 4-12

1. _h_ Depreciation expense, trucks
2. _g_ Lee Hale, capital
3. _d_ Interest receivable
4. _h_ Lee Hale, withdrawals
5. _c_ Automobiles
6. _f_ Notes payable (due in 3 years)
7. _e_ Accounts payable
8. _d_ Prepaid insurance
9. _b_ Land not currently used in business operations
10. _e_ Unearned services revenue

11. _c_ Accum. deprec., trucks
12. _d_ Cash
13. _c_ Building
14. _d_ Patent
15. _c_ Office equipment
16. _c_ Land (used in operations)
17. _h_ Repairs expense
18. _d_ Prepaid property taxes
19. _e_ Notes payable (due in 2 months)
20. _b_ Notes receivable (due in 2 years)

## Quick Study 4-13

| Partial Balance Sheet | | |
|---|---|---|
| | | |
| | | |
| | | |
| | | |
| | | |
| | | |
| | | |
| | | |
| | | |
| | | |
| | | |
| | | |
| | | |
| | | |

## *Quick Study 4-14

Name:_____

## Quick Study 4-15

_____
_____
_____
_____
_____
_____
_____
_____
_____
_____
_____

## Quick Study 4-16

|  | 2014 | 2013 |
|---|---|---|
| Debt to equity ratio |  |  |

Comments:
_____
_____
_____
_____
_____

## *Quick Study 4-17

### GENERAL JOURNAL

Page____

| Date | Account Titles and Explanation | PR | Debit | Credit |
|---|---|---|---|---|
|  |  |  |  |  |
|  |  |  |  |  |
|  |  |  |  |  |
|  |  |  |  |  |
|  |  |  |  |  |
|  |  |  |  |  |
|  |  |  |  |  |
|  |  |  |  |  |
|  |  |  |  |  |
|  |  |  |  |  |
|  |  |  |  |  |

# Chapter 4

Name:_____

## Exercise 4-1

| | | | | | |
|---|---|---|---|---|---|
| 1. | _____ | Roberta Jefferson, withdrawals | 9. | _____ | Cash |
| 2. | _____ | Interest income | 10. | _____ | Office supplies |
| 3. | _____ | Accum. deprec., machinery | 11. | _____ | Roberta Jefferson, capital |
| 4. | _____ | Service revenue | 12. | _____ | Wages payable |
| 5. | _____ | Accounts receivable | 13. | _____ | Machinery |
| 6. | _____ | Rent expense | 14. | _____ | Insurance expense |
| 7. | _____ | Deprec. exp., machinery | 15. | _____ | Interest expense |
| 8. | _____ | Accounts payable | 16. | _____ | Interest receivable |

## Exercise 4-2

| ACCOUNT | ADJUSTED TRIAL BALANCE Debit | ADJUSTED TRIAL BALANCE Credit | INCOME STATEMENT Debit | INCOME STATEMENT Credit | BALANCE SHEET AND STATEMENT OF CHANGES IN EQUITY Debit | BALANCE SHEET AND STATEMENT OF CHANGES IN EQUITY Credit |
|---|---|---|---|---|---|---|
| Cash | 21,000 | | | | | |
| Accounts receivable | 8,200 | | | | | |
| Trucks | 48,000 | | | | | |
| Accum. deprec., trucks | | 31,250 | | | | |
| Franchise | 6,500 | | | | | |
| Accounts payable | | 13,000 | | | | |
| Salaries payable | | 14,600 | | | | |
| Unearned revenue | | 2,450 | | | | |
| Bo Webber, capital | | 37,750 | | | | |
| Bo Webber, withdrls. | 7,200 | | | | | |
| Plumbing revenue | | 31,600 | | | | |
| Deprec. expense, trucks | 12,100 | | | | | |
| Salaries expense | 17,800 | | | | | |
| Rent expense | 6,000 | | | | | |
| Miscellaneous expense | 3,850 | | | | | |
| Totals | 130,650 | 130,650 | | | | |
| | | | | | | |
| | | | | | | |
| | | | | | | |

*Fundamental Accounting Principles*, 15ce, Working Papers

## Exercise 4-3

### Parts 1, 2, and 3

**Musical Sensations**

**Work Sheet**

**For Year Ended December 31, 2017**

| Account Title | Unadjusted Trial Balance | | Adjustments | | Adjusted Trial Balance | | Income Statement | | Balance Sheet and Statement of Changes in Equity | |
|---|---|---|---|---|---|---|---|---|---|---|
| | Debit | Credit | Debit | Credit | Debit | Credit | Debit | Credit | Debit | Credit |
| Cash | 7,500 | | | | | | | | | |
| Accounts receivable | 14,200 | | | | | | | | | |
| Office supplies | 790 | | | | | | | | | |
| Musical equipment | 125,000 | | | | | | | | | |
| Accum. dep., musical equip. | | 21,600 | | | | | | | | |
| Accounts payable | | 4,200 | | | | | | | | |
| Unearned performance rev. | | 12,400 | | | | | | | | |
| Jim Daley, capital | | 154,300 | | | | | | | | |
| Jim Daley, withdrawals | 52,000 | | | | | | | | | |
| Performance revenue | | 138,000 | | | | | | | | |
| Salaries expense | 86,000 | | | | | | | | | |
| Travelling expense | 45,010 | | | | | | | | | |
| Totals | 330,500 | 330,500 | | | | | | | | |

**Exercise 4-3 (concl'd.)**

**Part 4**

_____

_____

_____

_____

_____

Jim Daley, Capital

**Exercise 4-4**

**1(a)** _____

_____

**2(a)**                    **GENERAL JOURNAL**                    Page____

| Date | Account Titles and Explanation | PR | Debit | Credit |
|------|-------------------------------|----|-------|--------|
|      |                               |    |       |        |
|      |                               |    |       |        |
|      |                               |    |       |        |
|      |                               |    |       |        |

**3(a)**                                                    Owner's Capital

_____

_____

_____

_____

_____

**1(b)** _____

**2(b)**                    **GENERAL JOURNAL**                    Page____

| Date | Account Titles and Explanation | PR | Debit | Credit |
|------|-------------------------------|----|-------|--------|
|      |                               |    |       |        |
|      |                               |    |       |        |
|      |                               |    |       |        |
|      |                               |    |       |        |

**3(b)**                                                    Owner's Capital

_____

_____

_____

_____

**Exercise 4-5**

|  | Debit | Credit |
|---|---|---|
| Rent revenue |  | 99,000 |
| Salaries expense | 35,300 |  |
| Insurance expense | 4,400 |  |
| Dock rental expense | 12,000 |  |
| Boat supplies expense | 6,220 |  |
| Depreciation expense, boats | 21,500 | _____ |
| Totals |  |  |
| Profit | _____ | _____ |
| Totals | _____ | _____ |

**Closing Entries**

### GENERAL JOURNAL                                    Page_____

| Date | Account Titles and Explanation | PR | Debit | Credit |
|---|---|---|---|---|
|  |  |  |  |  |
|  |  |  |  |  |
|  |  |  |  |  |
|  |  |  |  |  |
|  |  |  |  |  |
|  |  |  |  |  |
|  |  |  |  |  |
|  |  |  |  |  |
|  |  |  |  |  |
|  |  |  |  |  |
|  |  |  |  |  |
|  |  |  |  |  |
|  |  |  |  |  |
|  |  |  |  |  |
|  |  |  |  |  |
|  |  |  |  |  |
|  |  |  |  |  |
|  |  |  |  |  |
|  |  |  |  |  |
|  |  |  |  |  |
|  |  |  |  |  |
|  |  |  |  |  |
|  |  |  |  |  |
|  |  |  |  |  |
|  |  |  |  |  |

Exercise 4-6

## GENERAL JOURNAL                                    Page_____

| Date | Account Titles and Explanation | PR | Debit | Credit |
|------|-------------------------------|----|-------|--------|
| 2017 30 | Plumbing Revenue | | 42,050 | |
| Apr | Income summary | | | 42,050 |
| | To close revenue to the inc summ | | | |
| | | | | |
| 30 | Income summary | | 32600 | |
| | Dep exp, Trucks | | | 4900 |
| | Salaries exp | | | 17800 |
| | Rent exp | | | 3000 |
| | Advertising exp | | | 6900 |
| | To close exp ac to inc summan | | | |
| | | | | |
| 30 | Income summary | | 9450 | |
| | Sid Willard, capital | | | 9450 |
| | To close income summ to capital | | | |
| | | | | |
| 30 | Sid Willard, capital | | 9600 | |
| | Sid Willard, Withdrawals | | | 9600 |
| | To close withdrawals to capital. | | | |
| | | | | |
| | | | | |

### Willard Co.
### Post-Closing Trial Balance
#### April 30, 2017

| Acct No. | Account | Debit | Credit |
|----------|---------|-------|--------|
| 101 | Cash | 3600 | |
| 106 | Accounts Receivable | 8500 | |
| 153 | Trucks | 26000 | |
| 154 | Accumulated dep, Trucks | | 8250 |
| 193 | Franchise | 13200 | |
| 201 | Accounts payable | | 9600 |
| 209 | Salaries payable | | 3200 |
| 233 | Unearned revenue | | 1300 |
| 301 | Sid Willard, capital | | 28950 |
| | Totals | $51,300 | $51,300 |

Sid Willard, capital

| (Withdraws) 9600 | 29100 |
| | 9450 (Profit) |
| | 28950 |

$29100 + 9450 - 9600 = 28950$

**Exercise 4-7**

### GENERAL JOURNAL                                    Page____

| Date | | Account Titles and Explanation | PR | Debit | Credit |
|---|---|---|---|---|---|
| 2017 | 31 | Subscription revenues | | 71000 | |
| January | | Interest income | | 450 | |
| | | Income summary | | | 71450 |
| | | To close subscrip rev to Income summary | | | |
| | | | | | |
| | 31 | Income summary | | 80000 | |
| | | Dep exp, equipment | | | 1500 |
| | | Rent exp | | | 17500 |
| | | Salaries exp. | | | 61000 |
| | | To close exp acc to inc summary | | | |
| | | | | | |
| | 31 | Trish Norris capital | | 8550 | |
| | | Income summary | | | 8550 |
| | | To close income summ to capital | | | |
| | | | | | |
| | 31 | Trish Norris, capital | | 19400 | |
| | | Trish Norris, withdrawals | | | 19400 |

**Exercise 4-8** To close withdrawals to capital.

**1.**

### Adjusted Trial Balance

| | Debit | Credit |
|---|---|---|
| | | |
| | | |
| | | |
| | | |
| | | |
| | | |
| | | |
| | | |
| | | |
| | | |
| | | |
| | | |
| | | |
| | | |
| | | |
| | | |
| | | |

Name:_____

**Exercise 4-8 (cont'd.)**

**Explanation:** _____

_____

_____

_____

_____

_____

**2. Closing entries:**

**GENERAL JOURNAL**　　　　　　　　　　　　　　　Page_____

| Date | Account Titles and Explanation | PR | Debit | Credit |
|---|---|---|---|---|
| | | | | |
| | | | | |
| | | | | |
| | | | | |
| | | | | |
| | | | | |
| | | | | |
| | | | | |
| | | | | |
| | | | | |
| | | | | |
| | | | | |
| | | | | |
| | | | | |
| | | | | |
| | | | | |
| | | | | |
| | | | | |
| | | | | |
| | | | | |
| | | | | |

**3.**

**Nick Stilz, Capital**
_____

Name:_____

**Exercise 4-9**

## GENERAL JOURNAL

| Date | Account Titles and Explanation | PR | Debit | Credit |
|------|-------------------------------|----|-------|--------|
|      |                               |    |       |        |
|      |                               |    |       |        |
|      |                               |    |       |        |
|      |                               |    |       |        |
|      |                               |    |       |        |
|      |                               |    |       |        |
|      |                               |    |       |        |
|      |                               |    |       |        |
|      |                               |    |       |        |
|      |                               |    |       |        |
|      |                               |    |       |        |
|      |                               |    |       |        |
|      |                               |    |       |        |
|      |                               |    |       |        |
|      |                               |    |       |        |
|      |                               |    |       |        |
|      |                               |    |       |        |

Name:_____

**Exercise 4-9 (concl'd.)**

**Posting to Accounts:**

| Assets | | | Liabilities | |
|---|---|---|---|---|
| Bal. Dec. 31 142,000 | | | 51,000 | Bal. Dec. 31 |

| Marcy Jones, Capital | | | Marcy Jones, Withdrawals | |
|---|---|---|---|---|
| | 71,800 Bal. Dec. 31 | | Bal. Dec. 31 38,000 | |

| Services Revenue | | | Salaries Expense | |
|---|---|---|---|---|
| | 103,000 Bal. Dec. 31 | | Bal. Dec. 31 27,000 | |

| Rent Expense | | | Insurance Expense | |
|---|---|---|---|---|
| Bal. Dec. 31 9,100 | | | Bal. Dec. 31 1,500 | |

| Depreciation Expense | | | Income Summary | |
|---|---|---|---|---|
| Bal. Dec. 31 8,200 | | | | |

**Exercise 4-10**

**Post-Closing Trial Balance**

| | Debit | Credit |
|---|---|---|
| | | |
| | | |
| | | |
| | | |
| | | |
| | | |
| | | |

Name:_____

**Exercise 4-11**

1. _____

2.                     **GENERAL JOURNAL**                     Page____

| Date | Account Titles and Explanation | PR | Debit | Credit |
|------|-------------------------------|----|-------|--------|
|      |                               |    |       |        |
|      |                               |    |       |        |
|      |                               |    |       |        |
|      |                               |    |       |        |
|      |                               |    |       |        |
|      |                               |    |       |        |

3.                                                    **Jozef Jones, Capital**

_____

_____

_____

_____

**Exercise 4-12**

a.

| Account Title | Adjusted Trial Balance Debit | Credit |
|---------------|------:|------:|
| Accounts payable............................................................... |  | $ 31,000 |
| Accounts receivable ......................................................... | $ 48,000 |  |
| Accumulated depreciation, equipment ............................... |  | 9,000 |
| Accumulated depreciation, truck....................................... |  | 21,000 |
| Cash .................................................................................. | 14,400 |  |
| Depreciation expense ....................................................... | 3,800 |  |
| Equipment ........................................................................ | 19,000 |  |
| Franchise........................................................................... | 21,000 |  |
| Gas and oil expense.......................................................... | 7,500 |  |
| Interest expense ............................................................... | 450 |  |
| Interest payable................................................................. |  | 750 |
| Land not currently used in business operations....................... | 148,000 |  |
| Long-term notes payable.................................................... |  | 35,000 |
| Notes payable, due February 1, 2018................................. |  | 7,000 |
| Notes receivable................................................................ | 6,000 |  |
| Patent ............................................................................... | 7,000 |  |
| Prepaid Rent...................................................................... | 14,000 |  |
| Rent expense .................................................................... | 51,000 |  |
| Repair revenue.................................................................. |  | 266,000 |
| Repair supplies .................................................................. | 13,100 |  |
| Repair supplies expense .................................................... | 29,000 |  |
| Truck.................................................................................. | 26,000 |  |
| Unearned repair revenue .................................................. |  | 12,600 |
| Vic Sopik, capital .............................................................. |  | 74,900 |
| Vic Sopik, withdrawals ..................................................... | 49,000 |  |
| Totals ................................................................................ | $457,250 | $457,250 |

**Exercise 4-12 (concl'd.)**

b. _____**Vic Sopik, Capital**_____

*Analysis component:*        _____

_____

_____

_____

_____

**Exercise 4-13**                                        **Calculations:**

a.    **Current assets =**

      [        ]

b.    **Property, plant and equipment =**

      [        ]

c.    **Intangible assets =**

      [        ]

d.    **Non-current investments =**

      [        ]

e.    **Total assets =**

      [        ]

f.    **Current liabilities =**

      [        ]

g.    **Non-current liabilities =**

      [        ]

h.    **Total liabilities =**

      [        ]

i.    **Total liabilities and equity =**

      [        ]

**Exercise 4-14**

| Sunshine Sushi | | | |
|---|---|---|---|
| Balance Sheet | | | |
| December 31, 2017 | | | |
| **Assets** | | | |
| Current assets: | | | |
| | | | |
| | | | |
| | | | |
| Total current assets | | | |
| Non-current investments: | | | |
| | | | |
| Property, plant and equipment: | | | |
| | | | |
| | | | |
| | | | |
| | | | |
| | | | |
| Total assets | | | |
| **Liabilities** | | | |
| Current liabilities: | | | |
| | | | |
| | | | |
| | | | |
| Total current liabilities......................................... | | | |
| Non-current liabilities: | | | |
| | | | |
| Total liabilities | | | |
| Equity | | | |
| | | | |
| Total liabilities and equity .......................................... | | | |

|  | Balance Sheet |  |  |  |
|---|---|---|---|---|
|  |  |  |  |  |
|  |  |  |  |  |
|  |  |  |  |  |
|  |  |  |  |  |
|  |  |  |  |  |
|  |  |  |  |  |
|  |  |  |  |  |
|  |  |  |  |  |
|  |  |  |  |  |
|  |  |  |  |  |
|  |  |  |  |  |
|  |  |  |  |  |
|  |  |  |  |  |
|  |  |  |  |  |
|  |  |  |  |  |
|  |  |  |  |  |
|  |  |  |  |  |
|  |  |  |  |  |
|  |  |  |  |  |
|  |  |  |  |  |
|  |  |  |  |  |
|  |  |  |  |  |
|  |  |  |  |  |
|  |  |  |  |  |
|  |  |  |  |  |
|  |  |  |  |  |
|  |  |  |  |  |
|  |  |  |  |  |
|  |  |  |  |  |
|  |  |  |  |  |
|  |  |  |  |  |
|  |  |  |  |  |

**Exercise 4-16**

### HANSON TRUCKING COMPANY
**Balance Sheet**
### December 31, 2017

| | $ | $ | $ |
|---|---|---|---|
| Assets | | | |
| Current assets: | | | |
| Cash | | 13000 | |
| Accounts receivable | | 29600 | |
| Office supplies | | 3100 | |
| Total current assets | | | $ 45700 |
| Property, plant & equipment: | | | |
| Land | | 275000 | |
| Trucks | 170000 | | |
| less: Accumulated depr. | 46000 | 124000 | |
| Total property, plant, equip | | | 399000 |
| Total assets | | | 444700 |
| | | | |
| Liabilities | | | |
| Current liabilities: | | | |
| Accounts payable | 31000 | | |
| Interest payable | 400 | | |
| Total current liabilities | | 31400 | |
| Long term notes payable | | 152000 | |
| Total liabilities | | | 183400 |
| | | | |
| Equity | | | |
| Stanley Hanson, capital | | | 261300 |
| Total liabilities & equity | | | 444700 |
| | | | |
| Calculation: | | | |
| $206200 - $19000 + $168000 | | | |
| - $22500 - $58000 - $6500 | | | |
| - $6900 = $261,300 | | | |
| OR | | | |
| Total assets - Total liabilities | | | |
| = $444700 - $163400 | | | |
| = $261,300 | | | |

Name:_____

**Exercise 4-17**

a. _____

_____

_____

_____

b. Journalizing:

### GENERAL JOURNAL

Page____

| Date | Account Titles and Explanation | PR | Debit | Credit |
|------|-------------------------------|----|-------|--------|
|      |                               |    |       |        |
|      |                               |    |       |        |
|      |                               |    |       |        |
|      |                               |    |       |        |
|      |                               |    |       |        |
|      |                               |    |       |        |
|      |                               |    |       |        |
|      |                               |    |       |        |
|      |                               |    |       |        |
|      |                               |    |       |        |
|      |                               |    |       |        |
|      |                               |    |       |        |
|      |                               |    |       |        |
|      |                               |    |       |        |
|      |                               |    |       |        |

c. _____

### Unadjusted Trial Balance

|  | Debit | Credit |
|--|-------|--------|
|  |       |        |
|  |       |        |
|  |       |        |
|  |       |        |
|  |       |        |
|  |       |        |
|  |       |        |
|  |       |        |
|  |       |        |
|  |       |        |
|  |       |        |

Name:_____

**Exercise 4-17 (cont'd.)**

**b, d, g.** Posting journal entries in (b), adjustments in (d), and closing entries in (g):

| Cash | |
|---|---|
| Bal. Dec. 31/16  2,000 | |

| Leda Svenson, Capital | |
|---|---|
| | 17,100  Bal. Dec. 31/16 |

| Accounts Receivable | |
|---|---|
| Bal. Dec. 31/16  5,000 | |

| Leda Svenson, Withdrawals | |
|---|---|
| Bal. Dec. 31/16  -0- | |

| Tutoring Revenue | |
|---|---|
| | -0-  Bal. Dec. 31/16 |

| Prepaid Rent | |
|---|---|
| Bal. Dec. 31/16  3,000 | |

| Office Equipment | |
|---|---|
| Bal. Dec. 31/16  20,000 | |

| Rent Expense | |
|---|---|
| Bal. Dec. 31/16  -0- | |

| Accum. Deprec., Office Equip. | |
|---|---|
| | 10,000  Bal. Dec. 31/16 |

| Depreciation Expense | |
|---|---|
| Bal. Dec. 31/16  -0- | |

| Unearned Revenue | |
|---|---|
| | 2,900  Bal. Dec. 31/16 |

| Advertising Expense | |
|---|---|
| Bal. Dec. 31/16  -0- | |

| Income Summary | |
|---|---|
| | |

**Exercise 4-17 (cont'd.)**

**d. Journalize adjustments:**

**GENERAL JOURNAL**                                    Page_____

| Date | Account Titles and Explanation | PR | Debit | Credit |
|---|---|---|---|---|
|  |  |  |  |  |
|  |  |  |  |  |
|  |  |  |  |  |
|  |  |  |  |  |
|  |  |  |  |  |
|  |  |  |  |  |
|  |  |  |  |  |
|  |  |  |  |  |
|  |  |  |  |  |
|  |  |  |  |  |
|  |  |  |  |  |
|  |  |  |  |  |

**e.**

**Adjusted Trial Balance**

|  | Debit | Credit |
|---|---|---|
|  |  |  |
|  |  |  |
|  |  |  |
|  |  |  |
|  |  |  |
|  |  |  |
|  |  |  |
|  |  |  |
|  |  |  |
|  |  |  |
|  |  |  |
|  |  |  |
|  |  |  |

Name:_____

**Exercise 4-17 (cont'd.)**

**f. Financial statement preparation:**

### Income Statement

| | | |
|---|---|---|
| | | |
| | | |
| | | |
| | | |
| | | |
| | | |
| | | |
| | | |
| | | |

### Statement of Changes in Equity

| | | |
|---|---|---|
| | | |
| | | |
| | | |
| | | |
| | | |
| | | |

### Balance Sheet

| | | | |
|---|---|---|---|
| | | | |
| | | | |
| | | | |
| | | | |
| | | | |
| | | | |
| | | | |
| | | | |
| | | | |
| | | | |
| | | | |
| | | | |
| | | | |
| | | | |

Name:_____

**Exercise 4-17 (cont'd.)**

**g. Journalize closing entries:**

### GENERAL JOURNAL

Page_____

| Date | | Account Titles and Explanation | PR | Debit | Credit |
|---|---|---|---|---|---|
| | | | | | |
| | | | | | |
| | | | | | |
| | | | | | |
| | | | | | |
| | | | | | |
| | | | | | |
| | | | | | |
| | | | | | |
| | | | | | |
| | | | | | |
| | | | | | |
| | | | | | |
| | | | | | |
| | | | | | |
| | | | | | |
| | | | | | |
| | | | | | |
| | | | | | |
| | | | | | |
| | | | | | |

**h.**

### Post-Closing Trial Balance

| | Debit | Credit |
|---|---|---|
| | | |
| | | |
| | | |
| | | |
| | | |
| | | |
| | | |
| | | |
| | | |
| | | |
| | | |
| | | |
| | | |
| | | |
| | | |

Name:_____

## Exercise 4-18

1. Prepare journal entries:

### GENERAL JOURNAL

Page_____

| Date | Account Titles and Explanation | PR | Debit | Credit |
|---|---|---|---|---|
| | | | | |
| | | | | |
| | | | | |
| | | | | |
| | | | | |
| | | | | |
| | | | | |
| | | | | |
| | | | | |
| | | | | |
| | | | | |
| | | | | |
| | | | | |
| | | | | |
| | | | | |
| | | | | |
| | | | | |
| | | | | |
| | | | | |
| | | | | |
| | | | | |
| | | | | |
| | | | | |
| | | | | |
| | | | | |
| | | | | |
| | | | | |
| | | | | |
| | | | | |
| | | | | |
| | | | | |
| | | | | |
| | | | | |
| | | | | |
| | | | | |
| | | | | |
| | | | | |
| | | | | |
| | | | | |
| | | | | |
| | | | | |
| | | | | |

**Exercise 4-18 (continued)**

**2, 3 and 5. Post journal entries, adjusting entries and closing entries to the general ledger :**

**Ledger as of May 31 (using the T-account format):**

| Cash | Supplies | Prepaid Insurance |
|------|----------|-------------------|

| Printer | Laptop | Accum. Dep., Laptop |
|---------|--------|---------------------|

|  | Accum. Dep., Printer | Accounts Payable |
|--|----------------------|------------------|

| Unearned Tour Revenue | Wages Payable | Emily Lee, Capital |
|-----------------------|---------------|--------------------|

| Emily Lee, Withdrawals | | |
|------------------------|--|--|

Name:_____

Exercise 4-18 (continued)

*Parts 2, 3, 5*

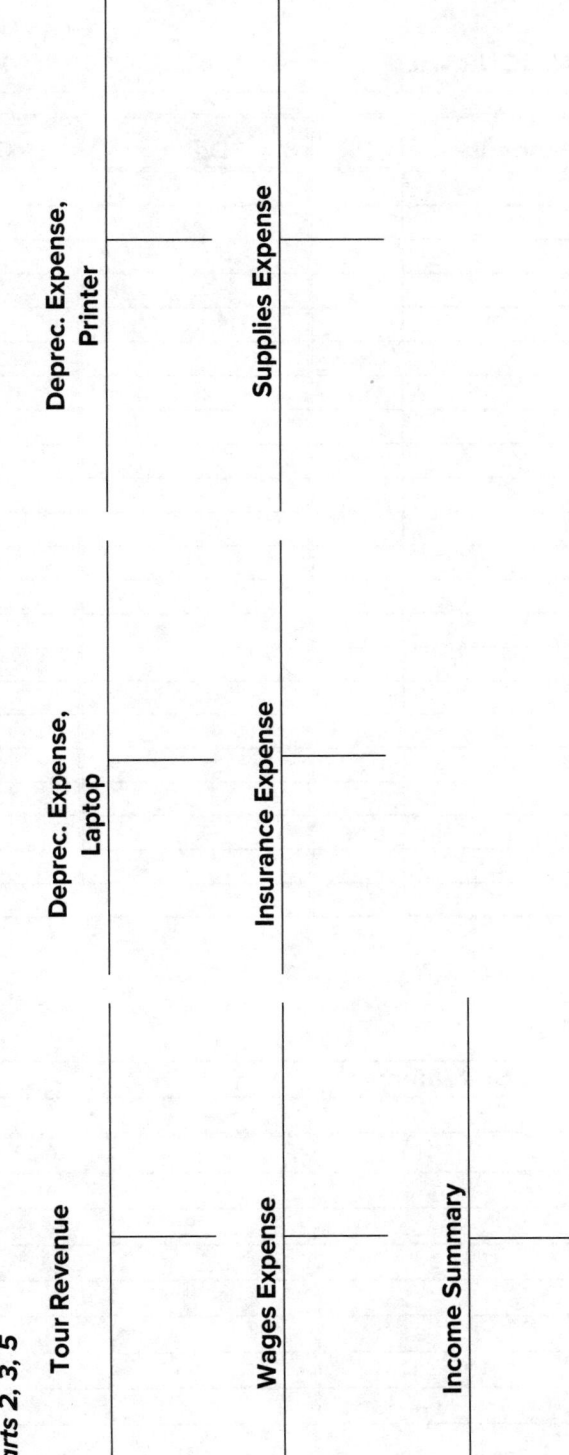

Tour Revenue

Deprec. Expense, Laptop

Deprec. Expense, Printer

Wages Expense

Insurance Expense

Supplies Expense

Income Summary

**Exercise 4-18 (cont'd.)**

**3. Prepare adjusting entries:**

GENERAL JOURNAL                                          Page_____

| Date | Account Titles and Explanation | PR | Debit | Credit |
|------|-------------------------------|----|-------|--------|
|      |                               |    |       |        |
|      |                               |    |       |        |
|      |                               |    |       |        |
|      |                               |    |       |        |
|      |                               |    |       |        |
|      |                               |    |       |        |
|      |                               |    |       |        |
|      |                               |    |       |        |
|      |                               |    |       |        |
|      |                               |    |       |        |
|      |                               |    |       |        |
|      |                               |    |       |        |
|      |                               |    |       |        |
|      |                               |    |       |        |
|      |                               |    |       |        |
|      |                               |    |       |        |
|      |                               |    |       |        |
|      |                               |    |       |        |
|      |                               |    |       |        |
|      |                               |    |       |        |
|      |                               |    |       |        |
|      |                               |    |       |        |

**4. Financial statement preparation:**

Income Statement

| | | |
|---|---|---|
|   |   |   |
|   |   |   |
|   |   |   |
|   |   |   |
|   |   |   |
|   |   |   |
|   |   |   |
|   |   |   |
|   |   |   |
|   |   |   |
|   |   |   |

**Exercise 4-18 (cont'd.)**

---

### Statement of Changes in Equity

| | | |
|---|---|---|
| | | |
| | | |
| | | |
| | | |
| | | |
| | | |

---

### Balance Sheet

| | | | |
|---|---|---|---|
| | | | |
| | | | |
| | | | |
| | | | |
| | | | |
| | | | |
| | | | |
| | | | |
| | | | |
| | | | |
| | | | |
| | | | |
| | | | |
| | | | |
| | | | |
| | | | |
| | | | |
| | | | |
| | | | |
| | | | |
| | | | |
| | | | |

**Exercise 4-18 (cont'd.)**

**5. Journalize closing entries:**

## GENERAL JOURNAL                                      Page_____

| Date | Account Titles and Explanation | PR | Debit | Credit |
|------|-------------------------------|----|-------|--------|
|      |                               |    |       |        |
|      |                               |    |       |        |
|      |                               |    |       |        |
|      |                               |    |       |        |
|      |                               |    |       |        |
|      |                               |    |       |        |
|      |                               |    |       |        |
|      |                               |    |       |        |
|      |                               |    |       |        |
|      |                               |    |       |        |
|      |                               |    |       |        |
|      |                               |    |       |        |
|      |                               |    |       |        |
|      |                               |    |       |        |
|      |                               |    |       |        |
|      |                               |    |       |        |
|      |                               |    |       |        |
|      |                               |    |       |        |

**6.** _____

## Post-Closing Trial Balance

|  | Debit | Credit |
|--|-------|--------|
|  |       |        |
|  |       |        |
|  |       |        |
|  |       |        |
|  |       |        |
|  |       |        |
|  |       |        |
|  |       |        |
|  |       |        |
|  |       |        |
|  |       |        |
|  |       |        |
|  |       |        |
|  |       |        |

Name:_____

**\*Exercise 4-19**

_____
_____
_____
_____
_____
_____
_____
_____
_____
_____
_____
_____
_____
_____
_____
_____
_____
_____
_____

**Exercise 4-20**

|  | 2013 | 2012 |
|---|---|---|
| **Current Ratio** |  |  |
| **Quick Ratio** |  |  |

**Comments:** _____
_____
_____
_____
_____
_____
_____
_____
_____
_____
_____
_____

### Exercise 4-21

|                     | 2013 | 2012 |
|---------------------|------|------|
| Debt to equity ratio |      |      |

**Comments:** _____

_____

_____

_____

_____

_____

_____

_____

_____

_____

_____

_____

### *Exercise 4-22

**GENERAL JOURNAL**                                    Page_____

| Date | | Account Titles and Explanation | PR | Debit | Credit |
|------|--|-------------------------------|----|-------|--------|
|      |  |                               |    |       |        |
|      |  |                               |    |       |        |
|      |  |                               |    |       |        |
|      |  |                               |    |       |        |
|      |  |                               |    |       |        |
|      |  |                               |    |       |        |
|      |  |                               |    |       |        |
|      |  |                               |    |       |        |
|      |  |                               |    |       |        |

Name:_____

*Exercise 4-23

1. Adjusting entries:

GENERAL JOURNAL          Page _____

| Date | Account Titles and Explanation | PR | Debit | Credit |
|------|-------------------------------|----|-------|--------|
|      |                               |    |       |        |
|      |                               |    |       |        |
|      |                               |    |       |        |
|      |                               |    |       |        |
|      |                               |    |       |        |
|      |                               |    |       |        |
|      |                               |    |       |        |
|      |                               |    |       |        |
|      |                               |    |       |        |
|      |                               |    |       |        |

2. Subsequent entries without reversing:

GENERAL JOURNAL          Page _____

| Date | Account Titles and Explanation | PR | Debit | Credit |
|------|-------------------------------|----|-------|--------|
|      |                               |    |       |        |
|      |                               |    |       |        |
|      |                               |    |       |        |
|      |                               |    |       |        |
|      |                               |    |       |        |
|      |                               |    |       |        |
|      |                               |    |       |        |
|      |                               |    |       |        |
|      |                               |    |       |        |
|      |                               |    |       |        |
|      |                               |    |       |        |
|      |                               |    |       |        |
|      |                               |    |       |        |
|      |                               |    |       |        |
|      |                               |    |       |        |
|      |                               |    |       |        |
|      |                               |    |       |        |
|      |                               |    |       |        |
|      |                               |    |       |        |
|      |                               |    |       |        |
|      |                               |    |       |        |
|      |                               |    |       |        |

*Exercise 4-23 (concl'd.)

3. Reversing entries and subsequent entries:

GENERAL JOURNAL                    Page _____

| Date | Account Titles and Explanation | PR | Debit | Credit |
|------|-------------------------------|----|-------|--------|
|  |  |  |  |  |
|  |  |  |  |  |
|  |  |  |  |  |
|  |  |  |  |  |
|  |  |  |  |  |
|  |  |  |  |  |
|  |  |  |  |  |
|  |  |  |  |  |
|  |  |  |  |  |
|  |  |  |  |  |
|  |  |  |  |  |
|  |  |  |  |  |
|  |  |  |  |  |
|  |  |  |  |  |
|  |  |  |  |  |
|  |  |  |  |  |
|  |  |  |  |  |
|  |  |  |  |  |
|  |  |  |  |  |
|  |  |  |  |  |
|  |  |  |  |  |
|  |  |  |  |  |
|  |  |  |  |  |
|  |  |  |  |  |
|  |  |  |  |  |
|  |  |  |  |  |
|  |  |  |  |  |

## Problem 4-1A

### Parts 1, 2, and 3

Nanimahoo Rentals

Work Sheet

For Year Ended March 31, 2017

| Account Title | Unadjusted Trial Balance | | Adjustments | | Adjusted Trial Balance | | Income Statement | | Balance Sheet and Statement of Changes in Equity | |
|---|---|---|---|---|---|---|---|---|---|---|
| | Debit | Credit | Debit | Credit | Debit | Credit | Debit | Credit | Debit | Credit |
| Cash | 7,000 | | | | | | | | | |
| Rent receivable | 31,000 | | | | | | | | | |
| Office supplies | 2,250 | | | | | | | | | |
| Notes receivable, due 2020 | 46,000 | | | | | | | | | |
| Furniture | 16,000 | | | | | | | | | |
| Building | 216,000 | | | | | | | | | |
| Land | 41,000 | | | | | | | | | |
| Patent | 9,600 | | | | | | | | | |
| Accounts payable | | 13,750 | | | | | | | | |
| Long-term note payable | | 175,000 | | | | | | | | |
| Stephen Silva, capital | | 90,250 | | | | | | | | |
| tephen Silva, withdrawals | 92,000 | | | | | | | | | |
| Rent revenue | | 328,800 | | | | | | | | |
| Office salaries expense | 52,000 | | | | | | | | | |
| Interest expense | 5,250 | | | | | | | | | |
| Advertising expense | 14,600 | | | | | | | | | |
| Janitorial expense | 41,000 | | | | | | | | | |
| Utilities expense | 34,100 | | | | | | | | | |
| Totals | 607,800 | 607,800 | | | | | | | | |

**Problem 4-2A**

**Parts 1, 2, and 3**

Trenton Consulting

Work Sheet

For Year Ended June 30, 2017

| Account Title | Unadjusted Trial Balance | | Adjustments | | Adjusted Trial Balance | | Income Statement | | Balance Sheet and Statement of Changes in Equity | |
|---|---|---|---|---|---|---|---|---|---|---|
| | Debit | Credit | Debit | Credit | Debit | Credit | Debit | Credit | Debit | Credit |
| Cash | 680 | | | | | | | | | |
| Accounts receivable | 2,900 | | | | | | | | | |
| Prepaid rent | 3,660 | | | | | | | | | |
| Equipment | 9,600 | | | | | | | | | |
| Accounts payable | | 1,730 | | | | | | | | |
| Toni Trenton, capital | | 26,650 | | | | | | | | |
| Toni Trenton, withdrawals | 6,880 | | | | | | | | | |
| Consulting revenue | | 30,200 | | | | | | | | |
| Wages expense | 24,920 | | | | | | | | | |
| Insurance expense | 1,620 | | | | | | | | | |
| Rent expense | 8,320 | | | | | | | | | |
| Totals | 58,580 | 58,580 | | | | | | | | |

**Problem 4-2A (concl'd.)**

**Part 4**

| | Toni Trenton, Capital |
|---|---|
| _____ | |
| _____ | |
| _____ | |
| _____ | |

*Analysis component:*

_____

_____

_____

_____

_____

_____

**Problem 4-3A**

**Part 1**

Challenger Construction

Work Sheet

For Year Ended September 30, 2017

| Account Title | Unadjusted Trial Balance | | Adjustments | | Adjusted Trial Balance | | Income Statement | | Balance Sheet and Statement of Changes in Equity | |
|---|---|---|---|---|---|---|---|---|---|---|
| | Debit | Credit | Debit | Credit | Debit | Credit | Debit | Credit | Debit | Credit |
| Cash | 22,000 | | | | | | | | | |
| Supplies | 17,200 | | | | | | | | | |
| Prepaid insurance | 9,600 | | | | | | | | | |
| Land not currently used | 50,000 | | | | | | | | | |
| Equipment | 106,000 | | | | | | | | | |
| Accum. deprec., equipment | | 40,500 | | | | | | | | |
| Copyright | 6,000 | | | | | | | | | |
| Accounts payable | | 8,100 | | | | | | | | |
| Interest payable | | | | | | | | | | |
| Wages payable | | | | | | | | | | |
| Long-term notes payable | | 50,000 | | | | | | | | |
| Chris Challenger, capital | | 71,000 | | | | | | | | |
| Chris Challenger, withdrawals | 68,000 | | | | | | | | | |
| Construction revenue | | 255,620 | | | | | | | | |
| Deprec. Expense, equipment | | | | | | | | | | |
| Wages expense | 96,000 | | | | | | | | | |
| Interest expense | 1,200 | | | | | | | | | |
| Insurance expense | | | | | | | | | | |
| Rent expense | 26,400 | | | | | | | | | |
| Supplies expense | | | | | | | | | | |
| Business taxes expense | 10,000 | | | | | | | | | |
| Repairs expense | 5,020 | | | | | | | | | |
| Utilities expense | 7,800 | | | | | | | | | |
| Totals | 425,220 | 425,220 | | | | | | | | |

Name:_____

**Problem 4-3A (cont'd.)**

**Part 2**
**Adjusting entries:**

**GENERAL JOURNAL** Page____

| Date | Account Titles and Explanation | PR | Debit | Credit |
|------|-------------------------------|----|-------|--------|
| a.   |                               |    |       |        |
|      |                               |    |       |        |
|      |                               |    |       |        |
|      |                               |    |       |        |
| b.   |                               |    |       |        |
|      |                               |    |       |        |
|      |                               |    |       |        |
|      |                               |    |       |        |
| c.   |                               |    |       |        |
|      |                               |    |       |        |
|      |                               |    |       |        |
|      |                               |    |       |        |
| d.   |                               |    |       |        |
|      |                               |    |       |        |
|      |                               |    |       |        |
|      |                               |    |       |        |
| e.   |                               |    |       |        |
|      |                               |    |       |        |
|      |                               |    |       |        |
|      |                               |    |       |        |
| f.   |                               |    |       |        |
|      |                               |    |       |        |
|      |                               |    |       |        |
|      |                               |    |       |        |
|      |                               |    |       |        |

**Problem 4-3A (cont'd.)**

**Part 2**
**Closing entries:**

**GENERAL JOURNAL**                                    Page_____

| Date | | Account Titles and Explanation | PR | Debit | Credit |
|---|---|---|---|---|---|
| | | | | | |
| | | | | | |
| | | | | | |
| | | | | | |
| | | | | | |
| | | | | | |
| | | | | | |
| | | | | | |
| | | | | | |
| | | | | | |
| | | | | | |
| | | | | | |
| | | | | | |
| | | | | | |
| | | | | | |
| | | | | | |
| | | | | | |
| | | | | | |
| | | | | | |
| | | | | | |
| | | | | | |
| | | | | | |
| | | | | | |
| | | | | | |
| | | | | | |
| | | | | | |
| | | | | | |
| | | | | | |
| | | | | | |
| | | | | | |
| | | | | | |
| | | | | | |
| | | | | | |
| | | | | | |
| | | | | | |

Name:_____

**Problem 4-3A (cont'd.)**

**Part 3**

| Income Statement | | |
|---|---|---|
| | | |
| | | |
| | | |
| | | |
| | | |
| | | |
| | | |
| | | |
| | | |
| | | |
| | | |
| | | |
| | | |
| | | |
| | | |
| | | |
| | | |
| | | |
| | | |
| | | |
| | | |
| | | |
| | | |
| | | |

| Statement of Changes in Equity | | |
|---|---|---|
| | | |
| | | |
| | | |
| | | |
| | | |
| | | |
| | | |
| | | |
| | | |

Name:_____

**Problem 4-3A (concl'd.)**

| | Balance Sheet | | |
|---|---|---|---|
| | | | |
| | | | |
| | | | |
| | | | |
| | | | |
| | | | |
| | | | |
| | | | |
| | | | |
| | | | |
| | | | |
| | | | |
| | | | |
| | | | |
| | | | |
| | | | |
| | | | |
| | | | |
| | | | |
| | | | |
| | | | |
| | | | |
| | | | |
| | | | |
| | | | |
| | | | |
| | | | |
| | | | |
| | | | |
| | | | |
| | | | |

*Analysis component:*

a._____

_____

_____

b._____

_____

_____

**Problem 4-4A**

| | | | |
|---|---|---|---|
| **Part 1** | **GENERAL JOURNAL** | | Page_____ |

| Date | Account Titles and Explanation | PR | Debit | Credit |
|---|---|---|---|---|
| 2017 Dec | 31 Repair Revenue | | 157630 | |
| | Income summary | | | 157630 |
| | To close revenue to the inc summn | | | |
| | | | | |
| | 31 Income summary | | 174990 | |
| | Dep exp, equipment | | | 8500 |
| | Wages exp | | | 104500 |
| | Insurance exp | | | 1900 |
| | Rent exp | | | 52350 |
| | Office supplies exp | | | 4800 |
| | Utilities exp | | | 2940 |
| | To close exp act to inc sum | | | |
| | | | | |
| | 31 Mike Yang, capited | | 17,360 | |
| | Income summary | | | 17,360 |
| | To close incom sum to cap | | | |
| | | | | |
| | 31 Mike Yang, capital | | 36000 | |
| | Mike Yang, withdrawals | | | 36000 |
| | To close withdrawals | | | |
| | to capital | | | |
| | | | | |
| | | | | |
| | | | | |

**Problem 4-4A**

**Part 2**

My Autobody
**Post-Closing Trial Balance**
December 31, 2017

| Acct No. | Account | Debit | Credit |
|---|---|---|---|
| 101 | Cash | 28000 | |
| 124 | Shop supplies | 1800 | |
| 128 | Prepaid insurance | 4200 | |
| 167 | Equipment | 88000 | |
| 168 | Accumulated dep. equip | | 7500 |
| 201 | Accounts payable | | 19000 |
| 210 | Wages payable | | 8860 |
| 301 | Mike Yang, capital | | 86640 |
| | Totals | $122000 | $122000 |
| | | | |
| | | | |
| | | | |

**Problem 4-5A**                          *Name* _____

**Income Statement**

| | | |
|---|---|---|
| | | |
| | | |
| | | |
| | | |
| | | |
| | | |
| | | |
| | | |
| | | |
| | | |
| | | |
| | | |
| | | |

**Statement of Changes in Equity**

| | | |
|---|---|---|
| | | |
| | | |
| | | |
| | | |

**Problem 4-5A (concl'd.)**

|  | Balance Sheet | | |
|---|---|---|---|
|  |  |  |  |
|  |  |  |  |
|  |  |  |  |
|  |  |  |  |
|  |  |  |  |
|  |  |  |  |
|  |  |  |  |
|  |  |  |  |
|  |  |  |  |
|  |  |  |  |
|  |  |  |  |
|  |  |  |  |
|  |  |  |  |
|  |  |  |  |
|  |  |  |  |
|  |  |  |  |
|  |  |  |  |
|  |  |  |  |
|  |  |  |  |
|  |  |  |  |
|  |  |  |  |
|  |  |  |  |
|  |  |  |  |
|  |  |  |  |
|  |  |  |  |
|  |  |  |  |
|  |  |  |  |
|  |  |  |  |
|  |  |  |  |
|  |  |  |  |
|  |  |  |  |
|  |  |  |  |
|  |  |  |  |
|  |  |  |  |

*Analysis component:*

_____
_____
_____
_____
_____
_____
_____

**Problem 4-6A**

## GENERAL JOURNAL

Page_____

| Date | | Account Titles and Explanation | PR | Debit | Credit |
|---|---|---|---|---|---|
| 2017 | | | | | |
| Dec | 31 | Professional rev | | 206,480 | |
| | | Rent revenue | | 26000 | |
| | | Income summary | | | 232,480 |
| | | To close the rev accounts. | | | |
| | | | | | |
| | 31 | Income summary | | 135,010 | |
| | | Dep exp, building | | | 20000 |
| | | Dep exp, equipment | | | 8000 |
| | | wages expense | | | 64000 |
| | | interest expense | | | 610 |
| | | Insurance expense | | | 18000 |
| | | Supplies expense | | | 12800 |
| | | Telephone exp. | | | 4400 |
| | | Utilities exp | | | 7200 |
| | | To close expense accounts. | | | |
| | | | | | |
| | 31 | Income summary | | 97470 | |
| | | Sig Lloyd, capital | | | 97470 |
| | | To close the income | | | |
| | | summary account. | | | |
| | | | | | |
| | 31 | Sig Lloyd, capital | | 3000 | |
| | | Sig Lloyd, withdrawals | | | 3000 |
| | | To close the | | | |
| | | withdrawals account. | | | |
| | | | | | |

**Problem 4-7A**

## LLOYD CONSTRUCTION
### Income Statement
### For Year Ended December 31, 2017

| | $ | $ |
|---|---|---|
| Revenues: | | |
| Professional revenue | 206480 | |
| Rent revenue | 26000 | |
| Total revenues | | 232480 |
| | | |
| Operating Expenses: | | |
| Wages expense | 64000 | |
| Depreciation exps, building | 20000 | |
| Insurance expense | 18000 | |
| Supplies expense | 12800 | |
| Interest expense | 610 | |
| Depreciation exps, equipment | 8000 | |
| Utilities expense | 7200 | |
| Telephone expense | 4400 | |
| Total operating expenses | | 135010 |
| | | |
| Profit | | $97,470 |

## LLOYD CONSTRUCTION
### Statement of Changes in Equity
### For Year Ended December 31, 2017

| | | |
|---|---|---|
| Sig Lloyd capital, January 1 | | $17000 |
| Add: Investments by owner | 75000 | |
| Profit | 97,470 | 172470 |
| Total | | $189,470 |
| Less: Withdrawals by owner | | 3000 |
| Sig Lloyd capital, December 31 | | $186,470 |

**Problem 4-7A (concl'd.)**

Lloyd Construction
**Balance Sheet**
December 31, 2017

| | $ | $ | $ |
|---|---|---|---|
| Assets | | | |
| Current assets: | | | |
| Cash | | 16000 | |
| Current investments | | 21000 | |
| Supplies | | 7600 | |
| Total current assets | | | $44,600 |
| Non Currents investments: | | | |
| Notes receivable | | | 42000 |
| Property, plant & equipment: | | | |
| Land | | 86000 | |
| Building | 260000 | | |
| Less: Accumulated depr. | 141000 | 119,000 | |
| Equipment | 78000 | | |
| Less: Accumulated depr | 38000 | 40000 | |
| Total property, plant, equip | | | 245000 |
| Intangible assets: | | | |
| Franchise | | | 31000 |
| Total assets | | | 362600 |
| | | | |
| Liabilities | | | |
| Current liabilities: | | | |
| Accounts Payable | 17000 | | |
| Interest Payable | 130 | | |
| Unearned professional rev | 27000 | | |
| Current portion of long term | 45000 | | |
| notes payable | | | |
| Total current liabilities | | $89130 | |
| Non current liabilities: | | | |
| Long term notes payable | | 87000 | |
| (less current portion) | | | |
| Total liabilites | | | $176130 |
| | | | |
| Equity | | | |
| Sig Lloyd, capital | | | 186470 |
| Total liabilities & equity | | | 362600 |

*Analysis component:*

_____
_____
_____
_____
_____

**Problem 4-8A**

**Part 1**

## GENERAL JOURNAL

Page_____

| Date | Account Titles and Explanation | PR | Debit | Credit |
|------|-------------------------------|----|-------|--------|
|      |                               |    |       |        |
|      |                               |    |       |        |
|      |                               |    |       |        |
|      |                               |    |       |        |
|      |                               |    |       |        |
|      |                               |    |       |        |
|      |                               |    |       |        |
|      |                               |    |       |        |
|      |                               |    |       |        |
|      |                               |    |       |        |
|      |                               |    |       |        |
|      |                               |    |       |        |
|      |                               |    |       |        |
|      |                               |    |       |        |
|      |                               |    |       |        |
|      |                               |    |       |        |
|      |                               |    |       |        |
|      |                               |    |       |        |
|      |                               |    |       |        |
|      |                               |    |       |        |
|      |                               |    |       |        |
|      |                               |    |       |        |

**Chapter 4**

Name:_____

**Problem 4-8A (cont'd.)**

**Part 2**

| Adjusted Trial Balance | | |
|---|---|---|
| | Debit | Credit |
| | | |
| | | |
| | | |
| | | |
| | | |
| | | |
| | | |
| | | |
| | | |
| | | |
| | | |
| | | |
| | | |
| | | |
| | | |
| | | |
| | | |
| | | |
| | | |
| | | |
| | | |
| | | |
| | | |
| | | |
| | | |
| | | |
| | | |
| | | |

*Fundamental Accounting Principles*, 15ce, Working Papers

**Problem 4-8A (cont'd.)**

**Part 3**

**GENERAL JOURNAL**

Page_____

| Date | Account Titles and Explanation | PR | Debit | Credit |
|------|-------------------------------|----|-------|--------|
|  |  |  |  |  |
|  |  |  |  |  |
|  |  |  |  |  |
|  |  |  |  |  |
|  |  |  |  |  |
|  |  |  |  |  |
|  |  |  |  |  |
|  |  |  |  |  |
|  |  |  |  |  |
|  |  |  |  |  |
|  |  |  |  |  |
|  |  |  |  |  |
|  |  |  |  |  |
|  |  |  |  |  |
|  |  |  |  |  |
|  |  |  |  |  |
|  |  |  |  |  |
|  |  |  |  |  |
|  |  |  |  |  |
|  |  |  |  |  |
|  |  |  |  |  |
|  |  |  |  |  |
|  |  |  |  |  |
|  |  |  |  |  |
|  |  |  |  |  |
|  |  |  |  |  |

**Chapter 4**

Name:_____

**Problem 4-9A**

| Income Statement | | |
|---|---|---|
| | | |
| | | |
| | | |
| | | |
| | | |
| | | |
| | | |
| | | |
| | | |
| | | |
| | | |
| | | |
| | | |
| | | |
| | | |
| | | |
| | | |
| | | |
| | | |

| Statement of Changes in Equity | | |
|---|---|---|
| | | |
| | | |
| | | |
| | | |
| | | |
| | | |
| | | |
| | | |

**Problem 4-9A (concl'd.)**

| Balance Sheet | | | |
|---|---|---|---|
| | | | |
| | | | |
| | | | |
| | | | |
| | | | |
| | | | |
| | | | |
| | | | |
| | | | |
| | | | |
| | | | |
| | | | |
| | | | |
| | | | |
| | | | |
| | | | |
| | | | |
| | | | |
| | | | |
| | | | |
| | | | |
| | | | |
| | | | |
| | | | |
| | | | |
| | | | |
| | | | |
| | | | |
| | | | |
| | | | |
| | | | |
| | | | |
| | | | |

*Analysis component:*

_____
_____
_____
_____
_____
_____
_____

Name:_____

**Problem 4-10A**

**Part 1**

|  | Income Statement | | |
|---|---|---|---|
|  |  |  |  |
|  |  |  |  |
|  |  |  |  |
|  |  |  |  |
|  |  |  |  |
|  |  |  |  |
|  |  |  |  |
|  |  |  |  |
|  |  |  |  |
|  |  |  |  |
|  |  |  |  |
|  |  |  |  |
|  |  |  |  |
|  |  |  |  |
|  |  |  |  |
|  |  |  |  |
|  |  |  |  |
|  |  |  |  |
|  |  |  |  |
|  |  |  |  |
|  |  |  |  |
|  |  |  |  |
|  |  |  |  |

**Part 2**

**Noel Apex, Capital**

Problem 4-11A

## IMPRESSIONS DANCE SCHOOL
### Income Statement
### For Year Ended September 30, 2017

| | | |
|---|---|---|
| Revenues: | | |
| Dance school revenue | | 154680 |
| Rent revenue | | 21000 |
| Total revenues | | $175,680 |
| Operating expenses: | | |
| Salaries expense | 174000 | |
| Gas, oil & repairs exp. | 29600 | |
| Depr exps, Building | 28400 | |
| Depr exps, automobiles | 7100 | |
| Total operating expenses | | 239100 |
| Loss | | $63420 |

## IMPRESSIONS DANCE SCHOOL
### Statement of Changes in Equity
### For Year Ended September 30, 2017

| | | |
|---|---|---|
| Alisha Bjorn capital, October 1 | | 168960 |
| Less: Loss | 63420 | |
| Withdrawals | 10000 | 73420 |
| Alisha Bjorn capital, September 30 | | $95,540 |

**Problem 4-11A (concl'd.)**

Impressions Dance school
**Balance Sheet**
September 30, 2017

| Assets | $ | $ | $ |
|---|---|---|---|
| Current assets: | | | |
| Cash | | 11600 | |
| Accounts receivable | | 13500 | |
| Store supplies | | 4380 | |
| Total Current assets | | | $29480 |
| | | | |
| Non Current investments: | | | |
| Land for future expansion | | | 50000 |
| | | | |
| Property, plant, equipment: | | | |
| Land | | 32900 | |
| Building | 236000 | | |
| less: Accumulated depr | 164000 | 72000 | |
| Automobiles | 71000 | | |
| less: Accumulated depr | 39360 | 31640 | |
| Total Property, plant, equipment | | | 136540 |
| | | | |
| Intangible assets: | | | |
| Copyrights | | 6900 | |
| Brand name | | 8800 | 15700 |
| Total assets | | | $231720 |
| | | | |
| Liabilities | | | |
| Current liabilities: | | | |
| Accounts payable | 22680 | | |
| Unearned revenue | 23500 | | |
| Total current liabilities | | 46180 | |
| Non current liabilities: | | | |
| Notes payable due in 18 months | | 90000 | |
| Total liabilities | | | 136180 |
| | | | |
| Equity | | | |
| Alisha Bjorn, capital | | | 95540 |
| Total liabilities & equity | | | $231720 |

*Analysis component:*

_____
_____
_____
_____
_____

Name:_____

**Problem 4-12A**

Wyett North capital = $415780 - $28000 + $132995

Part 1  Profit = Revenues - Expenses    $520775

= 398400 - (16200 + 25000

| | Wyett North, Capital | |

+ 3500 + 10260 + 41000

+ 126625 + 6100 + 36720)   (with/ 28000 | 415780 (Beg bal)

= 398400 - 265405 | 132995 (profit)

| 520,775 (End bal)

Part 2  = $132995

### North Country Rentals
**Balance Sheet**
### March 31, 2017

| Assets | | | |
|---|---|---|---|
| Current assets: | | | |
| Cash | | 17000 | |
| Rent receivable | | 16000 | |
| Office supplies | | 700 | |
| Prepaid advertising | | 400 | |
| Current portion of notes receiva | | 55000 | |
| Total current assets | | | $ 89100 |
| Non current investments: | | | |
| Notes receivable less current portion | | | 88000 |
| Property, Plant, equipment | | | |
| Land | | 110000 | |
| Building | 591000 | | |
| less: Accumulated depr | 25000 | 566000 | |
| Furniture | 42800 | | |
| Less: Accumulated depr | 3500 | 39300 | |
| Total property, plant, equipment | | | 715300 |
| Intengible assets: | | | |
| Brand name | | | 3000 |
| Total assets | | | $ 895400 |
| | | | |
| Liabilities | | | |
| Current liabilities: | | | |
| Account payable | 9100 | | |
| Interest payable | 900 | | |
| Salaries payable | 2625 | | |
| Current portion of long term | 215000 | | |
| notes payable | | | |
| Total current liabilities | | $ 227625 | |
| Non current liabilities | | | |
| Long term notes payable less current porti | | 147000 | |
| Total liabilities | | | $ 374625 |
| | | | |
| Equity | | | |
| Wyett North, capital | | | 520775 |
| Total liabilities & equity | | | $ 895400 |

Name:_____

**Problem 4-12A (concl'd.)**

***Analysis component:***

_____

_____

_____

_____

_____

_____

_____

**Problem 4-13A**

Part 1.  Use either the balance column format or T-accounts; both are provided.

## GENERAL LEDGER

### Cash                                                    ACCOUNT NO. 101

| DATE | EXPLANATION | PR | DEBIT | CREDIT | BALANCE |
|------|-------------|----|----|----|----|
|  |  |  |  |  |  |
|  |  |  |  |  |  |
|  |  |  |  |  |  |
|  |  |  |  |  |  |
|  |  |  |  |  |  |
|  |  |  |  |  |  |
|  |  |  |  |  |  |
|  |  |  |  |  |  |
|  |  |  |  |  |  |
|  |  |  |  |  |  |
|  |  |  |  |  |  |
|  |  |  |  |  |  |

### Accounts Receivable                                     ACCOUNT NO. 106

| DATE | EXPLANATION | PR | DEBIT | CREDIT | BALANCE |
|------|-------------|----|----|----|----|
|  |  |  |  |  |  |
|  |  |  |  |  |  |

### Office Supplies                                         ACCOUNT NO. 124

| DATE | EXPLANATION | PR | DEBIT | CREDIT | BALANCE |
|------|-------------|----|----|----|----|
|  |  |  |  |  |  |
|  |  |  |  |  |  |
|  |  |  |  |  |  |

### Prepaid Insurance                                       ACCOUNT NO. 128

| DATE | EXPLANATION | PR | DEBIT | CREDIT | BALANCE |
|------|-------------|----|----|----|----|
|  |  |  |  |  |  |
|  |  |  |  |  |  |
|  |  |  |  |  |  |

### Furniture                                               ACCOUNT NO. 160

| DATE | EXPLANATION | PR | DEBIT | CREDIT | BALANCE |
|------|-------------|----|----|----|----|
|  |  |  |  |  |  |
|  |  |  |  |  |  |

### Accumulated Depreciation, Furniture                     ACCOUNT NO. 161

| DATE | EXPLANATION | PR | DEBIT | CREDIT | BALANCE |
|------|-------------|----|----|----|----|
|  |  |  |  |  |  |
|  |  |  |  |  |  |

**Problem 4-13A (cont'd.)**

### Computer Equipment     ACCOUNT NO. 167

| DATE | EXPLANATION | PR | DEBIT | CREDIT | BALANCE |
|------|-------------|----|-------|--------|---------|
|      |             |    |       |        |         |
|      |             |    |       |        |         |

### Accumulated Depreciation, Computer Equipment     ACCOUNT NO. 168

| DATE | EXPLANATION | PR | DEBIT | CREDIT | BALANCE |
|------|-------------|----|-------|--------|---------|
|      |             |    |       |        |         |
|      |             |    |       |        |         |

### Accounts Payable     ACCOUNT NO. 201

| DATE | EXPLANATION | PR | DEBIT | CREDIT | BALANCE |
|------|-------------|----|-------|--------|---------|
|      |             |    |       |        |         |
|      |             |    |       |        |         |

### Salaries Payable     ACCOUNT NO. 209

| DATE | EXPLANATION | PR | DEBIT | CREDIT | BALANCE |
|------|-------------|----|-------|--------|---------|
|      |             |    |       |        |         |
|      |             |    |       |        |         |

### Sam Near, Capital     ACCOUNT NO. 301

| DATE | EXPLANATION | PR | DEBIT | CREDIT | BALANCE |
|------|-------------|----|-------|--------|---------|
|      |             |    |       |        |         |
|      |             |    |       |        |         |
|      |             |    |       |        |         |
|      |             |    |       |        |         |

### Sam Near, Withdrawals     ACCOUNT NO. 302

| DATE | EXPLANATION | PR | DEBIT | CREDIT | BALANCE |
|------|-------------|----|-------|--------|---------|
|      |             |    |       |        |         |
|      |             |    |       |        |         |
|      |             |    |       |        |         |

### Commissions Revenue     ACCOUNT NO. 405

| DATE | EXPLANATION | PR | DEBIT | CREDIT | BALANCE |
|------|-------------|----|-------|--------|---------|
|      |             |    |       |        |         |
|      |             |    |       |        |         |
|      |             |    |       |        |         |
|      |             |    |       |        |         |

### Depreciation Expense, Furniture     ACCOUNT NO. 610

| DATE | EXPLANATION | PR | DEBIT | CREDIT | BALANCE |
|------|-------------|----|-------|--------|---------|
|      |             |    |       |        |         |
|      |             |    |       |        |         |
|      |             |    |       |        |         |

**Problem 4-13A (cont'd.)**

### Depreciation Expense, Computer Equipment　　　ACCOUNT NO. 612

| DATE | EXPLANATION | PR | DEBIT | CREDIT | BALANCE |
|------|-------------|----|-------|--------|---------|
|      |             |    |       |        |         |
|      |             |    |       |        |         |
|      |             |    |       |        |         |

### Salaries Expense　　　ACCOUNT NO. 622

| DATE | EXPLANATION | PR | DEBIT | CREDIT | BALANCE |
|------|-------------|----|-------|--------|---------|
|      |             |    |       |        |         |
|      |             |    |       |        |         |
|      |             |    |       |        |         |
|      |             |    |       |        |         |

### Insurance Expense　　　ACCOUNT NO. 637

| DATE | EXPLANATION | PR | DEBIT | CREDIT | BALANCE |
|------|-------------|----|-------|--------|---------|
|      |             |    |       |        |         |
|      |             |    |       |        |         |
|      |             |    |       |        |         |

### Rent Expense　　　ACCOUNT NO. 640

| DATE | EXPLANATION | PR | DEBIT | CREDIT | BALANCE |
|------|-------------|----|-------|--------|---------|
|      |             |    |       |        |         |
|      |             |    |       |        |         |
|      |             |    |       |        |         |

### Office Supplies Expense　　　ACCOUNT NO. 650

| DATE | EXPLANATION | PR | DEBIT | CREDIT | BALANCE |
|------|-------------|----|-------|--------|---------|
|      |             |    |       |        |         |
|      |             |    |       |        |         |
|      |             |    |       |        |         |

### Repairs Expense　　　ACCOUNT NO. 684

| DATE | EXPLANATION | PR | DEBIT | CREDIT | BALANCE |
|------|-------------|----|-------|--------|---------|
|      |             |    |       |        |         |
|      |             |    |       |        |         |
|      |             |    |       |        |         |

### Telephone Expense　　　ACCOUNT NO. 688

| DATE | EXPLANATION | PR | DEBIT | CREDIT | BALANCE |
|------|-------------|----|-------|--------|---------|
|      |             |    |       |        |         |
|      |             |    |       |        |         |
|      |             |    |       |        |         |

**Problem 4-13A (cont'd.)**

| | Income Summary | | | | ACCOUNT NO. 901 |
|---|---|---|---|---|---|
| DATE | EXPLANATION | PR | DEBIT | CREDIT | BALANCE |
| | | | | | |
| | | | | | |
| | | | | | |
| | | | | | |

**Part 1. Use either T-accounts or the balance column format; both are provided.**

Cash                    101

Accum. Deprec, Furniture        161

Computer Equipment        167

Accum. Deprec, Computer Equip    168

Accounts Payable        201

Accounts Receivable        106

Salaries Payable        209

Office Supplies        124

Sam Near, Capital        301

Prepaid Insurance        128

Sam Near, Withdrawals        302

Commissions Earned        405

Furniture        160

**Problem 4-13A (cont'd.)**

Part 1.  Use either T-accounts or the balance column format; both are provided.

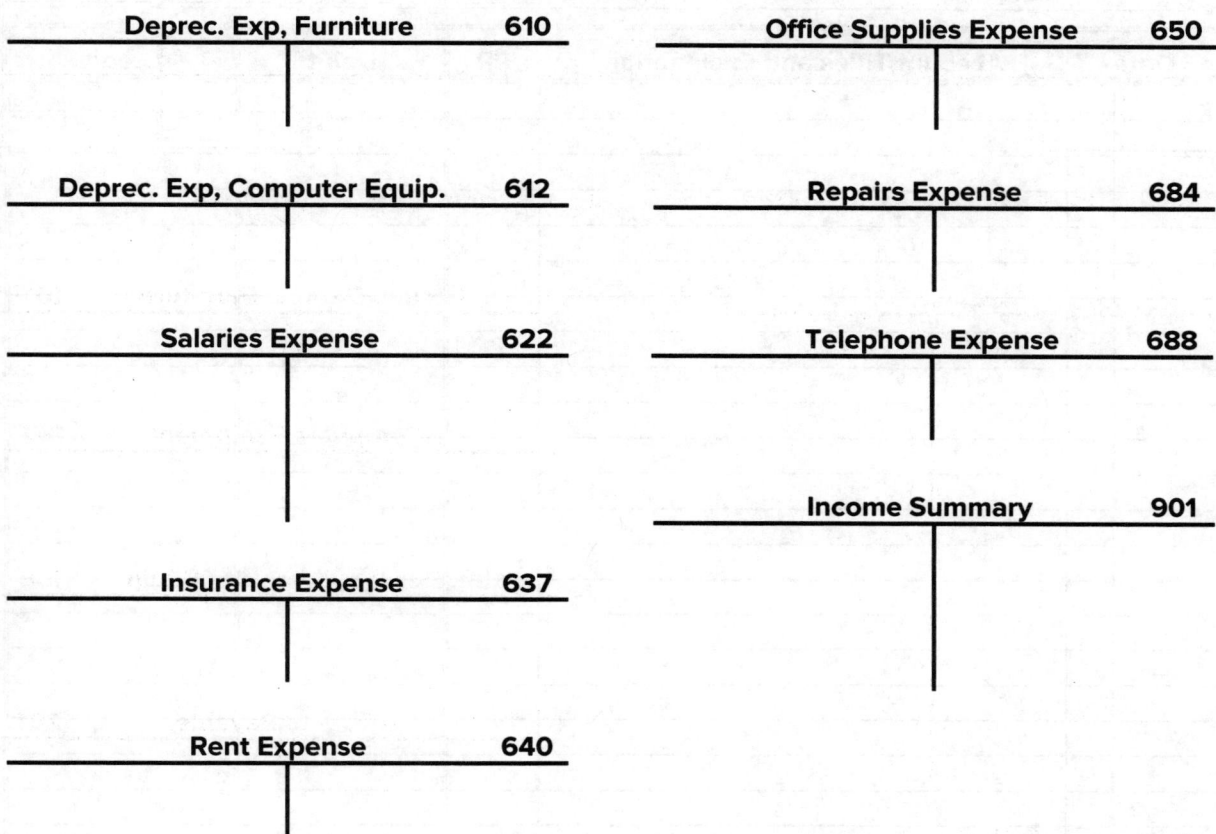

| Deprec. Exp, Furniture | 610 | | Office Supplies Expense | 650 |

| Deprec. Exp, Computer Equip. | 612 | | Repairs Expense | 684 |

| Salaries Expense | 622 | | Telephone Expense | 688 |

| | | | Income Summary | 901 |

| Insurance Expense | 637 |

| Rent Expense | 640 |

**Problem 4-13A (cont'd.)**

**Part 2. Transactions for June:**

## GENERAL JOURNAL                                    Page____

| Date | Account Titles and Explanation | PR | Debit | Credit |
|------|-------------------------------|----|-------|--------|
|      |                               |    |       |        |
|      |                               |    |       |        |
|      |                               |    |       |        |
|      |                               |    |       |        |
|      |                               |    |       |        |
|      |                               |    |       |        |
|      |                               |    |       |        |
|      |                               |    |       |        |
|      |                               |    |       |        |
|      |                               |    |       |        |
|      |                               |    |       |        |
|      |                               |    |       |        |
|      |                               |    |       |        |
|      |                               |    |       |        |
|      |                               |    |       |        |
|      |                               |    |       |        |
|      |                               |    |       |        |
|      |                               |    |       |        |
|      |                               |    |       |        |
|      |                               |    |       |        |
|      |                               |    |       |        |
|      |                               |    |       |        |
|      |                               |    |       |        |
|      |                               |    |       |        |
|      |                               |    |       |        |
|      |                               |    |       |        |
|      |                               |    |       |        |
|      |                               |    |       |        |
|      |                               |    |       |        |
|      |                               |    |       |        |
|      |                               |    |       |        |
|      |                               |    |       |        |
|      |                               |    |       |        |
|      |                               |    |       |        |
|      |                               |    |       |        |
|      |                               |    |       |        |
|      |                               |    |       |        |

**Problem 4-13A (cont'd.)**

**Part 2. Transactions for June (cont'd.)**

## GENERAL JOURNAL

Page_____

| Date | | Account Titles and Explanation | PR | Debit | Credit |
|---|---|---|---|---|---|
| | | | | | |
| | | | | | |
| | | | | | |
| | | | | | |
| | | | | | |
| | | | | | |
| | | | | | |
| | | | | | |
| | | | | | |
| | | | | | |
| | | | | | |
| | | | | | |
| | | | | | |
| | | | | | |
| | | | | | |
| | | | | | |
| | | | | | |
| | | | | | |
| | | | | | |
| | | | | | |
| | | | | | |
| | | | | | |
| | | | | | |
| | | | | | |
| | | | | | |
| | | | | | |
| | | | | | |
| | | | | | |
| | | | | | |
| | | | | | |
| | | | | | |
| | | | | | |
| | | | | | |
| | | | | | |
| | | | | | |
| | | | | | |
| | | | | | |
| | | | | | |
| | | | | | |
| | | | | | |

**Problem 4-13A (cont'd.)**

**Part 3.  Adjusting entries:**

### GENERAL JOURNAL                                            Page____

| Date | Account Titles and Explanation | PR | Debit | Credit |
|------|-------------------------------|-----|-------|--------|
|      |                               |     |       |        |
|      |                               |     |       |        |
|      |                               |     |       |        |
|      |                               |     |       |        |
|      |                               |     |       |        |
|      |                               |     |       |        |
|      |                               |     |       |        |
|      |                               |     |       |        |
|      |                               |     |       |        |
|      |                               |     |       |        |
|      |                               |     |       |        |
|      |                               |     |       |        |
|      |                               |     |       |        |
|      |                               |     |       |        |
|      |                               |     |       |        |
|      |                               |     |       |        |
|      |                               |     |       |        |
|      |                               |     |       |        |
|      |                               |     |       |        |
|      |                               |     |       |        |
|      |                               |     |       |        |
|      |                               |     |       |        |
|      |                               |     |       |        |
|      |                               |     |       |        |
|      |                               |     |       |        |

### Income Statement

| | | |
|---|---|---|
|   |   |   |
|   |   |   |
|   |   |   |
|   |   |   |
|   |   |   |
|   |   |   |
|   |   |   |
|   |   |   |
|   |   |   |
|   |   |   |
|   |   |   |

## Statement of Changes in Equity

| | | | |
|---|---|---|---|
| | | | |
| | | | |
| | | | |
| | | | |
| | | | |
| | | | |
| | | | |
| | | | |

## Balance Sheet

| | | | | |
|---|---|---|---|---|
| | | | | |
| | | | | |
| | | | | |
| | | | | |
| | | | | |
| | | | | |
| | | | | |
| | | | | |
| | | | | |
| | | | | |
| | | | | |
| | | | | |
| | | | | |
| | | | | |
| | | | | |
| | | | | |
| | | | | |
| | | | | |
| | | | | |
| | | | | |
| | | | | |
| | | | | |
| | | | | |
| | | | | |
| | | | | |

Name:_____

## Problem 4-13A (concl'd.)

### Part 5. Closing entries:

**GENERAL JOURNAL**                                      Page_____

| Date | Account Titles and Explanation | PR | Debit | Credit |
|------|-------------------------------|----|-------|--------|
|      |                               |    |       |        |
|      |                               |    |       |        |
|      |                               |    |       |        |
|      |                               |    |       |        |
|      |                               |    |       |        |
|      |                               |    |       |        |
|      |                               |    |       |        |
|      |                               |    |       |        |
|      |                               |    |       |        |
|      |                               |    |       |        |
|      |                               |    |       |        |
|      |                               |    |       |        |
|      |                               |    |       |        |
|      |                               |    |       |        |
|      |                               |    |       |        |
|      |                               |    |       |        |
|      |                               |    |       |        |
|      |                               |    |       |        |
|      |                               |    |       |        |
|      |                               |    |       |        |
|      |                               |    |       |        |
|      |                               |    |       |        |
|      |                               |    |       |        |

### Part 6

**Post-Closing Trial Balance**

|  | Debit | Credit |
|--|-------|--------|
|  |       |        |
|  |       |        |
|  |       |        |
|  |       |        |
|  |       |        |
|  |       |        |
|  |       |        |
|  |       |        |
|  |       |        |
|  |       |        |
|  |       |        |

Name:_____

**Problem 4-14A**

a.

|  | **2014** | **2013** |
|---|---|---|
| **Current ratio** |  |  |
| **Quick ratio** |  |  |
| **Debt to equity ratio** |  |  |

**b. Comments:** _____

_____

_____

_____

_____

_____

_____

_____

_____

_____

_____

_____

_____

Name:_____

**\*Problem 4-15A**

Part 1

### GENERAL JOURNAL

Page____

| Date | Account Titles and Explanation | PR | Debit | Credit |
|------|-------------------------------|----|----|------|
| a. | | | | |
| | | | | |
| | | | | |
| | | | | |
| b. | | | | |
| | | | | |
| | | | | |
| | | | | |
| c. | | | | |
| | | | | |
| | | | | |
| | | | | |
| d. | | | | |
| | | | | |
| | | | | |
| | | | | |
| e. | | | | |
| | | | | |
| | | | | |
| | | | | |
| f. | | | | |
| | | | | |
| | | | | |
| | | | | |

**\*Problem 4-15A (concl'd.)**

**Part 2**

### GENERAL JOURNAL                                    Page____

| Date | Account Titles and Explanation | PR | Debit | Credit |
|------|-------------------------------|----|-------|--------|
|      |                               |    |       |        |
|      |                               |    |       |        |
|      |                               |    |       |        |
|      |                               |    |       |        |
|      |                               |    |       |        |
|      |                               |    |       |        |
|      |                               |    |       |        |
|      |                               |    |       |        |
|      |                               |    |       |        |
|      |                               |    |       |        |
|      |                               |    |       |        |
|      |                               |    |       |        |
|      |                               |    |       |        |
|      |                               |    |       |        |
|      |                               |    |       |        |
|      |                               |    |       |        |
|      |                               |    |       |        |
|      |                               |    |       |        |
|      |                               |    |       |        |
|      |                               |    |       |        |

**Part 3**

### GENERAL JOURNAL                                    Page____

| Date | Account Titles and Explanation | PR | Debit | Credit |
|------|-------------------------------|----|-------|--------|
|      |                               |    |       |        |
|      |                               |    |       |        |
|      |                               |    |       |        |
|      |                               |    |       |        |
|      |                               |    |       |        |
|      |                               |    |       |        |
|      |                               |    |       |        |
|      |                               |    |       |        |
|      |                               |    |       |        |
|      |                               |    |       |        |
|      |                               |    |       |        |
|      |                               |    |       |        |
|      |                               |    |       |        |
|      |                               |    |       |        |
|      |                               |    |       |        |
|      |                               |    |       |        |

**Problem 4-1B**

**Parts 1, 2, and 3**

Daimler Tours

Work Sheet

For Year Ended July 31, 2017

| Account Title | Unadjusted Trial Balance | | Adjustments | | Adjusted Trial Balance | | Income Statement | | Balance Sheet and Statement of Changes in Equity | |
|---|---|---|---|---|---|---|---|---|---|---|
| | Debit | Credit | Debit | Credit | Debit | Credit | Debit | Credit | Debit | Credit |
| Cash | 9,100 | | | | | | | | | |
| Accounts receivable | 18,700 | | | | | | | | | |
| Notes receivable | 16,000 | | | | | | | | | |
| Prepaid insurance | 5,100 | | | | | | | | | |
| Furniture | 6,750 | | | | | | | | | |
| Accounts payable | | 6,925 | | | | | | | | |
| Unearned tour revenue | | 12,430 | | | | | | | | |
| Jan Rider, capital | | 60,975 | | | | | | | | |
| Jan Rider, withdrawals | -0- | | | | | | | | | |
| Tour revenue | | 16,700 | | | | | | | | |
| Wages expense | 41,380 | | | | | | | | | |
| Totals | 97,030 | 97,030 | | | | | | | | |

## Problem 4-2B

### Parts 1, 2, and 3

**Tucker Photographers**

**Work Sheet**

**For Year Ended December 31, 2017**

| Account Title | Unadjusted Trial Balance | | Adjustments | | Adjusted Trial Balance | | Income Statement | | Balance Sheet and Statement of Changes in Equity | |
|---|---|---|---|---|---|---|---|---|---|---|
| | Debit | Credit | Debit | Credit | Debit | Credit | Debit | Credit | Debit | Credit |
| Cash | 9,100 | | | | | | | | | |
| Accounts receivable | 13,000 | | | | | | | | | |
| Prepaid equipment rental | 3,860 | | | | | | | | | |
| Automobile | 49,000 | | | | | | | | | |
| Accum. deprec., automobile | | -0- | | | | | | | | |
| Accounts payable | | 1,920 | | | | | | | | |
| Unearned revenue | | 5,740 | | | | | | | | |
| Jim Tucker, capital | | 65,700 | | | | | | | | |
| Jim Tucker, withdrawals | 2,600 | | | | | | | | | |
| Service Revenue | | 8,400 | | | | | | | | |
| Deprec. Expense, automobile | -0- | | | | | | | | | |
| Equipment rental expense | 4,200 | | | | | | | | | |
| Totals | 94,860 | 94,860 | | | | | | | | |

Name:_____

**Problem 4-2B (concl'd.)**

**Part 4**

_____

**Jim Tucker, Capital**

_____

_____

_____

_____

*Analysis component:*

_____

_____

_____

_____

_____

_____

_____

## Problem 4-3B

### Part 1

**Webster Demolition Company**

**Work Sheet**

**For Year Ended June 30, 2017**

| Account Title | Unadjusted Trial Balance Debit | Unadjusted Trial Balance Credit | Adjustments Debit | Adjustments Credit | Adjusted Trial Balance Debit | Adjusted Trial Balance Credit | Income Statement Debit | Income Statement Credit | Balance Sheet and Statement of Changes in Equity Debit | Balance Sheet and Statement of Changes in Equity Credit |
|---|---|---|---|---|---|---|---|---|---|---|
| Cash | 4,500 | | | | | | | | | |
| Supplies | 8,200 | | | | | | | | | |
| Prepaid insurance | 7,300 | | | | | | | | | |
| Equipment | 72,000 | | | | | | | | | |
| Accum. deprec., equipment | | 5,000 | | | | | | | | |
| Accounts payable | | 9,100 | | | | | | | | |
| Interest payable | | | | | | | | | | |
| Wages payable | | | | | | | | | | |
| Long-term notes payable | | 45,000 | | | | | | | | |
| Rusty Webster, capital | | 21,400 | | | | | | | | |
| Rusty Webster, withdrawals | 2,100 | | | | | | | | | |
| Demolition revenue | | 83,300 | | | | | | | | |
| Deprec. expense, equipment | | | | | | | | | | |
| Wages expense | 27,400 | | | | | | | | | |
| Interest expense | 1,100 | | | | | | | | | |
| Insurance expense | | | | | | | | | | |
| Rent expense | 24,400 | | | | | | | | | |
| Supplies expense | | | | | | | | | | |
| Business tax expense | 4,200 | | | | | | | | | |
| Repairs expense | 4,200 | | | | | | | | | |
| Utilities expense | 8,400 | | | | | | | | | |
| Totals | 163,800 | 163,800 | | | | | | | | |

**Problem 4-3B (cont'd.)**

**Part 2**
**Adjusting entries:**

GENERAL JOURNAL                                    Page____

| Date | Account Titles and Explanation | PR | Debit | Credit |
|------|-------------------------------|----|----|----|
|      |                               |    |    |    |
| a.   |                               |    |    |    |
|      |                               |    |    |    |
|      |                               |    |    |    |
|      |                               |    |    |    |
| b.   |                               |    |    |    |
|      |                               |    |    |    |
|      |                               |    |    |    |
|      |                               |    |    |    |
| c.   |                               |    |    |    |
|      |                               |    |    |    |
|      |                               |    |    |    |
|      |                               |    |    |    |
| d.   |                               |    |    |    |
|      |                               |    |    |    |
|      |                               |    |    |    |
|      |                               |    |    |    |
| e.   |                               |    |    |    |
|      |                               |    |    |    |
|      |                               |    |    |    |
|      |                               |    |    |    |
| f.   |                               |    |    |    |
|      |                               |    |    |    |
|      |                               |    |    |    |
|      |                               |    |    |    |
|      |                               |    |    |    |
|      |                               |    |    |    |

Name:_____

**Problem 4-3B (cont'd.)**

**Part 2**

**Closing entries:**

### GENERAL JOURNAL

Page_____

| Date | Account Titles and Explanation | PR | Debit | Credit |
|---|---|---|---|---|
|  |  |  |  |  |
|  |  |  |  |  |
|  |  |  |  |  |
|  |  |  |  |  |
|  |  |  |  |  |
|  |  |  |  |  |
|  |  |  |  |  |
|  |  |  |  |  |
|  |  |  |  |  |
|  |  |  |  |  |
|  |  |  |  |  |
|  |  |  |  |  |
|  |  |  |  |  |
|  |  |  |  |  |
|  |  |  |  |  |
|  |  |  |  |  |
|  |  |  |  |  |
|  |  |  |  |  |
|  |  |  |  |  |
|  |  |  |  |  |
|  |  |  |  |  |
|  |  |  |  |  |
|  |  |  |  |  |
|  |  |  |  |  |
|  |  |  |  |  |
|  |  |  |  |  |
|  |  |  |  |  |
|  |  |  |  |  |
|  |  |  |  |  |
|  |  |  |  |  |
|  |  |  |  |  |
|  |  |  |  |  |
|  |  |  |  |  |
|  |  |  |  |  |
|  |  |  |  |  |
|  |  |  |  |  |
|  |  |  |  |  |
|  |  |  |  |  |
|  |  |  |  |  |

**Chapter 4**

Name:_____

**Problem 4-3B (cont'd.)**

**Part 3**

---

### Income Statement

| | | |
|---|---|---|
| | | |
| | | |
| | | |
| | | |
| | | |
| | | |
| | | |
| | | |
| | | |
| | | |
| | | |
| | | |
| | | |
| | | |
| | | |
| | | |
| | | |
| | | |
| | | |
| | | |

### Statement of Changes in Equity

| | | |
|---|---|---|
| | | |
| | | |
| | | |
| | | |
| | | |
| | | |
| | | |
| | | |
| | | |
| | | |

**Problem 4-3B (concl'd.)**

| Balance Sheet | | | |
|---|---|---|---|
| | | | |
| | | | |
| | | | |
| | | | |
| | | | |
| | | | |
| | | | |
| | | | |
| | | | |
| | | | |
| | | | |
| | | | |
| | | | |
| | | | |
| | | | |
| | | | |
| | | | |
| | | | |
| | | | |
| | | | |
| | | | |
| | | | |
| | | | |
| | | | |
| | | | |
| | | | |
| | | | |
| | | | |
| | | | |
| | | | |
| | | | |
| | | | |

*Analysis component:*

a._____

_____

_____

b._____

_____

_____

_____

Chapter 4                    Name:_____

**Problem 4-4B**

Part 1                    GENERAL JOURNAL                    Page____

| Date | Account Titles and Explanation | PR | Debit | Credit |
|------|-------------------------------|----|-------|--------|
|      |                               |    |       |        |
|      |                               |    |       |        |
|      |                               |    |       |        |
|      |                               |    |       |        |
|      |                               |    |       |        |
|      |                               |    |       |        |
|      |                               |    |       |        |
|      |                               |    |       |        |
|      |                               |    |       |        |
|      |                               |    |       |        |
|      |                               |    |       |        |
|      |                               |    |       |        |
|      |                               |    |       |        |
|      |                               |    |       |        |
|      |                               |    |       |        |
|      |                               |    |       |        |
|      |                               |    |       |        |
|      |                               |    |       |        |
|      |                               |    |       |        |
|      |                               |    |       |        |
|      |                               |    |       |        |
|      |                               |    |       |        |
|      |                               |    |       |        |
|      |                               |    |       |        |

Part 2

## Post-Closing Trial Balance

|  | Debit | Credit |
|--|-------|--------|
|  |       |        |
|  |       |        |
|  |       |        |
|  |       |        |
|  |       |        |
|  |       |        |
|  |       |        |
|  |       |        |
|  |       |        |
|  |       |        |
|  |       |        |
|  |       |        |

Name:_____

**Problem 4-5B**

### Income Statement

| | | |
|---|---|---|
| | | |
| | | |
| | | |
| | | |
| | | |
| | | |
| | | |
| | | |
| | | |
| | | |
| | | |
| | | |
| | | |
| | | |
| | | |
| | | |
| | | |
| | | |
| | | |
| | | |
| | | |
| | | |
| | | |
| | | |

### Statement of Changes in Equity

| | | |
|---|---|---|
| | | |
| | | |
| | | |
| | | |
| | | |
| | | |
| | | |
| | | |
| | | |

**Problem 4-5B (concl'd.)**

|  | Balance Sheet |  |  |
|---|---|---|---|
|  |  |  |  |
|  |  |  |  |
|  |  |  |  |
|  |  |  |  |
|  |  |  |  |
|  |  |  |  |
|  |  |  |  |
|  |  |  |  |
|  |  |  |  |
|  |  |  |  |
|  |  |  |  |
|  |  |  |  |
|  |  |  |  |
|  |  |  |  |
|  |  |  |  |
|  |  |  |  |
|  |  |  |  |
|  |  |  |  |
|  |  |  |  |
|  |  |  |  |
|  |  |  |  |
|  |  |  |  |
|  |  |  |  |
|  |  |  |  |
|  |  |  |  |
|  |  |  |  |
|  |  |  |  |
|  |  |  |  |
|  |  |  |  |
|  |  |  |  |
|  |  |  |  |
|  |  |  |  |

*Analysis component:*

_____

_____

_____

_____

_____

_____

Name:_____

**Problem 4-6B**

## GENERAL JOURNAL

Page____

| Date | Account Titles and Explanation | PR | Debit | Credit |
|------|-------------------------------|----|-------|--------|
|  |  |  |  |  |
|  |  |  |  |  |
|  |  |  |  |  |
|  |  |  |  |  |
|  |  |  |  |  |
|  |  |  |  |  |
|  |  |  |  |  |
|  |  |  |  |  |
|  |  |  |  |  |
|  |  |  |  |  |
|  |  |  |  |  |
|  |  |  |  |  |
|  |  |  |  |  |
|  |  |  |  |  |
|  |  |  |  |  |
|  |  |  |  |  |
|  |  |  |  |  |
|  |  |  |  |  |
|  |  |  |  |  |
|  |  |  |  |  |
|  |  |  |  |  |
|  |  |  |  |  |
|  |  |  |  |  |
|  |  |  |  |  |
|  |  |  |  |  |
|  |  |  |  |  |
|  |  |  |  |  |
|  |  |  |  |  |
|  |  |  |  |  |
|  |  |  |  |  |
|  |  |  |  |  |
|  |  |  |  |  |
|  |  |  |  |  |
|  |  |  |  |  |
|  |  |  |  |  |
|  |  |  |  |  |
|  |  |  |  |  |
|  |  |  |  |  |
|  |  |  |  |  |
|  |  |  |  |  |

**Problem 4-7B**

## Income Statement

| | | |
|---|---|---|
| | | |
| | | |
| | | |
| | | |
| | | |
| | | |
| | | |
| | | |
| | | |
| | | |
| | | |
| | | |
| | | |
| | | |
| | | |
| | | |
| | | |
| | | |
| | | |
| | | |
| | | |
| | | |

## Statement of Changes in Equity

| | | |
|---|---|---|
| | | |
| | | |
| | | |
| | | |
| | | |
| | | |
| | | |
| | | |
| | | |
| | | |
| | | |
| | | |

Name:_____

**Problem 4-7B (concl'd.)**

## Balance Sheet

| | | | |
|---|---|---|---|
| | | | |
| | | | |
| | | | |
| | | | |
| | | | |
| | | | |
| | | | |
| | | | |
| | | | |
| | | | |
| | | | |
| | | | |
| | | | |
| | | | |
| | | | |
| | | | |
| | | | |
| | | | |
| | | | |
| | | | |
| | | | |
| | | | |
| | | | |
| | | | |
| | | | |
| | | | |
| | | | |
| | | | |
| | | | |
| | | | |
| | | | |
| | | | |

*Analysis component:*

_____
_____
_____
_____
_____
_____

Name:_____

**Problem 4-8B**

**Part 1**

## GENERAL JOURNAL

Page_____

| Date | Account Titles and Explanation | PR | Debit | Credit |
|------|-------------------------------|----|-------|--------|
|      |                               |    |       |        |
|      |                               |    |       |        |
|      |                               |    |       |        |
|      |                               |    |       |        |
|      |                               |    |       |        |
|      |                               |    |       |        |
|      |                               |    |       |        |
|      |                               |    |       |        |
|      |                               |    |       |        |
|      |                               |    |       |        |
|      |                               |    |       |        |
|      |                               |    |       |        |
|      |                               |    |       |        |
|      |                               |    |       |        |
|      |                               |    |       |        |
|      |                               |    |       |        |
|      |                               |    |       |        |
|      |                               |    |       |        |
|      |                               |    |       |        |
|      |                               |    |       |        |
|      |                               |    |       |        |

Name:_____

**Problem 4-8B (cont'd.)**

**Part 2**

## Adjusted Trial Balance

|  | Debit | Credit |
|---|---|---|
|  |  |  |
|  |  |  |
|  |  |  |
|  |  |  |
|  |  |  |
|  |  |  |
|  |  |  |
|  |  |  |
|  |  |  |
|  |  |  |
|  |  |  |
|  |  |  |
|  |  |  |
|  |  |  |
|  |  |  |
|  |  |  |
|  |  |  |
|  |  |  |
|  |  |  |
|  |  |  |
|  |  |  |
|  |  |  |
|  |  |  |
|  |  |  |
|  |  |  |
|  |  |  |
|  |  |  |
|  |  |  |
|  |  |  |
|  |  |  |
|  |  |  |

Name:_____

**Problem 4-8B (cont'd.)**

**Part 3**

### GENERAL JOURNAL

Page____

| Date | Account Titles and Explanation | PR | Debit | Credit |
|------|-------------------------------|-----|-------|--------|
|      |                               |     |       |        |
|      |                               |     |       |        |
|      |                               |     |       |        |
|      |                               |     |       |        |
|      |                               |     |       |        |
|      |                               |     |       |        |
|      |                               |     |       |        |
|      |                               |     |       |        |
|      |                               |     |       |        |
|      |                               |     |       |        |
|      |                               |     |       |        |
|      |                               |     |       |        |
|      |                               |     |       |        |
|      |                               |     |       |        |
|      |                               |     |       |        |
|      |                               |     |       |        |
|      |                               |     |       |        |
|      |                               |     |       |        |
|      |                               |     |       |        |
|      |                               |     |       |        |
|      |                               |     |       |        |
|      |                               |     |       |        |
|      |                               |     |       |        |
|      |                               |     |       |        |
|      |                               |     |       |        |

**Problem 4-9B**

## Income Statement

| | | |
|---|---|---|
| | | |
| | | |
| | | |
| | | |
| | | |
| | | |
| | | |
| | | |
| | | |
| | | |
| | | |
| | | |
| | | |
| | | |
| | | |
| | | |
| | | |
| | | |
| | | |
| | | |
| | | |
| | | |
| | | |
| | | |
| | | |
| | | |
| | | |
| | | |

## Statement of Changes in Equity

| | | |
|---|---|---|
| | | |
| | | |
| | | |
| | | |
| | | |
| | | |
| | | |
| | | |
| | | |
| | | |
| | | |

**Problem 4-9B (concl'd.)**

Balance Sheet

| | | | |
|---|---|---|---|
| | | | |
| | | | |
| | | | |
| | | | |
| | | | |
| | | | |
| | | | |
| | | | |
| | | | |
| | | | |
| | | | |
| | | | |
| | | | |
| | | | |
| | | | |
| | | | |
| | | | |
| | | | |
| | | | |
| | | | |
| | | | |
| | | | |
| | | | |
| | | | |
| | | | |
| | | | |
| | | | |
| | | | |
| | | | |
| | | | |
| | | | |

*Analysis component:*

_____

_____

_____

_____

_____

_____

**Chapter 4**

Name:_____

**Problem 4-10B**

**Part 1**

| | | |
|---|---|---|
| **Income Statement** | | |

| | | |
|---|---|---|
| | | |
| | | |
| | | |
| | | |
| | | |
| | | |
| | | |
| | | |
| | | |
| | | |
| | | |
| | | |
| | | |
| | | |
| | | |
| | | |
| | | |
| | | |
| | | |
| | | |
| | | |
| | | |
| | | |
| | | |
| | | |
| | | |
| | | |

**Part 2**

**Grant Greenway, Capital**

**Problem 4-11B**

## Income Statement

| | | |
|---|---|---|
| | | |
| | | |
| | | |
| | | |
| | | |
| | | |
| | | |
| | | |
| | | |
| | | |
| | | |
| | | |
| | | |
| | | |
| | | |
| | | |
| | | |
| | | |
| | | |
| | | |
| | | |
| | | |
| | | |
| | | |

## Statement of Changes in Equity

| | | |
|---|---|---|
| | | |
| | | |
| | | |
| | | |
| | | |
| | | |
| | | |
| | | |
| | | |

**Problem 4-11B (concl'd.)**

## Balance Sheet

| | | | |
|---|---|---|---|
| | | | |
| | | | |
| | | | |
| | | | |
| | | | |
| | | | |
| | | | |
| | | | |
| | | | |
| | | | |
| | | | |
| | | | |
| | | | |
| | | | |
| | | | |
| | | | |
| | | | |
| | | | |
| | | | |
| | | | |
| | | | |
| | | | |
| | | | |
| | | | |
| | | | |
| | | | |
| | | | |
| | | | |
| | | | |
| | | | |
| | | | |
| | | | |
| | | | |
| | | | |

*Analysis component:*

Name:_____

**Problem 4-12B**

**Part 1**

_____

_____

_____

_____

**Jan Delta, Capital**

**Part 2**

_____

**Balance Sheet**

| | | | |
|---|---|---|---|
| | | | |
| | | | |
| | | | |
| | | | |
| | | | |
| | | | |
| | | | |
| | | | |
| | | | |
| | | | |
| | | | |
| | | | |
| | | | |
| | | | |
| | | | |
| | | | |
| | | | |
| | | | |
| | | | |
| | | | |
| | | | |
| | | | |
| | | | |
| | | | |
| | | | |
| | | | |
| | | | |
| | | | |
| | | | |
| | | | |
| | | | |
| | | | |
| | | | |
| | | | |
| | | | |
| | | | |
| | | | |
| | | | |
| | | | |

## Problem 4-13B

**Part 1.** Use either the balance column format or T-accounts; both are provided.

### GENERAL LEDGER

#### Cash                                                                    ACCOUNT NO. 101

| DATE | EXPLANATION | PR | DEBIT | CREDIT | BALANCE |
|------|-------------|----|-------|--------|---------|
|      |             |    |       |        |         |
|      |             |    |       |        |         |
|      |             |    |       |        |         |
|      |             |    |       |        |         |
|      |             |    |       |        |         |
|      |             |    |       |        |         |
|      |             |    |       |        |         |

#### Accounts Receivable                                                     ACCOUNT NO. 106

| DATE | EXPLANATION | PR | DEBIT | CREDIT | BALANCE |
|------|-------------|----|-------|--------|---------|
|      |             |    |       |        |         |
|      |             |    |       |        |         |

#### Office Supplies                                                         ACCOUNT NO. 124

| DATE | EXPLANATION | PR | DEBIT | CREDIT | BALANCE |
|------|-------------|----|-------|--------|---------|
|      |             |    |       |        |         |
|      |             |    |       |        |         |
|      |             |    |       |        |         |

#### Prepaid Insurance                                                       ACCOUNT NO. 128

| DATE | EXPLANATION | PR | DEBIT | CREDIT | BALANCE |
|------|-------------|----|-------|--------|---------|
|      |             |    |       |        |         |
|      |             |    |       |        |         |
|      |             |    |       |        |         |

#### Land                                                                    ACCOUNT NO. 170

| DATE | EXPLANATION | PR | DEBIT | CREDIT | BALANCE |
|------|-------------|----|-------|--------|---------|
|      |             |    |       |        |         |
|      |             |    |       |        |         |

#### Buildings                                                               ACCOUNT NO. 173

| DATE | EXPLANATION | PR | DEBIT | CREDIT | BALANCE |
|------|-------------|----|-------|--------|---------|
|      |             |    |       |        |         |
|      |             |    |       |        |         |

#### Accumulated Depreciation, Buildings                                     ACCOUNT NO. 174

| DATE | EXPLANATION | PR | DEBIT | CREDIT | BALANCE |
|------|-------------|----|-------|--------|---------|
|      |             |    |       |        |         |
|      |             |    |       |        |         |

## Problem 4-13B (cont'd.)

### Accounts Payable     ACCOUNT NO. 201

| DATE | EXPLANATION | PR | DEBIT | CREDIT | BALANCE |
|------|-------------|----|-------|--------|---------|
|      |             |    |       |        |         |
|      |             |    |       |        |         |

### Salaries Payable     ACCOUNT NO. 209

| DATE | EXPLANATION | PR | DEBIT | CREDIT | BALANCE |
|------|-------------|----|-------|--------|---------|
|      |             |    |       |        |         |
|      |             |    |       |        |         |

### Amy Young, Capital     ACCOUNT NO. 301

| DATE | EXPLANATION | PR | DEBIT | CREDIT | BALANCE |
|------|-------------|----|-------|--------|---------|
|      |             |    |       |        |         |
|      |             |    |       |        |         |
|      |             |    |       |        |         |
|      |             |    |       |        |         |

### Amy Young, Withdrawals     ACCOUNT NO. 302

| DATE | EXPLANATION | PR | DEBIT | CREDIT | BALANCE |
|------|-------------|----|-------|--------|---------|
|      |             |    |       |        |         |
|      |             |    |       |        |         |
|      |             |    |       |        |         |

### Storage Revenue     ACCOUNT NO. 401

| DATE | EXPLANATION | PR | DEBIT | CREDIT | BALANCE |
|------|-------------|----|-------|--------|---------|
|      |             |    |       |        |         |
|      |             |    |       |        |         |
|      |             |    |       |        |         |
|      |             |    |       |        |         |

### Depreciation Expense, Buildings     ACCOUNT NO. 606

| DATE | EXPLANATION | PR | DEBIT | CREDIT | BALANCE |
|------|-------------|----|-------|--------|---------|
|      |             |    |       |        |         |
|      |             |    |       |        |         |
|      |             |    |       |        |         |

### Salaries Expense     ACCOUNT NO. 622

| DATE | EXPLANATION | PR | DEBIT | CREDIT | BALANCE |
|------|-------------|----|-------|--------|---------|
|      |             |    |       |        |         |
|      |             |    |       |        |         |
|      |             |    |       |        |         |
|      |             |    |       |        |         |
|      |             |    |       |        |         |

**Problem 4-13B (cont'd.)**

### Insurance Expense ACCOUNT NO. 637

| DATE | EXPLANATION | PR | DEBIT | CREDIT | BALANCE |
|------|-------------|----|-------|--------|---------|
|      |             |    |       |        |         |
|      |             |    |       |        |         |
|      |             |    |       |        |         |

### Equipment Rental Expense ACCOUNT NO. 640

| DATE | EXPLANATION | PR | DEBIT | CREDIT | BALANCE |
|------|-------------|----|-------|--------|---------|
|      |             |    |       |        |         |
|      |             |    |       |        |         |
|      |             |    |       |        |         |

### Office Supplies Expense ACCOUNT NO. 650

| DATE | EXPLANATION | PR | DEBIT | CREDIT | BALANCE |
|------|-------------|----|-------|--------|---------|
|      |             |    |       |        |         |
|      |             |    |       |        |         |
|      |             |    |       |        |         |

### Repairs Expense ACCOUNT NO. 684

| DATE | EXPLANATION | PR | DEBIT | CREDIT | BALANCE |
|------|-------------|----|-------|--------|---------|
|      |             |    |       |        |         |
|      |             |    |       |        |         |
|      |             |    |       |        |         |

### Telephone Expense ACCOUNT NO. 688

| DATE | EXPLANATION | PR | DEBIT | CREDIT | BALANCE |
|------|-------------|----|-------|--------|---------|
|      |             |    |       |        |         |
|      |             |    |       |        |         |
|      |             |    |       |        |         |

### Income Summary ACCOUNT NO. 901

| DATE | EXPLANATION | PR | DEBIT | CREDIT | BALANCE |
|------|-------------|----|-------|--------|---------|
|      |             |    |       |        |         |
|      |             |    |       |        |         |
|      |             |    |       |        |         |
|      |             |    |       |        |         |

|  | Cash | 101 |  | Accounts Payable | 201 |
|---|---|---|---|---|---|

|  | Accounts Receivable | 106 |  | Salaries Payable | 209 |
|---|---|---|---|---|---|

|  |  |  |  | Amy Young, Capital | 301 |
|---|---|---|---|---|---|

|  |  |  |  | Amy Young, Withdrawals | 302 |
|---|---|---|---|---|---|

|  | Office Supplies | 124 |  | Storage Revenue | 405 |
|---|---|---|---|---|---|

|  | Prepaid Insurance | 128 |  | Deprec. Exp., Buildings | 606 |
|---|---|---|---|---|---|

|  | Land | 170 |  | Salaries Expense | 622 |
|---|---|---|---|---|---|

|  | Buildings | 173 |  | Insurance Expense | 637 |
|---|---|---|---|---|---|

|  | Accum. Deprec., Buildings | 174 |  | Equipment Rental Expense | 640 |
|---|---|---|---|---|---|

**Problem 4-13B (cont'd.)**

|  | Office Supplies Expense | 650 | | Telephone Expense | 688 |
|---|---|---|---|---|---|

|  | Repairs Expense | 684 | | Income Summary | 901 |
|---|---|---|---|---|---|

**Part 2. Transactions for July:**

GENERAL JOURNAL                  Page____

| Date | Account Titles and Explanation | PR | Debit | Credit |
|---|---|---|---|---|
|  |  |  |  |  |
|  |  |  |  |  |
|  |  |  |  |  |
|  |  |  |  |  |
|  |  |  |  |  |
|  |  |  |  |  |
|  |  |  |  |  |
|  |  |  |  |  |
|  |  |  |  |  |
|  |  |  |  |  |
|  |  |  |  |  |
|  |  |  |  |  |
|  |  |  |  |  |
|  |  |  |  |  |
|  |  |  |  |  |
|  |  |  |  |  |
|  |  |  |  |  |
|  |  |  |  |  |
|  |  |  |  |  |
|  |  |  |  |  |
|  |  |  |  |  |
|  |  |  |  |  |
|  |  |  |  |  |

Name:_____

**Problem 4-13B (cont'd.)**

**Part 2. Transactions for July (cont'd.)**

GENERAL JOURNAL

Page____

| Date | Account Titles and Explanation | PR | Debit | Credit |
|------|-------------------------------|----|-------|--------|
| | | | | |
| | | | | |
| | | | | |
| | | | | |
| | | | | |
| | | | | |
| | | | | |
| | | | | |
| | | | | |
| | | | | |
| | | | | |
| | | | | |
| | | | | |
| | | | | |
| | | | | |
| | | | | |
| | | | | |
| | | | | |
| | | | | |
| | | | | |
| | | | | |
| | | | | |
| | | | | |
| | | | | |
| | | | | |
| | | | | |
| | | | | |
| | | | | |
| | | | | |
| | | | | |
| | | | | |
| | | | | |
| | | | | |
| | | | | |
| | | | | |
| | | | | |
| | | | | |
| | | | | |
| | | | | |

**Problem 4-13B (cont'd.)**

**Part 3. Adjusting entries:**

GENERAL JOURNAL

| Date | Account Titles and Explanation | PR | Debit | Credit |
|------|-------------------------------|----|-------|--------|
|  |  |  |  |  |
|  |  |  |  |  |
|  |  |  |  |  |
|  |  |  |  |  |
|  |  |  |  |  |
|  |  |  |  |  |
|  |  |  |  |  |
|  |  |  |  |  |
|  |  |  |  |  |
|  |  |  |  |  |
|  |  |  |  |  |
|  |  |  |  |  |
|  |  |  |  |  |
|  |  |  |  |  |
|  |  |  |  |  |
|  |  |  |  |  |
|  |  |  |  |  |
|  |  |  |  |  |
|  |  |  |  |  |
|  |  |  |  |  |
|  |  |  |  |  |
|  |  |  |  |  |
|  |  |  |  |  |
|  |  |  |  |  |
|  |  |  |  |  |
|  |  |  |  |  |

**Part 4**

Income Statement

| | | |
|---|---|---|
|  |  |  |
|  |  |  |
|  |  |  |
|  |  |  |
|  |  |  |
|  |  |  |
|  |  |  |
|  |  |  |
|  |  |  |
|  |  |  |
|  |  |  |
|  |  |  |

**Problem 4-13B (cont'd.)**

### Statement of Changes in Equity

| | | |
|---|---|---|
| | | |
| | | |
| | | |
| | | |
| | | |
| | | |
| | | |
| | | |
| | | |

### Balance Sheet

| | | | |
|---|---|---|---|
| | | | |
| | | | |
| | | | |
| | | | |
| | | | |
| | | | |
| | | | |
| | | | |
| | | | |
| | | | |
| | | | |
| | | | |
| | | | |
| | | | |
| | | | |
| | | | |
| | | | |
| | | | |
| | | | |
| | | | |
| | | | |
| | | | |
| | | | |
| | | | |
| | | | |
| | | | |
| | | | |

**Problem 4-13B (concl'd.)**

**Part 5.  Closing entries:**

### GENERAL JOURNAL                                    Page_____

| Date | Account Titles and Explanation | PR | Debit | Credit |
|------|-------------------------------|-----|-------|--------|
|      |                               |     |       |        |
|      |                               |     |       |        |
|      |                               |     |       |        |
|      |                               |     |       |        |
|      |                               |     |       |        |
|      |                               |     |       |        |
|      |                               |     |       |        |
|      |                               |     |       |        |
|      |                               |     |       |        |
|      |                               |     |       |        |
|      |                               |     |       |        |
|      |                               |     |       |        |
|      |                               |     |       |        |
|      |                               |     |       |        |
|      |                               |     |       |        |
|      |                               |     |       |        |
|      |                               |     |       |        |
|      |                               |     |       |        |
|      |                               |     |       |        |
|      |                               |     |       |        |
|      |                               |     |       |        |
|      |                               |     |       |        |
|      |                               |     |       |        |
|      |                               |     |       |        |
|      |                               |     |       |        |
|      |                               |     |       |        |

**Part 6**

### Post-Closing Trial Balance

|  | Debit | Credit |
|--|-------|--------|
|  |       |        |
|  |       |        |
|  |       |        |
|  |       |        |
|  |       |        |
|  |       |        |
|  |       |        |
|  |       |        |
|  |       |        |
|  |       |        |
|  |       |        |

Name:_____

### Problem 4-14B

|                      | 2014 | 2013 |
|----------------------|------|------|
| **Current ratio**    |      |      |
| **Quick ratio**      |      |      |
| **Debt to equity ratio** |  |      |

**b. Comments:** _____

_____

_____

_____

_____

_____

_____

_____

_____

_____

_____

_____

_____

_____

_____

Chapter 4

Name:_____

**\*Problem 4-15B (cont'd.)**

**Part 1**

### GENERAL JOURNAL

Page_____

| Date | Account Titles and Explanation | PR | Debit | Credit |
|------|-------------------------------|-----|-------|--------|
|      |                               |     |       |        |
|      |                               |     |       |        |
|      |                               |     |       |        |
|      |                               |     |       |        |
|      |                               |     |       |        |
|      |                               |     |       |        |
|      |                               |     |       |        |
|      |                               |     |       |        |
|      |                               |     |       |        |
|      |                               |     |       |        |
|      |                               |     |       |        |
|      |                               |     |       |        |
|      |                               |     |       |        |
|      |                               |     |       |        |
|      |                               |     |       |        |
|      |                               |     |       |        |
|      |                               |     |       |        |
|      |                               |     |       |        |
|      |                               |     |       |        |
|      |                               |     |       |        |
|      |                               |     |       |        |
|      |                               |     |       |        |
|      |                               |     |       |        |
|      |                               |     |       |        |
|      |                               |     |       |        |
|      |                               |     |       |        |
|      |                               |     |       |        |
|      |                               |     |       |        |
|      |                               |     |       |        |
|      |                               |     |       |        |
|      |                               |     |       |        |
|      |                               |     |       |        |
|      |                               |     |       |        |
|      |                               |     |       |        |
|      |                               |     |       |        |
|      |                               |     |       |        |

Name:_____

**\*Problem 4-15B (concl'd.)**

**Part 2**                    GENERAL JOURNAL                    Page_____

| Date | Account Titles and Explanation | PR | Debit | Credit |
|------|-------------------------------|----|----|----|
|  |  |  |  |  |
|  |  |  |  |  |
|  |  |  |  |  |
|  |  |  |  |  |
|  |  |  |  |  |
|  |  |  |  |  |
|  |  |  |  |  |
|  |  |  |  |  |
|  |  |  |  |  |
|  |  |  |  |  |
|  |  |  |  |  |
|  |  |  |  |  |
|  |  |  |  |  |
|  |  |  |  |  |
|  |  |  |  |  |
|  |  |  |  |  |
|  |  |  |  |  |
|  |  |  |  |  |
|  |  |  |  |  |
|  |  |  |  |  |
|  |  |  |  |  |
|  |  |  |  |  |
|  |  |  |  |  |

**Part 3**

GENERAL JOURNAL                    Page_____

| Date | Account Titles and Explanation | PR | Debit | Credit |
|------|-------------------------------|----|----|----|
|  |  |  |  |  |
|  |  |  |  |  |
|  |  |  |  |  |
|  |  |  |  |  |
|  |  |  |  |  |
|  |  |  |  |  |
|  |  |  |  |  |
|  |  |  |  |  |
|  |  |  |  |  |
|  |  |  |  |  |
|  |  |  |  |  |

Name:_____

**Cumulative Problem**

**Part 1**  **Echo Systems**

### GENERAL JOURNAL

Page____

| Date | | Account Titles and Explanation | PR | Debit | Credit |
|---|---|---|---|---|---|
| | | | | | |
| | | | | | |
| | | | | | |
| | | | | | |
| | | | | | |
| | | | | | |
| | | | | | |
| | | | | | |
| | | | | | |
| | | | | | |
| | | | | | |
| | | | | | |
| | | | | | |
| | | | | | |
| | | | | | |
| | | | | | |
| | | | | | |
| | | | | | |
| | | | | | |
| | | | | | |
| | | | | | |
| | | | | | |
| | | | | | |
| | | | | | |
| | | | | | |
| | | | | | |
| | | | | | |
| | | | | | |
| | | | | | |
| | | | | | |
| | | | | | |
| | | | | | |
| | | | | | |
| | | | | | |
| | | | | | |
| | | | | | |
| | | | | | |
| | | | | | |
| | | | | | |
| | | | | | |
| | | | | | |
| | | | | | |
| | | | | | |
| | | | | | |

**Cumulative Problem (cont'd.)**

### GENERAL JOURNAL

Page_____

| Date | Account Titles and Explanation | PR | Debit | Credit |
|------|-------------------------------|----|-------|--------|
| | | | | |
| | | | | |
| | | | | |
| | | | | |
| | | | | |
| | | | | |
| | | | | |
| | | | | |
| | | | | |
| | | | | |
| | | | | |
| | | | | |
| | | | | |
| | | | | |
| | | | | |
| | | | | |
| | | | | |
| | | | | |
| | | | | |
| | | | | |
| | | | | |
| | | | | |
| | | | | |
| | | | | |
| | | | | |
| | | | | |
| | | | | |
| | | | | |
| | | | | |
| | | | | |
| | | | | |
| | | | | |
| | | | | |
| | | | | |
| | | | | |
| | | | | |
| | | | | |
| | | | | |
| | | | | |
| | | | | |
| | | | | |
| | | | | |

Name:_____

## Cumulative Problem (cont'd.)

### GENERAL LEDGER

#### Cash            ACCOUNT NO. 101

| DATE | EXPLANATION | PR | DEBIT | CREDIT | BALANCE |
|------|-------------|----|-------|--------|---------|
| 2017<br>Dec. 31 | Balance | | | | 89,090 |
| | | | | | |
| | | | | | |

#### Accounts Receivable     ACCOUNT NO. 106

| DATE | EXPLANATION | PR | DEBIT | CREDIT | BALANCE |
|------|-------------|----|-------|--------|---------|
| 2017<br>Dec. 31 | Balance | | | | 5,700 |
| | | | | | |
| | | | | | |

#### Computer Supplies     ACCOUNT NO. 126

| DATE | EXPLANATION | PR | DEBIT | CREDIT | BALANCE |
|------|-------------|----|-------|--------|---------|
| 2017<br>Dec. 31 | Balance | | | | 1,440 |
| | | | | | |
| | | | | | |

#### Prepaid Insurance     ACCOUNT NO. 128

| DATE | EXPLANATION | PR | DEBIT | CREDIT | BALANCE |
|------|-------------|----|-------|--------|---------|
| 2017<br>Dec. 31 | Balance | | | | 3,240 |
| | | | | | |
| | | | | | |

#### Prepaid Rent     ACCOUNT NO. 131

| DATE | EXPLANATION | PR | DEBIT | CREDIT | BALANCE |
|------|-------------|----|-------|--------|---------|
| 2017<br>Dec. 31 | Balance | | | | 2,250 |
| | | | | | |
| | | | | | |

#### Office Equipment     ACCOUNT NO. 163

| DATE | EXPLANATION | PR | DEBIT | CREDIT | BALANCE |
|------|-------------|----|-------|--------|---------|
| 2017<br>Dec. 31 | Balance | | | | 18,000 |
| | | | | | |
| | | | | | |

#### Accumulated Depreciation, Office Equipment     ACCOUNT NO. 164

| DATE | EXPLANATION | PR | DEBIT | CREDIT | BALANCE |
|------|-------------|----|-------|--------|---------|
| 2017<br>Dec. 31 | Balance | | | | 1,500 |
| | | | | | |

## Cumulative Problem (cont'd.)

### Computer Equipment                                   ACCOUNT NO. 167

| DATE | EXPLANATION | PR | DEBIT | CREDIT | BALANCE |
|---|---|---|---|---|---|
| 2017 Dec. 31 | Balance | | | | 36,000 |
| | | | | | |
| | | | | | |

### Accumulated Depreciation, Computer Equipment          ACCOUNT NO. 168

| DATE | EXPLANATION | PR | DEBIT | CREDIT | BALANCE |
|---|---|---|---|---|---|
| 2017 Dec. 31 | Balance | | | | 2,250 |
| | | | | | |
| | | | | | |

### Accounts Payable                                      ACCOUNT NO. 201

| DATE | EXPLANATION | PR | DEBIT | CREDIT | BALANCE |
|---|---|---|---|---|---|
| 2017 Dec. 31 | Balance | | | | 2,310 |
| | | | | | |
| | | | | | |

### Wages Payable                                         ACCOUNT NO. 210

| DATE | EXPLANATION | PR | DEBIT | CREDIT | BALANCE |
|---|---|---|---|---|---|
| 2017 Dec. 31 | Balance | | | | 800 |
| | | | | | |
| | | | | | |

### Unearned Computer Services Revenue                    ACCOUNT NO. 236

| DATE | EXPLANATION | PR | DEBIT | CREDIT | BALANCE |
|---|---|---|---|---|---|
| 2017 Dec. 31 | Balance | | | | 3,000 |
| | | | | | |
| | | | | | |

### Mary Graham, Capital                                  ACCOUNT NO. 301

| DATE | EXPLANATION | PR | DEBIT | CREDIT | BALANCE |
|---|---|---|---|---|---|
| 2017 Dec. 31 | Balance | | | | 144,000 |
| | | | | | |
| | | | | | |
| | | | | | |

### Mary Graham, Withdrawals                              ACCOUNT NO. 302

| DATE | EXPLANATION | PR | DEBIT | CREDIT | BALANCE |
|---|---|---|---|---|---|
| 2017 Dec. 31 | Balance | | | | 14,400 |
| | | | | | |
| | | | | | |

## Cumulative Problem (cont'd.)

### Computer Services Revenue ACCOUNT NO. 403

| DATE | EXPLANATION | PR | DEBIT | CREDIT | BALANCE |
|------|-------------|----|-------|--------|---------|
| 2017<br>Dec. 31 | Balance | | | | 52,200 |
| | | | | | |
| | | | | | |
| | | | | | |

### Depreciation Expense, Office Equipment ACCOUNT NO. 612

| DATE | EXPLANATION | PR | DEBIT | CREDIT | BALANCE |
|------|-------------|----|-------|--------|---------|
| 2017<br>Dec. 31 | Balance | | | | 1,500 |
| | | | | | |
| | | | | | |

### Depreciation Expense, Computer Equipment ACCOUNT NO. 613

| DATE | EXPLANATION | PR | DEBIT | CREDIT | BALANCE |
|------|-------------|----|-------|--------|---------|
| 2017<br>Dec. 31 | Balance | | | | 2,250 |
| | | | | | |
| | | | | | |

### Wages Expense ACCOUNT NO. 623

| DATE | EXPLANATION | PR | DEBIT | CREDIT | BALANCE |
|------|-------------|----|-------|--------|---------|
| 2017<br>Dec. 31 | Balance | | | | 6,200 |
| | | | | | |
| | | | | | |

### Insurance Expense ACCOUNT NO. 637

| DATE | EXPLANATION | PR | DEBIT | CREDIT | BALANCE |
|------|-------------|----|-------|--------|---------|
| 2017<br>Dec. 31 | Balance | | | | 1,080 |
| | | | | | |
| | | | | | |
| | | | | | |

### Rent Expense ACCOUNT NO. 640

| DATE | EXPLANATION | PR | DEBIT | CREDIT | BALANCE |
|------|-------------|----|-------|--------|---------|
| 2017<br>Dec. 31 | Balance | | | | 6,750 |
| | | | | | |
| | | | | | |

### Computer Supplies Expense ACCOUNT NO. 652

| DATE | EXPLANATION | PR | DEBIT | CREDIT | BALANCE |
|------|-------------|----|-------|--------|---------|
| 2017<br>Dec. 31 | Balance | | | | 5,430 |
| | | | | | |
| | | | | | |
| | | | | | |

## Cumulative Problem (cont'd.)

### Advertising Expense                                    ACCOUNT NO. 655

| DATE | EXPLANATION | PR | DEBIT | CREDIT | BALANCE |
|------|-------------|-----|-------|--------|---------|
| 2017 Dec. 31 | Balance | | | | 5,820 |
| | | | | | |
| | | | | | |

### Mileage Expense                                    ACCOUNT NO. 676

| DATE | EXPLANATION | PR | DEBIT | CREDIT | BALANCE |
|------|-------------|-----|-------|--------|---------|
| 2017 Dec. 31 | Balance | | | | 2,800 |
| | | | | | |
| | | | | | |

### Repairs Expense, Computer                                    ACCOUNT NO. 684

| DATE | EXPLANATION | PR | DEBIT | CREDIT | BALANCE |
|------|-------------|-----|-------|--------|---------|
| 2017 Dec. 31 | Balance | | | | 2,610 |
| | | | | | |
| | | | | | |

### Charitable Donations Expense                                    ACCOUNT NO. 699

| DATE | EXPLANATION | PR | DEBIT | CREDIT | BALANCE |
|------|-------------|-----|-------|--------|---------|
| 2017 Dec. 31 | Balance | | | | 1,500 |
| | | | | | |
| | | | | | |

### Income Summary                                    ACCOUNT NO. 901

| DATE | EXPLANATION | PR | DEBIT | CREDIT | BALANCE |
|------|-------------|-----|-------|--------|---------|
| 2017 Dec. 31 | Balance | | | | |
| | | | | | |
| | | | | | |
| | | | | | |

Name:_____

Cumulative Problem (concl'd.)

Part 2

## ECHO SYSTEMS
### Post-Closing Trial Balance
### December 31, 2017

|  | Debit | Credit |
|---|---|---|
|  |  |  |
|  |  |  |
|  |  |  |
|  |  |  |
|  |  |  |
|  |  |  |
|  |  |  |
|  |  |  |
|  |  |  |
|  |  |  |
|  |  |  |
|  |  |  |
|  |  |  |
|  |  |  |
|  |  |  |
|  |  |  |
|  |  |  |
|  |  |  |
|  |  |  |
|  |  |  |
|  |  |  |
|  |  |  |
|  |  |  |
|  |  |  |
|  |  |  |
|  |  |  |
|  |  |  |
|  |  |  |
|  |  |  |
|  |  |  |
|  |  |  |
|  |  |  |
|  |  |  |
|  |  |  |
|  |  |  |
|  |  |  |

**Chapter 5**                                    Name:_____

**Quick Study 5-1**

|                        | a. | b. | c. | d. | e. |
|------------------------|----|----|----|----|----|
| Net sales              |    |    |    |    |    |
| Cost of goods sold     |    |    |    |    |    |
| Gross profit from sales|    |    |    |    |    |
| Operating expenses     |    |    |    |    |    |
| Profit (loss)          |    |    |    |    |    |

**Quick Study 5-2**

a. _____

b. _____

c. _____

d. _____

e. _____

**Quick Study 5-3**

a. _____

_____

_____

b. _____

_____

_____

**Quick Study 5-4**

a. _____

_____

_____

b. _____

_____

_____

**Quick Study 5-5**

a. _____

_____

_____

b. _____

_____

_____

c. _____

_____

_____

Quick Study 5-5 (concl'd.)

## GENERAL JOURNAL　　　　　　　　　　　　Page____

| Date | Account Titles and Explanation | PR | Debit | Credit |
|------|-------------------------------|----|----|----|
|  |  |  |  |  |
|  |  |  |  |  |
|  |  |  |  |  |
|  |  |  |  |  |

d. _____

_____

_____

## GENERAL JOURNAL　　　　　　　　　　　　Page____

| Date | Account Titles and Explanation | PR | Debit | Credit |
|------|-------------------------------|----|----|----|
|  |  |  |  |  |
|  |  |  |  |  |
|  |  |  |  |  |
|  |  |  |  |  |

## Quick Study 5-6

## GENERAL JOURNAL　　　　　　　　　　　　Page____

| Date | Account Titles and Explanation | PR | Debit | Credit |
|------|-------------------------------|----|----|----|
| May 1 | Merchandise Inventory | | 1200 | |
|  | Accounts payable | | | 1200 |
|  | To record purchase of | | | |
|  | merchandise, terms 1/10, n/30. | | | |
|  |  | | | |
| 14 | Accounts payable | | 1200 | |
|  | Cash | | | 1200 |
|  | To record payment of | | | |
|  | credit purchase. | | | |

**Quick Study 5-6 (concl'd.)**

### GENERAL JOURNAL                                    Page____

| Date | | Account Titles and Explanation | PR | Debit | Credit |
|---|---|---|---|---|---|
| | 15 | Merchandise Inventory | | 3000 | |
| | |    Accounts payable | | | 3000 |
| | | To record purchase of | | | |
| | | merchandise, terms 2/15, n/30. | | | |
| | | | | | |
| | 30 | Accounts payable | | 3000 | |
| | |    Merchandise Inventory | | | 60 |
| | |    Cash | | | 2940 |
| | | To record pay of credit pur within | | | |
| | | dis period, $3000×2%, = $60. | | | |

**Quick Study 5-7**

### GENERAL JOURNAL                                    Page____

| Date | | Account Titles and Explanation | PR | Debit | Credit |
|---|---|---|---|---|---|
| Aug | 2 | Merchandise Inventory | | 14000 | |
| | |    Accounts payable | | | 14000 |
| | | To record pur of merchandis | | | |
| | | terms 1/5, n/15 | | | |
| | | | | | |
| | 4 | Accounts payable | | 1500 | |
| | |    Merchandise inventory | | | 1500 |
| | | To record allowance regarding | | | |
| | | Aug 2 credit purchase. | | | |
| | | | | | |
| | 17 | Accounts payable | | 12500 | |
| | |    Cash | | | 12500 |
| | | To record pay of credit pur | | | |
| | | less allowance, 14000-1500=12500 | | | |

**Quick Study 5-8**

### GENERAL JOURNAL                                    Page____

| Date | | Account Titles and Explanation | PR | Debit | Credit |
|---|---|---|---|---|---|
| | | | | | |
| | | | | | |
| | | | | | |
| | | | | | |
| | | | | | |
| | | | | | |
| | | | | | |

Name:_____

## Quick Study 5-8 (concl'd.)

### GENERAL JOURNAL                                    Page____

| Date | Account Titles and Explanation | PR | Debit | Credit |
|---|---|---|---|---|
|  |  |  |  |  |
|  |  |  |  |  |
|  |  |  |  |  |
|  |  |  |  |  |
|  |  |  |  |  |
|  |  |  |  |  |
|  |  |  |  |  |
|  |  |  |  |  |

## Quick Study 5-9

a. _____

_____

b. _____

_____

_____

### GENERAL JOURNAL                                    Page____

| Date | Account Titles and Explanation | PR | Debit | Credit |
|---|---|---|---|---|
| c. |  |  |  |  |
|  |  |  |  |  |
|  |  |  |  |  |
|  |  |  |  |  |
|  |  |  |  |  |
| d. |  |  |  |  |
|  |  |  |  |  |
|  |  |  |  |  |
|  |  |  |  |  |
|  |  |  |  |  |

Name:_____

## GENERAL JOURNAL

Page_____

| Date | | Account Titles and Explanation | PR | Debit | Credit |
|---|---|---|---|---|---|
| Sep | 1 | Account Receivable JenAir | | $ 6000 | |
| | | Sales | | | $ 6000 |
| | | To record sales 2/10, n/30. | | | |
| | | | | | |
| | 1 | Cost of goods sold | | $ 4200 | |
| | | Merchandise Inventory | | | 4200 |
| | | To record cost of sales. | | | |
| | | | | | |
| | 11 | Cash | | 6000 | |
| | | Account Receivable JenAir | | | 6000 |
| | | To record collection | | | |
| | | from credit customers. | | | |
| | | | | | |
| | 15 | Account Receivable Dennis level | | 1800 | |
| | | Sales | | | 1800. |
| | | | | | |
| | 15 | Cost of goods sold | | 1500 | |
| | | Merchandise invent | | | 1500 |
| | | | | | |
| | 25 | Cash | | 1764 | |
| | | Sales discount | | 36 | |
| | | Account Receivable Dennis level | | | 1800 |
| | | To record dis. | | | |
| | | collection within | | | |
| | | discount period | | | |
| | | $1800 X 2% = $36 | | | |
| | | | | | |
| | | | | | |

*Fundamental Accounting Principles*, 15ce, Working Papers

**Quick Study 5-11**

### GENERAL JOURNAL                                      Page____

| Date | Account Titles and Explanation | PR | Debit | Credit |
|------|-------------------------------|-----|-------|--------|
| Oct 15 | Account Receivable leslie | | 900 | |
| | Sales | | | 900 |
| 15 | Cost of goods sold | | 600 | |
| | Merchandise Inventory | | | 600 |
| 16 | Sales Return & allowance | | 100 | |
| | Account Receivable | | | 100 |
| 25 | Cash | | 800 | |
| | Sales discount | | | 800 |
| | Account Receivable | | | |
| | 900 - 100 | | | |
| | | | | |
| | | | | |
| | | | | |

**Quick Study 5-12**

### GENERAL JOURNAL                                      Page____

| Date | Account Titles and Explanation | PR | Debit | Credit |
|------|-------------------------------|-----|-------|--------|
| Apr 1 | Account Receivable | | $ 2000 | |
| | Sales | | | 2000 |
| 1 | Cost of goods sold | | 1400 | |
| | Merchandise Invent | | | 1400 |
| 4 | Sales Returns & allowances | | 500 | |
| | Account Receivable | | | 500 |
| 4 | Merchandise Inventory | | 350 | |
| | cost of goods sold | | | 350 |
| 11 | Cash | | 1470 | |
| | Sales discount | | 30 | |
| | Account Receiva | | | 1500 |
| | $500 × 2% = | | | |
| | 2000 - 500 = 1500 × 2% | | | |
| | = 30 | | | |

Name:_____

## Quick Study 5-12 (concl'd.)

### GENERAL JOURNAL

Page_____

| Date | Account Titles and Explanation | PR | Debit | Credit |
|------|-------------------------------|----|-------|--------|
|  |  |  |  |  |
|  |  |  |  |  |
|  |  |  |  |  |
|  |  |  |  |  |
|  |  |  |  |  |
|  |  |  |  |  |

## Quick Study 5-13

### GENERAL JOURNAL

Page_____

| Date | Account Titles and Explanation | PR | Debit | Credit |
|------|-------------------------------|----|-------|--------|
|  |  |  |  |  |
|  |  |  |  |  |
|  |  |  |  |  |
|  |  |  |  |  |
|  |  |  |  |  |
|  |  |  |  |  |
|  |  |  |  |  |

**Calculations:**

_____
_____
_____

*Fundamental Accounting Principles*, 15ce, Working Papers

Name:_____

**Quick Study 5-14**

a. **Classified Multi-Step**

| Income Statement | | | |
|---|---|---|---|
| | | | |
| | | | |
| | | | |
| | | | |
| | | | |
| | | | |
| | | | |
| | | | |
| | | | |
| | | | |
| | | | |
| | | | |
| | | | |
| | | | |
| | | | |
| | | | |
| | | | |
| | | | |
| | | | |
| | | | |
| | | | |
| | | | |

b. **Single-Step**

| Income Statement | | | |
|---|---|---|---|
| | | | |
| | | | |
| | | | |
| | | | |
| | | | |
| | | | |
| | | | |
| | | | |
| | | | |
| | | | |
| | | | |
| | | | |

Name:_____

**Quick Study 5-15**

|  | (a) | (b) | (c) | (d) |
|---|---|---|---|---|
|  |  |  |  |  |
|  |  |  |  |  |
|  |  |  |  |  |
|  |  |  |  |  |
|  |  |  |  |  |
|  |  |  |  |  |
|  |  |  |  |  |
|  |  |  |  |  |

**Calculations:**

_____

_____

_____

_____

_____

_____

_____

_____

Name:_____

**Quick Study 5-16**

_____
_____
_____
_____
_____
_____
_____
_____
_____

**Quick Study 5-17**

_____
_____
_____
_____
_____
_____
_____
_____
_____
_____

**Quick Study 5-18**

**1.**

**a.**

**b.**

**c.**

**2.**

**Quick Study 5-19**

**\*Quick Study 5-20**

**a. QS5-6 - Periodic**        **GENERAL JOURNAL**          Page_____

| Date | Account Titles and Explanation | PR | Debit | Credit |
|------|-------------------------------|-----|-------|--------|
|      |                               |     |       |        |
|      |                               |     |       |        |
|      |                               |     |       |        |
|      |                               |     |       |        |
|      |                               |     |       |        |
|      |                               |     |       |        |
|      |                               |     |       |        |
|      |                               |     |       |        |
|      |                               |     |       |        |
|      |                               |     |       |        |
|      |                               |     |       |        |
|      |                               |     |       |        |
|      |                               |     |       |        |
|      |                               |     |       |        |
|      |                               |     |       |        |

*Quick Study 5-20 (cont'd.)

b. QS5-7 - Periodic          GENERAL JOURNAL                    Page____

| Date | Account Titles and Explanation | PR | Debit | Credit |
|------|-------------------------------|----|----|----|
|  |  |  |  |  |
|  |  |  |  |  |
|  |  |  |  |  |
|  |  |  |  |  |
|  |  |  |  |  |
|  |  |  |  |  |
|  |  |  |  |  |
|  |  |  |  |  |
|  |  |  |  |  |
|  |  |  |  |  |
|  |  |  |  |  |
|  |  |  |  |  |
|  |  |  |  |  |
|  |  |  |  |  |
|  |  |  |  |  |
|  |  |  |  |  |

c. QS5-8 - Periodic          GENERAL JOURNAL                    Page____

| Date | Account Titles and Explanation | PR | Debit | Credit |
|------|-------------------------------|----|----|----|
|  |  |  |  |  |
|  |  |  |  |  |
|  |  |  |  |  |
|  |  |  |  |  |
|  |  |  |  |  |
|  |  |  |  |  |
|  |  |  |  |  |
|  |  |  |  |  |
|  |  |  |  |  |
|  |  |  |  |  |
|  |  |  |  |  |
|  |  |  |  |  |
|  |  |  |  |  |

*Quick Study 5-21

**a. QS5-10 - Periodic**                **GENERAL JOURNAL**                    Page____

| Date | Account Titles and Explanation | PR | Debit | Credit |
|------|-------------------------------|----|-------|--------|
|      |                               |    |       |        |
|      |                               |    |       |        |
|      |                               |    |       |        |
|      |                               |    |       |        |
|      |                               |    |       |        |
|      |                               |    |       |        |
|      |                               |    |       |        |
|      |                               |    |       |        |
|      |                               |    |       |        |
|      |                               |    |       |        |
|      |                               |    |       |        |
|      |                               |    |       |        |
|      |                               |    |       |        |
|      |                               |    |       |        |
|      |                               |    |       |        |
|      |                               |    |       |        |
|      |                               |    |       |        |
|      |                               |    |       |        |
|      |                               |    |       |        |
|      |                               |    |       |        |
|      |                               |    |       |        |

**b. QS5-11 - Periodic**                **GENERAL JOURNAL**                    Page____

| Date | Account Titles and Explanation | PR | Debit | Credit |
|------|-------------------------------|----|-------|--------|
|      |                               |    |       |        |
|      |                               |    |       |        |
|      |                               |    |       |        |
|      |                               |    |       |        |
|      |                               |    |       |        |
|      |                               |    |       |        |
|      |                               |    |       |        |
|      |                               |    |       |        |
|      |                               |    |       |        |
|      |                               |    |       |        |
|      |                               |    |       |        |
|      |                               |    |       |        |
|      |                               |    |       |        |
|      |                               |    |       |        |

Name:_____

*Quick Study 5-21 (concl'd.)

c. QS5-12 - Periodic          GENERAL JOURNAL          Page_____

| Date | Account Titles and Explanation | PR | Debit | Credit |
|------|-------------------------------|-----|-------|--------|
|      |                               |     |       |        |
|      |                               |     |       |        |
|      |                               |     |       |        |
|      |                               |     |       |        |
|      |                               |     |       |        |
|      |                               |     |       |        |
|      |                               |     |       |        |
|      |                               |     |       |        |
|      |                               |     |       |        |
|      |                               |     |       |        |
|      |                               |     |       |        |
|      |                               |     |       |        |
|      |                               |     |       |        |
|      |                               |     |       |        |
|      |                               |     |       |        |
|      |                               |     |       |        |

*Quick Study 5-22          Name _____

| | | |
|---|---|---|
| | | |
| | | |
| | | |
| | | |
| | | |
| | | |
| | | |
| | | |
| | | |

**\*Quick Study 5-23**

|  | (a) | (b) | (c) | (d) |
|---|---|---|---|---|
|  |  |  |  |  |
|  |  |  |  |  |
|  |  |  |  |  |
|  |  |  |  |  |
|  |  |  |  |  |
|  |  |  |  |  |
|  |  |  |  |  |
|  |  |  |  |  |
|  |  |  |  |  |
|  |  |  |  |  |
|  |  |  |  |  |
|  |  |  |  |  |

**Calculations:**

_____

_____

_____

_____

_____

**\*Quick Study 5-24**

### GENERAL JOURNAL                                    Page_____

| Date | | Account Titles and Explanation | PR | Debit | Credit |
|---|---|---|---|---|---|
|  |  |  |  |  |  |
|  |  |  |  |  |  |
|  |  |  |  |  |  |
|  |  |  |  |  |  |
|  |  |  |  |  |  |

**\*Quick Study 5-25**

### GENERAL JOURNAL                                    Page_____

| Date | | Account Titles and Explanation | PR | Debit | Credit |
|---|---|---|---|---|---|
|  |  |  |  |  |  |
|  |  |  |  |  |  |
|  |  |  |  |  |  |
|  |  |  |  |  |  |
|  |  |  |  |  |  |
|  |  |  |  |  |  |
|  |  |  |  |  |  |
|  |  |  |  |  |  |
|  |  |  |  |  |  |

Name:_____

**\*Quick Study 5-26**

### GENERAL JOURNAL

Page____

| Date | | Account Titles and Explanation | PR | Debit | Credit |
|------|---|-------------------------------|----|----|-----|
| | | | | | |
| | | | | | |
| | | | | | |
| | | | | | |

**\*Quick Study 5-27**

### GENERAL JOURNAL

Page____

| Date | | Account Titles and Explanation | PR | Debit | Credit |
|------|---|-------------------------------|----|----|-----|
| | | | | | |
| | | | | | |
| | | | | | |
| | | | | | |
| | | | | | |
| | | | | | |

## Exercise 5-1

|                          | a.      | b.      | c.      | d.      | e.      |
|--------------------------|---------|---------|---------|---------|---------|
| Sales                    | 240,000 | 140,000 | 75,000  |         |         |
| Cost of goods sold       |         |         | 42,000  | 268,000 | 46,000  |
| Gross profit from sales  | 114,000 |         |         |         | 39,000  |
| Operating expenses       | 95,000  | 82,000  |         | 146,000 |         |
| Profit (loss)            |         | (28,000)| (8,000) | 48,000  | (14,000)|

Name:_____

**Exercise 5-2**

### GENERAL JOURNAL

Page_____

| Date | Account Titles and Explanation | PR | Debit | Credit |
|------|-------------------------------|----|-------|--------|
|      |                               |    |       |        |
|      |                               |    |       |        |
|      |                               |    |       |        |
|      |                               |    |       |        |
|      |                               |    |       |        |
|      |                               |    |       |        |
|      |                               |    |       |        |
|      |                               |    |       |        |
|      |                               |    |       |        |
|      |                               |    |       |        |
|      |                               |    |       |        |
|      |                               |    |       |        |
|      |                               |    |       |        |
|      |                               |    |       |        |
|      |                               |    |       |        |
|      |                               |    |       |        |
|      |                               |    |       |        |
|      |                               |    |       |        |
|      |                               |    |       |        |
|      |                               |    |       |        |
|      |                               |    |       |        |
|      |                               |    |       |        |
|      |                               |    |       |        |
|      |                               |    |       |        |
|      |                               |    |       |        |
|      |                               |    |       |        |
|      |                               |    |       |        |
|      |                               |    |       |        |
|      |                               |    |       |        |
|      |                               |    |       |        |
|      |                               |    |       |        |
|      |                               |    |       |        |

**Exercise 5-3**

## GENERAL JOURNAL

| Date | Account Titles and Explanation | PR | Debit | Credit |
|------|-------------------------------|----|-------|--------|
| | | | | |
| | | | | |
| | | | | |
| | | | | |
| | | | | |
| | | | | |
| | | | | |
| | | | | |
| | | | | |
| | | | | |
| | | | | |
| | | | | |
| | | | | |
| | | | | |
| | | | | |
| | | | | |
| | | | | |
| | | | | |
| | | | | |
| | | | | |
| | | | | |
| | | | | |
| | | | | |
| | | | | |
| | | | | |
| | | | | |
| | | | | |
| | | | | |
| | | | | |
| | | | | |
| | | | | |
| | | | | |
| | | | | |
| | | | | |
| | | | | |
| | | | | |
| | | | | |
| | | | | |
| | | | | |
| | | | | |
| | | | | |
| | | | | |

**Exercise 5-4**

### GENERAL JOURNAL

Page_____

| Date | | Account Titles and Explanation | PR | Debit | Credit |
|---|---|---|---|---|---|
| | | | | | |
| | | | | | |
| | | | | | |
| | | | | | |
| | | | | | |
| | | | | | |
| | | | | | |
| | | | | | |
| | | | | | |
| | | | | | |
| | | | | | |
| | | | | | |
| | | | | | |
| | | | | | |
| | | | | | |
| | | | | | |
| | | | | | |
| | | | | | |
| | | | | | |
| | | | | | |
| | | | | | |
| | | | | | |
| | | | | | |
| | | | | | |
| | | | | | |
| | | | | | |
| | | | | | |
| | | | | | |
| | | | | | |
| | | | | | |
| | | | | | |
| | | | | | |
| | | | | | |
| | | | | | |
| | | | | | |
| | | | | | |
| | | | | | |
| | | | | | |
| | | | | | |
| | | | | | |

**Exercise 5-5**

**GENERAL JOURNAL**

Page____

| Date | Account Titles and Explanation | PR | Debit | Credit |
|------|-------------------------------|----|-------|--------|
| Feb 1 | Ac Receiv | | 2100 | |
| | Sales | | | 2100 |
| 1 | Cost of Goods Sold | | 1500 | |
| | Merchandise Invent | | | 1500 |
| 2 | Delivery expense | | 225 | |
| | Cash | | | 225 |
| 3 | Sales Returns & allow | | 1050 | |
| | Account Receir | | | 1050 |
| 3 | Merchandise Invt | | 750 | |
| | Cost of goods sold | | | 750 |
| 4 | Acount Receivable | | 3800 | |
| | Sales | | | 3800 |
| 4 | Cost of goods sold | | 2280 | |
| | Merchand Invt | | | 2280 |
| 11 | Cash | | 1029 | |
| | Sales discount | | 21 | |
| | Account Receivable | | | 1050 |
| | 1050 × 2% = $21 | | | |
| 23 | Cash | | 1200 | |
| | Sales | | | 1200 |
| 23 | Cost of goods sold | | 720 | |
| | Merchan Inventory | | | 720 |
| 28 | Cash | | 3800 | |
| | Ac Recei | | | 3800 |

**Exercise 5-5 (concl'd.)**

## GENERAL JOURNAL

Page____

| Date | Account Titles and Explanation | PR | Debit | Credit |
|------|-------------------------------|-----|-------|--------|
|      |                               |     |       |        |
|      |                               |     |       |        |
|      |                               |     |       |        |
|      |                               |     |       |        |
|      |                               |     |       |        |
|      |                               |     |       |        |
|      |                               |     |       |        |
|      |                               |     |       |        |
|      |                               |     |       |        |
|      |                               |     |       |        |
|      |                               |     |       |        |
|      |                               |     |       |        |
|      |                               |     |       |        |
|      |                               |     |       |        |
|      |                               |     |       |        |
|      |                               |     |       |        |
|      |                               |     |       |        |
|      |                               |     |       |        |
|      |                               |     |       |        |
|      |                               |     |       |        |
|      |                               |     |       |        |
|      |                               |     |       |        |
|      |                               |     |       |        |
|      |                               |     |       |        |
|      |                               |     |       |        |
|      |                               |     |       |        |
|      |                               |     |       |        |
|      |                               |     |       |        |

**Exercise 5-6**

**GENERAL JOURNAL**

| Date | Account Titles and Explanation | PR | Debit | Credit |
|------|-------------------------------|-----|-------|--------|
| Oct 1 | Merchandise Inventory | | 1400 | |
| | Account payable- Orbiteoo | | | 1400 |
| 1 | Merchandise Inventory | | 200 | |
| | Shipping Cost | | | 200 |
| 5 | Account Receiveble | | 600 | |
| | Sales | | | 600 |
| 5 | Cost of goods Sold | | 420 | |
| | Merchandise Inventory | | | 420 |
| 7 | Account Payable | | 500 | |
| | Merchandise Inventory | | | 500 |
| 10 | Account payable | | 900 | |
| | Merchandise Inventory | | | 27 |
| | Cash | | | 873 |
| | 1400 - 500 = 900 X3% = 27 | | | |
| 14 | Sales Returns & allowance | | 100 | |
| | Account Receivable | | | 100 |
| 14 | Merchandise inventory | | 70 | |
| 14 | Cost of goods sold | | | 70 |
| 22 | Cash | | 500 | |
| | Account Receivable | | | 500 |
| | 600 - 100 | | | |
| 23 | Merchan Inventory | | 2000 | |
| | Account payable | | | 2000 |
| 23 | Mercha Inventory | | 300 | |
| | Cash | | | 300 |
| 25 | Ac Rec | | 1000 | |
| | Sale | | | 1000 |

## GENERAL JOURNAL

Page____

| Date | Account Titles and Explanation | PR | Debit | Credit |
|------|-------------------------------|----|----|----|
| 25 | cost of goods s | | 700 | |
| | Merch inventory | | | 700 |
| 25 | freight exp | | 150 | |
| | cash | | | 150 |
| 26 | Account payable | | 2000 | |
| | cash | | | 1960 |
| | Merch inventory | | | 40 |
| | 2000 × 2% | | | |
| 31 | Cash | | 980 | |
| | sale discount | | 20 | |
| | Account Receivable | | | 1000 |
| | 1000 × 2% | | | |

Name:_____

**Exercise 5-7**

a.  **Entries journalized by Wilson Purchasing:**

**GENERAL JOURNAL**                                      Page____

| Date | Account Titles and Explanation | PR | Debit | Credit |
|------|-------------------------------|----|----|----|
|  |  |  |  |  |
|  |  |  |  |  |
|  |  |  |  |  |
|  |  |  |  |  |
|  |  |  |  |  |
|  |  |  |  |  |
|  |  |  |  |  |
|  |  |  |  |  |
|  |  |  |  |  |
|  |  |  |  |  |
|  |  |  |  |  |
|  |  |  |  |  |
|  |  |  |  |  |
|  |  |  |  |  |
|  |  |  |  |  |
|  |  |  |  |  |
|  |  |  |  |  |
|  |  |  |  |  |

b.  **Entries journalized by Hostel Sales:**

**GENERAL JOURNAL**                                      Page____

| Date | Account Titles and Explanation | PR | Debit | Credit |
|------|-------------------------------|----|----|----|
|  |  |  |  |  |
|  |  |  |  |  |
|  |  |  |  |  |
|  |  |  |  |  |
|  |  |  |  |  |
|  |  |  |  |  |
|  |  |  |  |  |
|  |  |  |  |  |
|  |  |  |  |  |
|  |  |  |  |  |
|  |  |  |  |  |
|  |  |  |  |  |
|  |  |  |  |  |

Name:_____

## Exercise 5-7 (concl'd.)

### GENERAL JOURNAL

Page_____

| Date | Account Titles and Explanation | PR | Debit | Credit |
|------|-------------------------------|----|----|----|
|  |  |  |  |  |
|  |  |  |  |  |
|  |  |  |  |  |
|  |  |  |  |  |
|  |  |  |  |  |
|  |  |  |  |  |
|  |  |  |  |  |
|  |  |  |  |  |
|  |  |  |  |  |
|  |  |  |  |  |
|  |  |  |  |  |
|  |  |  |  |  |
|  |  |  |  |  |
|  |  |  |  |  |

*Analysis component:*

_____
_____
_____
_____
_____
_____
_____
_____
_____
_____
_____
_____
_____
_____
_____

## Exercise 5-8

| 1. | 6. |
|----|----|
| 2. | 7. |
| 3. | 8. |
| 4. | 9. |
| 5. | 10. |

**Exercise 5-9**

| Merchandise Inventory | Cost of Goods Sold |
|---|---|
| | |

*Analysis component:*

_____
_____
_____
_____
_____
_____
_____
_____
_____
_____
_____
_____

**Exercise 5-10**

a._____
b._____
c._____
d._____

*Analysis component:*

_____
_____
_____
_____
_____
_____
_____
_____

## Exercise 5-11

| | Company A | | Company B | |
|---|---|---|---|---|
| | 2017 | 2016 | 2017 | 2016 |
| Sales | $ 256,000 | $ 180,000 | | $ 45,000 |
| Sales discounts | 2,560 | | $ 1,100 | 500 |
| Sales returns and allowances | _____ | 16,000 | 5,500 | _____ |
| Net sales | | 163,000 | | 42,000 |
| Cost of goods sold | 153,600 | _____ | 57,000 | _____ |
| Gross profit from sales | 51,000 | _____ | 48,400 | 20,000 |
| Selling expenses | 17,920 | 19,000 | 25,000 | |
| Administrative expenses | 25,600 | _____ | 29,700 | 9,000 |
| Total operating expenses | | 46,000 | | |
| Profit (loss) | | $ 14,400 | | $ 2,000 |
| Gross profit ratio | | | | |

Calculations:

_____
_____
_____
_____
_____
_____
_____

*Analysis component:*

_____
_____
_____
_____
_____
_____
_____

Name:_____

**Exercise 5-12**

a.

### Income Statement

| | | |
|---|---|---|
| | | |
| | | |
| | | |
| | | |
| | | |
| | | |
| | | |
| | | |
| | | |
| | | |
| | | |
| | | |
| | | |

*Analysis component:*

_____
_____
_____
_____
_____
_____
_____
_____

**Exercise 5-13**

Part a

### GENERAL JOURNAL

Page_____

| Date | Account Titles and Explanation | PR | Debit | Credit |
|---|---|---|---|---|
| | | | | |
| | | | | |
| | | | | |
| | | | | |
| | | | | |
| | | | | |
| | | | | |
| | | | | |
| | | | | |
| | | | | |

**Exercise 5-13 (cont'd.)**

**Part b**

### Income Statement

|  |  |  |  |
|---|---|---|---|
|  |  |  |  |
|  |  |  |  |
|  |  |  |  |
|  |  |  |  |
|  |  |  |  |
|  |  |  |  |
|  |  |  |  |
|  |  |  |  |
|  |  |  |  |
|  |  |  |  |
|  |  |  |  |
|  |  |  |  |
|  |  |  |  |
|  |  |  |  |
|  |  |  |  |
|  |  |  |  |

*Analysis component:*

_____

_____

_____

_____

_____

_____

_____

**Exercise 5-14**

**1.** _____

_____

**2.** _____

_____

**3.** _____

_____

_____

# Chapter 5

Name:_____

## *Exercise 5-15

|  | (a) | (b) | (c) |
|---|---|---|---|
| Purchases |  |  |  |
| Purchases discounts |  |  |  |
| Purchase returns and allowances |  |  |  |
| Transportation-in |  |  |  |
| Cost of goods purchased |  |  |  |
|  |  |  |  |
| Beginning inventory |  |  |  |
| Cost of goods purchased |  |  |  |
| Ending inventory |  |  |  |
| Cost of goods sold |  |  |  |

## *Exercise 5-16

|  | Company A | | Company B | |
|---|---|---|---|---|
|  | 2017 | 2016 | 2017 | 2016 |
| Sales | 110,000 | 185,000 | 90,000 |  |
| Cost of goods sold: |  |  |  |  |
|   Merch. inventory (beginning) | 8,700 | 27,300 | 8,875 | 8,000 |
|   Net cost of merchandise purchases | 62,000 |  |  | 26,100 |
|   Merch. Inventory (ending) |  | (20,000) | (8,920) | (9,875) |
|   Cost of goods sold | 64,300 | 106,000 |  |  |
| Gross profit from sales |  |  | 39,545 | 19,775 |
| Operating expenses | 26,000 | 54,000 | 27,000 |  |
| Profit (loss) | 1,700 | 18,000 |  | 6,275 |
| Gross profit ratio |  |  |  |  |

*Analysis component:*

_____
_____
_____
_____

*Fundamental Accounting Principles*, 15ce, Working Papers

*Exercise 5-17

|  | (a) | (b) | (c) |
|---|---|---|---|
| Invoice cost of merch. purchases | 44,400 | 21,000 | 16,250 |
| Purchase discounts | 2,000 |  | 325 |
| Purchase returns and allowances | 1,500 | 750 | 550 |
| Cost of transportation-in |  | 1,750 | 2,000 |
|  |  |  |  |
| Merchandise inventory (beginning) | 4,500 |  | 3,500 |
| Net cost of merchandise purchases | 44,700 | 19,750 |  |
| Merchandise inventory (ending) | 2,200 | 3,750 |  |
| Cost of goods sold |  | 20,800 | 17,065 |

*Exercise 5-18

### GENERAL JOURNAL                                    Page_____

| Date | Account Titles and Explanation | PR | Debit | Credit |
|---|---|---|---|---|
|  |  |  |  |  |
|  |  |  |  |  |
|  |  |  |  |  |
|  |  |  |  |  |
|  |  |  |  |  |
|  |  |  |  |  |
|  |  |  |  |  |
|  |  |  |  |  |
|  |  |  |  |  |
|  |  |  |  |  |
|  |  |  |  |  |
|  |  |  |  |  |
|  |  |  |  |  |
|  |  |  |  |  |
|  |  |  |  |  |
|  |  |  |  |  |
|  |  |  |  |  |
|  |  |  |  |  |
|  |  |  |  |  |
|  |  |  |  |  |
|  |  |  |  |  |
|  |  |  |  |  |
|  |  |  |  |  |
|  |  |  |  |  |
|  |  |  |  |  |
|  |  |  |  |  |

Name:_____

**\*Exercise 5-18 (cont'd.)**

### GENERAL JOURNAL

Page____

| Date | Account Titles and Explanation | PR | Debit | Credit |
|------|-------------------------------|-----|-------|--------|
|      |                               |     |       |        |
|      |                               |     |       |        |
|      |                               |     |       |        |
|      |                               |     |       |        |
|      |                               |     |       |        |
|      |                               |     |       |        |
|      |                               |     |       |        |
|      |                               |     |       |        |
|      |                               |     |       |        |
|      |                               |     |       |        |
|      |                               |     |       |        |
|      |                               |     |       |        |
|      |                               |     |       |        |
|      |                               |     |       |        |
|      |                               |     |       |        |
|      |                               |     |       |        |
|      |                               |     |       |        |
|      |                               |     |       |        |
|      |                               |     |       |        |
|      |                               |     |       |        |
|      |                               |     |       |        |
|      |                               |     |       |        |
|      |                               |     |       |        |
|      |                               |     |       |        |
|      |                               |     |       |        |
|      |                               |     |       |        |
|      |                               |     |       |        |
|      |                               |     |       |        |
|      |                               |     |       |        |
|      |                               |     |       |        |
|      |                               |     |       |        |
|      |                               |     |       |        |
|      |                               |     |       |        |
|      |                               |     |       |        |
|      |                               |     |       |        |
|      |                               |     |       |        |
|      |                               |     |       |        |
|      |                               |     |       |        |

Name:_____

**\*Exercise 5-18 (concl'd.)**

### GENERAL JOURNAL

Page____

| Date | Account Titles and Explanation | PR | Debit | Credit |
|------|-------------------------------|----|----|----|
|  |  |  |  |  |
|  |  |  |  |  |
|  |  |  |  |  |
|  |  |  |  |  |
|  |  |  |  |  |
|  |  |  |  |  |
|  |  |  |  |  |
|  |  |  |  |  |
|  |  |  |  |  |
|  |  |  |  |  |
|  |  |  |  |  |
|  |  |  |  |  |
|  |  |  |  |  |
|  |  |  |  |  |
|  |  |  |  |  |
|  |  |  |  |  |
|  |  |  |  |  |
|  |  |  |  |  |
|  |  |  |  |  |
|  |  |  |  |  |
|  |  |  |  |  |
|  |  |  |  |  |
|  |  |  |  |  |
|  |  |  |  |  |
|  |  |  |  |  |
|  |  |  |  |  |
|  |  |  |  |  |
|  |  |  |  |  |
|  |  |  |  |  |
|  |  |  |  |  |
|  |  |  |  |  |
|  |  |  |  |  |
|  |  |  |  |  |
|  |  |  |  |  |
|  |  |  |  |  |
|  |  |  |  |  |
|  |  |  |  |  |
|  |  |  |  |  |

Name:_____

*Exercise 5-19

## GENERAL JOURNAL

Page____

| Date | Account Titles and Explanation | PR | Debit | Credit |
|------|-------------------------------|----|-------|--------|
|  |  |  |  |  |
|  |  |  |  |  |
|  |  |  |  |  |
|  |  |  |  |  |
|  |  |  |  |  |
|  |  |  |  |  |
|  |  |  |  |  |
|  |  |  |  |  |
|  |  |  |  |  |
|  |  |  |  |  |
|  |  |  |  |  |
|  |  |  |  |  |
|  |  |  |  |  |
|  |  |  |  |  |
|  |  |  |  |  |
|  |  |  |  |  |
|  |  |  |  |  |
|  |  |  |  |  |
|  |  |  |  |  |
|  |  |  |  |  |
|  |  |  |  |  |
|  |  |  |  |  |
|  |  |  |  |  |
|  |  |  |  |  |
|  |  |  |  |  |
|  |  |  |  |  |
|  |  |  |  |  |
|  |  |  |  |  |
|  |  |  |  |  |
|  |  |  |  |  |
|  |  |  |  |  |
|  |  |  |  |  |
|  |  |  |  |  |
|  |  |  |  |  |
|  |  |  |  |  |
|  |  |  |  |  |
|  |  |  |  |  |
|  |  |  |  |  |
|  |  |  |  |  |
|  |  |  |  |  |
|  |  |  |  |  |
|  |  |  |  |  |

*Exercise 5-20

**GENERAL JOURNAL**

Page_____

| Date | Account Titles and Explanation | PR | Debit | Credit |
|------|-------------------------------|----|----|----|
|  |  |  |  |  |
|  |  |  |  |  |
|  |  |  |  |  |
|  |  |  |  |  |
|  |  |  |  |  |
|  |  |  |  |  |
|  |  |  |  |  |
|  |  |  |  |  |
|  |  |  |  |  |
|  |  |  |  |  |
|  |  |  |  |  |
|  |  |  |  |  |
|  |  |  |  |  |
|  |  |  |  |  |
|  |  |  |  |  |
|  |  |  |  |  |
|  |  |  |  |  |
|  |  |  |  |  |
|  |  |  |  |  |
|  |  |  |  |  |
|  |  |  |  |  |
|  |  |  |  |  |
|  |  |  |  |  |
|  |  |  |  |  |
|  |  |  |  |  |
|  |  |  |  |  |
|  |  |  |  |  |
|  |  |  |  |  |
|  |  |  |  |  |
|  |  |  |  |  |
|  |  |  |  |  |
|  |  |  |  |  |
|  |  |  |  |  |
|  |  |  |  |  |
|  |  |  |  |  |
|  |  |  |  |  |

Name:_____

*Exercise 5-21

## GENERAL JOURNAL                                      Page____

| Date | Account Titles and Explanation | PR | Debit | Credit |
|------|-------------------------------|----|----|------|
|  |  |  |  |  |
|  |  |  |  |  |
|  |  |  |  |  |
|  |  |  |  |  |
|  |  |  |  |  |
|  |  |  |  |  |
|  |  |  |  |  |
|  |  |  |  |  |
|  |  |  |  |  |
|  |  |  |  |  |
|  |  |  |  |  |
|  |  |  |  |  |
|  |  |  |  |  |
|  |  |  |  |  |
|  |  |  |  |  |
|  |  |  |  |  |
|  |  |  |  |  |
|  |  |  |  |  |
|  |  |  |  |  |
|  |  |  |  |  |
|  |  |  |  |  |
|  |  |  |  |  |
|  |  |  |  |  |
|  |  |  |  |  |
|  |  |  |  |  |
|  |  |  |  |  |

*Exercise 5-22

## GENERAL JOURNAL                                      Page____

| Date | Account Titles and Explanation | PR | Debit | Credit |
|------|-------------------------------|----|----|------|
|  |  |  |  |  |
|  |  |  |  |  |
|  |  |  |  |  |
|  |  |  |  |  |
|  |  |  |  |  |
|  |  |  |  |  |
|  |  |  |  |  |
|  |  |  |  |  |
|  |  |  |  |  |
|  |  |  |  |  |
|  |  |  |  |  |
|  |  |  |  |  |

*Exercise 5–22 (concl'd.)

GENERAL JOURNAL                                    Page____

| Date | Account Titles and Explanation | PR | Debit | Credit |
|------|-------------------------------|----|-------|--------|
|      |                               |    |       |        |
|      |                               |    |       |        |
|      |                               |    |       |        |
|      |                               |    |       |        |
|      |                               |    |       |        |
|      |                               |    |       |        |
|      |                               |    |       |        |
|      |                               |    |       |        |
|      |                               |    |       |        |
|      |                               |    |       |        |
|      |                               |    |       |        |
|      |                               |    |       |        |
|      |                               |    |       |        |
|      |                               |    |       |        |
|      |                               |    |       |        |
|      |                               |    |       |        |
|      |                               |    |       |        |
|      |                               |    |       |        |

*Exercise 5-23

GENERAL JOURNAL                                    Page____

| Date | Account Titles and Explanation | PR | Debit | Credit |
|------|-------------------------------|----|-------|--------|
|      |                               |    |       |        |
|      |                               |    |       |        |
|      |                               |    |       |        |
|      |                               |    |       |        |
|      |                               |    |       |        |
|      |                               |    |       |        |
|      |                               |    |       |        |
|      |                               |    |       |        |
|      |                               |    |       |        |
|      |                               |    |       |        |
|      |                               |    |       |        |
|      |                               |    |       |        |
|      |                               |    |       |        |
|      |                               |    |       |        |
|      |                               |    |       |        |
|      |                               |    |       |        |

**\*Exercise 5–23 (concl'd.)**

**GENERAL JOURNAL**                          Page____

| Date | | Account Titles and Explanation | PR | Debit | Credit |
|---|---|---|---|---|---|
| | | | | | |
| | | | | | |
| | | | | | |
| | | | | | |
| | | | | | |
| | | | | | |
| | | | | | |
| | | | | | |
| | | | | | |
| | | | | | |
| | | | | | |
| | | | | | |
| | | | | | |
| | | | | | |
| | | | | | |
| | | | | | |
| | | | | | |
| | | | | | |
| | | | | | |
| | | | | | |
| | | | | | |
| | | | | | |
| | | | | | |
| | | | | | |
| | | | | | |
| | | | | | |
| | | | | | |
| | | | | | |
| | | | | | |
| | | | | | |
| | | | | | |
| | | | | | |
| | | | | | |
| | | | | | |
| | | | | | |
| | | | | | |
| | | | | | |
| | | | | | |
| | | | | | |
| | | | | | |
| | | | | | |

Name:_____

*Exercise 5-24

### GENERAL JOURNAL

| Date | | Account Titles and Explanation | PR | Debit | Credit |
|------|---|-------------------------------|----|----|------|
| | | | | | |
| | | | | | |
| | | | | | |
| | | | | | |
| | | | | | |
| | | | | | |
| | | | | | |
| | | | | | |
| | | | | | |
| | | | | | |
| | | | | | |
| | | | | | |
| | | | | | |
| | | | | | |
| | | | | | |
| | | | | | |
| | | | | | |
| | | | | | |
| | | | | | |
| | | | | | |
| | | | | | |
| | | | | | |
| | | | | | |
| | | | | | |
| | | | | | |
| | | | | | |
| | | | | | |
| | | | | | |
| | | | | | |
| | | | | | |
| | | | | | |
| | | | | | |
| | | | | | |
| | | | | | |
| | | | | | |
| | | | | | |
| | | | | | |
| | | | | | |
| | | | | | |

**\*Exercise 5-25**

a.

| | | |
|---|---|---|
| | | |
| | | |
| | | |
| | | |
| | | |
| | | |
| | | |

b.

| | | |
|---|---|---|
| | | |
| | | |
| | | |
| | | |
| | | |
| | | |
| | | |

c.

| | | |
|---|---|---|
| | | |
| | | |
| | | |
| | | |
| | | |
| | | |
| | | |
| | | |
| | | |
| | | |

d. _____

_____

_____

*Analysis component:*

_____

_____

_____

_____

_____

_____

_____

Name:_____

*Exercise 5-26

a. _____

b. _____

c. _____

## Income Statement

| | | | | |
|---|---|---|---|---|
| | | | | |
| | | | | |
| | | | | |
| | | | | |
| | | | | |
| | | | | |
| | | | | |
| | | | | |
| | | | | |
| | | | | |
| | | | | |
| | | | | |
| | | | | |
| | | | | |
| | | | | |
| | | | | |
| | | | | |
| | | | | |
| | | | | |
| | | | | |
| | | | | |
| | | | | |
| | | | | |
| | | | | |
| | | | | |
| | | | | |
| | | | | |
| | | | | |
| | | | | |
| | | | | |
| | | | | |
| | | | | |
| | | | | |
| | | | | |

Name:_____

**\*Exercise 5-27**

## GENERAL JOURNAL                                Page_____

| Date | Account Titles and Explanation | PR | Debit | Credit |
|------|-------------------------------|----|----|----|
|  |  |  |  |  |
|  |  |  |  |  |
|  |  |  |  |  |
|  |  |  |  |  |
|  |  |  |  |  |
|  |  |  |  |  |
|  |  |  |  |  |
|  |  |  |  |  |
|  |  |  |  |  |
|  |  |  |  |  |
|  |  |  |  |  |
|  |  |  |  |  |
|  |  |  |  |  |
|  |  |  |  |  |
|  |  |  |  |  |
|  |  |  |  |  |
|  |  |  |  |  |
|  |  |  |  |  |
|  |  |  |  |  |
|  |  |  |  |  |
|  |  |  |  |  |

**\*Exercise 5-28**

## GENERAL JOURNAL                                Page_____

| Date | Account Titles and Explanation | PR | Debit | Credit |
|------|-------------------------------|----|----|----|
|  |  |  |  |  |
|  |  |  |  |  |
|  |  |  |  |  |
|  |  |  |  |  |
|  |  |  |  |  |
|  |  |  |  |  |
|  |  |  |  |  |
|  |  |  |  |  |
|  |  |  |  |  |
|  |  |  |  |  |
|  |  |  |  |  |
|  |  |  |  |  |

**Problem 5-1A**

Part 1                                    GENERAL JOURNAL                                    Page____

| Date | Account Titles and Explanation | PR | Debit | Credit |
|------|-------------------------------|----|-------|--------|
|      |                               |    |       |        |
|      |                               |    |       |        |
|      |                               |    |       |        |
|      |                               |    |       |        |
|      |                               |    |       |        |
|      |                               |    |       |        |
|      |                               |    |       |        |
|      |                               |    |       |        |
|      |                               |    |       |        |
|      |                               |    |       |        |
|      |                               |    |       |        |
|      |                               |    |       |        |
|      |                               |    |       |        |
|      |                               |    |       |        |
|      |                               |    |       |        |
|      |                               |    |       |        |
|      |                               |    |       |        |
|      |                               |    |       |        |
|      |                               |    |       |        |
|      |                               |    |       |        |
|      |                               |    |       |        |
|      |                               |    |       |        |
|      |                               |    |       |        |
|      |                               |    |       |        |
|      |                               |    |       |        |
|      |                               |    |       |        |
|      |                               |    |       |        |
|      |                               |    |       |        |
|      |                               |    |       |        |
|      |                               |    |       |        |
|      |                               |    |       |        |
|      |                               |    |       |        |
|      |                               |    |       |        |
|      |                               |    |       |        |
|      |                               |    |       |        |
|      |                               |    |       |        |
|      |                               |    |       |        |
|      |                               |    |       |        |
|      |                               |    |       |        |
|      |                               |    |       |        |
|      |                               |    |       |        |
|      |                               |    |       |        |

**Problem 5-1A (concl'd.)**

## GENERAL JOURNAL                                                Page_____

| Date | Account Titles and Explanation | PR | Debit | Credit |
|------|-------------------------------|----|----|-----|
|      |                               |    |    |     |
|      |                               |    |    |     |
|      |                               |    |    |     |
|      |                               |    |    |     |
|      |                               |    |    |     |
|      |                               |    |    |     |
|      |                               |    |    |     |
|      |                               |    |    |     |
|      |                               |    |    |     |
|      |                               |    |    |     |
|      |                               |    |    |     |
|      |                               |    |    |     |
|      |                               |    |    |     |
|      |                               |    |    |     |
|      |                               |    |    |     |
|      |                               |    |    |     |
|      |                               |    |    |     |
|      |                               |    |    |     |
|      |                               |    |    |     |
|      |                               |    |    |     |

**Part 2**

_____

_____

_____

_____

_____

**Problem 5-2A**

## GENERAL JOURNAL                                                Page_____

| Date | Account Titles and Explanation | PR | Debit | Credit |
|------|-------------------------------|----|----|-----|
|      |                               |    |    |     |
|      |                               |    |    |     |
|      |                               |    |    |     |
|      |                               |    |    |     |
|      |                               |    |    |     |
|      |                               |    |    |     |
|      |                               |    |    |     |
|      |                               |    |    |     |
|      |                               |    |    |     |
|      |                               |    |    |     |

Name:_____

**Problem 5-2A (cont'd.)**

**GENERAL JOURNAL**

Page____

| Date | Account Titles and Explanation | PR | Debit | Credit |
|---|---|---|---|---|
| | | | | |
| | | | | |
| | | | | |
| | | | | |
| | | | | |
| | | | | |
| | | | | |
| | | | | |
| | | | | |
| | | | | |
| | | | | |
| | | | | |
| | | | | |
| | | | | |
| | | | | |
| | | | | |
| | | | | |
| | | | | |
| | | | | |
| | | | | |
| | | | | |
| | | | | |
| | | | | |
| | | | | |
| | | | | |
| | | | | |
| | | | | |
| | | | | |
| | | | | |
| | | | | |
| | | | | |
| | | | | |
| | | | | |
| | | | | |
| | | | | |
| | | | | |
| | | | | |
| | | | | |
| | | | | |

Name:_____

**Problem 5-2A (concl'd.)**

## GENERAL JOURNAL

Page_____

| Date | Account Titles and Explanation | PR | Debit | Credit |
|------|-------------------------------|----|-------|--------|
|      |                               |    |       |        |
|      |                               |    |       |        |
|      |                               |    |       |        |
|      |                               |    |       |        |
|      |                               |    |       |        |
|      |                               |    |       |        |
|      |                               |    |       |        |
|      |                               |    |       |        |
|      |                               |    |       |        |
|      |                               |    |       |        |
|      |                               |    |       |        |
|      |                               |    |       |        |
|      |                               |    |       |        |
|      |                               |    |       |        |
|      |                               |    |       |        |
|      |                               |    |       |        |
|      |                               |    |       |        |
|      |                               |    |       |        |
|      |                               |    |       |        |
|      |                               |    |       |        |
|      |                               |    |       |        |
|      |                               |    |       |        |
|      |                               |    |       |        |
|      |                               |    |       |        |
|      |                               |    |       |        |

*Analysis component:*

_____
_____
_____
_____
_____
_____
_____
_____
_____
_____
_____

*Fundamental Accounting Principles*, **15ce, Working Papers**

Name:_____

**Problem 5-3A**

## GENERAL JOURNAL

Page____

| Date | Account Titles and Explanation | PR | Debit | Credit |
|---|---|---|---|---|
| | | | | |
| | | | | |
| | | | | |
| | | | | |
| | | | | |
| | | | | |
| | | | | |
| | | | | |
| | | | | |
| | | | | |
| | | | | |
| | | | | |
| | | | | |
| | | | | |
| | | | | |
| | | | | |
| | | | | |
| | | | | |
| | | | | |
| | | | | |
| | | | | |
| | | | | |
| | | | | |
| | | | | |
| | | | | |
| | | | | |
| | | | | |
| | | | | |
| | | | | |
| | | | | |
| | | | | |
| | | | | |
| | | | | |
| | | | | |
| | | | | |
| | | | | |
| | | | | |
| | | | | |
| | | | | |
| | | | | |
| | | | | |
| | | | | |
| | | | | |
| | | | | |

**Problem 5-3A (concl'd.)**

## GENERAL JOURNAL

Page_____

| Date | Account Titles and Explanation | PR | Debit | Credit |
|------|-------------------------------|----|-------|--------|
|      |                               |    |       |        |
|      |                               |    |       |        |
|      |                               |    |       |        |
|      |                               |    |       |        |
|      |                               |    |       |        |
|      |                               |    |       |        |
|      |                               |    |       |        |
|      |                               |    |       |        |
|      |                               |    |       |        |
|      |                               |    |       |        |
|      |                               |    |       |        |
|      |                               |    |       |        |
|      |                               |    |       |        |
|      |                               |    |       |        |
|      |                               |    |       |        |
|      |                               |    |       |        |
|      |                               |    |       |        |
|      |                               |    |       |        |
|      |                               |    |       |        |
|      |                               |    |       |        |
|      |                               |    |       |        |
|      |                               |    |       |        |
|      |                               |    |       |        |
|      |                               |    |       |        |
|      |                               |    |       |        |
|      |                               |    |       |        |
|      |                               |    |       |        |
|      |                               |    |       |        |
|      |                               |    |       |        |
|      |                               |    |       |        |
|      |                               |    |       |        |
|      |                               |    |       |        |
|      |                               |    |       |        |
|      |                               |    |       |        |
|      |                               |    |       |        |
|      |                               |    |       |        |

Name:_____

**Problem 5-4A**

Part 1

## GENERAL JOURNAL

Page_____

| Date | Account Titles and Explanation | PR | Debit | Credit |
|------|-------------------------------|----|-------|--------|
|      |                               |    |       |        |
|      |                               |    |       |        |
|      |                               |    |       |        |
|      |                               |    |       |        |
|      |                               |    |       |        |
|      |                               |    |       |        |
|      |                               |    |       |        |
|      |                               |    |       |        |
|      |                               |    |       |        |
|      |                               |    |       |        |
|      |                               |    |       |        |
|      |                               |    |       |        |
|      |                               |    |       |        |
|      |                               |    |       |        |
|      |                               |    |       |        |
|      |                               |    |       |        |
|      |                               |    |       |        |
|      |                               |    |       |        |
|      |                               |    |       |        |
|      |                               |    |       |        |
|      |                               |    |       |        |
|      |                               |    |       |        |
|      |                               |    |       |        |
|      |                               |    |       |        |
|      |                               |    |       |        |
|      |                               |    |       |        |
|      |                               |    |       |        |
|      |                               |    |       |        |
|      |                               |    |       |        |
|      |                               |    |       |        |
|      |                               |    |       |        |
|      |                               |    |       |        |
|      |                               |    |       |        |
|      |                               |    |       |        |
|      |                               |    |       |        |
|      |                               |    |       |        |
|      |                               |    |       |        |

**Part 2- Multiple-step**

### Income Statement

| | | |
|---|---|---|
| | | |
| | | |
| | | |
| | | |
| | | |
| | | |
| | | |
| | | |
| | | |
| | | |
| | | |
| | | |
| | | |
| | | |
| | | |
| | | |
| | | |
| | | |

*Analysis component:*

_____
_____
_____
_____
_____
_____
_____

**Problem 5-5A**

### Part 1 - Classified, multiple-step

| Income Statement | | | |
|---|---|---|---|
| | | | |
| | | | |
| | | | |
| | | | |
| | | | |
| | | | |
| | | | |
| | | | |
| | | | |
| | | | |
| | | | |
| | | | |
| | | | |
| | | | |
| | | | |
| | | | |
| | | | |
| | | | |
| | | | |
| | | | |
| | | | |
| | | | |
| | | | |

### Part 2 - Single-step

| Income Statement | | |
|---|---|---|
| | | |
| | | |
| | | |
| | | |
| | | |
| | | |
| | | |
| | | |
| | | |
| | | |
| | | |

**Problem 5-6A**

a. _____
_____
_____

b. _____
_____
_____

c. _____
_____
_____

|  | Tank Tops | Pullovers | Yoga Pants |
|---|---|---|---|
| Sale price |  |  |  |
| Cost |  |  |  |
| Gross Profit |  |  |  |
| Gross Profit % |  |  |  |
|  |  |  |  |

d. _____
_____
_____
_____
_____

**Problem 5-7A**

**Part 1 – Classified, multiple-step**

|  | Income Statement |  |  |  |
| --- | --- | --- | --- | --- |
|  |  |  |  |  |
|  |  |  |  |  |
|  |  |  |  |  |
|  |  |  |  |  |
|  |  |  |  |  |
|  |  |  |  |  |
|  |  |  |  |  |
|  |  |  |  |  |
|  |  |  |  |  |
|  |  |  |  |  |
|  |  |  |  |  |
|  |  |  |  |  |
|  |  |  |  |  |
|  |  |  |  |  |
|  |  |  |  |  |
|  |  |  |  |  |
|  |  |  |  |  |
|  |  |  |  |  |
|  |  |  |  |  |
|  |  |  |  |  |
|  |  |  |  |  |
|  |  |  |  |  |
|  |  |  |  |  |
|  |  |  |  |  |
|  |  |  |  |  |
|  |  |  |  |  |
|  |  |  |  |  |
|  |  |  |  |  |
|  |  |  |  |  |
|  |  |  |  |  |
|  |  |  |  |  |
|  |  |  |  |  |
|  |  |  |  |  |
|  |  |  |  |  |
|  |  |  |  |  |
|  |  |  |  |  |

Name:_____

**Problem 5-7A (concl'd.)**

**Part 2 – Single-step**

|  |  |  |
|---|---|---|
| **Income Statement** | | |

| | | |
|---|---|---|
| | | |
| | | |
| | | |
| | | |
| | | |
| | | |
| | | |
| | | |
| | | |
| | | |
| | | |
| | | |
| | | |
| | | |
| | | |

*Analysis component:*

**Problem 5-8A**

**Part 1 – Classified, multiple-step**

| Income Statement | | | |
|---|---|---|---|
| | | | |
| | | | |
| | | | |
| | | | |
| | | | |
| | | | |
| | | | |
| | | | |
| | | | |
| | | | |
| | | | |
| | | | |
| | | | |
| | | | |
| | | | |
| | | | |
| | | | |
| | | | |
| | | | |
| | | | |
| | | | |
| | | | |
| | | | |

**Part 2 – Multiple-step**

| Income Statement | | |
|---|---|---|
| | | |
| | | |
| | | |
| | | |
| | | |
| | | |
| | | |
| | | |
| | | |
| | | |
| | | |

Name:_____

**Problem 5-8A (concl'd.)**

**Part 3 – Single-step**

|  | Income Statement |  |  |
|---|---|---|---|
|  |  |  |  |
|  |  |  |  |
|  |  |  |  |
|  |  |  |  |
|  |  |  |  |
|  |  |  |  |
|  |  |  |  |
|  |  |  |  |
|  |  |  |  |
|  |  |  |  |

*Analysis component:*

_____

_____

_____

_____

_____

_____

_____

_____

**\*Problem 5-9A**

## GENERAL JOURNAL

Page_____

| Date | Account Titles and Explanation | PR | Debit | Credit |
|------|-------------------------------|----|----|----|
|  |  |  |  |  |
|  |  |  |  |  |
|  |  |  |  |  |
|  |  |  |  |  |
|  |  |  |  |  |
|  |  |  |  |  |
|  |  |  |  |  |
|  |  |  |  |  |
|  |  |  |  |  |
|  |  |  |  |  |
|  |  |  |  |  |
|  |  |  |  |  |
|  |  |  |  |  |
|  |  |  |  |  |
|  |  |  |  |  |
|  |  |  |  |  |
|  |  |  |  |  |
|  |  |  |  |  |
|  |  |  |  |  |
|  |  |  |  |  |
|  |  |  |  |  |
|  |  |  |  |  |
|  |  |  |  |  |
|  |  |  |  |  |
|  |  |  |  |  |
|  |  |  |  |  |
|  |  |  |  |  |
|  |  |  |  |  |
|  |  |  |  |  |
|  |  |  |  |  |
|  |  |  |  |  |
|  |  |  |  |  |
|  |  |  |  |  |
|  |  |  |  |  |
|  |  |  |  |  |
|  |  |  |  |  |
|  |  |  |  |  |

**\*Problem 5-10A**

## GENERAL JOURNAL

Page_____

| Date | Account Titles and Explanation | PR | Debit | Credit |
|------|-------------------------------|----|-------|--------|
|  |  |  |  |  |
|  |  |  |  |  |
|  |  |  |  |  |
|  |  |  |  |  |
|  |  |  |  |  |
|  |  |  |  |  |
|  |  |  |  |  |
|  |  |  |  |  |
|  |  |  |  |  |
|  |  |  |  |  |
|  |  |  |  |  |
|  |  |  |  |  |
|  |  |  |  |  |
|  |  |  |  |  |
|  |  |  |  |  |
|  |  |  |  |  |
|  |  |  |  |  |
|  |  |  |  |  |
|  |  |  |  |  |
|  |  |  |  |  |
|  |  |  |  |  |
|  |  |  |  |  |
|  |  |  |  |  |
|  |  |  |  |  |
|  |  |  |  |  |
|  |  |  |  |  |
|  |  |  |  |  |
|  |  |  |  |  |
|  |  |  |  |  |
|  |  |  |  |  |
|  |  |  |  |  |
|  |  |  |  |  |
|  |  |  |  |  |
|  |  |  |  |  |
|  |  |  |  |  |
|  |  |  |  |  |
|  |  |  |  |  |
|  |  |  |  |  |
|  |  |  |  |  |
|  |  |  |  |  |

**\*Problem 5-10A (concl'd.)**

## GENERAL JOURNAL

Page_____

| Date | Account Titles and Explanation | PR | Debit | Credit |
|------|-------------------------------|----|-------|--------|
| | | | | |
| | | | | |
| | | | | |
| | | | | |
| | | | | |
| | | | | |
| | | | | |
| | | | | |
| | | | | |
| | | | | |
| | | | | |
| | | | | |
| | | | | |
| | | | | |
| | | | | |
| | | | | |
| | | | | |
| | | | | |
| | | | | |
| | | | | |
| | | | | |
| | | | | |
| | | | | |
| | | | | |
| | | | | |
| | | | | |
| | | | | |
| | | | | |
| | | | | |
| | | | | |
| | | | | |
| | | | | |
| | | | | |
| | | | | |
| | | | | |
| | | | | |
| | | | | |

Name:_____

*Problem 5-11A

1. _____

2. _____

3. _____

**\*Problem 5-11A (concl'd.)**

### 4. Multi-step

**Income Statement**

| | | |
|---|---|---|
| | | |
| | | |
| | | |
| | | |
| | | |
| | | |
| | | |
| | | |
| | | |
| | | |
| | | |
| | | |
| | | |
| | | |
| | | |
| | | |
| | | |
| | | |
| | | |
| | | |

### 5. Single-step

**Income Statement**

| | | |
|---|---|---|
| | | |
| | | |
| | | |
| | | |
| | | |
| | | |
| | | |
| | | |
| | | |
| | | |
| | | |
| | | |
| | | |

Name:_____

**\*Problem 5-12A**

**Analysis and calculations:**

_____
_____
_____
_____
_____
_____
_____
_____
_____
_____
_____
_____
_____
_____
_____
_____
_____
_____
_____
_____
_____
_____
_____
_____
_____
_____
_____
_____
_____
_____
_____
_____
_____
_____
_____
_____
_____
_____
_____
_____
_____
_____
_____
_____

Chapter 5                                        Name:_____

**\*Problem 5-12A (cont'd.)**

| | | | | |
|---|---|---|---|---|
| **Income Statement** | | | | |

| | | | | |
|---|---|---|---|---|
| | | | | |
| | | | | |
| | | | | |
| | | | | |
| | | | | |
| | | | | |
| | | | | |
| | | | | |
| | | | | |
| | | | | |
| | | | | |
| | | | | |
| | | | | |
| | | | | |
| | | | | |
| | | | | |
| | | | | |
| | | | | |
| | | | | |
| | | | | |
| | | | | |
| | | | | |
| | | | | |
| | | | | |
| | | | | |
| | | | | |
| | | | | |
| | | | | |
| | | | | |
| | | | | |
| | | | | |
| | | | | |
| | | | | |
| | | | | |
| | | | | |

*Problem 5-13A

## GENERAL JOURNAL

Page____

| Date | Account Titles and Explanation | PR | Debit | Credit |
|------|-------------------------------|----|-------|--------|
|      |                               |    |       |        |
|      |                               |    |       |        |
|      |                               |    |       |        |
|      |                               |    |       |        |
|      |                               |    |       |        |
|      |                               |    |       |        |
|      |                               |    |       |        |
|      |                               |    |       |        |
|      |                               |    |       |        |
|      |                               |    |       |        |
|      |                               |    |       |        |
|      |                               |    |       |        |
|      |                               |    |       |        |
|      |                               |    |       |        |
|      |                               |    |       |        |
|      |                               |    |       |        |
|      |                               |    |       |        |
|      |                               |    |       |        |
|      |                               |    |       |        |
|      |                               |    |       |        |
|      |                               |    |       |        |
|      |                               |    |       |        |
|      |                               |    |       |        |
|      |                               |    |       |        |
|      |                               |    |       |        |
|      |                               |    |       |        |
|      |                               |    |       |        |
|      |                               |    |       |        |
|      |                               |    |       |        |
|      |                               |    |       |        |
|      |                               |    |       |        |
|      |                               |    |       |        |
|      |                               |    |       |        |
|      |                               |    |       |        |
|      |                               |    |       |        |
|      |                               |    |       |        |
|      |                               |    |       |        |
|      |                               |    |       |        |

*Problem 5-14A

## GENERAL JOURNAL

| Date | Account Titles and Explanation | PR | Debit | Credit |
|------|-------------------------------|----|----|----|
| | | | | |
| | | | | |
| | | | | |
| | | | | |
| | | | | |
| | | | | |
| | | | | |
| | | | | |
| | | | | |
| | | | | |
| | | | | |
| | | | | |
| | | | | |
| | | | | |
| | | | | |
| | | | | |
| | | | | |
| | | | | |
| | | | | |
| | | | | |
| | | | | |
| | | | | |
| | | | | |
| | | | | |
| | | | | |
| | | | | |
| | | | | |
| | | | | |
| | | | | |
| | | | | |
| | | | | |
| | | | | |
| | | | | |
| | | | | |
| | | | | |
| | | | | |
| | | | | |
| | | | | |
| | | | | |
| | | | | |
| | | | | |
| | | | | |

Name:_____

**\*Problem 5-14A (concl'd.)**

## GENERAL JOURNAL

Page_____

| Date | Account Titles and Explanation | PR | Debit | Credit |
|------|-------------------------------|----|-------|--------|
|      |                               |    |       |        |
|      |                               |    |       |        |
|      |                               |    |       |        |
|      |                               |    |       |        |
|      |                               |    |       |        |
|      |                               |    |       |        |
|      |                               |    |       |        |
|      |                               |    |       |        |
|      |                               |    |       |        |
|      |                               |    |       |        |
|      |                               |    |       |        |
|      |                               |    |       |        |
|      |                               |    |       |        |
|      |                               |    |       |        |
|      |                               |    |       |        |
|      |                               |    |       |        |
|      |                               |    |       |        |
|      |                               |    |       |        |
|      |                               |    |       |        |
|      |                               |    |       |        |
|      |                               |    |       |        |
|      |                               |    |       |        |
|      |                               |    |       |        |
|      |                               |    |       |        |
|      |                               |    |       |        |
|      |                               |    |       |        |
|      |                               |    |       |        |
|      |                               |    |       |        |
|      |                               |    |       |        |
|      |                               |    |       |        |
|      |                               |    |       |        |
|      |                               |    |       |        |
|      |                               |    |       |        |
|      |                               |    |       |        |
|      |                               |    |       |        |
|      |                               |    |       |        |
|      |                               |    |       |        |
|      |                               |    |       |        |

Name:_____

**Problem 5-1B**

Part 1                          **GENERAL JOURNAL**                          Page_____

| Date | Account Titles and Explanation | PR | Debit | Credit |
|---|---|---|---|---|
| | | | | |
| | | | | |
| | | | | |
| | | | | |
| | | | | |
| | | | | |
| | | | | |
| | | | | |
| | | | | |
| | | | | |
| | | | | |
| | | | | |
| | | | | |
| | | | | |
| | | | | |
| | | | | |
| | | | | |
| | | | | |
| | | | | |
| | | | | |
| | | | | |
| | | | | |
| | | | | |
| | | | | |
| | | | | |
| | | | | |
| | | | | |
| | | | | |
| | | | | |
| | | | | |
| | | | | |
| | | | | |
| | | | | |
| | | | | |
| | | | | |
| | | | | |
| | | | | |
| | | | | |
| | | | | |

Name:_____

**Problem 5-1B (concl'd.)**

### GENERAL JOURNAL

Page_____

| Date | Account Titles and Explanation | PR | Debit | Credit |
|------|-------------------------------|----|-------|--------|
|      |                               |    |       |        |
|      |                               |    |       |        |
|      |                               |    |       |        |
|      |                               |    |       |        |
|      |                               |    |       |        |
|      |                               |    |       |        |
|      |                               |    |       |        |
|      |                               |    |       |        |
|      |                               |    |       |        |
|      |                               |    |       |        |
|      |                               |    |       |        |
|      |                               |    |       |        |
|      |                               |    |       |        |
|      |                               |    |       |        |
|      |                               |    |       |        |

**Part 2**

_____

_____

_____

_____

_____

**Problem 5-2B**

### GENERAL JOURNAL

Page_____

| Date | Account Titles and Explanation | PR | Debit | Credit |
|------|-------------------------------|----|-------|--------|
|      |                               |    |       |        |
|      |                               |    |       |        |
|      |                               |    |       |        |
|      |                               |    |       |        |
|      |                               |    |       |        |
|      |                               |    |       |        |
|      |                               |    |       |        |
|      |                               |    |       |        |
|      |                               |    |       |        |
|      |                               |    |       |        |
|      |                               |    |       |        |
|      |                               |    |       |        |
|      |                               |    |       |        |
|      |                               |    |       |        |

**Problem 5-2B (cont'd.)**

### GENERAL JOURNAL

Page____

| Date | | Account Titles and Explanation | PR | Debit | Credit |
|------|--|-------------------------------|----|----|----|
| | | | | | |
| | | | | | |
| | | | | | |
| | | | | | |
| | | | | | |
| | | | | | |
| | | | | | |
| | | | | | |
| | | | | | |
| | | | | | |
| | | | | | |
| | | | | | |
| | | | | | |
| | | | | | |
| | | | | | |
| | | | | | |
| | | | | | |
| | | | | | |
| | | | | | |
| | | | | | |
| | | | | | |
| | | | | | |
| | | | | | |
| | | | | | |
| | | | | | |
| | | | | | |
| | | | | | |
| | | | | | |
| | | | | | |
| | | | | | |
| | | | | | |
| | | | | | |
| | | | | | |
| | | | | | |
| | | | | | |
| | | | | | |
| | | | | | |
| | | | | | |
| | | | | | |
| | | | | | |
| | | | | | |
| | | | | | |

**Problem 5-2B (concl'd.)**

## GENERAL JOURNAL

Page_____

| Date | Account Titles and Explanation | PR | Debit | Credit |
|------|-------------------------------|----|-------|--------|
|  |  |  |  |  |
|  |  |  |  |  |
|  |  |  |  |  |
|  |  |  |  |  |
|  |  |  |  |  |
|  |  |  |  |  |
|  |  |  |  |  |
|  |  |  |  |  |
|  |  |  |  |  |
|  |  |  |  |  |
|  |  |  |  |  |
|  |  |  |  |  |
|  |  |  |  |  |
|  |  |  |  |  |
|  |  |  |  |  |
|  |  |  |  |  |
|  |  |  |  |  |
|  |  |  |  |  |
|  |  |  |  |  |
|  |  |  |  |  |
|  |  |  |  |  |
|  |  |  |  |  |
|  |  |  |  |  |
|  |  |  |  |  |
|  |  |  |  |  |
|  |  |  |  |  |
|  |  |  |  |  |

*Analysis component:*

_____
_____
_____
_____
_____
_____
_____
_____
_____
_____
_____
_____

## GENERAL JOURNAL

Page____

| Date | Account Titles and Explanation | PR | Debit | Credit |
|---|---|---|---|---|
| | | | | |
| | | | | |
| | | | | |
| | | | | |
| | | | | |
| | | | | |
| | | | | |
| | | | | |
| | | | | |
| | | | | |
| | | | | |
| | | | | |
| | | | | |
| | | | | |
| | | | | |
| | | | | |
| | | | | |
| | | | | |
| | | | | |
| | | | | |
| | | | | |
| | | | | |
| | | | | |
| | | | | |
| | | | | |
| | | | | |
| | | | | |
| | | | | |
| | | | | |
| | | | | |
| | | | | |
| | | | | |
| | | | | |
| | | | | |
| | | | | |
| | | | | |
| | | | | |
| | | | | |
| | | | | |
| | | | | |
| | | | | |
| | | | | |

Name:_____

**Problem 5-3B (concl'd.)**

## GENERAL JOURNAL

Page_____

| Date | Account Titles and Explanation | PR | Debit | Credit |
|------|-------------------------------|----|-------|--------|
|  |  |  |  |  |
|  |  |  |  |  |
|  |  |  |  |  |
|  |  |  |  |  |
|  |  |  |  |  |
|  |  |  |  |  |
|  |  |  |  |  |
|  |  |  |  |  |
|  |  |  |  |  |
|  |  |  |  |  |
|  |  |  |  |  |
|  |  |  |  |  |
|  |  |  |  |  |
|  |  |  |  |  |
|  |  |  |  |  |
|  |  |  |  |  |
|  |  |  |  |  |
|  |  |  |  |  |
|  |  |  |  |  |
|  |  |  |  |  |
|  |  |  |  |  |
|  |  |  |  |  |
|  |  |  |  |  |
|  |  |  |  |  |
|  |  |  |  |  |
|  |  |  |  |  |
|  |  |  |  |  |
|  |  |  |  |  |
|  |  |  |  |  |
|  |  |  |  |  |
|  |  |  |  |  |
|  |  |  |  |  |

*Analysis component:*

_____
_____
_____
_____
_____
_____

**Problem 5-4B**
Part 1

## GENERAL JOURNAL

| Date | Account Titles and Explanation | PR | Debit | Credit |
|------|-------------------------------|----|-------|--------|
|  |  |  |  |  |
|  |  |  |  |  |
|  |  |  |  |  |
|  |  |  |  |  |
|  |  |  |  |  |
|  |  |  |  |  |
|  |  |  |  |  |
|  |  |  |  |  |
|  |  |  |  |  |
|  |  |  |  |  |
|  |  |  |  |  |
|  |  |  |  |  |
|  |  |  |  |  |
|  |  |  |  |  |
|  |  |  |  |  |
|  |  |  |  |  |
|  |  |  |  |  |
|  |  |  |  |  |
|  |  |  |  |  |
|  |  |  |  |  |
|  |  |  |  |  |
|  |  |  |  |  |
|  |  |  |  |  |
|  |  |  |  |  |
|  |  |  |  |  |
|  |  |  |  |  |
|  |  |  |  |  |
|  |  |  |  |  |
|  |  |  |  |  |
|  |  |  |  |  |
|  |  |  |  |  |
|  |  |  |  |  |
|  |  |  |  |  |
|  |  |  |  |  |
|  |  |  |  |  |
|  |  |  |  |  |
|  |  |  |  |  |
|  |  |  |  |  |
|  |  |  |  |  |
|  |  |  |  |  |
|  |  |  |  |  |
|  |  |  |  |  |
|  |  |  |  |  |

Name:_____

**Problem 5-4B (concl'd.)**

Part 2- Multiple-step

Income Statement

| | | |
|---|---|---|
| | | |
| | | |
| | | |
| | | |
| | | |
| | | |
| | | |
| | | |
| | | |
| | | |
| | | |
| | | |
| | | |
| | | |
| | | |
| | | |
| | | |
| | | |
| | | |
| | | |
| | | |
| | | |

*Analysis component:*

_____
_____
_____
_____
_____
_____
_____
_____

Name:_____

**Problem 5-5B**

**1. Classified, multiple-step**

Income Statement

| | | | |
|---|---|---|---|
| | | | |
| | | | |
| | | | |
| | | | |
| | | | |
| | | | |
| | | | |
| | | | |
| | | | |
| | | | |
| | | | |
| | | | |
| | | | |
| | | | |
| | | | |
| | | | |
| | | | |
| | | | |
| | | | |
| | | | |
| | | | |
| | | | |
| | | | |

**2. Single-step**

Income Statement

| | | |
|---|---|---|
| | | |
| | | |
| | | |
| | | |
| | | |
| | | |
| | | |
| | | |
| | | |
| | | |
| | | |

Name:_____

**Problem 5-6B**

a._____
_____
_____

b._____
_____
_____

c._____
_____
_____

|  | Small handbags | Medium Handbags | Large Handbags |
|---|---|---|---|
| Sale price |  |  |  |
| Cost |  |  |  |
| Gross Profit |  |  |  |
| Gross Profit % |  |  |  |
|  |  |  |  |

d._____
_____
_____
_____
_____
_____
_____
_____
_____
_____

Name:_____

**Problem 5-7B**

**Part 1 – Classified, multiple-step**

### Income Statement

| | | | |
|---|---|---|---|
| | | | |
| | | | |
| | | | |
| | | | |
| | | | |
| | | | |
| | | | |
| | | | |
| | | | |
| | | | |
| | | | |
| | | | |
| | | | |
| | | | |
| | | | |
| | | | |
| | | | |
| | | | |
| | | | |
| | | | |
| | | | |
| | | | |
| | | | |
| | | | |
| | | | |

**Part 2 – Single-step**

### Income Statement

| | | |
|---|---|---|
| | | |
| | | |
| | | |
| | | |
| | | |
| | | |
| | | |
| | | |

*Analysis component:*

_____

_____

_____

_____

**Problem 5-8B**

**Part 1 – Classified, multiple-step**

| | | | |
|---|---|---|---|
| **Income Statement** | | | |
| | | | |
| | | | |
| | | | |
| | | | |
| | | | |
| | | | |
| | | | |
| | | | |
| | | | |
| | | | |
| | | | |
| | | | |
| | | | |
| | | | |
| | | | |
| | | | |
| | | | |
| | | | |
| | | | |
| | | | |
| | | | |
| | | | |
| | | | |
| | | | |
| | | | |
| | | | |
| | | | |
| | | | |
| | | | |

Problem 5-8B (concl'd.)

## Part 2 – Multiple-step

| Income Statement | | |
|---|---|---|
| | | |
| | | |
| | | |
| | | |
| | | |
| | | |
| | | |
| | | |
| | | |
| | | |
| | | |
| | | |
| | | |
| | | |
| | | |
| | | |
| | | |

## Part 3 – Single-step

| Income Statement | | |
|---|---|---|
| | | |
| | | |
| | | |
| | | |
| | | |
| | | |
| | | |
| | | |

Name:_____

**\*Problem 5-9B**

**GENERAL JOURNAL**

Page_____

| Date | | Account Titles and Explanation | PR | Debit | Credit |
|---|---|---|---|---|---|
| | | | | | |
| | | | | | |
| | | | | | |
| | | | | | |
| | | | | | |
| | | | | | |
| | | | | | |
| | | | | | |
| | | | | | |
| | | | | | |
| | | | | | |
| | | | | | |
| | | | | | |
| | | | | | |
| | | | | | |
| | | | | | |
| | | | | | |
| | | | | | |
| | | | | | |
| | | | | | |
| | | | | | |
| | | | | | |
| | | | | | |
| | | | | | |
| | | | | | |
| | | | | | |
| | | | | | |
| | | | | | |
| | | | | | |
| | | | | | |
| | | | | | |
| | | | | | |
| | | | | | |
| | | | | | |
| | | | | | |
| | | | | | |
| | | | | | |

*Fundamental Accounting Principles*, 15ce, Working Papers

*Problem 5-10B

## GENERAL JOURNAL

Page____

| Date | Account Titles and Explanation | PR | Debit | Credit |
|------|-------------------------------|-----|-------|--------|
|      |                               |     |       |        |
|      |                               |     |       |        |
|      |                               |     |       |        |
|      |                               |     |       |        |
|      |                               |     |       |        |
|      |                               |     |       |        |
|      |                               |     |       |        |
|      |                               |     |       |        |
|      |                               |     |       |        |
|      |                               |     |       |        |
|      |                               |     |       |        |
|      |                               |     |       |        |
|      |                               |     |       |        |
|      |                               |     |       |        |
|      |                               |     |       |        |
|      |                               |     |       |        |
|      |                               |     |       |        |
|      |                               |     |       |        |
|      |                               |     |       |        |
|      |                               |     |       |        |
|      |                               |     |       |        |
|      |                               |     |       |        |
|      |                               |     |       |        |
|      |                               |     |       |        |
|      |                               |     |       |        |
|      |                               |     |       |        |
|      |                               |     |       |        |
|      |                               |     |       |        |
|      |                               |     |       |        |
|      |                               |     |       |        |
|      |                               |     |       |        |
|      |                               |     |       |        |
|      |                               |     |       |        |
|      |                               |     |       |        |
|      |                               |     |       |        |
|      |                               |     |       |        |
|      |                               |     |       |        |
|      |                               |     |       |        |
|      |                               |     |       |        |

**\*Problem 5-10B (concl'd.)**

## GENERAL JOURNAL

Page_____

| Date | Account Titles and Explanation | PR | Debit | Credit |
|------|-------------------------------|----|-------|--------|
| | | | | |
| | | | | |
| | | | | |
| | | | | |
| | | | | |
| | | | | |
| | | | | |
| | | | | |
| | | | | |
| | | | | |
| | | | | |
| | | | | |
| | | | | |
| | | | | |
| | | | | |
| | | | | |
| | | | | |
| | | | | |
| | | | | |
| | | | | |
| | | | | |
| | | | | |
| | | | | |
| | | | | |
| | | | | |
| | | | | |
| | | | | |
| | | | | |
| | | | | |
| | | | | |
| | | | | |
| | | | | |
| | | | | |
| | | | | |
| | | | | |
| | | | | |
| | | | | |
| | | | | |
| | | | | |
| | | | | |
| | | | | |

Name:_____

**\*Problem 5-11B**

**1.** _____
_____
_____
_____
_____
_____
_____
_____
_____

**2.** _____
_____
_____
_____
_____
_____
_____
_____
_____
_____
_____

**3.** _____
_____
_____
_____
_____
_____
_____
_____
_____
_____
_____
_____
_____
_____
_____
_____
_____

Name:_____

**\*Problem 5-11B (concl'd.)**

## 4. Multiple-step

| Income Statement | | |
|---|---|---|
| | | |
| | | |
| | | |
| | | |
| | | |
| | | |
| | | |
| | | |
| | | |
| | | |
| | | |
| | | |
| | | |
| | | |
| | | |
| | | |
| | | |
| | | |
| | | |
| | | |
| | | |

## 5. Single-step

| Income Statement | | |
|---|---|---|
| | | |
| | | |
| | | |
| | | |
| | | |
| | | |
| | | |
| | | |
| | | |

Name:_____

**\*Problem 5-12B**

**Analysis and calculations:**

Name:_____

**\*Problem 5-12B (concl'd.)**

| | Income Statement | | | | |
|---|---|---|---|---|---|
| | | | | | |
| | | | | | |
| | | | | | |
| | | | | | |
| | | | | | |
| | | | | | |
| | | | | | |
| | | | | | |
| | | | | | |
| | | | | | |
| | | | | | |
| | | | | | |
| | | | | | |
| | | | | | |
| | | | | | |
| | | | | | |
| | | | | | |
| | | | | | |
| | | | | | |
| | | | | | |
| | | | | | |
| | | | | | |
| | | | | | |
| | | | | | |
| | | | | | |
| | | | | | |
| | | | | | |
| | | | | | |
| | | | | | |
| | | | | | |
| | | | | | |
| | | | | | |

Name:_____

*Problem 5-13B

### GENERAL JOURNAL

Page____

| Date | | Account Titles and Explanation | PR | Debit | Credit |
|---|---|---|---|---|---|
| | | | | | |
| | | | | | |
| | | | | | |
| | | | | | |
| | | | | | |
| | | | | | |
| | | | | | |
| | | | | | |
| | | | | | |
| | | | | | |
| | | | | | |
| | | | | | |
| | | | | | |
| | | | | | |
| | | | | | |
| | | | | | |
| | | | | | |
| | | | | | |
| | | | | | |
| | | | | | |
| | | | | | |
| | | | | | |
| | | | | | |
| | | | | | |
| | | | | | |
| | | | | | |
| | | | | | |
| | | | | | |
| | | | | | |
| | | | | | |
| | | | | | |
| | | | | | |
| | | | | | |
| | | | | | |
| | | | | | |
| | | | | | |
| | | | | | |

Name:_____

**\*Problem 5-13B (concl'd.)**

## GENERAL JOURNAL

Page_____

| Date | | Account Titles and Explanation | PR | Debit | Credit |
|---|---|---|---|---|---|
| | | | | | |
| | | | | | |
| | | | | | |
| | | | | | |
| | | | | | |
| | | | | | |
| | | | | | |
| | | | | | |
| | | | | | |
| | | | | | |
| | | | | | |
| | | | | | |
| | | | | | |

**\*Problem 5-14B**

## GENERAL JOURNAL

Page_____

| Date | | Account Titles and Explanation | PR | Debit | Credit |
|---|---|---|---|---|---|
| | | | | | |
| | | | | | |
| | | | | | |
| | | | | | |
| | | | | | |
| | | | | | |
| | | | | | |
| | | | | | |
| | | | | | |
| | | | | | |
| | | | | | |
| | | | | | |
| | | | | | |
| | | | | | |
| | | | | | |
| | | | | | |
| | | | | | |
| | | | | | |
| | | | | | |
| | | | | | |
| | | | | | |
| | | | | | |
| | | | | | |

Name:_____

**\*Problem 5-14B (concl'd.)**

### GENERAL JOURNAL

Page____

| Date | | Account Titles and Explanation | PR | Debit | Credit |
|---|---|---|---|---|---|
| | | | | | |
| | | | | | |
| | | | | | |
| | | | | | |
| | | | | | |
| | | | | | |
| | | | | | |
| | | | | | |
| | | | | | |
| | | | | | |
| | | | | | |
| | | | | | |
| | | | | | |
| | | | | | |
| | | | | | |
| | | | | | |
| | | | | | |
| | | | | | |
| | | | | | |
| | | | | | |
| | | | | | |
| | | | | | |
| | | | | | |
| | | | | | |
| | | | | | |
| | | | | | |
| | | | | | |
| | | | | | |
| | | | | | |
| | | | | | |
| | | | | | |
| | | | | | |
| | | | | | |
| | | | | | |
| | | | | | |
| | | | | | |
| | | | | | |
| | | | | | |
| | | | | | |
| | | | | | |

Name:_____

**Cumulative Prob. (Perpetual)**

**Part 1**        **Echo Systems**

GENERAL JOURNAL                           Page_____

| Date | Account Titles and Explanation | PR | Debit | Credit |
|------|-------------------------------|----|----|----|
|  |  |  |  |  |
|  |  |  |  |  |
|  |  |  |  |  |
|  |  |  |  |  |
|  |  |  |  |  |
|  |  |  |  |  |
|  |  |  |  |  |
|  |  |  |  |  |
|  |  |  |  |  |
|  |  |  |  |  |
|  |  |  |  |  |
|  |  |  |  |  |
|  |  |  |  |  |
|  |  |  |  |  |
|  |  |  |  |  |
|  |  |  |  |  |
|  |  |  |  |  |
|  |  |  |  |  |
|  |  |  |  |  |
|  |  |  |  |  |
|  |  |  |  |  |
|  |  |  |  |  |
|  |  |  |  |  |
|  |  |  |  |  |
|  |  |  |  |  |
|  |  |  |  |  |
|  |  |  |  |  |
|  |  |  |  |  |
|  |  |  |  |  |
|  |  |  |  |  |
|  |  |  |  |  |
|  |  |  |  |  |
|  |  |  |  |  |
|  |  |  |  |  |
|  |  |  |  |  |
|  |  |  |  |  |

Name:_____

**Cumulative Prob. (Perpetual)**

**Part 1**  Echo Systems (cont'd.)

### GENERAL JOURNAL

Page_____

| Date | Account Titles and Explanation | PR | Debit | Credit |
|---|---|---|---|---|
|  |  |  |  |  |
|  |  |  |  |  |
|  |  |  |  |  |
|  |  |  |  |  |
|  |  |  |  |  |
|  |  |  |  |  |
|  |  |  |  |  |
|  |  |  |  |  |
|  |  |  |  |  |
|  |  |  |  |  |
|  |  |  |  |  |
|  |  |  |  |  |
|  |  |  |  |  |
|  |  |  |  |  |
|  |  |  |  |  |
|  |  |  |  |  |
|  |  |  |  |  |
|  |  |  |  |  |
|  |  |  |  |  |
|  |  |  |  |  |
|  |  |  |  |  |
|  |  |  |  |  |
|  |  |  |  |  |
|  |  |  |  |  |
|  |  |  |  |  |
|  |  |  |  |  |
|  |  |  |  |  |
|  |  |  |  |  |
|  |  |  |  |  |
|  |  |  |  |  |
|  |  |  |  |  |
|  |  |  |  |  |
|  |  |  |  |  |
|  |  |  |  |  |
|  |  |  |  |  |
|  |  |  |  |  |
|  |  |  |  |  |
|  |  |  |  |  |

**Cumulative Prob. (Perpetual)**

Part 1          Echo Systems (cont'd.)

### GENERAL JOURNAL                          Page_____

| Date | Account Titles and Explanation | PR | Debit | Credit |
|------|-------------------------------|----|-------|--------|
|      |                               |    |       |        |
|      |                               |    |       |        |
|      |                               |    |       |        |
|      |                               |    |       |        |
|      |                               |    |       |        |
|      |                               |    |       |        |
|      |                               |    |       |        |
|      |                               |    |       |        |
|      |                               |    |       |        |
|      |                               |    |       |        |
|      |                               |    |       |        |
|      |                               |    |       |        |
|      |                               |    |       |        |
|      |                               |    |       |        |
|      |                               |    |       |        |
|      |                               |    |       |        |
|      |                               |    |       |        |
|      |                               |    |       |        |
|      |                               |    |       |        |
|      |                               |    |       |        |
|      |                               |    |       |        |
|      |                               |    |       |        |
|      |                               |    |       |        |
|      |                               |    |       |        |
|      |                               |    |       |        |
|      |                               |    |       |        |
|      |                               |    |       |        |
|      |                               |    |       |        |
|      |                               |    |       |        |
|      |                               |    |       |        |
|      |                               |    |       |        |
|      |                               |    |       |        |
|      |                               |    |       |        |
|      |                               |    |       |        |
|      |                               |    |       |        |
|      |                               |    |       |        |
|      |                               |    |       |        |
|      |                               |    |       |        |
|      |                               |    |       |        |

## GENERAL JOURNAL

Page____

| Date | Account Titles and Explanation | PR | Debit | Credit |
|------|-------------------------------|----|-------|--------|
|      |                               |    |       |        |
|      |                               |    |       |        |
|      |                               |    |       |        |
|      |                               |    |       |        |
|      |                               |    |       |        |
|      |                               |    |       |        |
|      |                               |    |       |        |
|      |                               |    |       |        |
|      |                               |    |       |        |
|      |                               |    |       |        |
|      |                               |    |       |        |
|      |                               |    |       |        |
|      |                               |    |       |        |
|      |                               |    |       |        |
|      |                               |    |       |        |
|      |                               |    |       |        |
|      |                               |    |       |        |
|      |                               |    |       |        |
|      |                               |    |       |        |
|      |                               |    |       |        |
|      |                               |    |       |        |
|      |                               |    |       |        |
|      |                               |    |       |        |
|      |                               |    |       |        |
|      |                               |    |       |        |
|      |                               |    |       |        |
|      |                               |    |       |        |
|      |                               |    |       |        |
|      |                               |    |       |        |
|      |                               |    |       |        |
|      |                               |    |       |        |
|      |                               |    |       |        |
|      |                               |    |       |        |
|      |                               |    |       |        |

**Cumulative Prob. (Perpetual)**

**Part 2**　　　　**Echo Systems (cont'd.)**

## GENERAL LEDGER

Cash　　　　　　　　　　　　　　　　**ACCOUNT NO. 101**

| DATE | EXPLANATION | PR | DEBIT | CREDIT | BALANCE |
|------|-------------|----|----|----|----|
| 2017<br>Dec. 31 | Beginning Balance | | | | 89,090 |
| | | | | | |
| | | | | | |
| | | | | | |
| | | | | | |
| | | | | | |
| | | | | | |
| | | | | | |
| | | | | | |
| | | | | | |
| | | | | | |
| | | | | | |
| | | | | | |
| | | | | | |
| | | | | | |
| | | | | | |
| | | | | | |
| | | | | | |
| | | | | | |
| | | | | | |
| | | | | | |
| | | | | | |
| | | | | | |
| | | | | | |
| | | | | | |
| | | | | | |
| | | | | | |
| | | | | | |
| | | | | | |
| | | | | | |
| | | | | | |
| | | | | | |
| | | | | | |
| | | | | | |
| | | | | | |
| | | | | | |

**Cumulative Prob. (Perpetual)**

**Part 2          Echo Systems (cont'd.)**

### Accounts Receivable – Alamo Engineering          ACCOUNT NO. 106.1

| DATE | EXPLANATION | PR | DEBIT | CREDIT | BALANCE |
|------|-------------|----|-------|--------|---------|
| 2017<br>Dec. 31 | Beginning Balance | | | | -0- |
| | | | | | |
| | | | | | |
| | | | | | |
| | | | | | |

### Accounts Receivable – Buckman Services          ACCOUNT NO. 106.2

| DATE | EXPLANATION | PR | DEBIT | CREDIT | BALANCE |
|------|-------------|----|-------|--------|---------|
| 2017<br>Dec. 31 | Beginning Balance | | | | -0- |
| | | | | | |
| | | | | | |
| | | | | | |

### Accounts Receivable – Capital Leasing          ACCOUNT NO. 106.3

| DATE | EXPLANATION | PR | DEBIT | CREDIT | BALANCE |
|------|-------------|----|-------|--------|---------|
| 2017<br>Dec. 31 | Beginning Balance | | | | -0- |
| | | | | | |
| | | | | | |
| | | | | | |

### Accounts Receivable – Decker Co.          ACCOUNT NO. 106.4

| DATE | EXPLANATION | PR | DEBIT | CREDIT | BALANCE |
|------|-------------|----|-------|--------|---------|
| 2017<br>Dec. 31 | Beginning Balance | | | | 2,700 |
| | | | | | |
| | | | | | |
| | | | | | |

### Accounts Receivable – Elite Corporation          ACCOUNT NO. 106.5

| DATE | EXPLANATION | PR | DEBIT | CREDIT | BALANCE |
|------|-------------|----|-------|--------|---------|
| 2017<br>Dec. 31 | Beginning Balance | | | | -0- |
| | | | | | |
| | | | | | |
| | | | | | |
| | | | | | |

**Cumulative Prob. (Perpetual)**

**Part 2**  **Echo Systems (cont'd.)**

### Accounts Receivable – Fostek Co.  ACCOUNT NO. 106.6

| DATE | EXPLANATION | PR | DEBIT | CREDIT | BALANCE |
|------|-------------|----|-------|--------|---------|
| 2017<br>Dec. 31 | Beginning Balance | | | | 3,000 |
| | | | | | |
| | | | | | |

### Accounts Receivable – Grandview Co.  ACCOUNT NO. 106.7

| DATE | EXPLANATION | PR | DEBIT | CREDIT | BALANCE |
|------|-------------|----|-------|--------|---------|
| 2017<br>Dec. 31 | Beginning Balance | | | | -0- |
| | | | | | |
| | | | | | |
| | | | | | |

### Accounts Receivable – Hacienda, Inc.  ACCOUNT NO. 106.8

| DATE | EXPLANATION | PR | DEBIT | CREDIT | BALANCE |
|------|-------------|----|-------|--------|---------|
| 2017<br>Dec. 31 | Beginning Balance | | | | -0- |
| | | | | | |
| | | | | | |

### Accounts Receivable – Images, Inc.  ACCOUNT NO. 106.9

| DATE | EXPLANATION | PR | DEBIT | CREDIT | BALANCE |
|------|-------------|----|-------|--------|---------|
| 2017<br>Dec. 31 | Beginning Balance | | | | -0- |
| | | | | | |

*Fundamental Accounting Principles*, 15ce, Working Papers

**Cumulative Prob. (Perpetual)**

**Part 2**          **Echo Systems (cont'd.)**

### Merchandise Inventory                    ACCOUNT NO. 119

| DATE | EXPLANATION | PR | DEBIT | CREDIT | BALANCE |
|------|-------------|----|-------|--------|---------|
|      |             |    |       |        |         |
|      |             |    |       |        |         |
|      |             |    |       |        |         |
|      |             |    |       |        |         |
|      |             |    |       |        |         |
|      |             |    |       |        |         |
|      |             |    |       |        |         |
|      |             |    |       |        |         |
|      |             |    |       |        |         |
|      |             |    |       |        |         |
|      |             |    |       |        |         |
|      |             |    |       |        |         |
|      |             |    |       |        |         |
|      |             |    |       |        |         |

### Computer Supplies                        ACCOUNT NO. 126

| DATE | EXPLANATION | PR | DEBIT | CREDIT | BALANCE |
|------|-------------|----|-------|--------|---------|
| 2017 Dec. 31 | Balance |    |       |        | 1,440 |
|      |             |    |       |        |         |
|      |             |    |       |        |         |

### Prepaid Insurance                        ACCOUNT NO. 128

| DATE | EXPLANATION | PR | DEBIT | CREDIT | BALANCE |
|------|-------------|----|-------|--------|---------|
| 2017 Dec. 31 | Beginning Balance |    |       |        | 3,240 |
|      |             |    |       |        |         |

### Prepaid Rent                             ACCOUNT NO. 131

| DATE | EXPLANATION | PR | DEBIT | CREDIT | BALANCE |
|------|-------------|----|-------|--------|---------|
| 2017 Dec. 31 | Beginning Balance |    |       |        | 2,250 |
|      |             |    |       |        |         |
|      |             |    |       |        |         |

### Office Equipment                         ACCOUNT NO. 163

| DATE | EXPLANATION | PR | DEBIT | CREDIT | BALANCE |
|------|-------------|----|-------|--------|---------|
| 2017 Dec. 31 | Beginning Balance |    |       |        | 18,000 |
|      |             |    |       |        |         |
|      |             |    |       |        |         |

**Cumulative Prob. (Perpetual)**

**Part 2          Echo Systems (cont'd.)**

### Accumulated Depreciation, Office Equipment — ACCOUNT NO. 164

| DATE | EXPLANATION | PR | DEBIT | CREDIT | BALANCE |
|------|-------------|----|----|----|----|
| 2017<br>Dec. 31 | Beginning Balance | | | | 1,500 |
| | | | | | |

### Computer Equipment — ACCOUNT NO. 167

| DATE | EXPLANATION | PR | DEBIT | CREDIT | BALANCE |
|------|-------------|----|----|----|----|
| 2017<br>Dec. 31 | Beginning Balance | | | | 36,000 |
| | | | | | |

### Accumulated Depreciation, Computer Equipment — ACCOUNT NO. 168

| DATE | EXPLANATION | PR | DEBIT | CREDIT | BALANCE |
|------|-------------|----|----|----|----|
| 2017<br>Dec. 31 | Beginning Balance | | | | 2,250 |
| | | | | | |

### Accounts Payable — ACCOUNT NO. 201

| DATE | EXPLANATION | PR | DEBIT | CREDIT | BALANCE |
|------|-------------|----|----|----|----|
| 2017<br>Dec. 31 | Beginning Balance | | | | 2,310 |
| | | | | | |
| | | | | | |
| | | | | | |
| | | | | | |
| | | | | | |
| | | | | | |
| | | | | | |
| | | | | | |
| | | | | | |

### Wages Payable — ACCOUNT NO. 210

| DATE | EXPLANATION | PR | DEBIT | CREDIT | BALANCE |
|------|-------------|----|----|----|----|
| 2017<br>Dec. 31 | Beginning Balance | | | | 800 |
| | | | | | |
| | | | | | |

**Cumulative Prob. (Perpetual)**

**Part 2          Echo Systems (cont'd.)**

### Unearned Computer Services Revenue                    ACCOUNT NO. 236

| DATE | EXPLANATION | PR | DEBIT | CREDIT | BALANCE |
|------|-------------|----|-------|--------|---------|
| 2017<br>Dec. 31 | Beginning Balance | | | | 3,000 |
| | | | | | |
| | | | | | |

### Mary Graham, Capital                    ACCOUNT NO. 301

| DATE | EXPLANATION | PR | DEBIT | CREDIT | BALANCE |
|------|-------------|----|-------|--------|---------|
| 2017<br>Dec. 31 | Beginning Balance | | | | 145,860 |
| | | | | | |
| | | | | | |

### Mary Graham, Withdrawals                    ACCOUNT NO. 302

| DATE | EXPLANATION | PR | DEBIT | CREDIT | BALANCE |
|------|-------------|----|-------|--------|---------|
| | | | | | |
| | | | | | |

### Computer Services Revenue                    ACCOUNT NO. 403

| DATE | EXPLANATION | PR | DEBIT | CREDIT | BALANCE |
|------|-------------|----|-------|--------|---------|
| | | | | | |
| | | | | | |
| | | | | | |
| | | | | | |
| | | | | | |

### Sales                    ACCOUNT NO. 413

| DATE | EXPLANATION | PR | DEBIT | CREDIT | BALANCE |
|------|-------------|----|-------|--------|---------|
| | | | | | |
| | | | | | |
| | | | | | |
| | | | | | |
| | | | | | |
| | | | | | |

**Cumulative Prob. (Perpetual)**

**Part 2**      Echo Systems (cont'd.)

### Sales Discounts      ACCOUNT NO. 414

| DATE | EXPLANATION | PR | DEBIT | CREDIT | BALANCE |
|------|-------------|----|-------|--------|---------|
|      |             |    |       |        |         |
|      |             |    |       |        |         |
|      |             |    |       |        |         |

### Sales Returns and Allowances      ACCOUNT NO. 415

| DATE | EXPLANATION | PR | DEBIT | CREDIT | BALANCE |
|------|-------------|----|-------|--------|---------|
|      |             |    |       |        |         |
|      |             |    |       |        |         |
|      |             |    |       |        |         |

### Cost of Goods Sold      ACCOUNT NO. 502

| DATE | EXPLANATION | PR | DEBIT | CREDIT | BALANCE |
|------|-------------|----|-------|--------|---------|
|      |             |    |       |        |         |
|      |             |    |       |        |         |
|      |             |    |       |        |         |
|      |             |    |       |        |         |
|      |             |    |       |        |         |
|      |             |    |       |        |         |
|      |             |    |       |        |         |

### Depreciation Expense, Office Equipment      ACCOUNT NO. 612

| DATE | EXPLANATION | PR | DEBIT | CREDIT | BALANCE |
|------|-------------|----|-------|--------|---------|
|      |             |    |       |        |         |
|      |             |    |       |        |         |

### Depreciation Expense, Computer Equipment      ACCOUNT NO. 613

| DATE | EXPLANATION | PR | DEBIT | CREDIT | BALANCE |
|------|-------------|----|-------|--------|---------|
|      |             |    |       |        |         |
|      |             |    |       |        |         |

### Wages Expense      ACCOUNT NO. 623

| DATE | EXPLANATION | PR | DEBIT | CREDIT | BALANCE |
|------|-------------|----|-------|--------|---------|
|      |             |    |       |        |         |
|      |             |    |       |        |         |
|      |             |    |       |        |         |
|      |             |    |       |        |         |

**Cumulative Prob. (Perpetual)**

**Part 2**        **Echo Systems (cont'd.)**

### Insurance Expense                    ACCOUNT NO. 637

| DATE | EXPLANATION | PR | DEBIT | CREDIT | BALANCE |
|------|-------------|-----|-------|--------|---------|
|      |             |     |       |        |         |
|      |             |     |       |        |         |

### Rent Expense                    ACCOUNT NO. 640

| DATE | EXPLANATION | PR | DEBIT | CREDIT | BALANCE |
|------|-------------|-----|-------|--------|---------|
|      |             |     |       |        |         |
|      |             |     |       |        |         |

### Computer Supplies Expense                    ACCOUNT NO. 652

| DATE | EXPLANATION | P.R. | DEBIT | CREDIT | BALANCE |
|------|-------------|------|-------|--------|---------|
|      |             |      |       |        |         |
|      |             |      |       |        |         |

### Advertising Expense                    ACCOUNT NO. 655

| DATE | EXPLANATION | PR | DEBIT | CREDIT | BALANCE |
|------|-------------|-----|-------|--------|---------|
|      |             |     |       |        |         |
|      |             |     |       |        |         |
|      |             |     |       |        |         |

### Mileage Expense                    ACCOUNT NO. 676

| DATE | EXPLANATION | PR | DEBIT | CREDIT | BALANCE |
|------|-------------|-----|-------|--------|---------|
|      |             |     |       |        |         |
|      |             |     |       |        |         |
|      |             |     |       |        |         |
|      |             |     |       |        |         |

### Repairs Expense, Computer                    ACCOUNT NO. 684

| DATE | EXPLANATION | PR | DEBIT | CREDIT | BALANCE |
|------|-------------|-----|-------|--------|---------|
|      |             |     |       |        |         |
|      |             |     |       |        |         |
|      |             |     |       |        |         |

### Charitable Donations Expense                    ACCOUNT NO. 699

| DATE | EXPLANATION | PR | DEBIT | CREDIT | BALANCE |
|------|-------------|-----|-------|--------|---------|
|      |             |     |       |        |         |
|      |             |     |       |        |         |

**Cumulative Prob. (Perpetual)**

**Part 3          Echo Systems**

### ECHO SYSTEMS
### Partial Work Sheet
### For Three Months Ended March 31, 2018

| Acct. No. | Account Title | Unadjusted Trial Balance Dr. | Cr. | Adjustments Dr. | Cr. | Adjusted Trial Balance Dr. | Cr. |
|---|---|---|---|---|---|---|---|
| 101 | Cash | | | | | | |
| 106.1 | Alamo Engineering Co. | | | | | | |
| 106.2 | Buckman Services | | | | | | |
| 106.3 | Capital Leasing | | | | | | |
| 106.4 | Decker Co. | | | | | | |
| 106.5 | Elite Corporation | | | | | | |
| 106.6 | Fostek Co. | | | | | | |
| 106.7 | Grandview Co. | | | | | | |
| 106.8 | Hacienda Inc. | | | | | | |
| 106.9 | Images Inc. | | | | | | |
| 119 | Merchandise inventory | | | | | | |
| 126 | Computer supplies | | | | | | |
| 128 | Prepaid insurance | | | | | | |
| 131 | Prepaid rent | | | | | | |
| 163 | Office equipment | | | | | | |
| 164 | Accum. deprec., office equipment | | | | | | |
| 167 | Computer equipment | | | | | | |
| 168 | Accum. deprec., computer equip. | | | | | | |
| 201 | Accounts payable | | | | | | |
| 210 | Wages payable | | | | | | |
| 236 | Unearned computer services rev. | | | | | | |
| 301 | Mary Graham, capital | | | | | | |
| 302 | Mary Graham, withdrawals | | | | | | |
| 403 | Computer services revenue | | | | | | |
| 413 | Sales | | | | | | |
| 414 | Sales discounts | | | | | | |
| 415 | Sales returns and allowances | | | | | | |
| 502 | Cost of goods sold | | | | | | |
| 612 | Deprec. exp., office equipment | | | | | | |
| 613 | Deprec. exp., computer equip. | | | | | | |
| 623 | Wages expense | | | | | | |
| 637 | Insurance expense | | | | | | |
| 640 | Rent expense | | | | | | |
| 652 | Computer supplies expense | | | | | | |
| 655 | Advertising expense | | | | | | |
| 676 | Mileage expense | | | | | | |
| 684 | Repairs expense, computer | | | | | | |
| 699 | Charitable donations expense | | | | | | |
| | Totals | | | | | | |
| | | | | | | | |
| | | | | | | | |
| | | | | | | | |
| | | | | | | | |
| | | | | | | | |
| | | | | | | | |

**Cumulative Prob. (Perpetual)**

**Part 4**       Echo Systems (cont'd.)

| ECHO SYSTEMS | | |
|---|---|---|
| **Income Statement** | | |
| **For Three Months Ended March 31, 2018** | | |
| | | |
| | | |
| | | |
| | | |
| | | |
| | | |
| | | |
| | | |
| | | |
| | | |
| | | |
| | | |
| | | |
| | | |
| | | |
| | | |
| | | |
| | | |
| | | |
| | | |
| | | |
| | | |
| | | |
| | | |

**Part 5**

| ECHO SYSTEMS | | |
|---|---|---|
| **Statement of Changes in Equity** | | |
| **For Three Months Ended March 31, 2018** | | |
| | | |
| | | |
| | | |
| | | |
| | | |
| | | |
| | | |
| | | |
| | | |

**Cumulative Prob. (Perpetual)**

**Part 6**  **Echo Systems (concl'd.)**

### ECHO SYSTEMS
### Balance Sheet
### March 31, 2018

| | | | |
|---|---|---|---|
| | | | |
| | | | |
| | | | |
| | | | |
| | | | |
| | | | |
| | | | |
| | | | |
| | | | |
| | | | |
| | | | |
| | | | |
| | | | |
| | | | |
| | | | |
| | | | |
| | | | |
| | | | |
| | | | |
| | | | |
| | | | |
| | | | |
| | | | |
| | | | |
| | | | |
| | | | |
| | | | |
| | | | |
| | | | |
| | | | |
| | | | |
| | | | |
| | | | |
| | | | |
| | | | |
| | | | |

**Chapter 5**

Name:_____

**Cumulative Prob. (Periodic)**

**Part 1**          **Echo Systems**
**Journal Entries**

GENERAL JOURNAL          Page _____

| Date | Account Titles and Explanation | PR | Debit | Credit |
|------|-------------------------------|----|-------|--------|
|  |  |  |  |  |
|  |  |  |  |  |
|  |  |  |  |  |
|  |  |  |  |  |
|  |  |  |  |  |
|  |  |  |  |  |
|  |  |  |  |  |
|  |  |  |  |  |
|  |  |  |  |  |
|  |  |  |  |  |
|  |  |  |  |  |
|  |  |  |  |  |
|  |  |  |  |  |
|  |  |  |  |  |
|  |  |  |  |  |
|  |  |  |  |  |
|  |  |  |  |  |
|  |  |  |  |  |
|  |  |  |  |  |
|  |  |  |  |  |
|  |  |  |  |  |
|  |  |  |  |  |
|  |  |  |  |  |
|  |  |  |  |  |
|  |  |  |  |  |
|  |  |  |  |  |
|  |  |  |  |  |
|  |  |  |  |  |
|  |  |  |  |  |
|  |  |  |  |  |
|  |  |  |  |  |
|  |  |  |  |  |
|  |  |  |  |  |
|  |  |  |  |  |
|  |  |  |  |  |
|  |  |  |  |  |
|  |  |  |  |  |
|  |  |  |  |  |
|  |  |  |  |  |
|  |  |  |  |  |
|  |  |  |  |  |
|  |  |  |  |  |

**Cumulative Prob. (Periodic)**

**Part 1**　　　　　**Echo Systems (cont'd.)**

| Date | Account Titles and Explanation | PR | Debit | Credit |
|---|---|---|---|---|
| | | | | |
| | | | | |
| | | | | |
| | | | | |
| | | | | |
| | | | | |
| | | | | |
| | | | | |
| | | | | |
| | | | | |
| | | | | |
| | | | | |
| | | | | |
| | | | | |
| | | | | |
| | | | | |
| | | | | |
| | | | | |
| | | | | |
| | | | | |
| | | | | |
| | | | | |
| | | | | |
| | | | | |
| | | | | |
| | | | | |
| | | | | |
| | | | | |
| | | | | |
| | | | | |
| | | | | |
| | | | | |
| | | | | |
| | | | | |
| | | | | |
| | | | | |
| | | | | |

**Cumulative Prob. (Periodic)**

**Part 1**          Echo Systems (cont'd.)

| Date | | Account Titles and Explanation | PR | Debit | Credit |
|---|---|---|---|---|---|
| | | | | | |
| | | | | | |
| | | | | | |
| | | | | | |
| | | | | | |
| | | | | | |
| | | | | | |
| | | | | | |
| | | | | | |
| | | | | | |
| | | | | | |
| | | | | | |
| | | | | | |
| | | | | | |
| | | | | | |
| | | | | | |
| | | | | | |
| | | | | | |
| | | | | | |
| | | | | | |
| | | | | | |
| | | | | | |
| | | | | | |
| | | | | | |
| | | | | | |
| | | | | | |
| | | | | | |
| | | | | | |
| | | | | | |
| | | | | | |
| | | | | | |
| | | | | | |
| | | | | | |
| | | | | | |
| | | | | | |
| | | | | | |
| | | | | | |
| | | | | | |
| | | | | | |
| | | | | | |

**Part 1**          **Echo Systems (cont'd.)**

| Date | Account Titles and Explanation | PR | Debit | Credit |
|------|-------------------------------|-----|-------|--------|
|      |                               |     |       |        |
|      |                               |     |       |        |
|      |                               |     |       |        |
|      |                               |     |       |        |
|      |                               |     |       |        |
|      |                               |     |       |        |
|      |                               |     |       |        |
|      |                               |     |       |        |
|      |                               |     |       |        |
|      |                               |     |       |        |
|      |                               |     |       |        |
|      |                               |     |       |        |
|      |                               |     |       |        |
|      |                               |     |       |        |
|      |                               |     |       |        |
|      |                               |     |       |        |
|      |                               |     |       |        |
|      |                               |     |       |        |
|      |                               |     |       |        |
|      |                               |     |       |        |
|      |                               |     |       |        |
|      |                               |     |       |        |
|      |                               |     |       |        |
|      |                               |     |       |        |
|      |                               |     |       |        |
|      |                               |     |       |        |
|      |                               |     |       |        |
|      |                               |     |       |        |
|      |                               |     |       |        |
|      |                               |     |       |        |
|      |                               |     |       |        |
|      |                               |     |       |        |
|      |                               |     |       |        |
|      |                               |     |       |        |
|      |                               |     |       |        |
|      |                               |     |       |        |
|      |                               |     |       |        |
|      |                               |     |       |        |
|      |                               |     |       |        |

## GENERAL LEDGER

Cash                                                             ACCOUNT NO. 101

| DATE | EXPLANATION | PR | DEBIT | CREDIT | BALANCE |
|------|-------------|----|-------|--------|---------|
| 2017 Dec. 31 | Beginning Balance | | | | 89,090 |
| | | | | | |
| | | | | | |
| | | | | | |
| | | | | | |
| | | | | | |
| | | | | | |
| | | | | | |
| | | | | | |
| | | | | | |
| | | | | | |
| | | | | | |
| | | | | | |
| | | | | | |
| | | | | | |
| | | | | | |
| | | | | | |
| | | | | | |
| | | | | | |
| | | | | | |
| | | | | | |
| | | | | | |
| | | | | | |
| | | | | | |
| | | | | | |
| | | | | | |
| | | | | | |
| | | | | | |
| | | | | | |
| | | | | | |
| | | | | | |
| | | | | | |
| | | | | | |

**Cumulative Prob. (Periodic)**

**Part 2          Echo Systems (cont'd.)**

### Accounts Receivable – Alamo Engineering          ACCOUNT NO. 106.1

| DATE | EXPLANATION | PR | DEBIT | CREDIT | BALANCE |
|------|-------------|----|-------|--------|---------|
| 2017 Dec. 31 | Beginning Balance | | | | -0- |
| | | | | | |
| | | | | | |
| | | | | | |
| | | | | | |

### Accounts Receivable – Buckman Services          ACCOUNT NO. 106.2

| DATE | EXPLANATION | PR | DEBIT | CREDIT | BALANCE |
|------|-------------|----|-------|--------|---------|
| 2017 Dec. 31 | Beginning Balance | | | | -0- |
| | | | | | |
| | | | | | |
| | | | | | |

### Accounts Receivable – Capital Leasing          ACCOUNT NO. 106.3

| DATE | EXPLANATION | PR | DEBIT | CREDIT | BALANCE |
|------|-------------|----|-------|--------|---------|
| 2017 Dec. 31 | Beginning Balance | | | | -0- |
| | | | | | |
| | | | | | |
| | | | | | |

### Accounts Receivable – Decker Co.          ACCOUNT NO. 106.4

| DATE | EXPLANATION | PR | DEBIT | CREDIT | BALANCE |
|------|-------------|----|-------|--------|---------|
| 2017 Dec. 31 | Beginning Balance | | | | 2,700 |
| | | | | | |
| | | | | | |
| | | | | | |

### Accounts Receivable – Elite Corporation          ACCOUNT NO. 106.5

| DATE | EXPLANATION | PR | DEBIT | CREDIT | BALANCE |
|------|-------------|----|-------|--------|---------|
| 2017 Dec. 31 | Beginning Balance | | | | -0- |
| | | | | | |
| | | | | | |
| | | | | | |
| | | | | | |

Name:_____

**Cumulative Prob. (Periodic)**

**Part 2**          **Echo Systems (cont'd.)**

### Accounts Receivable – Fostek Co.          ACCOUNT NO. 106.6

| DATE | EXPLANATION | PR | DEBIT | CREDIT | BALANCE |
|------|-------------|----|-------|--------|---------|
| 2017 Dec. 31 | Beginning Balance | | | | 3,000 |
| | | | | | |
| | | | | | |

### Accounts Receivable – Grandview Co.          ACCOUNT NO. 106.7

| DATE | EXPLANATION | PR | DEBIT | CREDIT | BALANCE |
|------|-------------|----|-------|--------|---------|
| 2017 Dec. 31 | Beginning Balance | | | | -0- |
| | | | | | |
| | | | | | |

### Accounts Receivable – Hacienda, Inc.          ACCOUNT NO. 106.8

| DATE | EXPLANATION | PR | DEBIT | CREDIT | BALANCE |
|------|-------------|----|-------|--------|---------|
| 2017 Dec. 31 | Beginning Balance | | | | -0- |
| | | | | | |
| | | | | | |

### Accounts Receivable – Images, Inc.          ACCOUNT NO. 106.9

| DATE | EXPLANATION | PR | DEBIT | CREDIT | BALANCE |
|------|-------------|----|-------|--------|---------|
| 2017 Dec. 31 | Beginning Balance | | | | -0- |
| | | | | | |

### Merchandise Inventory          ACCOUNT NO. 119

| DATE | EXPLANATION | PR | DEBIT | CREDIT | BALANCE |
|------|-------------|----|-------|--------|---------|
| 2017 Dec. 31 | Beginning Balance | | | | -0- |
| | | | | | |
| | | | | | |
| | | | | | |

### Computer Supplies          ACCOUNT NO. 126

| DATE | EXPLANATION | PR | DEBIT | CREDIT | BALANCE |
|------|-------------|----|-------|--------|---------|
| 2017 Dec. 31 | Beginning Balance | | | | 1,440 |
| | | | | | |
| | | | | | |

## Cumulative Prob. (Periodic)

**Part 2**        Echo Systems (cont'd.)

### Prepaid Insurance                                        ACCOUNT NO. 128

| DATE | EXPLANATION | PR | DEBIT | CREDIT | BALANCE |
|------|-------------|----|----|----|----|
| 2017 Dec. 31 | Beginning Balance | | | | 3,240 |
| | | | | | |

### Prepaid Rent                                            ACCOUNT NO. 131

| DATE | EXPLANATION | PR | DEBIT | CREDIT | BALANCE |
|------|-------------|----|----|----|----|
| 2017 Dec. 31 | Beginning Balance | | | | 2,250 |
| | | | | | |
| | | | | | |

### Office Equipment                                        ACCOUNT NO. 163

| DATE | EXPLANATION | PR | DEBIT | CREDIT | BALANCE |
|------|-------------|----|----|----|----|
| 2017 Dec. 31 | Beginning Balance | | | | 18,000 |
| | | | | | |
| | | | | | |

### Accumulated Depreciation, Office Equipment              ACCOUNT NO. 164

| DATE | EXPLANATION | PR | DEBIT | CREDIT | BALANCE |
|------|-------------|----|----|----|----|
| 2017 Dec. 31 | Beginning Balance | | | | 1,500 |
| | | | | | |

### Computer Equipment                                      ACCOUNT NO. 167

| DATE | EXPLANATION | PR | DEBIT | CREDIT | BALANCE |
|------|-------------|----|----|----|----|
| 2017 Dec. 31 | Beginning Balance | | | | 36,000 |
| | | | | | |

### Accumulated Depreciation, Computer Equipment            ACCOUNT NO. 168

| DATE | EXPLANATION | PR | DEBIT | CREDIT | BALANCE |
|------|-------------|----|----|----|----|
| 2017 Dec. 31 | Beginning Balance | | | | 2,250 |
| | | | | | |

**Cumulative Prob. (Periodic)**

**Part 2**          **Echo Systems (cont'd.)**

## Accounts Payable                          ACCOUNT NO. 201

| DATE | EXPLANATION | PR | DEBIT | CREDIT | BALANCE |
|------|-------------|-----|-------|--------|---------|
| 2017<br>Dec. 31 | Beginning Balance | | | | 2,310 |
| | | | | | |
| | | | | | |
| | | | | | |
| | | | | | |
| | | | | | |
| | | | | | |
| | | | | | |
| | | | | | |
| | | | | | |

## Wages Payable                            ACCOUNT NO. 210

| DATE | EXPLANATION | PR | DEBIT | CREDIT | BALANCE |
|------|-------------|-----|-------|--------|---------|
| 2017<br>Dec. 31 | Beginning Balance | | | | 800 |
| | | | | | |
| | | | | | |

## Unearned Computer Services Revenue            ACCOUNT NO. 236

| DATE | EXPLANATION | PR | DEBIT | CREDIT | BALANCE |
|------|-------------|-----|-------|--------|---------|
| 2017<br>Dec. 31 | Beginning Balance | | | | 3,000 |
| | | | | | |
| | | | | | |

## Mary Graham, Capital                          ACCOUNT NO. 301

| DATE | EXPLANATION | PR | DEBIT | CREDIT | BALANCE |
|------|-------------|-----|-------|--------|---------|
| 2017<br>Dec. 31 | Beginning Balance | | | | 145,860 |
| | | | | | |
| | | | | | |

## Mary Graham, Withdrawals                       ACCOUNT NO. 302

| DATE | EXPLANATION | PR | DEBIT | CREDIT | BALANCE |
|------|-------------|-----|-------|--------|---------|
| | | | | | |
| | | | | | |
| | | | | | |

**Cumulative Prob. (Periodic)**

**Part 2**          **Echo Systems (cont'd.)**

### Computer Services Revenue — ACCOUNT NO. 403

| DATE | EXPLANATION | PR | DEBIT | CREDIT | BALANCE |
|------|-------------|----|-------|--------|---------|
|      |             |    |       |        |         |
|      |             |    |       |        |         |
|      |             |    |       |        |         |
|      |             |    |       |        |         |
|      |             |    |       |        |         |

### Sales — ACCOUNT NO. 413

| DATE | EXPLANATION | PR | DEBIT | CREDIT | BALANCE |
|------|-------------|----|-------|--------|---------|
|      |             |    |       |        |         |
|      |             |    |       |        |         |
|      |             |    |       |        |         |
|      |             |    |       |        |         |
|      |             |    |       |        |         |
|      |             |    |       |        |         |

### Sales Discounts — ACCOUNT NO. 414

| DATE | EXPLANATION | PR | DEBIT | CREDIT | BALANCE |
|------|-------------|----|-------|--------|---------|
|      |             |    |       |        |         |
|      |             |    |       |        |         |
|      |             |    |       |        |         |

### Sales Returns and Allowances — ACCOUNT NO. 415

| DATE | EXPLANATION | PR | DEBIT | CREDIT | BALANCE |
|------|-------------|----|-------|--------|---------|
|      |             |    |       |        |         |
|      |             |    |       |        |         |
|      |             |    |       |        |         |

### Purchases — ACCOUNT NO. 505

| DATE | EXPLANATION | PR | DEBIT | CREDIT | BALANCE |
|------|-------------|----|-------|--------|---------|
|      |             |    |       |        |         |
|      |             |    |       |        |         |
|      |             |    |       |        |         |
|      |             |    |       |        |         |

**Cumulative Prob. (Periodic)**

**Part 2**        Echo Systems (cont'd.)

### Purchase Returns and Allowances                    ACCOUNT NO. 506

| DATE | EXPLANATION | PR | DEBIT | CREDIT | BALANCE |
|------|-------------|----|-------|--------|---------|
|      |             |    |       |        |         |
|      |             |    |       |        |         |
|      |             |    |       |        |         |

### Purchase Discounts                    ACCOUNT NO.507

| DATE | EXPLANATION | PR | DEBIT | CREDIT | BALANCE |
|------|-------------|----|-------|--------|---------|
|      |             |    |       |        |         |
|      |             |    |       |        |         |
|      |             |    |       |        |         |

### Transportation-In                    ACCOUNT NO. 508

| DATE | EXPLANATION | PR | DEBIT | CREDIT | BALANCE |
|------|-------------|----|-------|--------|---------|
|      |             |    |       |        |         |
|      |             |    |       |        |         |
|      |             |    |       |        |         |

### Depreciation Expense, Office Equipment                    ACCOUNT NO. 612

| DATE | EXPLANATION | PR | DEBIT | CREDIT | BALANCE |
|------|-------------|----|-------|--------|---------|
|      |             |    |       |        |         |
|      |             |    |       |        |         |

### Depreciation Expense, Computer Equipment                    ACCOUNT NO. 613

| DATE | EXPLANATION | PR | DEBIT | CREDIT | BALANCE |
|------|-------------|----|-------|--------|---------|
|      |             |    |       |        |         |
|      |             |    |       |        |         |

### Wages Expense                    ACCOUNT NO. 623

| DATE | EXPLANATION | PR | DEBIT | CREDIT | BALANCE |
|------|-------------|----|-------|--------|---------|
|      |             |    |       |        |         |
|      |             |    |       |        |         |
|      |             |    |       |        |         |

Cumulative Prob. (Periodic)

Part 2        Echo Systems (cont'd.)

### Insurance Expense                                    ACCOUNT NO. 637

| DATE | EXPLANATION | PR | DEBIT | CREDIT | BALANCE |
|------|-------------|-----|-------|--------|---------|
|      |             |     |       |        |         |
|      |             |     |       |        |         |

### Rent Expense                                         ACCOUNT NO. 640

| DATE | EXPLANATION | PR | DEBIT | CREDIT | BALANCE |
|------|-------------|-----|-------|--------|---------|
|      |             |     |       |        |         |
|      |             |     |       |        |         |

### Computer Supplies Expense                            ACCOUNT NO. 652

| DATE | EXPLANATION | P.R. | DEBIT | CREDIT | BALANCE |
|------|-------------|------|-------|--------|---------|
|      |             |      |       |        |         |
|      |             |      |       |        |         |

### Advertising Expense                                  ACCOUNT NO. 655

| DATE | EXPLANATION | PR | DEBIT | CREDIT | BALANCE |
|------|-------------|-----|-------|--------|---------|
|      |             |     |       |        |         |
|      |             |     |       |        |         |
|      |             |     |       |        |         |

### Mileage Expense                                      ACCOUNT NO. 676

| DATE | EXPLANATION | PR | DEBIT | CREDIT | BALANCE |
|------|-------------|-----|-------|--------|---------|
|      |             |     |       |        |         |
|      |             |     |       |        |         |
|      |             |     |       |        |         |
|      |             |     |       |        |         |

### Repairs Expense, Computer                            ACCOUNT NO. 684

| DATE | EXPLANATION | PR | DEBIT | CREDIT | BALANCE |
|------|-------------|-----|-------|--------|---------|
|      |             |     |       |        |         |
|      |             |     |       |        |         |
|      |             |     |       |        |         |

### Charitable Donations Expense                         ACCOUNT NO. 699

| DATE | EXPLANATION | PR | DEBIT | CREDIT | BALANCE |
|------|-------------|-----|-------|--------|---------|
|      |             |     |       |        |         |
|      |             |     |       |        |         |

**Cumulative Prob. (Periodic)**

**Part 3            Echo Systems (concl'd.)**

## ECHO SYSTEMS
## Partial Work Sheet
## March 31, 2018

| Acct. No. | Account Title | Unadjusted Trial Balance | | Adjustments | | Adjusted Trial Balance | |
|---|---|---|---|---|---|---|---|
| | | Debit | Credit | Debit | Credit | Debit | Credit |
| 101 | Cash | | | | | | |
| 106.1 | Alamo Engineering Co. | | | | | | |
| 106.2 | Buckman Services | | | | | | |
| 106.3 | Capital Leasing | | | | | | |
| 106.4 | Decker Co. | | | | | | |
| 106.5 | Elite Corporation | | | | | | |
| 106.6 | Fostek Co. | | | | | | |
| 106.7 | Grandview Co. | | | | | | |
| 106.8 | Hacienda Inc. | | | | | | |
| 106.9 | Images Inc. | | | | | | |
| 119 | Merchandise inventory | | | | | | |
| 126 | Computer supplies | | | | | | |
| 128 | Prepaid insurance | | | | | | |
| 131 | Prepaid rent | | | | | | |
| 163 | Office equipment | | | | | | |
| 164 | Accum. deprec., office equipment | | | | | | |
| 167 | Computer equipment | | | | | | |
| 168 | Accum. deprec., computer equip. | | | | | | |
| 201 | Accounts payable | | | | | | |
| 210 | Wages payable | | | | | | |
| 236 | Unearned computer services rev. | | | | | | |
| 301 | Mary Graham, capital | | | | | | |
| 302 | Mary Graham, withdrawals | | | | | | |
| 403 | Computer services revenue | | | | | | |
| 413 | Sales | | | | | | |
| 414 | Sales discounts | | | | | | |
| 415 | Sales returns and allowances | | | | | | |
| 505 | Purchases | | | | | | |
| 506 | Purchase returns and allowances | | | | | | |
| 507 | Purchase discounts | | | | | | |
| 508 | Transportation-in | | | | | | |
| 612 | Deprec. exp., office equipment | | | | | | |
| 613 | Deprec. exp., computer equip. | | | | | | |
| 623 | Wages expense | | | | | | |
| 637 | Insurance expense | | | | | | |
| 640 | Rent expense | | | | | | |
| 652 | Computer supplies expense | | | | | | |
| 655 | Advertising expense | | | | | | |
| 676 | Mileage expense | | | | | | |
| 684 | Repairs expense, computer | | | | | | |
| 699 | Charitable donations expense | | | | | | |
| | Totals | | | | | | |
| | | | | | | | |

**Parts 4, 5, and 6:  Use the forms provided earlier.**

**Quick Study 6-1**

1. _____
_____
_____

2. _____
_____
_____

**Quick Study 6-2**

_____
_____
_____
_____
_____

**Quick Study 6-3**

_____
_____
_____
_____
_____
_____

**Quick Study 6-4**

_____
_____
_____
_____
_____

**Quick Study 6-5**

_____
_____
_____
_____
_____
_____
_____
_____

**Chapter 6**

Name:_____

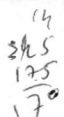

## Quick Study 6-6

### a. FIFO Perpetual

| Date | Purchases | | | Sales (at cost) | | | Inventory Balance | | |
|---|---|---|---|---|---|---|---|---|---|
| | Units | Unit Cost | Total Cost | Units | Unit cost | cost of goods sold | Units | Unit cost | Total cost |
| Jan 1 Beginning Inventory | | | | | | | | | |
| | 310 | @3.00 | =$930 | | | | 310 | @3.00 | $930 |
| 9 | 75 | @3.20 | =$240 | | | | 310 | @3.00 | $930 |
| | | | | | | | 75 | @3.20 | $240 |
| 25 | 100 | @3.35 | =$335 | | | | 310 | @3.00 | $930 |
| | | | | | | | 75 | @3.20 | $240 |
| | | | | | | | 100 | @3.35 | =$335 |
| 28 | | | | 310 | @3.00 | $930 | 40 | @3.20 | =$128 |
| | | | | 35 | @3.20 | $112 | 100 | @3.35 | =$335 |
| Total | 485 | | $1505 | 345 | | $1042 | 140 | | $463 |

### b. Moving Weighted Average Perpetual

| Date | Purchases | Sales (at cost) | Inventory Balance | | |
|---|---|---|---|---|---|
| | | | 310 | @3.00 | $930 |
| | | | 310 | @3.00 | $930 |
| | | | 75 | @3.20 | $240 |
| | | | 310 | @3.00 | $930 |
| | | | 75 | @3.20 | $240 |
| | | | 100 | @3.35 | $335 |
| | | 100 @3.35 | | | |
| | | 75 @3.20 | | | |
| | | 170 @3.00 | 140 | @3.00 | |

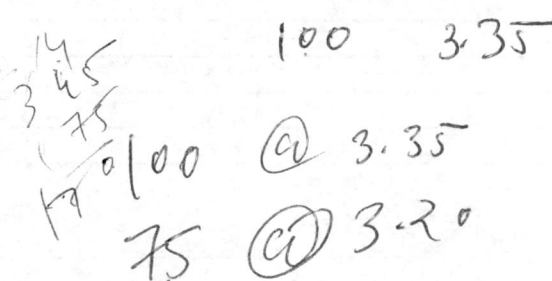

100    3.35

345
75
170   100 @ 3.35

75 @ 3.20

## Quick Study 6-7

| Date | Purchases | Sales (at cost) | Inventory Balance |
|------|-----------|-----------------|-------------------|
|      |           |                 |                   |
|      |           |                 |                   |
|      |           |                 |                   |
|      |           |                 |                   |
|      |           |                 |                   |
|      |           |                 |                   |
|      |           |                 |                   |
|      |           |                 |                   |
|      |           |                 |                   |
|      |           |                 |                   |
|      |           |                 |                   |
|      |           |                 |                   |

## Quick Study 6-8

| Date | Purchases/ Transportation-In/ (Purchase Returns/Discounts) | | | Cost of Goods Sold/ (Returns to Inventory) | | | Balance in Inventory | | |
|------|-------|------------------|----------|-------|------------------|----------|-------|---------------------|----------|
|        | Units | Cost Per Unit | Total $ | Units | Cost Per Unit | Total $ | Units | AvgCost Per Unit | Total $ |
| Jan. 1 |       | BFWD          |          |       |               |         | 10    | $15.00           | $150.00  |
| 3      |       |               |          | 6     |               |         |       |                  |          |
| 7      | 25    | $18.50        | $462.50  |       |               |         |       |                  |          |
| 8      |       |               | 50.00    |       |               |         |       |                  |          |
| 17     |       |               | (46.25)  |       |               |         |       |                  |          |
| 18     |       |               |          | 14    |               |         |       |                  |          |

*Calculations:*

## Quick Study 6-9

a.

b.

c.

**Quick Study 6-10**

**Parts a and b**

| Inventory Items | Units on Hand | Per Unit Cost | Per Unit NRV | Total Cost | Total NRV | LCNRV applied to: a. Inventory as a Group | LCNRV applied to: b. Each Product |
|---|---|---|---|---|---|---|---|
| Aprons | 9 | $6.00 | $5.50 | | | | |
| Bottles | 12 | 3.50 | 4.25 | | | | |
| Candles | 25 | 8.00 | 7.00 | | | | |
| | | | | | | | |

**Part c**     **GENERAL JOURNAL**     Page____

| Date | Account Titles and Explanation | PR | Debit | Credit |
|---|---|---|---|---|
| | | | | |
| | | | | |
| | | | | |
| | | | | |

**Quick Study 6-11**

a. _____
b. _____
c. _____
d. _____
e. _____
f. _____

**Quick Study 6-12**

_____
_____
_____
_____
_____
_____
_____
_____
_____
_____
_____
_____
_____
_____
_____
_____

**Quick Study 6-13**

**a.**
_____
_____
_____
_____
_____
_____
_____
_____
_____
_____
_____
_____

**b.**
_____
_____

**Quick Study 6-14**

_____
_____
_____
_____
_____
_____
_____
_____
_____
_____
_____

**Quick Study 6-15**

_____
_____
_____
_____
_____
_____
_____
_____
_____
_____
_____
_____
_____

**\*Quick Study 6-16**

_____
_____
_____
_____
_____
_____
_____
_____
_____

**Quick Study 6-17**

**a. Days' sales in inventory:**

_____
_____
_____
_____
_____
_____
_____

**b. Merchandise turnover:**

_____
_____
_____
_____
_____
_____
_____
_____

**\*Quick Study 6-18**

**a.** _____
_____
_____

**b.** _____
_____
_____

**Exercise 6-1**

|     | Include / Exclude? | Explanation and if applicable, correct inventory cost |
|-----|---------------------|-------------------------------------------------------|
| a.  |                     |                                                       |
| b.  |                     |                                                       |
| c.  |                     |                                                       |
| d.  |                     |                                                       |

**Exercise 6-2**

**a. FIFO Perpetual**

| Date | Purchases | Sales (at cost) | Inventory Balance |
|------|-----------|-----------------|-------------------|
|      |           |                 |                   |
|      |           |                 |                   |
|      |           |                 |                   |
|      |           |                 |                   |
|      |           |                 |                   |
|      |           |                 |                   |
|      |           |                 |                   |
|      |           |                 |                   |
|      |           |                 |                   |
|      |           |                 |                   |
|      |           |                 |                   |
|      |           |                 |                   |
|      |           |                 |                   |
|      |           |                 |                   |
|      |           |                 |                   |
|      |           |                 |                   |
|      |           |                 |                   |

**Exercise 6-2 (cont'd.)**

**Gross profit calculation under FIFO:**

_____
_____
_____
_____
_____
_____

**b. Moving weighted Average Perpetual**

| Date | Purchases | Sales (at cost) | Inventory Balance |
|------|-----------|-----------------|-------------------|
|      |           |                 |                   |
|      |           |                 |                   |
|      |           |                 |                   |
|      |           |                 |                   |
|      |           |                 |                   |
|      |           |                 |                   |
|      |           |                 |                   |
|      |           |                 |                   |
|      |           |                 |                   |
|      |           |                 |                   |
|      |           |                 |                   |
|      |           |                 |                   |
|      |           |                 |                   |
|      |           |                 |                   |
|      |           |                 |                   |
|      |           |                 |                   |
|      |           |                 |                   |

**Gross Profit Calculation under Moving Weighted Average:**

_____
_____
_____
_____
_____

**Exercise 6-3**

**Specific Identification**

| Date | Purchases | Sales (at cost) | Inventory Balance |
|------|-----------|-----------------|-------------------|
|      |           |                 |                   |
|      |           |                 |                   |
|      |           |                 |                   |
|      |           |                 |                   |
|      |           |                 |                   |
|      |           |                 |                   |
|      |           |                 |                   |
|      |           |                 |                   |
|      |           |                 |                   |
|      |           |                 |                   |
|      |           |                 |                   |
|      |           |                 |                   |
|      |           |                 |                   |
|      |           |                 |                   |

**Gross Profit Calculation under Specific Identification:**

Name:_____

**Exercise 6-4**

**1. FIFO Perpetual**

| Date | Purchases | Sales (at cost) | Inventory Balance |
|------|-----------|-----------------|-------------------|
|      |           |                 |                   |
|      |           |                 |                   |
|      |           |                 |                   |
|      |           |                 |                   |
|      |           |                 |                   |
|      |           |                 |                   |
|      |           |                 |                   |
|      |           |                 |                   |
|      |           |                 |                   |
|      |           |                 |                   |
|      |           |                 |                   |
|      |           |                 |                   |
|      |           |                 |                   |
|      |           |                 |                   |
|      |           |                 |                   |
|      |           |                 |                   |
|      |           |                 |                   |

**2. Moving weighted Average Perpetual**

| Date | Purchases | Sales (at cost) | Inventory Balance |
|------|-----------|-----------------|-------------------|
|      |           |                 |                   |
|      |           |                 |                   |
|      |           |                 |                   |
|      |           |                 |                   |
|      |           |                 |                   |
|      |           |                 |                   |
|      |           |                 |                   |
|      |           |                 |                   |
|      |           |                 |                   |
|      |           |                 |                   |
|      |           |                 |                   |
|      |           |                 |                   |
|      |           |                 |                   |
|      |           |                 |                   |
|      |           |                 |                   |
|      |           |                 |                   |

**Exercise 6-5**

**1.** _____

_____

_____

_____

_____

_____

_____

_____

**2.** _____

_____

_____

_____

_____

_____

**3(a). FIFO perpetual**

| Date | Purchases | Sales (at cost) | Inventory Balance |
|------|-----------|-----------------|-------------------|
|      |           |                 |                   |

**Exercise 6-5(concl'd.)**

**3(b). Moving weighted-average perpetual**

| Date | Purchases | Sales (at cost) | Inventory Balance |
|------|-----------|-----------------|-------------------|
|      |           |                 |                   |
|      |           |                 |                   |
|      |           |                 |                   |
|      |           |                 |                   |
|      |           |                 |                   |
|      |           |                 |                   |
|      |           |                 |                   |
|      |           |                 |                   |
|      |           |                 |                   |
|      |           |                 |                   |
|      |           |                 |                   |
|      |           |                 |                   |
|      |           |                 |                   |
|      |           |                 |                   |
|      |           |                 |                   |
|      |           |                 |                   |

**Exercise 6-6**

**Specific Identification**

| Date | Purchases | Sales (at cost) | Inventory Balance |
|------|-----------|-----------------|-------------------|
|      |           |                 |                   |
|      |           |                 |                   |
|      |           |                 |                   |
|      |           |                 |                   |
|      |           |                 |                   |
|      |           |                 |                   |
|      |           |                 |                   |
|      |           |                 |                   |
|      |           |                 |                   |
|      |           |                 |                   |
|      |           |                 |                   |
|      |           |                 |                   |
|      |           |                 |                   |
|      |           |                 |                   |
|      |           |                 |                   |
|      |           |                 |                   |
|      |           |                 |                   |
|      |           |                 |                   |
|      |           |                 |                   |
|      |           |                 |                   |
|      |           |                 |                   |
|      |           |                 |                   |

Name:_____

## Exercise 6-7

| | FIFO | Moving Weighted Average | Specific Identification |
|---|---|---|---|
| Car Armour | | | |
| Income Statements | | | |
| For the Year Ended December 31, 2017 | | | |
| | | | |
| | | | |
| | | | |
| | | | |
| | | | |
| | | | |
| | | | |
| | | | |
| | | | |

1. _____

2. _____
_____

## Exercise 6-8

| Date | Purchases/ Transportation-In/ (Purchase Returns/Discounts) Units | Cost Per Unit | Total $ | Cost of Goods Sold/ (Returns to Inventory) Units | Cost Per Unit | Total $ | Balance in Inventory Units | AvgCost Per Unit | Total $ |
|---|---|---|---|---|---|---|---|---|---|
| Mar. 1 | | BFWD | | | | | 60 | $94.00 | $5,640.00 |
| 2 | 35 | $96.00 | | | | | | | |
| 3 | | | | 22 | | | | | |
| 4 | | | | (2) | | | | | |
| 7 | | | | 65 | | | | | |
| 17 | 40 | 97.00 | | | | | | | |
| 28 | | | | 43 | | | | | |
| Totals | | | | | | | | | |

*Calculations:*

_____
_____
_____
_____
_____

*Fundamental Accounting Principles, 15ce, Working Papers*

Name:_____

*Analysis component:*

_____

_____

_____

**Exercise 6-9**

**Parts a and b**

| Inventory Items | Units on Hand | Per Unit | | Total Cost | Total NRV | LCNRV applied to: | |
| | | Cost | NRV | | | a. Inventory as a Group | b. Each Product |
|---|---|---|---|---|---|---|---|
| BB | 22 | $110 | $115 | | | | |
| FM | 15 | 145 | 138 | | | | |
| MB | 36 | 186 | 172 | | | | |
| SL | 40 | 78 | 92 | | | | |
| | | | | | | | |

**Part c**                    **GENERAL JOURNAL**                    Page_____

| Date | | Account Titles and Explanation | PR | Debit | Credit |
|---|---|---|---|---|---|
| | | | | | |
| | | | | | |
| | | | | | |
| | | | | | |

**Exercise 6-10**

1. _____

_____

_____

2.

| | For years ended December 31, 2017, 2018, and 2019 Income statement information should have been reported as: | Income statement information actually reported for years ended December 31, | | |
|---|---|---|---|---|
| | | 2017 | 2018 | 2019 |
| Sales | | | | |
| Cost of goods sold: | | | | |
| Beginning inventory | | | | |
| + Purchases | | | | |
| − Ending inventory | | | | |
| = Cost of goods sold | | | | |
| Gross profit | | | | |

**Exercise 6-11**

_____
_____
_____
_____
_____
_____
_____
_____
_____
_____
_____
_____

**Exercise 6-12**

| | *At Cost* | *At Retail* |
|---|---|---|
| | | |
| | | |
| | | |
| | | |
| | | |
| | | |
| | | |
| | | |
| | | |
| | | |
| | | |
| | | |
| | | |

**Exercise 6-13**

**a. Estimated cost of physical inventory:**

_____
_____
_____

**b. Shrinkage at cost and at retail:**

| | At Cost | At Retail |
|---|---|---|
| | | |
| | | |
| | | |
| | | |
| | | |
| | | |
| | | |

**Exercise 6-14**

**Merchandise turnover (2018):**
_____
_____
_____
_____

**Merchandise turnover (2017):**
_____
_____
_____
_____

**Days' sales in inventory (2018):**
_____
_____
_____
_____

**Days' sales in inventory (2017):**
_____
_____
_____
_____

**Comment on Russo's efficiency in using its assets to support increasing sales from 2017 to 2018.**
_____
_____
_____
_____

Name:_____

*Exercise 6-15

|  | Ending<br>Inventory | Cost of<br>Goods Sold |
|---|---|---|
| a. FIFO periodic: | | |

b. Weighted-average cost periodic:

Which method provides the lower profit and why?

*Exercise 6-16

|  | Ending<br>Inventory | Cost of<br>Goods Sold |
|---|---|---|
| a. FIFO periodic: | | |

b. Weighted-average cost periodic:

Which method provides the lower profit and why?

**\*Exercise 6-17**

_____
_____
_____
_____
_____
_____
_____
_____
_____
_____
_____
_____
_____
_____
_____
_____

**Problem 6-1A**

**Part 1**

|     | Include / Exclude? | Explanation and if applicable, inventory cost. |
| --- | --- | --- |
| a. | | |
| b. | | |
| c. | | |
| d. | | |
| e. | | |

**Part 2**

**Merchandise Inventory**

| | |
| --- | --- |
| Unadjusted Balance. | |
| Adjusted Bal. | |

Name:_____

**Problem 6-2A**

**1a. FIFO Perpetual**

| Date | Purchases | Sales (at cost) | Inventory Balance |
|------|-----------|-----------------|-------------------|
|      |           |                 |                   |
|      |           |                 |                   |
|      |           |                 |                   |
|      |           |                 |                   |
|      |           |                 |                   |
|      |           |                 |                   |
|      |           |                 |                   |
|      |           |                 |                   |
|      |           |                 |                   |
|      |           |                 |                   |
|      |           |                 |                   |
|      |           |                 |                   |
|      |           |                 |                   |
|      |           |                 |                   |
|      |           |                 |                   |
|      |           |                 |                   |
|      |           |                 |                   |
|      |           |                 |                   |
|      |           |                 |                   |

*Fundamental Accounting Principles,* **15ce, Working Papers**

Problem 6-2A (cont'd.)

## 1b. Moving Weighted-Average Perpetual

| Date | Purchases | Cost of Goods Sold | Inventory Balance |
|------|-----------|--------------------|--------------------|
|      |           |                    |                    |
|      |           |                    |                    |
|      |           |                    |                    |
|      |           |                    |                    |
|      |           |                    |                    |
|      |           |                    |                    |
|      |           |                    |                    |
|      |           |                    |                    |
|      |           |                    |                    |
|      |           |                    |                    |
|      |           |                    |                    |
|      |           |                    |                    |
|      |           |                    |                    |
|      |           |                    |                    |
|      |           |                    |                    |
|      |           |                    |                    |
|      |           |                    |                    |
|      |           |                    |                    |
|      |           |                    |                    |

**Problem 6-2A (cont'd.)**

**2. Specific Identification**

| Date | Purchases | Cost of Goods Sold | Inventory Balance |
|------|-----------|--------------------|--------------------|
|      |           |                    |                    |
|      |           |                    |                    |
|      |           |                    |                    |
|      |           |                    |                    |
|      |           |                    |                    |
|      |           |                    |                    |
|      |           |                    |                    |
|      |           |                    |                    |
|      |           |                    |                    |
|      |           |                    |                    |
|      |           |                    |                    |
|      |           |                    |                    |
|      |           |                    |                    |
|      |           |                    |                    |
|      |           |                    |                    |
|      |           |                    |                    |

**3.**                   **GENERAL JOURNAL**             Page____

|     | Date | Account Titles and Explanation | PR | Debit | Credit |
|-----|------|--------------------------------|----|----|----|
| a.  |      |                                |    |    |    |
|     |      |                                |    |    |    |
|     |      |                                |    |    |    |
|     |      |                                |    |    |    |
|     |      |                                |    |    |    |
|     |      |                                |    |    |    |
|     |      |                                |    |    |    |
|     |      |                                |    |    |    |
|     |      |                                |    |    |    |
|     |      |                                |    |    |    |
|     |      |                                |    |    |    |
|     |      |                                |    |    |    |
| b.  |      |                                |    |    |    |
|     |      |                                |    |    |    |
|     |      |                                |    |    |    |
|     |      |                                |    |    |    |
|     |      |                                |    |    |    |
|     |      |                                |    |    |    |

**Problem 6-2A (concl'd.)**

GENERAL JOURNAL                          Page____

| Date | Account Titles and Explanation | PR | Debit | Credit |
|------|-------------------------------|----|-------|--------|
|      |                               |    |       |        |
|      |                               |    |       |        |
|      |                               |    |       |        |
|      |                               |    |       |        |
|      |                               |    |       |        |
|      |                               |    |       |        |
|      |                               |    |       |        |
|      |                               |    |       |        |
|      |                               |    |       |        |
|      |                               |    |       |        |
| c.   |                               |    |       |        |
|      |                               |    |       |        |
|      |                               |    |       |        |
|      |                               |    |       |        |
|      |                               |    |       |        |
|      |                               |    |       |        |
|      |                               |    |       |        |
|      |                               |    |       |        |
|      |                               |    |       |        |
|      |                               |    |       |        |
|      |                               |    |       |        |
|      |                               |    |       |        |
|      |                               |    |       |        |
|      |                               |    |       |        |
|      |                               |    |       |        |

Name:_____

**\*Problem 6-3A**

**a. FIFO basis:**

_____
_____
_____
_____
_____
_____
_____

**b. Weighted Average basis:**

_____
_____
_____
_____
_____
_____
_____
_____

**Problem 6-4A**

**Calculation of cost of goods available for sale and units available for sale:**

_____
_____
_____
_____
_____
_____
_____
_____
_____
_____

**Calculation of units in ending inventory:**

_____
_____
_____
_____
_____
_____

Name:_____

**Problem 6-4A (cont'd.)**

**1a. FIFO Perpetual**

| Date | Purchases | Cost of Goods Sold | Inventory Balance |
|------|-----------|--------------------|--------------------|
|      |           |                    |                    |
|      |           |                    |                    |
|      |           |                    |                    |
|      |           |                    |                    |
|      |           |                    |                    |
|      |           |                    |                    |
|      |           |                    |                    |
|      |           |                    |                    |
|      |           |                    |                    |
|      |           |                    |                    |
|      |           |                    |                    |
|      |           |                    |                    |
|      |           |                    |                    |
|      |           |                    |                    |
|      |           |                    |                    |
|      |           |                    |                    |
|      |           |                    |                    |
|      |           |                    |                    |

**1b. Moving Weighted-Average Perpetual**

| Date | Purchases | Cost of Goods Sold | Inventory Balance |
|------|-----------|--------------------|--------------------|
|      |           |                    |                    |
|      |           |                    |                    |
|      |           |                    |                    |
|      |           |                    |                    |
|      |           |                    |                    |
|      |           |                    |                    |
|      |           |                    |                    |
|      |           |                    |                    |
|      |           |                    |                    |
|      |           |                    |                    |
|      |           |                    |                    |
|      |           |                    |                    |
|      |           |                    |                    |
|      |           |                    |                    |
|      |           |                    |                    |
|      |           |                    |                    |
|      |           |                    |                    |

**Problem 6-4A (concl'd.)**

**2.**

|  | FIFO | Moving Weighted Average |
| --- | --- | --- |
| Sales ............................................ |  |  |
| Cost of goods sold.................... |  |  |
| Gross profit .............................. |  |  |

*Analysis component:*       _____

_____

_____

_____

_____



**\*Problem 6-5A**

**a. FIFO basis:**

_____

_____

_____

_____

_____

_____

_____

_____

**b. Weighted Average basis:**

_____

_____

_____

_____

_____

_____

_____

_____

Name:_____

**Problem 6-6A**

**1a. FIFO Perpetual**

| Date | Purchases | Cost of Goods Sold | Inventory Balance |
|------|-----------|--------------------|-------------------|
|      |           |                    |                   |
|      |           |                    |                   |
|      |           |                    |                   |
|      |           |                    |                   |
|      |           |                    |                   |
|      |           |                    |                   |
|      |           |                    |                   |
|      |           |                    |                   |
|      |           |                    |                   |
|      |           |                    |                   |
|      |           |                    |                   |
|      |           |                    |                   |
|      |           |                    |                   |
|      |           |                    |                   |
|      |           |                    |                   |
|      |           |                    |                   |
|      |           |                    |                   |
|      |           |                    |                   |
|      |           |                    |                   |
|      |           |                    |                   |
|      |           |                    |                   |

Name:_____

**Problem 6-6A (cont'd)**

**1b. Moving Weighted-Average Perpetual**

| Date | Purchases | Cost of Goods Sold | Inventory Balance |
|------|-----------|--------------------|-------------------|
|      |           |                    |                   |
|      |           |                    |                   |
|      |           |                    |                   |
|      |           |                    |                   |
|      |           |                    |                   |
|      |           |                    |                   |
|      |           |                    |                   |
|      |           |                    |                   |
|      |           |                    |                   |
|      |           |                    |                   |
|      |           |                    |                   |
|      |           |                    |                   |
|      |           |                    |                   |
|      |           |                    |                   |
|      |           |                    |                   |
|      |           |                    |                   |
|      |           |                    |                   |
|      |           |                    |                   |
|      |           |                    |                   |

**Part 2**

|  | FIFO | Weighted moving average |
|--|------|-------------------------|
| **Sales** | | |
| **Cost of goods sold** | | |
| **Gross Profit** | | |

**Part 3**

_____
_____
_____
_____
_____
_____

Name:_____

## Problem 6-6A (concl'd.)

### Part 4

_____
_____
_____
_____
_____
_____

## Problem 6-7A

**Fresh Express Company**
**Income Statement Comparing FIFO and Moving Weighted Average Cost**
**For Year Ended December 31, 2017**

|  | FIFO | Moving Weighted Average |
|---|---|---|
| Sales |  |  |
| Cost of goods sold |  |  |
| Gross profit |  |  |
| Operating expenses |  |  |
| Profit |  |  |

**Supporting calculations:**

_____
_____
_____
_____
_____
_____
_____
_____
_____
_____
_____
_____
_____

Name:_____

**Problem 6-7A (cont'd.)**

**a. FIFO Perpetual**

| Date | Purchases | Cost of Goods Sold | Inventory Balance |
|------|-----------|--------------------|-------------------|
|      |           |                    |                   |
|      |           |                    |                   |
|      |           |                    |                   |
|      |           |                    |                   |
|      |           |                    |                   |
|      |           |                    |                   |
|      |           |                    |                   |
|      |           |                    |                   |
|      |           |                    |                   |
|      |           |                    |                   |
|      |           |                    |                   |
|      |           |                    |                   |
|      |           |                    |                   |
|      |           |                    |                   |
|      |           |                    |                   |
|      |           |                    |                   |
|      |           |                    |                   |
|      |           |                    |                   |
|      |           |                    |                   |

**b. Moving Weighted-Average Perpetual**

| Date | Purchases | Cost of Goods Sold | Inventory Balance |
|------|-----------|--------------------|-------------------|
|      |           |                    |                   |
|      |           |                    |                   |
|      |           |                    |                   |
|      |           |                    |                   |
|      |           |                    |                   |
|      |           |                    |                   |
|      |           |                    |                   |
|      |           |                    |                   |
|      |           |                    |                   |
|      |           |                    |                   |
|      |           |                    |                   |
|      |           |                    |                   |
|      |           |                    |                   |
|      |           |                    |                   |
|      |           |                    |                   |
|      |           |                    |                   |
|      |           |                    |                   |

*Fundamental Accounting Principles, 15ce, Working Papers*

**Problem 6-7A (concl'd.)**

*Analysis component:*

_____
_____
_____
_____
_____
_____
_____
_____


***Problem 6-8A**

| | FIFO | Weighted Average |
|---|---|---|
| **Fresh Express Company** | | |
| **Income Statement Comparing FIFO and Weighted Average Periodic** | | |
| **For Year Ended December 31, 2017** | | |
| Sales | | |
| Cost of goods sold | | |
| Gross profit | | |
| Operating expenses | | |
| Profit | | |

*Supporting calculations:*

_____
_____
_____
_____
_____
_____
_____
_____
_____
_____
_____
_____
_____
_____
_____
_____

Name:_____

**Problem 6-9A**

**Part 1**

| a. Cost of Goods Sold: | | 2017 | 2018 | 2019 |
|---|---|---|---|---|
| Reported .......................................... | | _____ | _____ | _____ |
| Adjustments: | 12/31/2017 error | _____ | _____ | _____ |
| | 12/31/2018 error | _____ | _____ | _____ |
| Corrected ......................................... | | _____ | _____ | _____ |

| b. Profit: | | 2017 | 2018 | 2019 |
|---|---|---|---|---|
| Reported .......................................... | | _____ | _____ | _____ |
| Adjustments: | 12/31/2017 error | _____ | _____ | _____ |
| | 12/31/2018 error | _____ | _____ | _____ |
| Corrected ......................................... | | _____ | _____ | _____ |

| c. Total Current Assets: | | 2017 | 2018 | 2019 |
|---|---|---|---|---|
| Reported .......................................... | | _____ | _____ | _____ |
| Adjustments: | 12/31/2017 error | _____ | _____ | _____ |
| | 12/31/2018 error | _____ | _____ | _____ |
| Corrected ......................................... | | _____ | _____ | _____ |

| d. Equity: | | 2017 | 2018 | 2019 |
|---|---|---|---|---|
| Reported .......................................... | | _____ | _____ | _____ |
| Adjustments: | 12/31/2017 error | _____ | _____ | _____ |
| | 12/31/2018 error | _____ | _____ | _____ |
| Corrected ......................................... | | _____ | _____ | _____ |

*Analysis component:*

_____
_____
_____
_____
_____
_____
_____
_____
_____
_____
_____
_____
_____
_____
_____
_____

Name:_____

## Problem 6-10A

| | 2017 | 2018 | 2019 |
|---|---|---|---|
| **Corrected Ending Inventory** | | | |
| **Corrected Cost of Goods Sold** | | | |
| **Corrected Profit** | | | |

## Problem 6-11A

| | | Per Unit | | | | LCNRV applied to: | |
|---|---|---|---|---|---|---|---|
| Inventory Items | Units on Hand | Cost | NRV | Total Cost | Total NRV | a. Major Group | b. Separately to Each Product |
| **Audio equip:** | | | | | | | |
| Receivers | 335 | $185 | $ 196 | | | | |
| MP3 players | 250 | 220 | 200 | | | | |
| Mixers | 316 | 174 | 190 | | | | |
| Stands | 194 | 100 | 82 | | | | |
| | | | | | | | |
| **Video:** | | | | | | | |
| Televisions | 470 | 295 | 250 | | | | |
| Video cards | 281 | 180 | 168 | | | | |
| Video recorders | 202 | 615 | 644 | | | | |
| | | | | | | | |
| **Car Audio:** | | | | | | | |
| GPS navigators | 175 | 142 | 168 | | | | |
| Receivers | 160 | 195 | 210 | | | | |
| | | | | | | | |
| | | | | | | | |

Name:_____

**Problem 6-11A (concl'd)**

**2a.** GENERAL JOURNAL                                                    Page____

| Date | Account Titles and Explanation | PR | Debit | Credit |
|------|-------------------------------|----|-------|--------|
|      |                               |    |       |        |
|      |                               |    |       |        |
|      |                               |    |       |        |
|      |                               |    |       |        |
|      |                               |    |       |        |

**2b.** GENERAL JOURNAL                                                    Page____

| Date | Account Titles and Explanation | PR | Debit | Credit |
|------|-------------------------------|----|-------|--------|
|      |                               |    |       |        |
|      |                               |    |       |        |
|      |                               |    |       |        |
|      |                               |    |       |        |
|      |                               |    |       |        |

**Problem 6-12A**

_____
_____
_____
_____
_____
_____
_____
_____
_____
_____
_____
_____
_____
_____
_____
_____
_____
_____
_____
_____
_____
_____
_____
_____

**Problem 6-13A**

_____
_____
_____
_____
_____
_____
_____
_____
_____
_____
_____
_____
_____
_____
_____
_____
_____
_____
_____
_____
_____

Name:_____

**Problem 6-14A**

**Part 1**

|  | At Cost | At Retail |
|---|---|---|
| **Earthly Goods** | | |
| **Estimated Inventory** | | |
| **December 31, 2017** | | |

**Part 2**

|  | At Cost | At Retail |
|---|---|---|
| **Earthly Goods** | | |
| **Inventory Shortage** | | |
| **December 31, 2017** | | |

Name:_____

## Problem 6-15A

### Part 1

| | At Cost | At Retail |
|---|---|---|
| | | |
| | | |
| | | |
| | | |
| | | |
| | | |
| | | |
| | | |
| | | |
| | | |
| | | |
| | | |
| | | |
| | | |
| | | |
| | | |

### Part 2

_____
_____
_____
_____

## Problem 6-16A

| | 2014 | 2013 |
|---|---|---|
| a. Inventory turnover ratio | | |
| b. Days' sales in inventory | | |

**Comments:** _____
_____
_____
_____
_____
_____

Chapter 6

Name:_____

**\*Problem 6-17A**

**Part 1**

_____
_____
_____
_____
_____
_____
_____
_____
_____
_____
_____
_____
_____
_____
_____
_____
_____
_____
_____

**Part 2**
**a.  FIFO basis:**

_____
_____
_____
_____
_____
_____
_____

**b.  Weighted Average basis:**

_____
_____
_____
_____
_____
_____

*Fundamental Accounting Principles,* **15ce, Working Papers**

Name:_____

**Problem 6-1B**

**Part 1**

|     | Include / Exclude? | Explanation and if applicable, inventory cost. |
| --- | --- | --- |
| a.  |     |     |
| b.  |     |     |
| c.  |     |     |
| d.  |     |     |
| e.  |     |     |

**Part 2**

**Merchandise Inventory**

| Unadjusted Balance. |     |
| --- | --- |
| Adjusted Bal. |     |

**Problem 6-2B**

### 1a. FIFO Perpetual

| Date | Purchases | Sales (at cost) | Inventory Balance |
|------|-----------|-----------------|-------------------|
|      |           |                 |                   |
|      |           |                 |                   |
|      |           |                 |                   |
|      |           |                 |                   |
|      |           |                 |                   |
|      |           |                 |                   |
|      |           |                 |                   |
|      |           |                 |                   |
|      |           |                 |                   |
|      |           |                 |                   |
|      |           |                 |                   |
|      |           |                 |                   |
|      |           |                 |                   |
|      |           |                 |                   |
|      |           |                 |                   |
|      |           |                 |                   |

### 1b. Moving Weighted-Average Perpetual

| Date | Purchases | Sales (at cost) | Inventory Balance |
|------|-----------|-----------------|-------------------|
|      |           |                 |                   |
|      |           |                 |                   |
|      |           |                 |                   |
|      |           |                 |                   |
|      |           |                 |                   |
|      |           |                 |                   |
|      |           |                 |                   |
|      |           |                 |                   |
|      |           |                 |                   |
|      |           |                 |                   |
|      |           |                 |                   |
|      |           |                 |                   |
|      |           |                 |                   |
|      |           |                 |                   |
|      |           |                 |                   |
|      |           |                 |                   |
|      |           |                 |                   |
|      |           |                 |                   |

Name:_____

Problem 6-2B (cont'd.)

## 2. Specific Identification

| Date | Purchases | Cost of Goods Sold | Inventory Balance |
|------|-----------|--------------------|--------------------|
|      |           |                    |                    |
|      |           |                    |                    |
|      |           |                    |                    |
|      |           |                    |                    |
|      |           |                    |                    |
|      |           |                    |                    |
|      |           |                    |                    |
|      |           |                    |                    |
|      |           |                    |                    |
|      |           |                    |                    |
|      |           |                    |                    |
|      |           |                    |                    |
|      |           |                    |                    |
|      |           |                    |                    |
|      |           |                    |                    |
|      |           |                    |                    |

**Problem 6-2B (cont'd.)**

3.                    GENERAL JOURNAL                    Page_____

| Date | Account Titles and Explanation | PR | Debit | Credit |
|------|-------------------------------|-----|-------|--------|
| a. | | | | |
| | | | | |
| | | | | |
| | | | | |
| | | | | |
| | | | | |
| | | | | |
| | | | | |
| | | | | |
| | | | | |
| | | | | |
| | | | | |
| b. | | | | |
| | | | | |
| | | | | |
| | | | | |
| | | | | |
| | | | | |
| | | | | |
| | | | | |
| | | | | |
| | | | | |
| | | | | |
| | | | | |
| c. | | | | |
| | | | | |
| | | | | |
| | | | | |
| | | | | |
| | | | | |
| | | | | |
| | | | | |
| | | | | |
| | | | | |

Name:_____

**\*Problem 6-3B**

**a. FIFO basis:**

_____
_____
_____
_____
_____
_____
_____

**b. Weighted Average basis:**

_____
_____
_____
_____
_____
_____

**Problem 6-4B**

### 1a. FIFO Perpetual

| Date | Purchases | Cost of Goods Sold | Inventory Balance |
|------|-----------|--------------------|-------------------|
|      |           |                    |                   |
|      |           |                    |                   |
|      |           |                    |                   |
|      |           |                    |                   |
|      |           |                    |                   |
|      |           |                    |                   |
|      |           |                    |                   |
|      |           |                    |                   |
|      |           |                    |                   |
|      |           |                    |                   |
|      |           |                    |                   |
|      |           |                    |                   |
|      |           |                    |                   |
|      |           |                    |                   |
|      |           |                    |                   |
|      |           |                    |                   |
|      |           |                    |                   |
|      |           |                    |                   |
|      |           |                    |                   |
|      |           |                    |                   |

### 1b. Moving Weighted-Average Perpetual

| Date | Purchases | Cost of Goods Sold | Inventory Balance |
|------|-----------|--------------------|-------------------|
|      |           |                    |                   |
|      |           |                    |                   |
|      |           |                    |                   |
|      |           |                    |                   |
|      |           |                    |                   |
|      |           |                    |                   |
|      |           |                    |                   |
|      |           |                    |                   |
|      |           |                    |                   |
|      |           |                    |                   |
|      |           |                    |                   |
|      |           |                    |                   |
|      |           |                    |                   |
|      |           |                    |                   |
|      |           |                    |                   |
|      |           |                    |                   |
|      |           |                    |                   |
|      |           |                    |                   |
|      |           |                    |                   |

Name:_____

**Problem 6-4B (concl'd.)**

**2.**

|  | FIFO | Moving Weighted Average |
|---|---|---|
| Sales ........................................... |  |  |
| Cost of goods sold.................... |  |  |
| Gross profit ............................... |  |  |

*Analysis component:* _____

_____

_____

_____

_____

_____


**\*Problem 6-5B**

**a. FIFO basis:**

_____

_____

_____

_____

_____

_____

_____


**b. Weighted Average basis:**

_____

_____

_____

_____

_____

_____

_____

_____

Name:_____

Problem 6-6B

## 1a. FIFO Perpetual

| Date | Purchases | Cost of Goods Sold | Inventory Balance |
|------|-----------|--------------------|-------------------|
|      |           |                    |                   |
|      |           |                    |                   |
|      |           |                    |                   |
|      |           |                    |                   |
|      |           |                    |                   |
|      |           |                    |                   |
|      |           |                    |                   |
|      |           |                    |                   |
|      |           |                    |                   |
|      |           |                    |                   |
|      |           |                    |                   |
|      |           |                    |                   |
|      |           |                    |                   |
|      |           |                    |                   |
|      |           |                    |                   |
|      |           |                    |                   |
|      |           |                    |                   |
|      |           |                    |                   |
|      |           |                    |                   |
|      |           |                    |                   |
|      |           |                    |                   |

Problem 6-6B (cont'd.)

1b. Moving Weighted-Average Perpetual

| Date | Purchases | Cost of Goods Sold | Inventory Balance |
|------|-----------|--------------------|--------------------|
|      |           |                    |                    |
|      |           |                    |                    |
|      |           |                    |                    |
|      |           |                    |                    |
|      |           |                    |                    |
|      |           |                    |                    |
|      |           |                    |                    |
|      |           |                    |                    |
|      |           |                    |                    |
|      |           |                    |                    |
|      |           |                    |                    |
|      |           |                    |                    |
|      |           |                    |                    |
|      |           |                    |                    |
|      |           |                    |                    |
|      |           |                    |                    |
|      |           |                    |                    |
|      |           |                    |                    |
|      |           |                    |                    |

Part 2

|                    | FIFO | Weighted moving average |
|--------------------|------|--------------------------|
| Sales              |      |                          |
| **Cost of goods sold** |   |                          |
| Gross Profit       |      |                          |

Part 3

_____

_____

_____

_____

_____

_____

Problem 6-6B (concl'd.)

Part 4

_____
_____
_____
_____
_____
_____

Problem 6-7B                              _____

**Blizzard Company**
**Income Statement Comparing FIFO and Moving Weighted Average Cost**
**For Year Ended December 31, 2017**

|                        | FIFO | Moving Weighted Average |
|------------------------|------|-------------------------|
| Sales                  |      |                         |
| Cost of goods sold     |      |                         |
| Gross profit           |      |                         |
| Operating expenses     |      |                         |
| Profit                 |      |                         |

**Supporting calculations:**

_____
_____
_____
_____
_____
_____
_____
_____
_____
_____
_____
_____
_____
_____

Name:_____

**Problem 6-7B (cont'd.)**

**a. FIFO Perpetual**

| Date | Purchases | Cost of Goods Sold | Inventory Balance |
|------|-----------|--------------------|--------------------|
|      |           |                    |                    |
|      |           |                    |                    |
|      |           |                    |                    |
|      |           |                    |                    |
|      |           |                    |                    |
|      |           |                    |                    |
|      |           |                    |                    |
|      |           |                    |                    |
|      |           |                    |                    |
|      |           |                    |                    |
|      |           |                    |                    |
|      |           |                    |                    |
|      |           |                    |                    |
|      |           |                    |                    |
|      |           |                    |                    |
|      |           |                    |                    |
|      |           |                    |                    |
|      |           |                    |                    |
|      |           |                    |                    |
|      |           |                    |                    |

**b. Moving Weighted-Average Perpetual**

| Date | Purchases | Cost of Goods Sold | Inventory Balance |
|------|-----------|--------------------|--------------------|
|      |           |                    |                    |
|      |           |                    |                    |
|      |           |                    |                    |
|      |           |                    |                    |
|      |           |                    |                    |
|      |           |                    |                    |
|      |           |                    |                    |
|      |           |                    |                    |
|      |           |                    |                    |
|      |           |                    |                    |
|      |           |                    |                    |
|      |           |                    |                    |
|      |           |                    |                    |
|      |           |                    |                    |

**Problem 6-7B (concl'd.)**

*Analysis component:*

_____
_____
_____
_____
_____
_____
_____
_____
_____

**\*Problem 6-8B**

<table>
<tr><td colspan="3" align="center">**Blizzard Company**</td></tr>
<tr><td colspan="3" align="center">**Income Statement Comparing FIFO and Weighted Average Periodic**</td></tr>
<tr><td colspan="3" align="center">**For Year Ended December 31, 2017**</td></tr>
<tr><td></td><td align="center">**FIFO**</td><td align="center">**Weighted Average**</td></tr>
<tr><td>**Sales**</td><td></td><td></td></tr>
<tr><td>**Cost of goods sold**</td><td></td><td></td></tr>
<tr><td>**Gross profit**</td><td></td><td></td></tr>
<tr><td>**Operating expenses**</td><td></td><td></td></tr>
<tr><td>**Profit**</td><td></td><td></td></tr>
</table>

**Supporting calculations:**

_____
_____
_____
_____
_____
_____
_____
_____
_____

**a. FIFO Periodic**

_____
_____
_____
_____
_____
_____
_____
_____

**b. Weighted Average Periodic**

_____
_____
_____
_____
_____
_____
_____
_____

Name:_____

**Problem 6-9B**

**Part 1**

| a. Cost of Goods Sold: | | 2017 | 2018 | 2019 |
|---|---|---|---|---|
| Reported ............................................. | | _____ | _____ | _____ |
| Adjustments: | 12/31/2017 error | _____ | _____ | _____ |
| | 12/31/2018 error | _____ | _____ | _____ |
| Corrected ............................................. | | _____ | _____ | _____ |

| b. Profit: | | 2017 | 2018 | 2019 |
|---|---|---|---|---|
| Reported ............................................. | | _____ | _____ | _____ |
| Adjustments: | 12/31/2017 error | _____ | _____ | _____ |
| | 12/31/2018 error | _____ | _____ | _____ |
| Corrected ............................................. | | _____ | _____ | _____ |

| c. Total Current Assets: | | 2017 | 2018 | 2019 |
|---|---|---|---|---|
| Reported ............................................. | | _____ | _____ | _____ |
| Adjustments: | 12/31/2017 error | _____ | _____ | _____ |
| | 12/31/2018 error | _____ | _____ | _____ |
| Corrected ............................................. | | _____ | _____ | _____ |

| d. Equity: | | 2017 | 2018 | 2019 |
|---|---|---|---|---|
| Reported ............................................. | | _____ | _____ | _____ |
| Adjustments: | 12/31/2017 error | _____ | _____ | _____ |
| | 12/31/2018 error | _____ | _____ | _____ |
| Corrected ............................................. | | _____ | _____ | _____ |

*Analysis component:*

_____
_____
_____
_____
_____
_____
_____
_____
_____
_____
_____
_____
_____
_____

Name:_____

## Problem 6-10B

### Part 1

| | Incorrect Income Statement Information For Years Ended December 31 | | | | Corrected Income Statement Information For Years Ended December 31 | | | |
|---|---|---|---|---|---|---|---|---|
| | 2017 | % | 2018 | % | 2017 | % | 2018 | % |
| Sales ............................ | | | | | | | | |
| Cost of goods sold...... | | | | | | | | |
| Gross profit ................. | | | | | | | | |

### Part 2

_____

_____
_____
_____

## Problem 6-11B

| Inventory Items | Units on Hand | Per Unit Cost | Per Unit NRV | Total Cost | Total NRV | LCNRV applied to: a. Major Category | LCNRV applied to: b. Separately to Each Product |
|---|---|---|---|---|---|---|---|
| Office furniture: | | | | | | | |
| Desks | 430 | $261 | $305 | | | | |
| Credenzas | 290 | 227 | 256 | | | | |
| Chairs | 585 | 49 | 43 | | | | |
| Bookshelves | 320 | 93 | 82 | | | | |
| | | | | | | | |
| Filing cabinets: | | | | | | | |
| Two-drawer | 215 | 81 | 70 | | | | |
| Four-drawer | 400 | 135 | 122 | | | | |
| Lateral | 178 | 104 | 118 | | | | |
| | | | | | | | |
| Office Equip.: | | | | | | | |
| Fax machines | 415 | 168 | 200 | | | | |
| Copiers | 544 | 317 | 288 | | | | |
| Typewriters | 355 | 125 | 117 | | | | |
| | | | | | | | |
| | | | | | | | |

Name:_____

**Problem 6-11B (concl'd)**

**2a.** GENERAL JOURNAL Page_____

| Date | Account Titles and Explanation | PR | Debit | Credit |
|------|-------------------------------|----|----|----|
|  |  |  |  |  |
|  |  |  |  |  |
|  |  |  |  |  |
|  |  |  |  |  |
|  |  |  |  |  |

**2b.** GENERAL JOURNAL Page_____

| Date | Account Titles and Explanation | PR | Debit | Credit |
|------|-------------------------------|----|----|----|
|  |  |  |  |  |
|  |  |  |  |  |
|  |  |  |  |  |
|  |  |  |  |  |
|  |  |  |  |  |

**Problem 6-12B**

Name:_____

## Problem 6-13B

_____
_____
_____
_____
_____
_____
_____
_____
_____
_____
_____
_____
_____
_____
_____
_____
_____
_____
_____
_____
_____

Name:_____

**Problem 6-14B**

**Part 1**

THE WILKE CO.
Estimated Inventory
December 31, 2017

|  | At Cost | At Retail |
| --- | --- | --- |
|  |  |  |
|  |  |  |
|  |  |  |
|  |  |  |
|  |  |  |
|  |  |  |
|  |  |  |
|  |  |  |
|  |  |  |
|  |  |  |
|  |  |  |
|  |  |  |
|  |  |  |
|  |  |  |

**Part 2**

THE WILKE CO.
Inventory Shortage
December 31, 2017

|  | At Cost | At Retail |
| --- | --- | --- |
|  |  |  |
|  |  |  |
|  |  |  |
|  |  |  |
|  |  |  |
|  |  |  |

Name:_____

## Problem 6-15B

**Part 1**

| | At Cost | At Retail |
| --- | --- | --- |
| | | |
| | | |
| | | |
| | | |
| | | |
| | | |
| | | |
| | | |
| | | |
| | | |
| | | |
| | | |
| | | |
| | | |
| | | |
| | | |
| | | |

## Problem 6-16B

| | 2014 | 2013 |
| --- | --- | --- |
| c. Inventory turnover ratio | | |
| d. Days' sales in inventory | | |

**Comments:** _____
_____
_____
_____
_____
_____
_____
_____

**\*Problem 6-17B**
**Part 1**
_____
_____
_____
_____
_____
_____
_____
_____
_____

**Part 2**
**a. FIFO basis:**
_____
_____
_____
_____
_____
_____

**b. Weighted Average basis:**
_____
_____
_____
_____
_____
_____

## Quick Study 7-1

**(a)** _____
_____
_____
_____
_____
_____

**(b)** _____
_____
_____
_____
_____
_____

**(c)** _____
_____
_____

## Quick Study 7-2

_____
_____
_____
_____
_____
_____
_____
_____
_____

| **Weakness #1** | |
|---|---|
| **Implication** | |
| **Recommendation** | |
| **Weakness #2** | |
| **Implication** | |
| **Recommendation** | |
| **Weakness #3** | |
| **Implication** | |
| **Recommendation** | |

Name:_____

**Quick Study 7-4**

**(1) Establishment of the fund:**

GENERAL JOURNAL

Page_____

| Date | Account Titles and Explanation | PR | Debit | Credit |
|------|-------------------------------|----|-------|--------|
|      |                               |    |       |        |
|      |                               |    |       |        |
|      |                               |    |       |        |
|      |                               |    |       |        |

**(2) Summary of petty cash receipts and entry to reimburse the fund at month-end:**

Wee Ones Agency
Petty Cash Payments Report
May 1 – 31, 2017

Receipts:
_____
_____
_____
_____
_____
_____

Fund total
Less:  Cash remaining
Equals:  Cash required to replenish petty cash
Cash over/(short)

GENERAL JOURNAL

Page_____

| Date | Account Titles and Explanation | PR | Debit | Credit |
|------|-------------------------------|----|-------|--------|
|      |                               |    |       |        |
|      |                               |    |       |        |
|      |                               |    |       |        |
|      |                               |    |       |        |
|      |                               |    |       |        |

**(3)** _____
_____
_____
_____
_____

Chapter 7

Name:_____

## Quick Study 7-5

### GENERAL JOURNAL

Page____

| Date | Account Titles and Explanation | PR | Debit | Credit |
|---|---|---|---|---|
| March 1 2017 | Printing exp | | 75 | |
| | taxi fare | | 48 | |
| | Delivery exp | | 55 | |
| | Cash over and short | | 3 | |
| | Cash | | | 181 |
| | | | | |
| | | | | |
| | | | | |
| | | | | |

## Quick Study 7-6

### GENERAL JOURNAL

Page____

| Date | Account Titles and Explanation | PR | Debit | Credit |
|---|---|---|---|---|
| Sep 1 2017 | Entertainment exp. | | 32 | |
| | Computer repair | | 45 | |
| | Delivery exp | | 18 | |
| | Cash over & short | | | 2 |
| | Cash | | | 93 |
| | | | | |
| | | | | |
| | | | | |
| | | | | |
| | | | | |
| | | | | |
| | | | | |

**Quick Study 7-7**

### GENERAL JOURNAL

Page____

| Date | Account Titles and Explanation | PR | Debit | Credit |
|---|---|---|---|---|
| Feb 1 | Cash | | $73125 | |
| | Credit card exp | | $1875 | |
| | Sales | | | $75000 |
| 1 | Cost of goods sold | | 62000 | |
| | Merchandise inventory | | | 62000 |
| 10 | Cash | | 28000 | |
| | Sales | | | 28000 |
| 10 | Cost of goods sold | | 23000 | |
| | Merchandise inventory | | | 23000 |
| | | | | |
| | | | | |
| | | | | |
| | | | | |
| | | | | |
| | | | | |
| | | | | |
| | | | | |
| | | | | |
| | | | | |

**Quick Study 7-8**

## GENERAL JOURNAL                                               Page____

| Date | | Account Titles and Explanation | PR | Debit | Credit |
|------|---|------------------------------|-----|-------|--------|
| Oct | 1 | Cash | | 13965 | |
| | | Debit card exp. | | 35 | |
| | | Sales | | | 14000 |
| | 1 | Cost of goods sold | | 8000 | |
| | | Merchandise inventory | | | 8000 |
| | 7 | Cash | | 3500 | |
| | | Sales | | | 3500 |
| | 7 | Cost of goods sold | | 2800 | |
| | | Merchandise inventory | | | 2800 |
| | | | | | |
| | | | | | |
| | | | | | |
| | | | | | |
| | | | | | |
| | | | | | |

**Quick Study 7-9     Parts 1 and 2:**

| | Bank or Book Effect | Add or Subtract | Journal Entry Required or Not |
|---|--------------------|-----------------|------------------------------|
| (a) | Bank | add | — |
| (b) | Book | add | Required |
| (c) | Book | add | required |
| (d) | Book | Subtract | Required |
| (e) | Bank | Subtract | — |
| (f) | Book | Subtract | Required |
| (g) | Book | Subtract | Required |

**Quick Study 7-10**

| | | | Bank Reconciliation | | | |
|---|---|---|---|---|---|---|
| | | | | | | |
| | | | | | | |
| | | | | | | |
| | | | | | | |
| | | | | | | |
| | | | | | | |
| | | | | | | |
| | | | | | | |
| | | | | | | |

**GENERAL JOURNAL**                                          Page____

| Date | | Account Titles and Explanation | PR | Debit | Credit |
|---|---|---|---|---|---|
| | | | | | |
| | | | | | |
| | | | | | |
| | | | | | |

**Quick Study 7-11**

**Part A**

| | | | |
|---|---|---|---|
| | | | |
| | | | |
| | | | |
| | | | |
| | | | |
| | | | |
| | | | |
| | | | |
| | | | |
| | | | |
| | | | |

Name:_____

## Quick Study 7-11 (cont'd.)

**Part B**

**GENERAL JOURNAL**

Page____

| Date | Account Titles and Explanation | PR | Debit | Credit |
|------|-------------------------------|----|-------|--------|
|      |                               |    |       |        |
|      |                               |    |       |        |
|      |                               |    |       |        |
|      |                               |    |       |        |
|      |                               |    |       |        |
|      |                               |    |       |        |
|      |                               |    |       |        |
|      |                               |    |       |        |
|      |                               |    |       |        |
|      |                               |    |       |        |
|      |                               |    |       |        |
|      |                               |    |       |        |
|      |                               |    |       |        |
|      |                               |    |       |        |
|      |                               |    |       |        |
|      |                               |    |       |        |
|      |                               |    |       |        |
|      |                               |    |       |        |

## Quick Study 7-12

*Fundamental Accounting Principles, 15ce, Working Papers*

Name:_____

**Exercise 7-1**

_____
_____
_____
_____
_____
_____
_____
_____
_____
_____

**Exercise 7-2**

_____
_____
_____
_____
_____
_____
_____
_____
_____
_____
_____
_____
_____
_____
_____
_____
_____
_____
_____
_____
_____
_____
_____
_____
_____

**Chapter 7**

Name:_____

**Exercise 7-3**

(a)_____
_____
_____
_____
_____
_____

(b)_____
_____
_____
_____
_____
_____

**Exercise 7-4**

**Internal Control Problem:**_____
_____
_____
_____
_____
_____
_____
_____

**Internal Control Recommendation:**_____
_____
_____
_____
_____

Name:_____

## Exercise 7-5

### (a) Establish the Fund

GENERAL JOURNAL          Page_____

| Date | Account Titles and Explanation | PR | Debit | Credit |
|------|-------------------------------|----|-------|--------|
|      |                               |    |       |        |
|      |                               |    |       |        |
|      |                               |    |       |        |
|      |                               |    |       |        |
|      |                               |    |       |        |
|      |                               |    |       |        |

### (b) Prepare a summary of petty cash receipts

Cameron Co.
**Petty Cash Payments Report**
**January 1 – 8, 2017**

Receipts:
_____
_____
_____
_____
_____
_____

Fund total
Less:  Cash remaining
Equals:  Cash required to replenish petty cash
Cash over/(short)

## Exercise 7-5 (concl'd.)

**Record the reimbursement:**

GENERAL JOURNAL                                    Page____

| Date | Account Titles and Explanation | PR | Debit | Credit |
|------|-------------------------------|----|----|----|
|      |                               |    |    |    |
|      |                               |    |    |    |
|      |                               |    |    |    |
|      |                               |    |    |    |
|      |                               |    |    |    |
|      |                               |    |    |    |
|      |                               |    |    |    |

*Analysis component:* _____

_____

_____

_____

_____

_____

## Exercise 7-6

**(a) Establish the Fund**

GENERAL JOURNAL                                    Page____

| Date | Account Titles and Explanation | PR | Debit | Credit |
|------|-------------------------------|----|----|----|
|      |                               |    |    |    |
|      |                               |    |    |    |
|      |                               |    |    |    |
|      |                               |    |    |    |
|      |                               |    |    |    |
|      |                               |    |    |    |
|      |                               |    |    |    |
|      |                               |    |    |    |

**Exercise 7-6 (concl'd.)**

**(b) Prepare a summary of petty cash receipts**

**Willard Company**
**Petty Cash Payments Report**
**September 9 – 30, 2017**

Receipts:

_____

_____

_____

_____

_____

_____

_____

Fund total

Less:  Cash remaining

Equals:  Cash required to replenish petty cash

Cash over/(short)

**Reimburse and reduce the fund**

**GENERAL JOURNAL**                                           Page_____

| Date | Account Titles and Explanation | PR | Debit | Credit |
|------|-------------------------------|----|-------|--------|
|      |                               |    |       |        |
|      |                               |    |       |        |
|      |                               |    |       |        |
|      |                               |    |       |        |
|      |                               |    |       |        |
|      |                               |    |       |        |
|      |                               |    |       |        |

*Analysis component:*

_____

_____

_____

_____

_____

_____

_____

_____

# Chapter 7

## Exercise 7-7

### GENERAL JOURNAL

Page____

| Date | | | Account Titles and Explanation | PR | Debit | Credit |
|------|---|---|-------------------------------|-----|-------|--------|
| **a.** Oct | 31 | | Cleaning exp. | | 100 | |
| 2017 | | | postage | | 26 | |
| | | | Delivery | | 45 | |
| | | | Cash over & short | | 6 | |
| | | | Cash | | | 177 |
| | | | | | | |
| | | | | | | |
| **b.** Nov | 30 | | Computer repair | | 78 | |
| | | | Entertainment exp | | 95 | |
| | | | Cash over & short | | | 5 |
| | | | Cash | | | 168 |
| | | | | | | |
| | | | | | | |
| | | | | | | |
| **c.** | | | Gxces exp | | 49 | |
| | | | Office supplies | | 92 | |
| | | | Entertainment exp | | 41 | |
| | | | petty cash | | 50 | |
| | | | Cash | | | 232 |
| | | | | | | |
| | | | | | | |

## Exercise 7-8

### GENERAL JOURNAL

Page____

| Date | | Account Titles and Explanation | PR | Debit | Credit |
|------|---|-------------------------------|-----|-------|--------|
| | | | | | |
| | | | | | |
| | | | | | |
| | | | | | |
| | | | | | |
| | | | | | |
| | | | | | |
| | | | | | |
| | | | | | |
| | | | | | |
| | | | | | |

Name:_____

**Exercise 7-8 (concl'd.)**

### GENERAL JOURNAL

Page_____

| Date | Account Titles and Explanation | PR | Debit | Credit |
|------|-------------------------------|----|----|----|
|  |  |  |  |  |
|  |  |  |  |  |
|  |  |  |  |  |
|  |  |  |  |  |
|  |  |  |  |  |
|  |  |  |  |  |
|  |  |  |  |  |
|  |  |  |  |  |
|  |  |  |  |  |
|  |  |  |  |  |
|  |  |  |  |  |
|  |  |  |  |  |
|  |  |  |  |  |
|  |  |  |  |  |
|  |  |  |  |  |
|  |  |  |  |  |

**Exercise 7-9**

### GENERAL JOURNAL

Page_____

| Date | Account Titles and Explanation | PR | Debit | Credit |
|------|-------------------------------|----|----|----|
|  |  |  |  |  |
|  |  |  |  |  |
|  |  |  |  |  |
|  |  |  |  |  |
|  |  |  |  |  |
|  |  |  |  |  |
|  |  |  |  |  |
|  |  |  |  |  |
|  |  |  |  |  |
|  |  |  |  |  |
|  |  |  |  |  |
|  |  |  |  |  |
|  |  |  |  |  |
|  |  |  |  |  |
|  |  |  |  |  |
|  |  |  |  |  |
|  |  |  |  |  |
|  |  |  |  |  |
|  |  |  |  |  |
|  |  |  |  |  |

Exercise 7-9 (concl'd.)

| | GENERAL JOURNAL | | | Page_____ |

| Date | Account Titles and Explanation | PR | Debit | Credit |
|------|-------------------------------|----|-------|--------|
| | | | | |
| | | | | |
| | | | | |
| | | | | |
| | | | | |
| | | | | |
| | | | | |
| | | | | |
| | | | | |
| | | | | |
| | | | | |
| | | | | |
| | | | | |
| | | | | |
| | | | | |
| | | | | |
| | | | | |
| | | | | |
| | | | | |
| | | | | |
| | | | | |
| | | | | |
| | | | | |
| | | | | |

*Analysis component:*

_____
_____
_____
_____
_____
_____
_____
_____
_____
_____
_____

Name:_____

**Exercise 7-10**

**Part 1**

_____

_____

_____

| | | | |
|---|---|---|---|
| | | | |
| | | | |
| | | | |
| | | | |
| | | | |
| | | | |
| | | | |
| | | | |
| | | | |

**Part 2**

**GENERAL JOURNAL**                           Page_____

| Date | Account Titles and Explanation | PR | Debit | Credit |
|---|---|---|---|---|
| | | | | |
| | | | | |
| | | | | |
| | | | | |

*Analysis component:*         _____

_____

_____

_____

**Exercise 7-11**

a. _____

_____

_____

| | | | |
|---|---|---|---|
| | | | |
| | | | |
| | | | |
| | | | |
| | | | |
| | | | |
| | | | |

**Exercise 7-11 (concl'd.)**

b.                                    GENERAL JOURNAL                              Page_____

| Date | Account Titles and Explanation | PR | Debit | Credit |
|------|-------------------------------|----|-------|--------|
|      |                               |    |       |        |
|      |                               |    |       |        |
|      |                               |    |       |        |
|      |                               |    |       |        |
|      |                               |    |       |        |
|      |                               |    |       |        |
|      |                               |    |       |        |
|      |                               |    |       |        |
|      |                               |    |       |        |
|      |                               |    |       |        |

*Analysis component:*

_____
_____
_____
_____
_____
_____
_____

Name:_____

**Exercise 7-12**

| | | Bank Balance | | Book Balance | | | Not Shown on the Reconciliation | |
|---|---|---|---|---|---|---|---|---|
| | | Add | Deduct | Add | Deduct | Adjust | | |
| 1. | Interest income earned on the account. | | | | | | | |
| 2. | Deposit made on September 30 after the bank was closed. | | | | | | | |
| 3. | Cheques outstanding on August 31 that cleared the bank in September. | | | | | | | |
| 4. | NSF cheque from customer returned on September 15 but not recorded by the company. | | | | | | | |
| 5. | Cheques written and mailed to payees on September 30. | | | | | | | |
| 6. | Deposit made on September 5 that was processed on September 8. | | | | | | | |
| 7. | Bank service charge. | | | | | | | |
| 8. | Cheques written and mailed to payees on October 5. | | | | | | | |
| 9. | Cheque written by another company but charged against the company's account in error. | | | | | | | |
| 10. | Principal and interest collected by the bank but not recorded by the company. | | | | | | | |
| 11. | Special charge for collection of note in No. 10 on company's behalf. | | | | | | | |
| 12. | Cheque written against the account and cleared by the bank; not recorded by the bookkeeper. | | | | | | | |

Name:_____

**\*Exercise 7-13**

|  | Case X | Case Y | Case Z |
|---|---|---|---|
|  |  |  |  |
|  |  |  |  |
|  |  |  |  |
|  |  |  |  |
|  |  |  |  |
|  |  |  |  |
|  |  |  |  |
|  |  |  |  |
|  |  |  |  |
|  |  |  |  |
|  |  |  |  |
|  |  |  |  |
|  |  |  |  |
|  |  |  |  |

**Problem 7-1A**

**(1) Principle Violated:**
    Recommendation:



**(2) Principle Violated:**
    Recommendation:



**(3) Principle Violated:**
    Recommendation:



**(4) Principle Violated:**
    Recommendation:



**(5) Principle Violated:**
    Recommendation:

# Chapter 7

Name:_____

## Problem 7-2A

### Part 1

**GENERAL JOURNAL**                          Page____

| Date | Account Titles and Explanation | PR | Debit | Credit |
|------|-------------------------------|-----|-------|--------|
|      | Petty cash                    |     | 400   |        |
|      |       cash                    |     |       | 400    |
|      |                               |     |       |        |
|      |                               |     |       |        |

### Part 2

**Milton Consulting**
**Petty Cash Payments Report**
**February 2 – 28, 2017**

Receipts:

Fund total

Less: Cash remaining

Equals: Cash required to replenish petty cash

Cash over/(short)

### Part 3

**GENERAL JOURNAL**                          Page____

| Date | Account Titles and Explanation | PR | Debit | Credit |
|------|-------------------------------|-----|-------|--------|
|      | Delivery exp                  |     | 32.45 |        |
|      | Auto                          |     | 135   |        |
|      | Postage                       |     | 65.65 |        |
|      | Merchse invent                |     | 74.60 |        |
|      | Office supplies exp           |     | 81.15 |        |
|      | Cash over & short             |     | 3     |        |
|      | Petty cash                    |     | 100   |        |
|      |      cash                     |     |       | 491.85 |
|      |                               |     |       |        |
|      |                               |     |       |        |

**Problem 7-2A (concl'd.)**

*Analysis component:*                    _____

_____

_____

_____

_____

_____

_____

_____

**Problem 7-3A**

### GENERAL JOURNAL

Page____

| Date | Account Titles and Explanation | PR | Debit | Credit |
|------|--------------------------------|----|-------|--------|
| Apr 1 | Petty cash | | 300 | |
| | cash | | | 300 |
| | | | | |
| 15 | Advertising exp. | | 92.50 | |
| | Janitorial exp | | 62 | |
| | Postage exp | | 25 | |
| | Office supplies exp. | | 78.15 | |
| | Petty cash | | 100 | |
| | Cash over & short | | | 2 |
| | Cash | | | 375.65 |
| | | | | |
| 30 | Delivery exp | | 14.80 | |
| | Auto exp. | | 45.60 | |
| | Office supplies exp | | 94.65 | |
| | Petty cash | | | 50 |
| | Cash | | | 105.05 |
| | | | | |
| | | | | |
| | | | | |
| | | | | |
| | | | | |
| | | | | |

*Analysis component:*

_____

_____

_____

_____

_____

_____

_____

**Problem 7-4A**

**a.**

| | | | |
|---|---|---|---|
| | | | |
| | | | |
| | | | |
| | | | |
| | | | |
| | | | |
| | | | |
| | | | |
| | | | |
| | | | |
| | | | |
| | | | |
| | | | |

**b.**

**GENERAL JOURNAL**                                        Page____

| Date | Account Titles and Explanation | PR | Debit | Credit |
|---|---|---|---|---|
| | | | | |
| | | | | |
| | | | | |
| | | | | |
| | | | | |
| | | | | |
| | | | | |
| | | | | |
| | | | | |
| | | | | |
| | | | | |
| | | | | |
| | | | | |

*Analysis component:*  _____

_____

_____

_____

_____

_____

_____

**Problem 7-5A**

a.

_____

_____

_____

|  |  |  |  |
|---|---|---|---|
|  |  |  |  |
|  |  |  |  |
|  |  |  |  |
|  |  |  |  |
|  |  |  |  |
|  |  |  |  |
|  |  |  |  |
|  |  |  |  |
|  |  |  |  |
|  |  |  |  |
|  |  |  |  |
|  |  |  |  |
|  |  |  |  |

b.

## GENERAL JOURNAL

Page_____

| Date | Account Titles and Explanation | PR | Debit | Credit |
|---|---|---|---|---|
|  |  |  |  |  |
|  |  |  |  |  |
|  |  |  |  |  |
|  |  |  |  |  |
|  |  |  |  |  |
|  |  |  |  |  |
|  |  |  |  |  |
|  |  |  |  |  |
|  |  |  |  |  |
|  |  |  |  |  |
|  |  |  |  |  |
|  |  |  |  |  |
|  |  |  |  |  |
|  |  |  |  |  |
|  |  |  |  |  |
|  |  |  |  |  |
|  |  |  |  |  |
|  |  |  |  |  |
|  |  |  |  |  |
|  |  |  |  |  |

**Problem 7-5A (concl'd.)**

### GENERAL JOURNAL

Page____

| Date | Account Titles and Explanation | PR | Debit | Credit |
|------|-------------------------------|----|----|-----|
|  |  |  |  |  |
|  |  |  |  |  |
|  |  |  |  |  |
|  |  |  |  |  |
|  |  |  |  |  |
|  |  |  |  |  |
|  |  |  |  |  |
|  |  |  |  |  |
|  |  |  |  |  |
|  |  |  |  |  |
|  |  |  |  |  |
|  |  |  |  |  |
|  |  |  |  |  |
|  |  |  |  |  |
|  |  |  |  |  |
|  |  |  |  |  |

**Problem 7-6A**

**Part 1**

| | | | |
|---|---|---|---|
|  |  |  |  |
|  |  |  |  |
|  |  |  |  |
|  |  |  |  |
|  |  |  |  |
|  |  |  |  |
|  |  |  |  |
|  |  |  |  |
|  |  |  |  |
|  |  |  |  |
|  |  |  |  |
|  |  |  |  |
|  |  |  |  |
|  |  |  |  |
|  |  |  |  |
|  |  |  |  |

**Problem 7-6A (concl'd.)**

**Part 2**

GENERAL JOURNAL

| Date | Account Titles and Explanation | PR | Debit | Credit |
|------|-------------------------------|----|-------|--------|
|      |                               |    |       |        |
|      |                               |    |       |        |
|      |                               |    |       |        |
|      |                               |    |       |        |
|      |                               |    |       |        |
|      |                               |    |       |        |
|      |                               |    |       |        |
|      |                               |    |       |        |
|      |                               |    |       |        |
|      |                               |    |       |        |
|      |                               |    |       |        |
|      |                               |    |       |        |
|      |                               |    |       |        |
|      |                               |    |       |        |
|      |                               |    |       |        |
|      |                               |    |       |        |
|      |                               |    |       |        |
|      |                               |    |       |        |
|      |                               |    |       |        |
|      |                               |    |       |        |
|      |                               |    |       |        |
|      |                               |    |       |        |
|      |                               |    |       |        |

*Analysis component:*  _____

_____
_____
_____
_____
_____
_____
_____
_____
_____
_____
_____
_____

**Problem 7-7A**

**Part 1**

_____

_____

| | | | |
|---|---|---|---|
| | | | |
| | | | |
| | | | |
| | | | |
| | | | |
| | | | |
| | | | |
| | | | |
| | | | |
| | | | |
| | | | |

**Part 2**

### GENERAL JOURNAL

Page_____

| Date | Account Titles and Explanation | PR | Debit | Credit |
|---|---|---|---|---|
| | | | | |
| | | | | |
| | | | | |
| | | | | |
| | | | | |
| | | | | |
| | | | | |
| | | | | |
| | | | | |
| | | | | |
| | | | | |
| | | | | |
| | | | | |
| | | | | |
| | | | | |
| | | | | |
| | | | | |
| | | | | |
| | | | | |
| | | | | |
| | | | | |

**Problem 7-7A (concl'd.)**

*Analysis component:*          _____

_____

_____

_____

_____

_____

_____

_____

_____

_____


**Problem 7-8A**

**a.**          _____

_____

| | | | |
|---|---|---|---|
| | | | |
| | | | |
| | | | |
| | | | |
| | | | |
| | | | |
| | | | |
| | | | |
| | | | |
| | | | |
| | | | |
| | | | |
| | | | |
| | | | |
| | | | |
| | | | |
| | | | |

Name:_____

**Problem 7-8A (concl'd.)**

b.                               **GENERAL JOURNAL**                          Page____

| Date | Account Titles and Explanation | PR | Debit | Credit |
|------|-------------------------------|-----|-------|--------|
|      |                               |     |       |        |
|      |                               |     |       |        |
|      |                               |     |       |        |
|      |                               |     |       |        |
|      |                               |     |       |        |
|      |                               |     |       |        |
|      |                               |     |       |        |
|      |                               |     |       |        |
|      |                               |     |       |        |
|      |                               |     |       |        |
|      |                               |     |       |        |
|      |                               |     |       |        |
|      |                               |     |       |        |
|      |                               |     |       |        |
|      |                               |     |       |        |
|      |                               |     |       |        |
|      |                               |     |       |        |
|      |                               |     |       |        |
|      |                               |     |       |        |
|      |                               |     |       |        |
|      |                               |     |       |        |

**Problem 7-9A**

a. _____
_____
_____

| | | | |
|---|---|---|---|
|   |   |   |   |
|   |   |   |   |
|   |   |   |   |
|   |   |   |   |
|   |   |   |   |
|   |   |   |   |
|   |   |   |   |
|   |   |   |   |
|   |   |   |   |
|   |   |   |   |
|   |   |   |   |
|   |   |   |   |
|   |   |   |   |

**Problem 7-9A (concl'd.)**

b.            **GENERAL JOURNAL**         Page_____

| Date | Account Titles and Explanation | PR | Debit | Credit |
|------|-------------------------------|----|-------|--------|
|      |                               |    |       |        |
|      |                               |    |       |        |
|      |                               |    |       |        |
|      |                               |    |       |        |
|      |                               |    |       |        |
|      |                               |    |       |        |
|      |                               |    |       |        |
|      |                               |    |       |        |
|      |                               |    |       |        |
|      |                               |    |       |        |
|      |                               |    |       |        |
|      |                               |    |       |        |
|      |                               |    |       |        |

**Problem 7-10A**

**Part 1**

| | | | |
|---|---|---|---|
| | | | |
| | | | |
| | | | |
| | | | |
| | | | |
| | | | |
| | | | |
| | | | |
| | | | |
| | | | |
| | | | |
| | | | |
| | | | |
| | | | |
| | | | |
| | | | |
| | | | |
| | | | |

**Problem 7-10A (concl'd.)**

**Part 2**

### GENERAL JOURNAL                    Page_____

| Date | Account Titles and Explanation | PR | Debit | Credit |
|------|-------------------------------|----|----|----|
|  |  |  |  |  |
|  |  |  |  |  |
|  |  |  |  |  |
|  |  |  |  |  |
|  |  |  |  |  |
|  |  |  |  |  |
|  |  |  |  |  |
|  |  |  |  |  |
|  |  |  |  |  |
|  |  |  |  |  |
|  |  |  |  |  |
|  |  |  |  |  |
|  |  |  |  |  |
|  |  |  |  |  |
|  |  |  |  |  |
|  |  |  |  |  |
|  |  |  |  |  |
|  |  |  |  |  |
|  |  |  |  |  |

*Analysis component:*

_____

_____

_____

_____

_____

_____

| (1) Principle Violated: |
|---|
| Recommendation: |
| |
| |
| |

| (2) Principle Violated: |
|---|
| Recommendation: |
| |
| |
| |
| |

| (3) Principle Violated: |
|---|
| Recommendation: |
| |
| |
| |
| |

| (4) Principle Violated: |
|---|
| Recommendation: |
| |
| |
| |
| |

| (5) Principle Violated: |
|---|
| Recommendation: |
| |
| |
| |

*Fundamental Accounting Principles*, 15ce, Working Papers

Chapter 7                                    Name:_____

Problem 7-2B

Part 1                        GENERAL JOURNAL                        Page_____

| Date | Account Titles and Explanation | PR | Debit | Credit |
|------|-------------------------------|----|----|----|
|  |  |  |  |  |
|  |  |  |  |  |
|  |  |  |  |  |

Part 2

**Stihl Repairs**
**Petty Cash Payments Report**
**July 5 – 31, 2017**

Receipts:

_____

_____

_____

_____

_____

_____

_____

_____

_____

_____

_____

_____

_____

Fund total

Less:  Cash remaining

Equals:  Cash required to replenish petty cash

Cash over/(short)

Part 3                        GENERAL JOURNAL                        Page_____

| Date | Account Titles and Explanation | PR | Debit | Credit |
|------|-------------------------------|----|----|----|
|  |  |  |  |  |
|  |  |  |  |  |
|  |  |  |  |  |
|  |  |  |  |  |
|  |  |  |  |  |
|  |  |  |  |  |
|  |  |  |  |  |
|  |  |  |  |  |
|  |  |  |  |  |
|  |  |  |  |  |
|  |  |  |  |  |

**Problem 7-2B (concl'd.)**

*Analysis component:*

_____
_____
_____
_____
_____
_____
_____
_____

**Problem 7-3B**

**GENERAL JOURNAL**

Page_____

| Date | Account Titles and Explanation | PR | Debit | Credit |
|------|-------------------------------|-----|-------|--------|
|      |                               |     |       |        |
|      |                               |     |       |        |
|      |                               |     |       |        |
|      |                               |     |       |        |
|      |                               |     |       |        |
|      |                               |     |       |        |
|      |                               |     |       |        |
|      |                               |     |       |        |
|      |                               |     |       |        |
|      |                               |     |       |        |
|      |                               |     |       |        |
|      |                               |     |       |        |
|      |                               |     |       |        |
|      |                               |     |       |        |
|      |                               |     |       |        |
|      |                               |     |       |        |
|      |                               |     |       |        |
|      |                               |     |       |        |
|      |                               |     |       |        |
|      |                               |     |       |        |
|      |                               |     |       |        |
|      |                               |     |       |        |
|      |                               |     |       |        |

*Analysis component:*

_____
_____
_____
_____
_____
_____
_____

**a.**

_____

| | | | |
|---|---|---|---|
| | | | |
| | | | |
| | | | |
| | | | |
| | | | |
| | | | |
| | | | |
| | | | |
| | | | |
| | | | |
| | | | |
| | | | |
| | | | |
| | | | |
| | | | |
| | | | |
| | | | |
| | | | |
| | | | |

**b.**            **GENERAL JOURNAL**            Page_____

| Date | Account Titles and Explanation | PR | Debit | Credit |
|---|---|---|---|---|
| | | | | |
| | | | | |
| | | | | |
| | | | | |
| | | | | |
| | | | | |
| | | | | |

**Analysis component:**      _____

_____
_____
_____
_____
_____
_____
_____

**Problem 7-5B**

**a.**

_____

_____

| | | | |
|---|---|---|---|
| | | | |
| | | | |
| | | | |
| | | | |
| | | | |
| | | | |
| | | | |
| | | | |
| | | | |
| | | | |
| | | | |
| | | | |
| | | | |
| | | | |

**b.**                    GENERAL JOURNAL                    Page____

| Date | Account Titles and Explanation | PR | Debit | Credit |
|---|---|---|---|---|
| | | | | |
| | | | | |
| | | | | |
| | | | | |
| | | | | |
| | | | | |
| | | | | |
| | | | | |
| | | | | |
| | | | | |
| | | | | |
| | | | | |
| | | | | |

**Problem 7-6B**

**Part 1**

_____

_____

_____

| | | | |
|---|---|---|---|
| | | | |
| | | | |
| | | | |
| | | | |
| | | | |
| | | | |
| | | | |
| | | | |
| | | | |
| | | | |
| | | | |
| | | | |
| | | | |
| | | | |
| | | | |
| | | | |
| | | | |

**Part 2**

**GENERAL JOURNAL**                                    Page_____

| Date | Account Titles and Explanation | PR | Debit | Credit |
|---|---|---|---|---|
| | | | | |
| | | | | |
| | | | | |
| | | | | |
| | | | | |
| | | | | |
| | | | | |
| | | | | |
| | | | | |
| | | | | |
| | | | | |
| | | | | |
| | | | | |
| | | | | |
| | | | | |
| | | | | |
| | | | | |
| | | | | |

Name:_____

**Problem 7-6B (concl'd.)**

*Analysis component:* _____

_____
_____
_____
_____
_____
_____
_____
_____
_____
_____

**Problem 7-7B   Part 1**

_____
_____

| | | | |
|---|---|---|---|
| | | | |
| | | | |
| | | | |
| | | | |
| | | | |
| | | | |
| | | | |
| | | | |
| | | | |
| | | | |
| | | | |
| | | | |

**Part 2**　　　　　　　　**GENERAL JOURNAL**　　　　　　　　Page____

| Date | Account Titles and Explanation | PR | Debit | Credit |
|---|---|---|---|---|
| | | | | |
| | | | | |
| | | | | |
| | | | | |
| | | | | |
| | | | | |
| | | | | |
| | | | | |
| | | | | |
| | | | | |

**Problem 7-7B (concl'd.)**

### GENERAL JOURNAL

Page____

| Date | Account Titles and Explanation | PR | Debit | Credit |
|------|-------------------------------|----|-------|--------|
|      |                               |    |       |        |
|      |                               |    |       |        |
|      |                               |    |       |        |
|      |                               |    |       |        |
|      |                               |    |       |        |
|      |                               |    |       |        |
|      |                               |    |       |        |
|      |                               |    |       |        |
|      |                               |    |       |        |
|      |                               |    |       |        |
|      |                               |    |       |        |

*Analysis component:*

_____
_____
_____
_____
_____
_____
_____
_____
_____
_____
_____

**Problem 7-8B    Part 1**

_____
_____
_____

| | | | |
|---|---|---|---|
| | | | |
| | | | |
| | | | |
| | | | |
| | | | |
| | | | |
| | | | |
| | | | |
| | | | |
| | | | |
| | | | |

**Problem 7-8B (concl'd.)**

**Part 2**        GENERAL JOURNAL        Page_____

| Date | Account Titles and Explanation | PR | Debit | Credit |
|------|-------------------------------|----|-------|--------|
|      |                               |    |       |        |
|      |                               |    |       |        |
|      |                               |    |       |        |
|      |                               |    |       |        |
|      |                               |    |       |        |
|      |                               |    |       |        |
|      |                               |    |       |        |
|      |                               |    |       |        |
|      |                               |    |       |        |
|      |                               |    |       |        |
|      |                               |    |       |        |
|      |                               |    |       |        |
|      |                               |    |       |        |
|      |                               |    |       |        |
|      |                               |    |       |        |
|      |                               |    |       |        |
|      |                               |    |       |        |
|      |                               |    |       |        |
|      |                               |    |       |        |
|      |                               |    |       |        |

**Problem 7-9B     Part 1**

| | | | |
|--|--|--|--|
| | | | |
| | | | |
| | | | |
| | | | |
| | | | |
| | | | |
| | | | |
| | | | |
| | | | |
| | | | |
| | | | |
| | | | |

Chapter 7 Name:_____

Problem 7-9B (concl'd.)

Part 2 GENERAL JOURNAL Page____

| Date | Account Titles and Explanation | PR | Debit | Credit |
|------|-------------------------------|----|-------|--------|
|  |  |  |  |  |
|  |  |  |  |  |
|  |  |  |  |  |
|  |  |  |  |  |
|  |  |  |  |  |
|  |  |  |  |  |
|  |  |  |  |  |
|  |  |  |  |  |
|  |  |  |  |  |
|  |  |  |  |  |
|  |  |  |  |  |
|  |  |  |  |  |
|  |  |  |  |  |
|  |  |  |  |  |
|  |  |  |  |  |
|  |  |  |  |  |
|  |  |  |  |  |
|  |  |  |  |  |
|  |  |  |  |  |
|  |  |  |  |  |
|  |  |  |  |  |
|  |  |  |  |  |
|  |  |  |  |  |
|  |  |  |  |  |

Problem 7-10B    Part 1

| | | | |
|--|--|--|--|
|  |  |  |  |
|  |  |  |  |
|  |  |  |  |
|  |  |  |  |
|  |  |  |  |
|  |  |  |  |
|  |  |  |  |
|  |  |  |  |

Name:_____

**Problem 7-10B (concl'd.)**

**Part 2**

**GENERAL JOURNAL**

Page____

| Date | Account Titles and Explanation | PR | Debit | Credit |
|------|-------------------------------|-----|-------|--------|
|      |                               |     |       |        |
|      |                               |     |       |        |
|      |                               |     |       |        |
|      |                               |     |       |        |
|      |                               |     |       |        |
|      |                               |     |       |        |
|      |                               |     |       |        |
|      |                               |     |       |        |
|      |                               |     |       |        |
|      |                               |     |       |        |
|      |                               |     |       |        |
|      |                               |     |       |        |
|      |                               |     |       |        |
|      |                               |     |       |        |
|      |                               |     |       |        |
|      |                               |     |       |        |
|      |                               |     |       |        |
|      |                               |     |       |        |
|      |                               |     |       |        |
|      |                               |     |       |        |
|      |                               |     |       |        |
|      |                               |     |       |        |
|      |                               |     |       |        |
|      |                               |     |       |        |
|      |                               |     |       |        |
|      |                               |     |       |        |
|      |                               |     |       |        |

*Analysis component:* _____

_____

_____

_____

_____

_____

_____

Name:_____

## Quick Study 8-1

### GENERAL JOURNAL

| Date | | Account Titles and Explanation | PR | Debit | Credit |
|------|---|--------------------------------|-----|-------|--------|
| | | | | | |
| | | | | | |
| | | | | | |
| | | | | | |
| | | | | | |
| | | | | | |
| | | | | | |
| | | | | | |
| | | | | | |
| | | | | | |
| | | | | | |
| | | | | | |
| | | | | | |
| | | | | | |
| | | | | | |

## Quick Study 8-2

(a) _____

_____

_____

_____

_____

(b) _____

_____

_____

_____

_____

(c) _____

_____

_____

_____

(d) _____

_____

_____

_____

## GENERAL JOURNAL

| Date | Account Titles and Explanation | PR | Debit | Credit |
|------|-------------------------------|-----|-------|--------|
|      |                               |     |       |        |
|      |                               |     |       |        |
|      |                               |     |       |        |
|      |                               |     |       |        |
|      |                               |     |       |        |
|      |                               |     |       |        |
|      |                               |     |       |        |
|      |                               |     |       |        |
|      |                               |     |       |        |
|      |                               |     |       |        |
|      |                               |     |       |        |
|      |                               |     |       |        |
|      |                               |     |       |        |
|      |                               |     |       |        |
|      |                               |     |       |        |
|      |                               |     |       |        |
|      |                               |     |       |        |
|      |                               |     |       |        |
|      |                               |     |       |        |
|      |                               |     |       |        |
|      |                               |     |       |        |
|      |                               |     |       |        |
|      |                               |     |       |        |
|      |                               |     |       |        |
|      |                               |     |       |        |
|      |                               |     |       |        |
|      |                               |     |       |        |
|      |                               |     |       |        |
|      |                               |     |       |        |
|      |                               |     |       |        |
|      |                               |     |       |        |
|      |                               |     |       |        |
|      |                               |     |       |        |
|      |                               |     |       |        |
|      |                               |     |       |        |
|      |                               |     |       |        |
|      |                               |     |       |        |

**Quick Study 8-4**

| Biatech | | |
|---|---|---|
| **Partial Balance Sheet** | | |
| **December 31, 2017** | | |
|  |  |  |
|  |  |  |
|  |  |  |
|  |  |  |
|  |  |  |
|  |  |  |
|  |  |  |
|  |  |  |
|  |  |  |
|  |  |  |

**Quick Study 8-5**

**GENERAL JOURNAL**

| Date | Account Titles and Explanation | PR | Debit | Credit |
|---|---|---|---|---|
|  |  |  |  |  |
|  |  |  |  |  |
|  |  |  |  |  |
|  |  |  |  |  |
|  |  |  |  |  |
|  |  |  |  |  |
|  |  |  |  |  |
|  |  |  |  |  |

Quick Study 8-6

a.

_____Allowance for Doubtful Accounts_____

b. _____
_____
_____
_____
_____

c.

### GENERAL JOURNAL                                         Page____

| Date | | Account Titles and Explanation | PR | Debit | Credit |
|------|--|-------------------------------|----|-------|--------|
|      |  |                               |    |       |        |
|      |  |                               |    |       |        |
|      |  |                               |    |       |        |
|      |  |                               |    |       |        |
|      |  |                               |    |       |        |

Quick Study 8-7

_____Allowance for Doubtful Accounts_____

### GENERAL JOURNAL                                         Page____

| Date | | Account Titles and Explanation | PR | Debit | Credit |
|------|--|-------------------------------|----|-------|--------|
|      |  |                               |    |       |        |
|      |  |                               |    |       |        |
|      |  |                               |    |       |        |
|      |  |                               |    |       |        |
|      |  |                               |    |       |        |

**Quick Study 8-8**

a.                    GENERAL JOURNAL                    Page____

| Date | Account Titles and Explanation | PR | Debit | Credit |
|------|-------------------------------|----|-------|--------|
|      |                               |    |       |        |
|      |                               |    |       |        |
|      |                               |    |       |        |
|      |                               |    |       |        |
|      |                               |    |       |        |

b. _____

_____

c. _____

_____

**Quick Study 8-9**

GENERAL JOURNAL                    Page____

| Date | Account Titles and Explanation | PR | Debit | Credit |
|------|-------------------------------|----|-------|--------|
|      |                               |    |       |        |
|      |                               |    |       |        |
|      |                               |    |       |        |
|      |                               |    |       |        |

**Allowance for Doubtful Accounts**

**Quick Study 8-10**

GENERAL JOURNAL                    Page____

| Date | Account Titles and Explanation | PR | Debit | Credit |
|------|-------------------------------|----|-------|--------|
|      |                               |    |       |        |
|      |                               |    |       |        |
|      |                               |    |       |        |
|      |                               |    |       |        |
|      |                               |    |       |        |

Name:_____

**Quick Study 8-11**

## GENERAL JOURNAL

Page____

| Date | | Account Titles and Explanation | PR | Debit | Credit |
|---|---|---|---|---|---|
| | | | | | |
| | | | | | |
| | | | | | |
| | | | | | |
| | | | | | |
| | | | | | |
| | | | | | |
| | | | | | |
| | | | | | |
| | | | | | |

**Quick Study 8-12**

## GENERAL JOURNAL

| Date | | Account Titles and Explanation | PR | Debit | Credit |
|---|---|---|---|---|---|
| | | | | | |
| | | | | | |
| | | | | | |
| | | | | | |
| | | | | | |
| | | | | | |
| | | | | | |
| | | | | | |
| | | | | | |
| | | | | | |
| | | | | | |
| | | | | | |
| | | | | | |

**Quick Study 8-13**

## GENERAL JOURNAL

| Date | | Account Titles and Explanation | PR | Debit | Credit |
|---|---|---|---|---|---|
| | | | | | |
| | | | | | |
| | | | | | |
| | | | | | |
| | | | | | |
| | | | | | |
| | | | | | |

Name:_____

**\*Quick Study 8-14**

a. _____
b. _____
c. _____

**\*Quick Study 8-15**

### GENERAL JOURNAL

| Date | | Account Titles and Explanation | PR | Debit | Credit |
|------|---|-------------------------------|----|----|------|
| | | | | | |
| | | | | | |
| | | | | | |
| | | | | | |
| | | | | | |
| | | | | | |
| | | | | | |
| | | | | | |

**\*Quick Study 8-16**

### GENERAL JOURNAL

| Date | | Account Titles and Explanation | PR | Debit | Credit |
|------|---|-------------------------------|----|----|------|
| | | | | | |
| | | | | | |
| | | | | | |
| | | | | | |
| | | | | | |
| | | | | | |

*Calculations:*

_____
_____
_____
_____
_____
_____
_____

Name:_____

**Exercise 8-1**

**Part 1**

## GENERAL LEDGER

| Accounts Receivable | Sales | Sales Returns and Allowances |
|---|---|---|
| | | |

## ACCOUNTS RECEIVABLE SUBLEDGER

| ABC Shop | Colt Enterprises | Red McKenzie |
|---|---|---|
| | | |

**Part 2**

| | | | |
|---|---|---|---|
| | | | |
| | | | |
| | | | |
| | | | |
| | | | |
| | | | |
| | | | |

<u>Comparison:</u>

*Fundamental Accounting Principles*, 15ce, Working Papers

Name:_____

**Exercise 8-2**

**(a)**

_____

_____

_____

_____

_____

**(b)**

_____

_____

_____

_____

_____

**(c)**

_____

_____

_____

_____

**(d)**

_____

_____

_____

_____

**Exercise 8-3**

**1.**

| Weakness #1 | |
| --- | --- |
| Implication | |
| Recommendation | |
| Weakness #2 | |
| Implication | |
| Recommendation | |

**Exercise 8-3 (cont'd.)**

| Weakness #3 | |
|---|---|
| **Implication** | |
| **Recommendation** | |
| Weakness #4 | |
| **Implication** | |
| **Recommendation** | |

**2.** _____

_____
_____
_____
_____
_____
_____
_____
_____
_____

**Exercise 8-4**

## GENERAL JOURNAL

| Date | Account Titles and Explanation | PR | Debit | Credit |
|------|-------------------------------|----|-------|--------|
|      |                               |    |       |        |
|      |                               |    |       |        |
|      |                               |    |       |        |
|      |                               |    |       |        |
|      |                               |    |       |        |
|      |                               |    |       |        |
|      |                               |    |       |        |
|      |                               |    |       |        |
|      |                               |    |       |        |
|      |                               |    |       |        |
|      |                               |    |       |        |
|      |                               |    |       |        |
|      |                               |    |       |        |

**Exercise 8-5**

## GENERAL JOURNAL

| Date | Account Titles and Explanation | PR | Debit | Credit |
|------|-------------------------------|----|-------|--------|
|      |                               |    |       |        |
|      |                               |    |       |        |
|      |                               |    |       |        |
|      |                               |    |       |        |
|      |                               |    |       |        |
|      |                               |    |       |        |
|      |                               |    |       |        |
|      |                               |    |       |        |
|      |                               |    |       |        |
|      |                               |    |       |        |
|      |                               |    |       |        |
|      |                               |    |       |        |
|      |                               |    |       |        |
|      |                               |    |       |        |
|      |                               |    |       |        |
|      |                               |    |       |        |
|      |                               |    |       |        |
|      |                               |    |       |        |
|      |                               |    |       |        |
|      |                               |    |       |        |

Exercise 8-6

a.

| Accounts Receivable | Allowance for Doubtful Accounts |
|---|---|
|  |  |

### GENERAL JOURNAL

| Date | Account Titles and Explanation | PR | Debit | Credit |
|---|---|---|---|---|
|  |  |  |  |  |
|  |  |  |  |  |
|  |  |  |  |  |
|  |  |  |  |  |

b.

| Accounts Receivable | Allowance for Doubtful Accounts |
|---|---|
|  |  |

### GENERAL JOURNAL

| Date | Account Titles and Explanation | PR | Debit | Credit |
|---|---|---|---|---|
|  |  |  |  |  |
|  |  |  |  |  |
|  |  |  |  |  |
|  |  |  |  |  |

**Exercise 8-7**

1.

### GENERAL JOURNAL

| Date | Account Titles and Explanation | PR | Debit | Credit |
|------|-------------------------------|----|-------|--------|
|      |                               |    |       |        |
|      |                               |    |       |        |
|      |                               |    |       |        |
|      |                               |    |       |        |
|      |                               |    |       |        |
|      |                               |    |       |        |
|      |                               |    |       |        |
|      |                               |    |       |        |
|      |                               |    |       |        |
|      |                               |    |       |        |
|      |                               |    |       |        |
|      |                               |    |       |        |
|      |                               |    |       |        |
|      |                               |    |       |        |
|      |                               |    |       |        |
|      |                               |    |       |        |
|      |                               |    |       |        |
|      |                               |    |       |        |
|      |                               |    |       |        |
|      |                               |    |       |        |

2.

Accounts Receivable

Allowance for Doubtful Accounts

Bad debt expense

Name:_____

## Exercise 8-8

a. _____

b. _____

c. _____

d. _____

e. _____

## Exercise 8-9

| **Partial Balance Sheet** | | |
|---|---|---|
| | | |
| | | |
| | | |
| | | |
| | | |
| | | |
| | | |
| | | |
| | | |
| | | |

## Exercise 8-10

a, b, and c                    **GENERAL JOURNAL**                    Page____

| Date | | Account Titles and Explanation | PR | Debit | Credit |
|---|---|---|---|---|---|
| | | | | | |
| | | | | | |
| | | | | | |
| | | | | | |
| | | | | | |
| | | | | | |
| | | | | | |
| | | | | | |
| | | | | | |
| | | | | | |
| | | | | | |
| | | | | | |
| | | | | | |
| | | | | | |
| | | | | | |

Name:_____

**Exercise 8-10 (concl'd.)**

| | | | | | |
|---|---|---|---|---|---|
| | | | | | |
| | | | | | |
| | | | | | |
| | | | | | |
| | | | | | |
| | | | | | |
| | | | | | |
| | | | | | |
| | | | | | |
| | | | | | |
| | | | | | |
| | | | | | |

*Calculations:*

| **Accounts Receivable** | **Allowance for Doubtful Accounts** |
|---|---|
| | |

**Exercise 8-10 (concl'd.)**

**d.**

|  |  |  |
|---|---|---|
| **Partial Balance Sheet** | | |
|  |  |  |
|  |  |  |
|  |  |  |
|  |  |  |
|  |  |  |

*Analysis component:*

_____
_____
_____
_____
_____

**Exercise 8-11**

**a, b, and c.**                **GENERAL JOURNAL**                Page____

| Date | Account Titles and Explanation | PR | Debit | Credit |
|---|---|---|---|---|
|  |  |  |  |  |
|  |  |  |  |  |
|  |  |  |  |  |
|  |  |  |  |  |
|  |  |  |  |  |
|  |  |  |  |  |
|  |  |  |  |  |
|  |  |  |  |  |
|  |  |  |  |  |
|  |  |  |  |  |
|  |  |  |  |  |
|  |  |  |  |  |
|  |  |  |  |  |
|  |  |  |  |  |
|  |  |  |  |  |
|  |  |  |  |  |
|  |  |  |  |  |
|  |  |  |  |  |
|  |  |  |  |  |
|  |  |  |  |  |

**Exercise 8-11 (concl'd.)**

| Date | | Account Titles and Explanation | PR | Debit | Credit |
|---|---|---|---|---|---|
| | | | | | |
| | | | | | |
| | | | | | |
| | | | | | |
| | | | | | |
| | | | | | |
| | | | | | |
| | | | | | |

*Calculations:*

| Accounts Receivable | Allowance for Doubtful Accounts |
|---|---|
| | |

**d.**

**Partial Balance Sheet**

| | | |
|---|---|---|
| | | |
| | | |
| | | |
| | | |
| | | |

*Analysis component:*

_____
_____
_____
_____
_____

Name:_____

Exercise 8-12

**a and b.**                    **GENERAL JOURNAL**                    Page____

| Date | | Account Titles and Explanation | PR | Debit | Credit |
|---|---|---|---|---|---|
| | | | | | |
| | | | | | |
| | | | | | |
| | | | | | |
| | | | | | |
| | | | | | |
| | | | | | |
| | | | | | |
| | | | | | |
| | | | | | |
| | | | | | |

*Calculations:*

**Accounts Receivable**                    **Allowance for Doubtful Accounts**

**c.**

**Partial Balance Sheet**

| | | |
|---|---|---|
| | | |
| | | |
| | | |
| | | |

*Analysis component:*

_____
_____
_____
_____
_____

**Exercise 8-13**

**GENERAL JOURNAL**　　　　　　　　　　　　　　　　Page_____

| Date | | Account Titles and Explanation | PR | Debit | Credit |
|---|---|---|---|---|---|
| | | | | | |
| | | | | | |
| | | | | | |
| | | | | | |
| | | | | | |
| | | | | | |
| | | | | | |
| | | | | | |

*Analysis component:*

_____
_____
_____
_____
_____
_____
_____

**Exercise 8-14**

1. _____
_____
_____
_____

2. _____
_____

3. 　　　　　　　　　　　**GENERAL JOURNAL**　　　　　　　　　　Page_____

| Date | | Account Titles and Explanation | PR | Debit | Credit |
|---|---|---|---|---|---|
| | | | | | |
| | | | | | |
| | | | | | |
| | | | | | |
| | | | | | |
| | | | | | |
| | | | | | |
| | | | | | |
| | | | | | |

Name:_____

**Exercise 8-15**

## GENERAL JOURNAL

| Date | Account Titles and Explanation | PR | Debit | Credit |
|------|-------------------------------|-----|-------|--------|
|      |                               |     |       |        |
|      |                               |     |       |        |
|      |                               |     |       |        |
|      |                               |     |       |        |
|      |                               |     |       |        |
|      |                               |     |       |        |
|      |                               |     |       |        |
|      |                               |     |       |        |
|      |                               |     |       |        |
|      |                               |     |       |        |
|      |                               |     |       |        |
|      |                               |     |       |        |
|      |                               |     |       |        |
|      |                               |     |       |        |

**Exercise 8-16**

## GENERAL JOURNAL

| Date | Account Titles and Explanation | PR | Debit | Credit |
|------|-------------------------------|-----|-------|--------|
|      |                               |     |       |        |
|      |                               |     |       |        |
|      |                               |     |       |        |
|      |                               |     |       |        |
|      |                               |     |       |        |
|      |                               |     |       |        |
|      |                               |     |       |        |
|      |                               |     |       |        |
|      |                               |     |       |        |
|      |                               |     |       |        |
|      |                               |     |       |        |
|      |                               |     |       |        |
|      |                               |     |       |        |
|      |                               |     |       |        |
|      |                               |     |       |        |
|      |                               |     |       |        |
|      |                               |     |       |        |
|      |                               |     |       |        |

**Exercise 8-17**

## GENERAL JOURNAL

| Date | Account Titles and Explanation | PR | Debit | Credit |
|------|-------------------------------|----|-------|--------|
|  |  |  |  |  |
|  |  |  |  |  |
|  |  |  |  |  |
|  |  |  |  |  |
|  |  |  |  |  |
|  |  |  |  |  |
|  |  |  |  |  |
|  |  |  |  |  |
|  |  |  |  |  |
|  |  |  |  |  |
|  |  |  |  |  |
|  |  |  |  |  |
|  |  |  |  |  |
|  |  |  |  |  |
|  |  |  |  |  |
|  |  |  |  |  |
|  |  |  |  |  |
|  |  |  |  |  |
|  |  |  |  |  |
|  |  |  |  |  |
|  |  |  |  |  |
|  |  |  |  |  |
|  |  |  |  |  |
|  |  |  |  |  |
|  |  |  |  |  |
|  |  |  |  |  |
|  |  |  |  |  |
|  |  |  |  |  |
|  |  |  |  |  |
|  |  |  |  |  |
|  |  |  |  |  |
|  |  |  |  |  |
|  |  |  |  |  |
|  |  |  |  |  |
|  |  |  |  |  |
|  |  |  |  |  |
|  |  |  |  |  |
|  |  |  |  |  |
|  |  |  |  |  |
|  |  |  |  |  |
|  |  |  |  |  |
|  |  |  |  |  |
|  |  |  |  |  |

*Exercise 8-18

## Part 1

| Accounts Receivable Turnover | Days' Sales Uncollected |
|---|---|
|  |  |
|  |  |
|  |  |
|  |  |
|  |  |
|  |  |
|  |  |

## Part 2

_____
_____
_____
_____
_____
_____
_____

*Exercise 8-19

### GENERAL JOURNAL

| Date | Account Titles and Explanation | PR | Debit | Credit |
|---|---|---|---|---|
|  |  |  |  |  |
|  |  |  |  |  |
|  |  |  |  |  |
|  |  |  |  |  |
|  |  |  |  |  |
|  |  |  |  |  |
|  |  |  |  |  |
|  |  |  |  |  |
|  |  |  |  |  |
|  |  |  |  |  |
|  |  |  |  |  |
|  |  |  |  |  |
|  |  |  |  |  |
|  |  |  |  |  |
|  |  |  |  |  |
|  |  |  |  |  |

Name:_____

**\*Exercise 8-19**

## GENERAL JOURNAL

| Date | Account Titles and Explanation | PR | Debit | Credit |
|------|-------------------------------|----|-------|--------|
|      |                               |    |       |        |
|      |                               |    |       |        |
|      |                               |    |       |        |
|      |                               |    |       |        |
|      |                               |    |       |        |
|      |                               |    |       |        |

**Financial Statement Note(s):**

_____

_____

_____

_____

**\*Exercise 8-20**

## GENERAL JOURNAL

| Date | Account Titles and Explanation | PR | Debit | Credit |
|------|-------------------------------|----|-------|--------|
|      |                               |    |       |        |
|      |                               |    |       |        |
|      |                               |    |       |        |
|      |                               |    |       |        |
|      |                               |    |       |        |
|      |                               |    |       |        |
|      |                               |    |       |        |
|      |                               |    |       |        |
|      |                               |    |       |        |
|      |                               |    |       |        |
|      |                               |    |       |        |

*Calculations:*

_____

_____

_____

_____

_____

_____

**Problem 8-1A**

_____
_____
_____
_____
_____
_____
_____
_____
_____
_____
_____
_____
_____
_____
_____
_____
_____
_____

**Problem 8-2A**

a. **Expense is 2% of credit sales:**

### GENERAL JOURNAL

| Date | Account Titles and Explanation | PR | Debit | Credit |
|------|-------------------------------|----|-------|--------|
|      |                               |    |       |        |
|      |                               |    |       |        |
|      |                               |    |       |        |
|      |                               |    |       |        |

b. **Allowance is 5% of accounts receivable:**

### GENERAL JOURNAL

| Date | Account Titles and Explanation | PR | Debit | Credit |
|------|-------------------------------|----|-------|--------|
|      |                               |    |       |        |
|      |                               |    |       |        |
|      |                               |    |       |        |
|      |                               |    |       |        |

*Calculations for Part b:*

**Allowance for
Doubtful Accounts**

**Chapter 8**

**Problem 8-2A (cont'd.)**

**Part 2**

| | | |
|---|---|---|
| | | |
| | | |
| | | |

**Part 3**

| | | |
|---|---|---|
| | | |
| | | |
| | | |

*Analysis component:*

_____

_____

_____

_____

_____

**Problem 8-3A     Part 1**

**Calculation of the required balance of the allowance (using an aging analysis):**

_____
_____
_____
_____
_____
_____
_____

**Allowance for Doubtful Accounts**

**Part 2**

### GENERAL JOURNAL

| Date | Account Titles and Explanation | PR | Debit | Credit |
|------|-------------------------------|----|-------|--------|
|      |                               |    |       |        |
|      |                               |    |       |        |
|      |                               |    |       |        |

*Analysis component:*

_____
_____
_____
_____
_____
_____

**Problem 8-4A   Part A**

Part 1                              **GENERAL JOURNAL**                              Page____

| Date | Account Titles and Explanation | PR | Debit | Credit |
|------|-------------------------------|----|-------|--------|
|      |                               |    |       |        |
|      |                               |    |       |        |
|      |                               |    |       |        |
|      |                               |    |       |        |
|      |                               |    |       |        |
|      |                               |    |       |        |
|      |                               |    |       |        |
|      |                               |    |       |        |
|      |                               |    |       |        |
|      |                               |    |       |        |
|      |                               |    |       |        |
|      |                               |    |       |        |
|      |                               |    |       |        |
|      |                               |    |       |        |
|      |                               |    |       |        |
|      |                               |    |       |        |
|      |                               |    |       |        |
|      |                               |    |       |        |
|      |                               |    |       |        |
|      |                               |    |       |        |
|      |                               |    |       |        |
|      |                               |    |       |        |
|      |                               |    |       |        |
|      |                               |    |       |        |
|      |                               |    |       |        |
|      |                               |    |       |        |
|      |                               |    |       |        |
|      |                               |    |       |        |
|      |                               |    |       |        |
|      |                               |    |       |        |
|      |                               |    |       |        |
|      |                               |    |       |        |
|      |                               |    |       |        |
|      |                               |    |       |        |
|      |                               |    |       |        |

**Problem 8-4A (concl'd.)**

Part B

Part 2                              GENERAL JOURNAL                              Page____

| Date | Account Titles and Explanation | PR | Debit | Credit |
|------|-------------------------------|----|-------|--------|
|      |                               |    |       |        |
|      |                               |    |       |        |
|      |                               |    |       |        |

Part 3

| | | | |
|---|---|---|---|
|   |   |   |   |
|   |   |   |   |
|   |   |   |   |

Part 4

_____

_____

Part C

Part 5                              GENERAL JOURNAL                              Page____

| Date | Account Titles and Explanation | PR | Debit | Credit |
|------|-------------------------------|----|-------|--------|
|      |                               |    |       |        |
|      |                               |    |       |        |
|      |                               |    |       |        |

*Calculations:*

| Accounts Receivable | Allowance for Doubtful Accounts |
|---------------------|----------------------------------|
|                     |                                  |

Part 6

| | | | |
|---|---|---|---|
|   |   |   |   |
|   |   |   |   |
|   |   |   |   |

Part 7

_____

_____

Problem 8-5A

## GENERAL JOURNAL

| Date | Account Titles and Explanation | PR | Debit | Credit |
|---|---|---|---|---|
| **2017** | | | | |
| a. | | | | |
| | | | | |
| | | | | |
| | | | | |
| | | | | |
| | | | | |
| | | | | |
| | | | | |
| | | | | |
| b. | | | | |
| | | | | |
| | | | | |
| | | | | |
| c. | | | | |
| | | | | |
| | | | | |
| | | | | |
| d. | | | | |
| | | | | |
| | | | | |
| | | | | |

*Calculations:*

| Accounts Receivable | | Allowance for Doubtful Accounts |
|---|---|---|

**Problem 8-5A (concl'd.)**

### GENERAL JOURNAL

| Date | Account Titles and Explanation | PR | Debit | Credit |
|------|-------------------------------|----|-------|--------|
| 2018 | | | | |
| e. | | | | |
| | | | | |
| | | | | |
| | | | | |
| | | | | |
| | | | | |
| | | | | |
| | | | | |
| f. | | | | |
| | | | | |
| | | | | |
| | | | | |
| | | | | |
| g. | | | | |
| | | | | |
| | | | | |
| | | | | |
| h. | | | | |
| | | | | |
| | | | | |
| | | | | |
| | | | | |

*Calculations:*

**Accounts Receivable**

**Allowance for Doubtful Accounts**

**Problem 8-6A**

**Part 1**
**Part a.**

### GENERAL JOURNAL

| Date | Account Titles and Explanation | PR | Debit | Credit |
|------|-------------------------------|----|----|----|
| **2017** | | | | |
| | | | | |
| | | | | |
| | | | | |

**Allowance for Doubtful Accounts**

**Part b.**

| | | |
|---|---|---|
| | | |
| | | |
| | | |
| | | |

**Part 2**
**Part c.**

### GENERAL JOURNAL

| Date | Account Titles and Explanation | PR | Debit | Credit |
|------|-------------------------------|----|----|----|
| **2017** | | | | |
| | | | | |
| | | | | |
| | | | | |

*Calculations:*

**Allowance for Doubtful Accounts**

**Part d.**

| | | |
|---|---|---|
| | | |
| | | |
| | | |
| | | |

Name:_____

## Problem 8-7A

### Part 1

#### GENERAL JOURNAL

| Date | Account Titles and Explanation | PR | Debit | Credit |
|---|---|---|---|---|
|  |  |  |  |  |
|  |  |  |  |  |
|  |  |  |  |  |
|  |  |  |  |  |

### Part 2

#### GENERAL JOURNAL

| Date | Account Titles and Explanation | PR | Debit | Credit |
|---|---|---|---|---|
|  |  |  |  |  |
|  |  |  |  |  |
|  |  |  |  |  |
|  |  |  |  |  |

*Calculations:*

| Accounts Receivable | Allowance for Doubtful Accounts |
|---|---|
|  |  |

## Problem 8-8A

a.

### Month

| Customer | Not yet due 0.5% | 1 to 29 days past due 1% | 30 to 59 days past due 4% | 60 to 89 days past due 10% | 90 to 119 days past due 20% | Over 119 days past due 50% |
|---|---|---|---|---|---|---|
| B. Axley |  |  |  |  |  |  |
| T. Holton |  |  |  |  |  |  |
| W. Nix |  |  |  |  |  |  |
| C. Percy |  |  |  |  |  |  |
| K. Willis |  |  |  |  |  |  |
|  |  |  |  |  |  |  |
|  |  |  |  |  |  |  |
|  |  |  |  |  |  |  |
|  |  |  |  |  |  |  |

Name:_____

**Problem 8-8A (concl'd.)**

**b.** GENERAL JOURNAL Page_____

| Date | Account Titles and Explanation | PR | Debit | Credit |
|---|---|---|---|---|
|  |  |  |  |  |
|  |  |  |  |  |
|  |  |  |  |  |
|  |  |  |  |  |

*Calculations:*

|  Accounts Receivable  |  |  Allowance for Doubtful Accounts  |  |
|---|---|---|---|
|  |  |  |  |

**Problem 8-9A**

**a.** GENERAL JOURNAL Page_____

| Date | Account Titles and Explanation | PR | Debit | Credit |
|---|---|---|---|---|
| **2017** |  |  |  |  |
|  |  |  |  |  |
|  |  |  |  |  |
|  |  |  |  |  |
|  |  |  |  |  |
|  |  |  |  |  |
| **2018** |  |  |  |  |
|  |  |  |  |  |
|  |  |  |  |  |
|  |  |  |  |  |
|  |  |  |  |  |
| **2019** |  |  |  |  |
|  |  |  |  |  |
|  |  |  |  |  |
|  |  |  |  |  |
|  |  |  |  |  |
|  |  |  |  |  |

**Problem 8-9A (concl'd.)**

*Calculations:*

| Accounts Receivable | Allowance for Doubtful Accounts |
|---|---|
| | |

*Analysis component:*

_____
_____
_____
_____
_____

**Problem 8-10A**

Parts a, b, and c.

| Date of Note | Principal | Interest Rate | Term | Maturity Date | Days of Accrued Interest at Dec. 31, 2017 | Accrued Interest at Dec. 31, 2017 |
|---|---|---|---|---|---|---|
| Nov. 1/16 | $240,000 | 4% | 180 days | | | |
| Jan. 5/17 | $100,000 | 5% | 90 days | | | |
| Nov. 20/17 | $90,000 | 4.5% | 45 days | | | |
| Dec. 10/17 | $120,000 | 5.5% | 30 days | | | |

*Calculations:*

_____
_____
_____
_____
_____
_____
_____
_____
_____
_____
_____
_____
_____
_____
_____

Problem 8-10A (concl'd.)

d.                          GENERAL JOURNAL                          Page____

| Date | Account Titles and Explanation | PR | Debit | Credit |
|------|-------------------------------|----|-------|--------|
|      |                               |    |       |        |
|      |                               |    |       |        |
|      |                               |    |       |        |

e.                          GENERAL JOURNAL                          Page____

| Date | Account Titles and Explanation | PR | Debit | Credit |
|------|-------------------------------|----|-------|--------|
|      |                               |    |       |        |
|      |                               |    |       |        |
|      |                               |    |       |        |
|      |                               |    |       |        |

Problem 8-11A

a.                          GENERAL JOURNAL                          Page____

| Date | Account Titles and Explanation | PR | Debit | Credit |
|------|-------------------------------|----|-------|--------|
|      |                               |    |       |        |
|      |                               |    |       |        |
|      |                               |    |       |        |
|      |                               |    |       |        |
|      |                               |    |       |        |
|      |                               |    |       |        |
|      |                               |    |       |        |
|      |                               |    |       |        |
|      |                               |    |       |        |
|      |                               |    |       |        |
|      |                               |    |       |        |
|      |                               |    |       |        |
|      |                               |    |       |        |
|      |                               |    |       |        |
|      |                               |    |       |        |
|      |                               |    |       |        |
|      |                               |    |       |        |
|      |                               |    |       |        |
|      |                               |    |       |        |

Problem 8-11A (concl'd.)

## GENERAL JOURNAL                                    Page____

| Date | Account Titles and Explanation | PR | Debit | Credit |
|------|-------------------------------|----|-------|--------|
|      |                               |    |       |        |
|      |                               |    |       |        |
|      |                               |    |       |        |
|      |                               |    |       |        |
|      |                               |    |       |        |
|      |                               |    |       |        |
|      |                               |    |       |        |
|      |                               |    |       |        |
|      |                               |    |       |        |
|      |                               |    |       |        |
|      |                               |    |       |        |
|      |                               |    |       |        |
|      |                               |    |       |        |
|      |                               |    |       |        |
|      |                               |    |       |        |
|      |                               |    |       |        |
|      |                               |    |       |        |
|      |                               |    |       |        |
|      |                               |    |       |        |
|      |                               |    |       |        |

b. Determine the maturity date of the note dated March 2:

_____

_____

_____

_____

_____

_____

Prepare the entry on the maturity date:

## GENERAL JOURNAL                                    Page____

| Date | Account Titles and Explanation | PR | Debit | Credit |
|------|-------------------------------|----|-------|--------|
|      |                               |    |       |        |
|      |                               |    |       |        |
|      |                               |    |       |        |
|      |                               |    |       |        |
|      |                               |    |       |        |

**Problem 8-12A**

**Parts (a) to (f)**

**GENERAL JOURNAL**

Page_____

| Date | Account Titles and Explanation | PR | Debit | Credit |
|---|---|---|---|---|
| | | | | |
| | | | | |
| | | | | |
| | | | | |
| | | | | |
| | | | | |
| | | | | |
| | | | | |
| | | | | |
| | | | | |
| | | | | |
| | | | | |
| | | | | |
| | | | | |
| | | | | |
| | | | | |
| | | | | |
| | | | | |
| | | | | |
| | | | | |
| | | | | |
| | | | | |
| | | | | |
| | | | | |
| | | | | |
| | | | | |
| | | | | |
| | | | | |
| | | | | |
| | | | | |
| | | | | |
| | | | | |
| | | | | |
| | | | | |
| | | | | |

*Analysis component:*

_____

_____

_____

_____

_____

_____

**\*Problem 8-13A**

|  | **2014** | **2013** |
|---|---|---|
| a. Accounts receivable turnover ratio |  |  |
| b. Days' sales uncollected |  |  |

**Comments:** _____
_____
_____
_____
_____
_____
_____

**\*Problem 8-14A**

**GENERAL JOURNAL**                              Page_____

| Date | Account Titles and Explanation | PR | Debit | Credit |
|---|---|---|---|---|
|  |  |  |  |  |
|  |  |  |  |  |
|  |  |  |  |  |
|  |  |  |  |  |
|  |  |  |  |  |
|  |  |  |  |  |
|  |  |  |  |  |
|  |  |  |  |  |
|  |  |  |  |  |
|  |  |  |  |  |
|  |  |  |  |  |
|  |  |  |  |  |
|  |  |  |  |  |
|  |  |  |  |  |
|  |  |  |  |  |
|  |  |  |  |  |
|  |  |  |  |  |

**\*Problem 8-14A (cont'd.)**

**GENERAL JOURNAL**                    Page____

| Date | Account Titles and Explanation | PR | Debit | Credit |
|------|-------------------------------|----|-------|--------|
|      |                               |    |       |        |
|      |                               |    |       |        |
|      |                               |    |       |        |
|      |                               |    |       |        |
|      |                               |    |       |        |
|      |                               |    |       |        |
|      |                               |    |       |        |
|      |                               |    |       |        |
|      |                               |    |       |        |
|      |                               |    |       |        |
|      |                               |    |       |        |
|      |                               |    |       |        |
|      |                               |    |       |        |
|      |                               |    |       |        |

*Analysis component:* _____

_____

_____

_____

_____

_____

**\*Problem 8-15A**

**GENERAL JOURNAL**                    Page____

| Date | Account Titles and Explanation | PR | Debit | Credit |
|------|-------------------------------|----|-------|--------|
|      |                               |    |       |        |
|      |                               |    |       |        |
|      |                               |    |       |        |
|      |                               |    |       |        |
|      |                               |    |       |        |
|      |                               |    |       |        |
|      |                               |    |       |        |
|      |                               |    |       |        |
|      |                               |    |       |        |
|      |                               |    |       |        |
|      |                               |    |       |        |
|      |                               |    |       |        |
|      |                               |    |       |        |
|      |                               |    |       |        |
|      |                               |    |       |        |
|      |                               |    |       |        |

Name:_____

**\*Problem 8-15A (cont'd.)**

## GENERAL JOURNAL

Page____

| Date | Account Titles and Explanation | PR | Debit | Credit |
|------|-------------------------------|----|----|----|
|  |  |  |  |  |
|  |  |  |  |  |
|  |  |  |  |  |
|  |  |  |  |  |
|  |  |  |  |  |
|  |  |  |  |  |
|  |  |  |  |  |
|  |  |  |  |  |
|  |  |  |  |  |
|  |  |  |  |  |
|  |  |  |  |  |
|  |  |  |  |  |
|  |  |  |  |  |
|  |  |  |  |  |
|  |  |  |  |  |
|  |  |  |  |  |
|  |  |  |  |  |
|  |  |  |  |  |
|  |  |  |  |  |
|  |  |  |  |  |
|  |  |  |  |  |
|  |  |  |  |  |
|  |  |  |  |  |
|  |  |  |  |  |
|  |  |  |  |  |
|  |  |  |  |  |
|  |  |  |  |  |
|  |  |  |  |  |
|  |  |  |  |  |
|  |  |  |  |  |
|  |  |  |  |  |
|  |  |  |  |  |
|  |  |  |  |  |

*Problem 8-15A (cont'd.)

## GENERAL JOURNAL                                        Page____

| Date | Account Titles and Explanation | PR | Debit | Credit |
|------|-------------------------------|----|-------|--------|
|      |                               |    |       |        |
|      |                               |    |       |        |
|      |                               |    |       |        |
|      |                               |    |       |        |
|      |                               |    |       |        |
|      |                               |    |       |        |
|      |                               |    |       |        |
|      |                               |    |       |        |
|      |                               |    |       |        |
|      |                               |    |       |        |
|      |                               |    |       |        |
|      |                               |    |       |        |
|      |                               |    |       |        |
|      |                               |    |       |        |
|      |                               |    |       |        |
|      |                               |    |       |        |
|      |                               |    |       |        |
|      |                               |    |       |        |
|      |                               |    |       |        |
|      |                               |    |       |        |
|      |                               |    |       |        |
|      |                               |    |       |        |
|      |                               |    |       |        |
|      |                               |    |       |        |
|      |                               |    |       |        |
|      |                               |    |       |        |
|      |                               |    |       |        |
|      |                               |    |       |        |
|      |                               |    |       |        |
|      |                               |    |       |        |
|      |                               |    |       |        |
|      |                               |    |       |        |
|      |                               |    |       |        |
|      |                               |    |       |        |
|      |                               |    |       |        |
|      |                               |    |       |        |
|      |                               |    |       |        |
|      |                               |    |       |        |
|      |                               |    |       |        |
|      |                               |    |       |        |

**Problem 8-1B**

_____
_____
_____
_____
_____
_____
_____
_____
_____
_____
_____
_____
_____
_____
_____

**Problem 8-2B**

a. Expense is 3% of credit sales:

### GENERAL JOURNAL

| Date | Account Titles and Explanation | PR | Debit | Credit |
|------|-------------------------------|----|-------|--------|
|      |                               |    |       |        |
|      |                               |    |       |        |
|      |                               |    |       |        |

b. Allowance is 6% of accounts receivable:

### GENERAL JOURNAL

| Date | Account Titles and Explanation | PR | Debit | Credit |
|------|-------------------------------|----|-------|--------|
|      |                               |    |       |        |
|      |                               |    |       |        |
|      |                               |    |       |        |

*Calculations for Part b:*

**Allowance for Doubtful Accounts**

Name:_____

**Problem 8-2B (concl'd.)**

**Part 2**

|  |  |  |
|---|---|---|
|  |  |  |
|  |  |  |
|  |  |  |

**Part 3**

|  |  |  |
|---|---|---|
|  |  |  |
|  |  |  |

*Analysis component:*

_____

_____

_____

_____

_____

_____

**Chapter 8**

Name:_____

**Problem 8-3B    Part 1**

Calculation of the required balance of the allowance (using an aging analysis):

_____
_____
_____
_____
_____
_____
_____

**Allowance for Doubtful Accounts**

**Part 2**

### GENERAL JOURNAL

| Date | Account Titles and Explanation | PR | Debit | Credit |
|------|-------------------------------|----|-------|--------|
|      |                               |    |       |        |
|      |                               |    |       |        |
|      |                               |    |       |        |

*Analysis component:*

_____
_____
_____
_____
_____
_____

**Problem 8-4B   Part A**

Part 1                          **GENERAL JOURNAL**                          Page____

| Date | Account Titles and Explanation | PR | Debit | Credit |
|------|-------------------------------|----|-------|--------|
|      |                               |    |       |        |
|      |                               |    |       |        |
|      |                               |    |       |        |
|      |                               |    |       |        |
|      |                               |    |       |        |
|      |                               |    |       |        |
|      |                               |    |       |        |
|      |                               |    |       |        |
|      |                               |    |       |        |
|      |                               |    |       |        |
|      |                               |    |       |        |
|      |                               |    |       |        |
|      |                               |    |       |        |
|      |                               |    |       |        |
|      |                               |    |       |        |
|      |                               |    |       |        |
|      |                               |    |       |        |
|      |                               |    |       |        |
|      |                               |    |       |        |
|      |                               |    |       |        |
|      |                               |    |       |        |
|      |                               |    |       |        |
|      |                               |    |       |        |
|      |                               |    |       |        |
|      |                               |    |       |        |
|      |                               |    |       |        |
|      |                               |    |       |        |
|      |                               |    |       |        |
|      |                               |    |       |        |
|      |                               |    |       |        |
|      |                               |    |       |        |
|      |                               |    |       |        |
|      |                               |    |       |        |
|      |                               |    |       |        |
|      |                               |    |       |        |
|      |                               |    |       |        |
|      |                               |    |       |        |
|      |                               |    |       |        |

**Problem 8-4B (concl'd.)**

**Part B**

**Part 2**                 **GENERAL JOURNAL**                        Page____

| Date | | Account Titles and Explanation | PR | Debit | Credit |
|---|---|---|---|---|---|
| | | | | | |
| | | | | | |
| | | | | | |

**Part 3**

| | | | | | |
|---|---|---|---|---|---|
| | | | | | |
| | | | | | |
| | | | | | |

**Part 4**

_____

_____

**Part C**

**Part 5**                 **GENERAL JOURNAL**                        Page____

| Date | | Account Titles and Explanation | PR | Debit | Credit |
|---|---|---|---|---|---|
| | | | | | |
| | | | | | |
| | | | | | |

*Calculations:*

| Accounts Receivable | Allowance for Doubtful Accounts |
|---|---|
| | |

**Part 6**

| | | | |
|---|---|---|---|
| | | | |
| | | | |
| | | | |

**Part 7**

_____

_____

Problem 8-5B

## GENERAL JOURNAL

| Date | Account Titles and Explanation | PR | Debit | Credit |
|------|-------------------------------|-----|-------|--------|
| 2017 | | | | |
| a. | | | | |
| | | | | |
| | | | | |
| | | | | |
| | | | | |
| | | | | |
| | | | | |
| | | | | |
| b. | | | | |
| | | | | |
| | | | | |
| | | | | |
| c. | | | | |
| | | | | |
| | | | | |
| | | | | |
| d. | | | | |
| | | | | |
| | | | | |
| | | | | |
| | | | | |

*Calculations:*

| Accounts Receivable | Allowance for Doubtful Accounts |
|---------------------|--------------------------------|
| | |

Name:_____

**Problem 8-5B (concl'd.)**

## GENERAL JOURNAL

| Date | Account Titles and Explanation | PR | Debit | Credit |
|------|-------------------------------|----|----|----|
| **2018** | | | | |
| e. | | | | |
| | | | | |
| | | | | |
| | | | | |
| | | | | |
| | | | | |
| | | | | |
| | | | | |
| f. | | | | |
| | | | | |
| | | | | |
| | | | | |
| g. | | | | |
| | | | | |
| | | | | |
| | | | | |
| h. | | | | |
| | | | | |
| | | | | |
| | | | | |

*Calculations:*

Accounts Receivable

Allowance for Doubtful Accounts

Name:_____

**Problem 8-6B**

**Part a**

GENERAL JOURNAL

| Date | Account Titles and Explanation | PR | Debit | Credit |
|------|-------------------------------|-----|-------|--------|
| 2017 | | | | |
| | | | | |
| | | | | |
| | | | | |
| | | | | |

**Allowance for Doubtful Accounts**

**Part b**

| | | |
|--|--|--|
| | | |
| | | |
| | | |
| | | |

**Part c**

GENERAL JOURNAL

| Date | Account Titles and Explanation | PR | Debit | Credit |
|------|-------------------------------|-----|-------|--------|
| 2017 | | | | |
| | | | | |
| | | | | |
| | | | | |

*Calculations:*

**Allowance for Doubtful Accounts**

**Part d**

| | | |
|--|--|--|
| | | |
| | | |
| | | |
| | | |

**Problem 8-7B**

**Part 1**

### GENERAL JOURNAL

| Date | | Account Titles and Explanation | PR | Debit | Credit |
|---|---|---|---|---|---|
| | | | | | |
| | | | | | |
| | | | | | |

**Part 2**

### GENERAL JOURNAL

| Date | | Account Titles and Explanation | PR | Debit | Credit |
|---|---|---|---|---|---|
| | | | | | |
| | | | | | |
| | | | | | |

*Calculations:*

| Accounts Receivable | Allowance for Doubtful Accounts |
|---|---|
| | |

**Problem 8-8B**

**a.**

**Month**

| Customer | Not yet due 1.5% | 1 to 29 days past due 2% | 30 to 59 days past due 5% | 60 to 89 days past due 20% | 90 to 119 days past due 35% | Over 119 days past due 50% |
|---|---|---|---|---|---|---|
| A. Leslie | | | | | | |
| T. Meston | | | | | | |
| P. Obrian | | | | | | |
| L. Timms | | | | | | |
| W. Victor | | | | | | |
| | | | | | | |
| | | | | | | |
| | | | | | | |

**Problem 8-8B (concl'd.)**

b.                                   GENERAL JOURNAL                                    Page____

| Date | Account Titles and Explanation | PR | Debit | Credit |
|------|-------------------------------|----|-------|--------|
|      |                               |    |       |        |
|      |                               |    |       |        |
|      |                               |    |       |        |
|      |                               |    |       |        |

*Calculations:*

| Accounts Receivable | | Allowance for Doubtful Accounts | |
|---|---|---|---|
| | | | |

**Problem 8-9B**

a.                                   GENERAL JOURNAL                                    Page____

| Date | Account Titles and Explanation | PR | Debit | Credit |
|------|-------------------------------|----|-------|--------|
| 2017 |                               |    |       |        |
|      |                               |    |       |        |
|      |                               |    |       |        |
|      |                               |    |       |        |
|      |                               |    |       |        |
| 2018 |                               |    |       |        |
|      |                               |    |       |        |
|      |                               |    |       |        |
|      |                               |    |       |        |
|      |                               |    |       |        |
| 2019 |                               |    |       |        |
|      |                               |    |       |        |
|      |                               |    |       |        |
|      |                               |    |       |        |
|      |                               |    |       |        |
|      |                               |    |       |        |

## Problem 8-9B (concl'd.)

*Calculations:*

| Accounts Receivable | Allowance for Doubtful Accounts |
|---|---|
|  |  |

*Analysis component:*

_____
_____
_____
_____
_____

## Problem 8-10B

**Parts a, b, and c.**

| Date of Note | Principal | Interest Rate | Term | Maturity Date | Days of Accrued Interest at Dec. 31, 2017 | Accrued Interest at Dec. 31, 2017 |
|---|---|---|---|---|---|---|
| Sept. 20/16 | $490,000 | 3% | 120 days |  |  |  |
| June 01/17 | $240,000 | 3.5% | 45 days |  |  |  |
| Nov. 23/17 | $164,000 | 4.5% | 90 days |  |  |  |
| Dec. 18/17 | $120,000 | 4% | 30 days |  |  |  |

*Calculations:*

_____
_____
_____
_____
_____
_____
_____
_____
_____
_____
_____
_____
_____
_____

**Problem 8-10B (concl'd.)**

d.                          GENERAL JOURNAL                          Page____

| Date | Account Titles and Explanation | PR | Debit | Credit |
|------|-------------------------------|----|----|----|
|  |  |  |  |  |
|  |  |  |  |  |
|  |  |  |  |  |
|  |  |  |  |  |

e.                          GENERAL JOURNAL                          Page____

| Date | Account Titles and Explanation | PR | Debit | Credit |
|------|-------------------------------|----|----|----|
|  |  |  |  |  |
|  |  |  |  |  |
|  |  |  |  |  |
|  |  |  |  |  |
|  |  |  |  |  |

**Problem 8-11B**

a.                          GENERAL JOURNAL                          Page____

| Date | Account Titles and Explanation | PR | Debit | Credit |
|------|-------------------------------|----|----|----|
|  |  |  |  |  |
|  |  |  |  |  |
|  |  |  |  |  |
|  |  |  |  |  |
|  |  |  |  |  |
|  |  |  |  |  |
|  |  |  |  |  |
|  |  |  |  |  |
|  |  |  |  |  |
|  |  |  |  |  |
|  |  |  |  |  |
|  |  |  |  |  |
|  |  |  |  |  |
|  |  |  |  |  |
|  |  |  |  |  |
|  |  |  |  |  |
|  |  |  |  |  |
|  |  |  |  |  |
|  |  |  |  |  |
|  |  |  |  |  |
|  |  |  |  |  |

**Problem 8-11B (concl'd.)**

### GENERAL JOURNAL
Page_____

| Date | Account Titles and Explanation | PR | Debit | Credit |
|------|-------------------------------|-----|-------|--------|
|      |                               |     |       |        |
|      |                               |     |       |        |
|      |                               |     |       |        |
|      |                               |     |       |        |
|      |                               |     |       |        |
|      |                               |     |       |        |
|      |                               |     |       |        |
|      |                               |     |       |        |
|      |                               |     |       |        |
|      |                               |     |       |        |
|      |                               |     |       |        |
|      |                               |     |       |        |
|      |                               |     |       |        |
|      |                               |     |       |        |
|      |                               |     |       |        |

**b. Determine the maturity date of the note dated March 1:**

_____

_____

_____

_____

_____

_____

**Prepare the entry on the maturity date:**

### GENERAL JOURNAL
Page_____

| Date | Account Titles and Explanation | PR | Debit | Credit |
|------|-------------------------------|-----|-------|--------|
|      |                               |     |       |        |
|      |                               |     |       |        |
|      |                               |     |       |        |
|      |                               |     |       |        |
|      |                               |     |       |        |

**Problem 8-12B**

**Parts (a) to (f)**

**GENERAL JOURNAL**

Page____

| Date | Account Titles and Explanation | PR | Debit | Credit |
|---|---|---|---|---|
| | | | | |
| | | | | |
| | | | | |
| | | | | |
| | | | | |
| | | | | |
| | | | | |
| | | | | |
| | | | | |
| | | | | |
| | | | | |
| | | | | |
| | | | | |
| | | | | |
| | | | | |
| | | | | |
| | | | | |
| | | | | |
| | | | | |
| | | | | |
| | | | | |
| | | | | |
| | | | | |
| | | | | |
| | | | | |
| | | | | |
| | | | | |
| | | | | |
| | | | | |
| | | | | |
| | | | | |
| | | | | |

*Analysis component:* _____

_____

_____

_____

_____

_____

Name:_____

**\*Problem 8-13B**

|  | **2014** | **2013** |
|---|---|---|
| **c. Accounts receivable turnover ratio** | | |
| **d. Days' sales uncollected** | | |

**Comments:**

_____
_____
_____
_____
_____
_____
_____

**\*Problem 8-14B**

**GENERAL JOURNAL**                                           Page_____

| Date | Account Titles and Explanation | PR | Debit | Credit |
|---|---|---|---|---|
|  |  |  |  |  |
|  |  |  |  |  |
|  |  |  |  |  |
|  |  |  |  |  |
|  |  |  |  |  |
|  |  |  |  |  |
|  |  |  |  |  |
|  |  |  |  |  |
|  |  |  |  |  |
|  |  |  |  |  |
|  |  |  |  |  |
|  |  |  |  |  |
|  |  |  |  |  |
|  |  |  |  |  |
|  |  |  |  |  |

*Problem 8-14B (cont'd.)

## GENERAL JOURNAL                          Page____

| Date | Account Titles and Explanation | PR | Debit | Credit |
|------|-------------------------------|-----|-------|--------|
|      |                               |     |       |        |
|      |                               |     |       |        |
|      |                               |     |       |        |
|      |                               |     |       |        |
|      |                               |     |       |        |
|      |                               |     |       |        |

*Analysis component:*

_____
_____
_____
_____
_____

*Problem 8-15B

## GENERAL JOURNAL                          Page____

| Date | Account Titles and Explanation | PR | Debit | Credit |
|------|-------------------------------|-----|-------|--------|
|      |                               |     |       |        |
|      |                               |     |       |        |
|      |                               |     |       |        |
|      |                               |     |       |        |
|      |                               |     |       |        |
|      |                               |     |       |        |
|      |                               |     |       |        |
|      |                               |     |       |        |
|      |                               |     |       |        |
|      |                               |     |       |        |
|      |                               |     |       |        |
|      |                               |     |       |        |
|      |                               |     |       |        |
|      |                               |     |       |        |
|      |                               |     |       |        |
|      |                               |     |       |        |
|      |                               |     |       |        |
|      |                               |     |       |        |
|      |                               |     |       |        |
|      |                               |     |       |        |
|      |                               |     |       |        |

Name:_____

**\*Problem 8-15B (cont'd.)**

### GENERAL JOURNAL

Page____

| Date | Account Titles and Explanation | PR | Debit | Credit |
|------|-------------------------------|-----|-------|--------|
|      |                               |     |       |        |
|      |                               |     |       |        |
|      |                               |     |       |        |
|      |                               |     |       |        |
|      |                               |     |       |        |
|      |                               |     |       |        |
|      |                               |     |       |        |
|      |                               |     |       |        |
|      |                               |     |       |        |
|      |                               |     |       |        |
|      |                               |     |       |        |
|      |                               |     |       |        |
|      |                               |     |       |        |
|      |                               |     |       |        |
|      |                               |     |       |        |
|      |                               |     |       |        |
|      |                               |     |       |        |
|      |                               |     |       |        |
|      |                               |     |       |        |
|      |                               |     |       |        |
|      |                               |     |       |        |
|      |                               |     |       |        |
|      |                               |     |       |        |
|      |                               |     |       |        |
|      |                               |     |       |        |
|      |                               |     |       |        |
|      |                               |     |       |        |
|      |                               |     |       |        |
|      |                               |     |       |        |
|      |                               |     |       |        |
|      |                               |     |       |        |
|      |                               |     |       |        |
|      |                               |     |       |        |
|      |                               |     |       |        |

**\*Problem 8-15B (concl'd.)**

## GENERAL JOURNAL

Page____

| Date | Account Titles and Explanation | PR | Debit | Credit |
|------|-------------------------------|----|----|----|
| | | | | |
| | | | | |
| | | | | |
| | | | | |
| | | | | |
| | | | | |
| | | | | |
| | | | | |
| | | | | |
| | | | | |
| | | | | |
| | | | | |
| | | | | |
| | | | | |
| | | | | |
| | | | | |
| | | | | |
| | | | | |
| | | | | |
| | | | | |
| | | | | |
| | | | | |
| | | | | |
| | | | | |
| | | | | |
| | | | | |
| | | | | |
| | | | | |
| | | | | |
| | | | | |
| | | | | |
| | | | | |
| | | | | |
| | | | | |
| | | | | |
| | | | | |
| | | | | |
| | | | | |
| | | | | |

**Quick Study AI-1**

_____

_____

_____

_____

_____

_____

**Quick Study AI-2**

### GENERAL JOURNAL

| Date | Account Titles and Explanation | PR | Debit | Credit |
|------|-------------------------------|----|-------|--------|
|  |  |  |  |  |
|  |  |  |  |  |
|  |  |  |  |  |
|  |  |  |  |  |
|  |  |  |  |  |
|  |  |  |  |  |
|  |  |  |  |  |
|  |  |  |  |  |

**Quick Study AI-3**

### GENERAL JOURNAL

| Date | Account Titles and Explanation | PR | Debit | Credit |
|------|-------------------------------|----|-------|--------|
|  |  |  |  |  |
|  |  |  |  |  |
|  |  |  |  |  |
|  |  |  |  |  |
|  |  |  |  |  |

**Quick Study AI-4**

| Employee | Gross Pay | Deductions: EI Premium | Taxes | CPP | Deductions Total | Pay: Net Pay | Distribution: Office Salaries | Distribution: Sales Salaries |
|----------|-----------|------------|-------|-----|-------------------|--------------|-----------------|----------------|
| Johnson, S. | 1,200.00 | 22.56 | 256.35 | 55.86 |  |  |  |  |
| Waverley, N. | 530.00 | 9.96 | 60.05 | 22.90 |  |  |  |  |
| Zender, B. | 675.00 | 12.69 | 95.40 | 30.08 |  |  |  |  |
| Totals | 2,405.00 | 45.21 | 411.80 | 108.84 |  |  |  |  |

Name:_____

## Quick Study AI-5

| Employee | Gross Pay | Deductions | | | | Pay | Salaries Expense |
|---|---|---|---|---|---|---|---|
| | | EI Premium | Taxes | CPP | Total Deductions | Net Pay | |
| Bentley, A. | 2,010.00 | | | | | | |
| Craig, T. | 2,115.00 | | | | | | |
| Totals | 4,125.00 | | | | | | |

## Quick Study AI-6

| Employee | Gross Pay | Deductions | | | | Pay | Distribution | |
|---|---|---|---|---|---|---|---|---|
| | | EI Premium | Income Taxes | CPP | Total Deductions | Net Pay | Office Salaries | Sales Salaries |
| Withers, S. | 2,500.00 | | | | | | 2,500.00 | |
| Volt. C. | 1,800.00 | | | | | | | 1,800.00 |
| Totals | | | | | | | | |

*Calculations:*

_____
_____
_____
_____
_____
_____
_____
_____

## Quick Study AI-7

### GENERAL JOURNAL                                                    Page____

| Date | Account Titles and Explanation | PR | Debit | Credit |
|---|---|---|---|---|
| | | | | |
| | | | | |
| | | | | |
| | | | | |
| | | | | |
| | | | | |
| | | | | |
| | | | | |
| | | | | |

**Quick Study AI-8**

### GENERAL JOURNAL

| Date | | Account Titles and Explanation | PR | Debit | Credit |
|------|---|-------------------------------|----|-------|--------|
| | | | | | |
| | | | | | |
| | | | | | |
| | | | | | |
| | | | | | |
| | | | | | |
| | | | | | |
| | | | | | |
| | | | | | |
| | | | | | |
| | | | | | |

**Quick Study AI-9**

### GENERAL JOURNAL

| Date | | Account Titles and Explanation | PR | Debit | Credit |
|------|---|-------------------------------|----|-------|--------|
| | | | | | |
| | | | | | |
| | | | | | |
| | | | | | |
| | | | | | |
| | | | | | |
| | | | | | |
| | | | | | |
| | | | | | |
| | | | | | |
| | | | | | |

**Quick Study AI-10**

### GENERAL JOURNAL

| Date | | Account Titles and Explanation | PR | Debit | Credit |
|------|---|-------------------------------|----|-------|--------|
| | | | | | |
| | | | | | |
| | | | | | |
| | | | | | |
| | | | | | |
| | | | | | |
| | | | | | |
| | | | | | |
| | | | | | |
| | | | | | |
| | | | | | |

Name:_____

## Quick Study AI-11

### GENERAL JOURNAL

| Date | | Account Titles and Explanation | PR | Debit | Credit |
|---|---|---|---|---|---|
| | | | | | |
| | | | | | |
| | | | | | |
| | | | | | |
| | | | | | |
| | | | | | |
| | | | | | |
| | | | | | |

## Exercise AI-1

| | | |
|---|---|---|
| | | |
| | | |
| | | |
| | | |
| | | |
| | | |
| | | |
| | | |
| | | |
| | | |
| | | |

## Exercise AI-2

| | | Deductions | | | | | Pay |
|---|---|---|---|---|---|---|---|
| Employee | Gross Pay | EI Premium | Income Taxes | CPP | Health Insurance | Total Deductions | Net Pay |
| H. Craig | 720.00 | | 106.20 | | 24.00 | | |
| J. Lim | 610.00 | | 79.70 | | 24.00 | | |
| D. Patelli | 830.00 | | 132.25 | | 36.00 | | |
| S. McFee | 1,700.00 | | 432.55 | | 24.00 | | |
| Totals | 3,860.00 | | 750.70 | | 108.00 | | |

*Calculations:*

_____
_____
_____
_____
_____
_____
_____

## Exercise AI-2 (concl'd.)

### GENERAL JOURNAL

| Date | Account Titles and Explanation | PR | Debit | Credit |
|------|-------------------------------|----|-------|--------|
|      |                               |    |       |        |
|      |                               |    |       |        |
|      |                               |    |       |        |
|      |                               |    |       |        |
|      |                               |    |       |        |
|      |                               |    |       |        |
|      |                               |    |       |        |
|      |                               |    |       |        |

## Exercise AI-3

| Employee | Gross Pay | Deductions EI Prem. | Income Taxes | United Way | CPP | Total Deductions | Pay Net Pay | Distribution Admin. Salaries | Sales Salaries |
|----------|-----------|---------|--------------|------------|-----|------------------|---------|-----------------|----------------|
| Akerley, D. | 1,900.00 | 35.72 | 338.55 | 80.00 | 87.39 | | | | |
| Nesbitt, M. | 1,260.00 | 23.69 | 167.75 | 50.00 | 55.71 | | | | |
| Trent, F. | 1,680.00 | 31.58 | 272.00 | 40.00 | 76.50 | | | | |
| Vacon, M. | 3,000.00 | 56.40 | 722.40 | 300.00 | 141.84 | | | | |
| Totals | 7,840.00 | 147.39 | 1,500.70 | 470.00 | 361.44 | | | | |

## Exercise AI-4

| Employee | Gross Pay | EI Prem. | Income Taxes | Canada Savings Bonds | CPP | United Way | Total Deductions | Net Pay | Office Salaries | Sales Salaries |
|----------|-----------|----------|--------------|----------------------|-----|------------|------------------|---------|-----------------|----------------|
| Crimson | 1,995.00 | | | | | | | | 1,995.00 | |
| Long | 2,040.00 | | | | | | | | | 2,040.00 |
| Morris | 2,000.00 | | | | | | | | | 2,000.00 |
| Peterson | 2,280.00 | | | | | | | | | 2,280.00 |
| Totals | 8,315.00 | | | | | | | | | |

Name:_____

## Exercise AI-5

| Employee | Gross Pay | Deductions | | | | | | Payment | Distribution | |
| | | EI Prem. | Income Taxes | Medical Ins. | CPP | United Way | Total Deductions | Net Pay | Office Salaries | Guide Salaries |
|---|---|---|---|---|---|---|---|---|---|---|
| Wynne | 1,200.00 | | | 65.00 | | 40.00 | | | | 1,200.00 |
| Short | 950.00 | | | 65.00 | | 100.00 | | | 950.00 | |
| Pearl | 1,150.00 | | | 65.00 | | 0 | | | | 1,150.00 |
| Quince | 875.00 | | | 65.00 | | 50.00 | | | | 875.00 |
| Totals | 4,175.00 | | | | | | | | | |

*Calculations:*

_____

_____

_____

_____

_____

_____

_____

_____

_____

## Exercise AI-6

| | | |
|---|---|---|
| | | |
| | | |
| | | |
| | | |
| | | |
| | | |
| | | |
| | | |
| | | |

### GENERAL JOURNAL

| Date | Account Titles and Explanation | PR | Debit | Credit |
|---|---|---|---|---|
| | | | | |
| | | | | |
| | | | | |
| | | | | |
| | | | | |
| | | | | |
| | | | | |

Name:_____

**Exercise AI-7**

### GENERAL JOURNAL

| Date | Account Titles and Explanation | PR | Debit | Credit |
|---|---|---|---|---|
| | | | | |
| | | | | |
| | | | | |
| | | | | |
| | | | | |
| | | | | |
| | | | | |
| | | | | |
| | | | | |
| | | | | |
| | | | | |
| | | | | |

**Exercise AI-8**

### GENERAL JOURNAL

| Date | Account Titles and Explanation | PR | Debit | Credit |
|---|---|---|---|---|
| | | | | |
| | | | | |
| | | | | |
| | | | | |
| | | | | |
| | | | | |
| | | | | |
| | | | | |

**Exercise AI-9**

### GENERAL JOURNAL

| Date | Account Titles and Explanation | PR | Debit | Credit |
|---|---|---|---|---|
| | | | | |
| | | | | |
| | | | | |
| | | | | |
| | | | | |
| | | | | |
| | | | | |
| | | | | |
| | | | | |

**Exercise AI-10**

### GENERAL JOURNAL

| Date | | Account Titles and Explanation | PR | Debit | Credit |
|---|---|---|---|---|---|
| | | | | | |
| | | | | | |
| | | | | | |
| | | | | | |
| | | | | | |
| | | | | | |
| | | | | | |
| | | | | | |
| | | | | | |
| | | | | | |
| | | | | | |
| | | | | | |
| | | | | | |
| | | | | | |
| | | | | | |

**Exercise AI-11**

| Employee | CPP Contribution | EI Contribution | Retirement Fund Contributions | Health Insurance |
|---|---|---|---|---|
| | | | | |
| | | | | |
| | | | | |
| | | | | |
| | | | | |
| | | | | |
| | | | | |

*Calculations:*

_____
_____
_____
_____
_____
_____
_____
_____
_____
_____

**Exercise AI-12**

## GENERAL JOURNAL

| Date | | Account Titles and Explanation | PR | Debit | Credit |
|---|---|---|---|---|---|
| | | | | | |
| | | | | | |
| | | | | | |
| | | | | | |
| | | | | | |
| | | | | | |
| | | | | | |
| | | | | | |
| | | | | | |
| | | | | | |
| | | | | | |
| | | | | | |
| | | | | | |
| | | | | | |
| | | | | | |
| | | | | | |
| | | | | | |
| | | | | | |
| | | | | | |
| | | | | | |
| | | | | | |
| | | | | | |
| | | | | | |
| | | | | | |
| | | | | | |
| | | | | | |
| | | | | | |
| | | | | | |
| | | | | | |

**Exercise AI-13**

## GENERAL JOURNAL

| Date | | Account Titles and Explanation | PR | Debit | Credit |
|---|---|---|---|---|---|
| | | | | | |
| | | | | | |
| | | | | | |
| | | | | | |
| | | | | | |
| | | | | | |
| | | | | | |

## Problem AI-1A

### Part 1

| Employee | M | T | W | T | F | S | S | Total Hrs. | O.T. Hrs. | Reg. Pay Rate | Regular Pay | O.T. Premium Pay | Gross Pay |
|----------|---|---|---|---|---|---|---|------------|-----------|---------------|-------------|------------------|-----------|
| | | | Daily Time | | | | | | | | | Earnings | |
| Loran | 8 | 8 | 8 | 8 | 8 | 4 | 0 | | | 40.00 | | | |
| Sousa | 7 | 8 | 6 | 7 | 8 | 4 | 0 | | | 36.00 | | | |
| Smith | 8 | 8 | 0 | 8 | 8 | 4 | 4 | | | 32.00 | | | |
| Parton | 8 | 8 | 8 | 8 | 8 | 0 | 0 | | | 40.00 | | | |
| Wood | 0 | 6 | 6 | 6 | 6 | 8 | 8 | | | 36.00 | | | |
| | | | | | | | | | | | | | |

| Employee | EI Prem. | CPP | Income Tax | Hosp. Ins. | Union Dues | Total Deductions | Net Pay | Office Salaries Expense | Service Wages Expense |
|----------|----------|-----|------------|-----------|-----------|------------------|---------|-------------------------|-----------------------|
| | | | Deductions | | | | Payment | Distribution | |
| Loran | | | | 40.00 | 16.00 | | | | |
| Sousa | | | | 40.00 | 15.00 | | | | |
| Smith | | | | 40.00 | 14.00 | | | | |
| Parton | | | | 40.00 | 16.00 | | | | |
| Wood | | | | 40.00 | 15.00 | | | | |
| Totals | | | | 200.00 | 76.00 | | | | |

### Part 2

#### GENERAL JOURNAL

| Date | Account Titles and Explanation | PR | Debit | Credit |
|------|-------------------------------|----|-------|--------|
| | | | | |
| | | | | |
| | | | | |
| | | | | |
| | | | | |
| | | | | |
| | | | | |
| | | | | |
| | | | | |
| | | | | |
| | | | | |
| | | | | |
| | | | | |
| | | | | |
| | | | | |
| | | | | |

Name:_____

**Problem AI-2A**

Part 1

### GENERAL JOURNAL

| Date | | Account Titles and Explanation | PR | Debit | Credit |
|------|--|-------------------------------|----|-------|--------|
| | | | | | |
| | | | | | |
| | | | | | |
| | | | | | |
| | | | | | |
| | | | | | |
| | | | | | |
| | | | | | |
| | | | | | |
| | | | | | |
| | | | | | |

Part 2

### GENERAL JOURNAL

| Date | | Account Titles and Explanation | PR | Debit | Credit |
|------|--|-------------------------------|----|-------|--------|
| | | | | | |
| | | | | | |
| | | | | | |
| | | | | | |
| | | | | | |
| | | | | | |

**Problem AI-3A**

Part 1

### GENERAL JOURNAL

| Date | | Account Titles and Explanation | PR | Debit | Credit |
|------|--|-------------------------------|----|-------|--------|
| | | | | | |
| | | | | | |
| | | | | | |
| | | | | | |
| | | | | | |
| | | | | | |
| | | | | | |
| | | | | | |
| | | | | | |
| | | | | | |
| | | | | | |
| | | | | | |

**Problem AI-3A (concl.)**

**Part 2**

### GENERAL JOURNAL

| Date | | Account Titles and Explanation | PR | Debit | Credit |
|---|---|---|---|---|---|
| | | | | | |
| | | | | | |
| | | | | | |
| | | | | | |
| | | | | | |
| | | | | | |

**Part 3**

### GENERAL JOURNAL

| Date | | Account Titles and Explanation | PR | Debit | Credit |
|---|---|---|---|---|---|
| | | | | | |
| | | | | | |
| | | | | | |
| | | | | | |
| | | | | | |
| | | | | | |
| | | | | | |
| | | | | | |

**Problem AI-4A**

### GENERAL JOURNAL

| Date | | Account Titles and Explanation | PR | Debit | Credit |
|---|---|---|---|---|---|
| | | | | | |
| | | | | | |
| | | | | | |
| | | | | | |
| | | | | | |
| | | | | | |
| | | | | | |
| | | | | | |
| | | | | | |
| | | | | | |
| | | | | | |
| | | | | | |
| | | | | | |
| | | | | | |
| | | | | | |

**Problem AI-4A (concl.)**

## GENERAL JOURNAL

| Date | Account Titles and Explanation | PR | Debit | Credit |
|---|---|---|---|---|
| | | | | |
| | | | | |
| | | | | |
| | | | | |
| | | | | |
| | | | | |
| | | | | |
| | | | | |
| | | | | |
| | | | | |
| | | | | |
| | | | | |
| | | | | |
| | | | | |
| | | | | |
| | | | | |
| | | | | |
| | | | | |
| | | | | |
| | | | | |
| | | | | |
| | | | | |
| | | | | |
| | | | | |
| | | | | |
| | | | | |
| | | | | |
| | | | | |
| | | | | |
| | | | | |
| | | | | |
| | | | | |
| | | | | |
| | | | | |
| | | | | |
| | | | | |
| | | | | |
| | | | | |
| | | | | |
| | | | | |
| | | | | |
| | | | | |

## Problem AI-1B

### Part 1

| Employee | Daily Time | | | | | | | Total Hrs. | O.T. Hrs. | Reg. Pay Rate | Earnings | | |
| | M | T | W | T | F | S | S | | | | Regular Pay | O.T. Premium Pay | Gross Pay |
|---|---|---|---|---|---|---|---|---|---|---|---|---|---|
| Amoko | 8 | 8 | 8 | 8 | 8 | 0 | 0 | | | 34.00 | | | |
| Carson | 7 | 8 | 8 | 7 | 8 | 4 | 0 | | | 36.00 | | | |
| Cheng | 8 | 8 | 0 | 8 | 8 | 4 | 4 | | | 36.00 | | | |
| Deszca | 8 | 8 | 8 | 8 | 8 | 0 | 0 | | | 30.00 | | | |
| Tan | 0 | 6 | 6 | 6 | 6 | 8 | 8 | | | 30.00 | | | |
| | | | | | | | | | | | | | |

| Employee | Deductions | | | | | | Payment | Distribution | |
| | EI Prem. | CPP | Income Tax | Hosp. Ins. | Union Dues | Total Deductions | Net Pay | Office Wages Expense | Service Wages Expense |
|---|---|---|---|---|---|---|---|---|---|
| Amoko | | | | 30.00 | 12.00 | | | | |
| Carson | | | | 30.00 | 12.00 | | | | |
| Cheng | | | | 30.00 | 12.00 | | | | |
| Deszca | | | | 30.00 | 12.00 | | | | |
| Tan | | | | 30.00 | 12.00 | | | | |
| Totals | | | | 150.00 | 60.00 | | | | |

### Part 2

## GENERAL JOURNAL

| Date | Account Titles and Explanation | PR | Debit | Credit |
|---|---|---|---|---|
| | | | | |
| | | | | |
| | | | | |
| | | | | |
| | | | | |
| | | | | |
| | | | | |
| | | | | |
| | | | | |
| | | | | |
| | | | | |
| | | | | |
| | | | | |
| | | | | |
| | | | | |
| | | | | |
| | | | | |

**Problem AI-2B**

**Part 1**

### GENERAL JOURNAL

| Date | | Account Titles and Explanation | PR | Debit | Credit |
|------|---|-------------------------------|----|-------|--------|
| | | | | | |
| | | | | | |
| | | | | | |
| | | | | | |
| | | | | | |
| | | | | | |
| | | | | | |
| | | | | | |
| | | | | | |
| | | | | | |
| | | | | | |
| | | | | | |
| | | | | | |

**Part 2**

### GENERAL JOURNAL

| Date | | Account Titles and Explanation | PR | Debit | Credit |
|------|---|-------------------------------|----|-------|--------|
| | | | | | |
| | | | | | |
| | | | | | |
| | | | | | |
| | | | | | |
| | | | | | |

**Problem AI-3B**

**Part 1**

### GENERAL JOURNAL

| Date | | Account Titles and Explanation | PR | Debit | Credit |
|------|---|-------------------------------|----|-------|--------|
| | | | | | |
| | | | | | |
| | | | | | |
| | | | | | |
| | | | | | |
| | | | | | |
| | | | | | |
| | | | | | |
| | | | | | |
| | | | | | |
| | | | | | |
| | | | | | |

**Problem AI-3B (concl.)**

**Part 2**

## GENERAL JOURNAL

| Date | | Account Titles and Explanation | PR | Debit | Credit |
|------|--|-------------------------------|-----|-------|--------|
| | | | | | |
| | | | | | |
| | | | | | |
| | | | | | |
| | | | | | |
| | | | | | |

**Part 3**

## GENERAL JOURNAL

| Date | | Account Titles and Explanation | PR | Debit | Credit |
|------|--|-------------------------------|-----|-------|--------|
| | | | | | |
| | | | | | |
| | | | | | |
| | | | | | |
| | | | | | |
| | | | | | |
| | | | | | |
| | | | | | |
| | | | | | |

**Problem AI-4B**

## GENERAL JOURNAL

| Date | | Account Titles and Explanation | PR | Debit | Credit |
|------|--|-------------------------------|-----|-------|--------|
| | | | | | |
| | | | | | |
| | | | | | |
| | | | | | |
| | | | | | |
| | | | | | |
| | | | | | |
| | | | | | |
| | | | | | |
| | | | | | |
| | | | | | |
| | | | | | |
| | | | | | |
| | | | | | |

**Problem AI-4B (concl.)**

## GENERAL JOURNAL

| Date | Account Titles and Explanation | PR | Debit | Credit |
|---|---|---|---|---|
| | | | | |
| | | | | |
| | | | | |
| | | | | |
| | | | | |
| | | | | |
| | | | | |
| | | | | |
| | | | | |
| | | | | |
| | | | | |
| | | | | |
| | | | | |
| | | | | |
| | | | | |
| | | | | |
| | | | | |
| | | | | |
| | | | | |
| | | | | |
| | | | | |
| | | | | |
| | | | | |
| | | | | |
| | | | | |
| | | | | |
| | | | | |
| | | | | |
| | | | | |
| | | | | |
| | | | | |
| | | | | |
| | | | | |
| | | | | |
| | | | | |
| | | | | |
| | | | | |
| | | | | |
| | | | | |

**Appendix II**                                      Name:_____

## Quick Study AII-1

1._____    3._____
2._____    4._____

## Quick Study AII-2

1._____    5._____
2._____    6._____
3._____    7._____
4._____    8._____

## Quick Study AII-3

a._____    e._____
b._____    f._____
c._____    g._____
d._____

## Quick Study AII-4

**GENERAL JOURNAL**                                      Page_____

| Date | Account Titles and Explanation | PR | Debit | Credit |
|------|-------------------------------|-----|-------|--------|
|  |  |  |  |  |
|  |  |  |  |  |
|  |  |  |  |  |
|  |  |  |  |  |
|  |  |  |  |  |
|  |  |  |  |  |
|  |  |  |  |  |
|  |  |  |  |  |
|  |  |  |  |  |
|  |  |  |  |  |
|  |  |  |  |  |
|  |  |  |  |  |
|  |  |  |  |  |
|  |  |  |  |  |
|  |  |  |  |  |
|  |  |  |  |  |
|  |  |  |  |  |
|  |  |  |  |  |
|  |  |  |  |  |

### Quick Study AII-5

| | | | |
|---|---|---|---|
| 1. | _____ | 5. | _____ |
| 2. | _____ | 6. | _____ |
| 3. | _____ | 7. | _____ |
| 4. | _____ | | |

### Quick Study AII-6

| | | | |
|---|---|---|---|
| 1. | _____ | 5. | _____ |
| 2. | _____ | 6. | _____ |
| 3. | _____ | 7. | _____ |
| 4. | _____ | | |

### Quick Study AII-7

| | | Sales Journal | | | Page |
|---|---|---|---|---|---|
| Date | Account Debited | Invoice Number | PR | Accounts Receivable Dr. Sales Cr. | Cost of Goods Sold Dr. Merchandise Inventory Cr. |
| | | | | | |
| | | | | | |
| | | | | | |
| | | | | | |
| | | | | | |

### Quick Study AII-8

| | | | Cash Receipts Journal | | | | | | Page |
|---|---|---|---|---|---|---|---|---|---|
| Date | Account Credited | PR | Explanation | Cash Dr. | Sales Disc. Dr. | Accts. Rec. Cr. | Sales Cr. | Other Accts. Cr. | COGS Dr. Merch. Inv. Cr. |
| | | | | | | | | | |
| | | | | | | | | | |
| | | | | | | | | | |
| | | | | | | | | | |
| | | | | | | | | | |

### Quick Study AII-9

| | | | | Purchases Journal | | | | Page |
|---|---|---|---|---|---|---|---|---|
| Date | Account Credited | Date of Invoice | Terms | PR | Accounts Payable Cr. | Merch. Inventory Dr. | Office Supplies Dr. | Other Accounts Dr. |
| | | | | | | | | |
| | | | | | | | | |
| | | | | | | | | |
| | | | | | | | | |
| | | | | | | | | |

### Quick Study AII-10

| | | | | | | | | | Page |
|---|---|---|---|---|---|---|---|---|---|
| | | **Cash Disbursements Journal** | | | | | | | |
| Date | Ch. No. | Payee | Account Debited | PR | Cash Cr. | Merch. Inventory Cr. | Other Accounts Dr. | Accounts Payable Dr. | |
| | | | | | | | | | |
| | | | | | | | | | |
| | | | | | | | | | |
| | | | | | | | | | |
| | | | | | | | | | |

### Exercise AII-1

| | | | | | | Page |
|---|---|---|---|---|---|---|
| | **Sales Journal** | | | | | |
| Date | Account Debited | Invoice Number | PR | Accounts Receivable Dr. Sales Cr. | Cost of Goods Sold Dr. Merchandise Inventory Cr. | |
| | | | | | | |
| | | | | | | |
| | | | | | | |
| | | | | | | |
| | | | | | | |
| | | | | | | |

### *Exercise AII-2

| | | | | Page |
|---|---|---|---|---|
| | **Sales Journal** | | | |
| Date | Account Debited | Invoice No. | PR | Accounts Receivable Dr. Sales Cr. |
| | | | | |
| | | | | |
| | | | | |
| | | | | |
| | | | | |

### Exercise AII-3

| | | | | | | | | | Page |
|---|---|---|---|---|---|---|---|---|---|
| | | **Cash Receipts Journal** | | | | | | | |
| Date | Account Credited | PR | Explanation | Cash Dr. | Sales Disc. Dr. | Accts. Rec. Cr. | Sales Cr. | Other Accts. Cr. | COGS Dr. Merch. Inv. Cr. |
| | | | | | | | | | |
| | | | | | | | | | |
| | | | | | | | | | |
| | | | | | | | | | |
| | | | | | | | | | |
| | | | | | | | | | |
| | | | | | | | | | |

**Appendix II**

Name:_____

**\*Exercise AII-4**

| | | | Cash Receipts Journal | | | | | Page | |
|---|---|---|---|---|---|---|---|---|---|
| Date | Account Credited | PR | Explanation | Cash Dr. | Sales Disc. Dr. | Accts. Rec. Cr. | Sales Cr. | | Other Accts. Cr. |
| | | | | | | | | | |
| | | | | | | | | | |
| | | | | | | | | | |
| | | | | | | | | | |
| | | | | | | | | | |

**Exercise AII-5**

| | | | | | Purchases Journal | | | | Page |
|---|---|---|---|---|---|---|---|---|---|
| Date | Account Credited | Date of Invoice | Terms | PR | Accounts Payable Cr. | Merch. Inventory Dr. | Office Supplies Dr. | | Other Accounts Dr. |
| | | | | | | | | | |
| | | | | | | | | | |
| | | | | | | | | | |
| | | | | | | | | | |
| | | | | | | | | | |

**\*Exercise AII-6**

| | | | | | Purchases Journal | | | | Page |
|---|---|---|---|---|---|---|---|---|---|
| Date | Account Credited | Date of Invoice | Terms | PR | Accts. Payable Cr. | Purchases Dr. | Office Supplies Dr. | | Other Accts. Dr. |
| | | | | | | | | | |
| | | | | | | | | | |
| | | | | | | | | | |
| | | | | | | | | | |
| | | | | | | | | | |

**Exercise AII-7**

| | | | | | Cash Disbursements Journal | | | | Page |
|---|---|---|---|---|---|---|---|---|---|
| Date | Ch. No. | Payee | Account Debited | PR | Cash Cr. | Merch. Inventory Cr. | Other Accounts Dr. | | Accounts Payable Dr. |
| | | | | | | | | | |
| | | | | | | | | | |
| | | | | | | | | | |
| | | | | | | | | | |
| | | | | | | | | | |
| | | | | | | | | | |
| | | | | | | | | | |

**\*Exercise AII-8**

| Cash Disbursements Journal | | | | | | | | Page | |
|---|---|---|---|---|---|---|---|---|---|
| Date | Ch. No. | Payee | Account Debited | PR | Cash Cr. | Purch. Disc. Cr. | Other Accounts Dr. | Accts. Payable Dr. | |
|  |  |  |  |  |  |  |  |  | |
|  |  |  |  |  |  |  |  |  | |
|  |  |  |  |  |  |  |  |  | |
|  |  |  |  |  |  |  |  |  | |
|  |  |  |  |  |  |  |  |  | |
|  |  |  |  |  |  |  |  |  | |
|  |  |  |  |  |  |  |  |  | |

**Exercise AII-9**

**Part 1 – Wilson Purchasing**

| Purchases Journal | | | | | | | | | Page |
|---|---|---|---|---|---|---|---|---|---|
| Date | Account Credited | Date of Invoice | Terms | PR | Accounts Payable Cr. | Merch. Inventory Dr. | Office Supplies Dr. | Other Accounts Dr. | |
|  |  |  |  |  |  |  |  |  | |
|  |  |  |  |  |  |  |  |  | |
|  |  |  |  |  |  |  |  |  | |

| Cash Disbursements Journal | | | | | | | | Page | |
|---|---|---|---|---|---|---|---|---|---|
| Date | Ch. No. | Payee | Account Debited | PR | Cash Cr. | Merch. Inventory Cr. | Other Accounts Dr. | Accounts Payable Dr. | |
|  |  |  |  |  |  |  |  |  | |
|  |  |  |  |  |  |  |  |  | |
|  |  |  |  |  |  |  |  |  | |
|  |  |  |  |  |  |  |  |  | |

## GENERAL JOURNAL                                    Page____

| Date | | Account Titles and Explanation | PR | Debit | Credit |
|---|---|---|---|---|---|
|  |  |  |  |  |  |
|  |  |  |  |  |  |
|  |  |  |  |  |  |
|  |  |  |  |  |  |
|  |  |  |  |  |  |
|  |  |  |  |  |  |

**Exercise AII-9 (concl'd.)**

**Part 2 – Hostel Sales**

| | Sales Journal | | | | | Page |
|---|---|---|---|---|---|---|
| Date | Account Debited | Invoice Number | PR | Accounts Receivable Dr. Sales Cr. | | Cost of Goods Sold Dr. Merchandise Inventory Cr. |
| | | | | | | |
| | | | | | | |
| | | | | | | |

| | Cash Receipts Journal | | | | | | | | Page |
|---|---|---|---|---|---|---|---|---|---|
| Date | Account Credited | PR | Explanation | Cash Dr. | Sales Disc. Dr. | Accts. Rec. Cr. | Sales Cr. | Other Accts. Cr. | COGS Dr. Merch. Inv. Cr. |
| | | | | | | | | | |
| | | | | | | | | | |
| | | | | | | | | | |

### GENERAL JOURNAL                                               Page_____

| Date | | Account Titles and Explanation | PR | Debit | Credit |
|---|---|---|---|---|---|
| | | | | | |
| | | | | | |
| | | | | | |
| | | | | | |
| | | | | | |
| | | | | | |
| | | | | | |
| | | | | | |
| | | | | | |
| | | | | | |
| | | | | | |

**\*Exercise AII-10**

**Part 1 – Wilson Purchasing**

| | Purchases Journal | | | | | | | Page |
|---|---|---|---|---|---|---|---|---|
| Date | Account Credited | Date of Invoice | Terms | PR | Accts. Payable Cr. | Purchases Dr. | Office Supplies Dr. | Other Accts. Dr. |
| | | | | | | | | |
| | | | | | | | | |
| | | | | | | | | |
| | | | | | | | | |
| | | | | | | | | |

Name:_____

**\*Exercise AII-10 (concl'd.)**

| | | | Cash Disbursements Journal | | | | | | Page |
|---|---|---|---|---|---|---|---|---|---|
| Date | Ch. No. | Payee | Account Debited | PR | Cash Cr. | Purch. Disc. Cr. | Other Accounts Dr. | Accts. Payable Dr. |  |
| | | | | | | | | | |
| | | | | | | | | | |
| | | | | | | | | | |
| | | | | | | | | | |
| | | | | | | | | | |

### GENERAL JOURNAL

Page____

| Date | | Account Titles and Explanation | PR | Debit | Credit |
|---|---|---|---|---|---|
| | | | | | |
| | | | | | |
| | | | | | |
| | | | | | |
| | | | | | |

**Part 2 – Hostel Sales**

| | Sales Journal | | | | Page |
|---|---|---|---|---|---|
| Date | Account Debited | Invoice No. | PR | Accounts Receivable Dr. Sales Cr. | |
| | | | | | |
| | | | | | |
| | | | | | |
| | | | | | |
| | | | | | |

| | | | Cash Receipts Journal | | | | | | Page |
|---|---|---|---|---|---|---|---|---|---|
| Date | Account Credited | PR | Explanation | Cash Dr. | Sales Disc. Dr. | Accts. Rec. Cr. | Sales Cr. | Other Accts. Cr. | |
| | | | | | | | | | |
| | | | | | | | | | |
| | | | | | | | | | |
| | | | | | | | | | |
| | | | | | | | | | |

### GENERAL JOURNAL

Page____

| Date | | Account Titles and Explanation | PR | Debit | Credit |
|---|---|---|---|---|---|
| | | | | | |
| | | | | | |
| | | | | | |
| | | | | | |
| | | | | | |

**Exercise AII-11**

_____
_____
_____
_____
_____
_____
_____
_____
_____
_____
_____

**Exercise AII-12**

a. _____

b. _____

c. _____

d. _____

e. _____

**Exercise AII-13**

Part 1

### ACCOUNTS RECEIVABLE SUBLEDGER

| Sanders Farrell | Don Holland | Brad Smithers |
|---|---|---|
| | | |

Part 2

### GENERAL LEDGER

| Accounts Receivable | Sales | Sales Returns and Allowances |
|---|---|---|
| | | |

**Exercise AII-13 (concl'd.)**

**Part 3**

| Schedule of Accounts Receivable | | |
|---|---|---|
| | | |
| | | |
| | | |
| | | |
| | | |
| | | |
| | | |
| | | |
| | | |
| | | |

**\*Exercise AII-14**

**Parts 1 and 2**

| GENERAL LEDGER |
|---|

**Cash**

**Accounts Payable**

**Sales Discounts**

**Accts. Receivable**

**Notes Payable**

**Purchases**

**Prepaid Insurance**

**Sales**

**Purchase
Returns and Allowances**

**Store Equipment**

**Sales
Returns and Allowances**

**Purchase Discounts**

**Exercise AII-14 (concl'd.)**

| ACCOUNTS RECEIVABLE SUBLEDGER | | |
|:---:|:---:|:---:|
| **Jack Hertz** | **Trudy Stone** | **Dave Waylon** |

| ACCOUNTS PAYABLE SUBLEDGER | | |
|:---:|:---:|:---:|
| **Grass Corp.** | **McGrew Company** | **Sulter Inc.** |

**Problem AII-1A**

| Special Journal | | Subledger | |
|---|---|---|---|
| Sales................................. | S | Accounts Receivable ....... | AR |
| Purchases........................ | P | Accounts Payable ............ | AP |
| Cash Receipts ................. | CR | Merchandise Inventory ... | MI |
| Cash Disbursements...... | CD | No Effect ........................... | NE |
| General Journal .............. | G | | |

| Date | Transaction | Special Journal | Subledger |
|---|---|---|---|
| *Mar. 1* | *Sold merchandise on credit.* | *S* | *AR/MI* |
| 2 | Defective merchandise sold on March 1 was returned by the customer. It was scrapped. | | |
| 3 | Purchased office equipment on credit; terms n/30. | | |
| 5 | Received payment regarding the March 1 sale. | | |
| 10 | Received a credit memorandum from the supplier regarding defective equipment purchased on March 3. | | |
| 14 | Sold merchandise for cash. | | |
| 16 | Purchased merchandise inventory on credit; terms 1/5, n30. | | |
| 17 | Paid the balance owing regarding the March 3 transaction. | | |
| 18 | Purchased merchandise inventory for cash. | | |
| 21 | Paid for the merchandise purchased on March 16. | | |
| 22 | Sold old equipment for cash. | | |
| 30 | Paid salaries for the month of March. | | |
| 30 | Accrued utilities for the month of March. | | |
| 30 | Closed the credit balance in the income summary to Capital. | | |

## Problem AII-2A

| Sales Journal | | | | | Page 3 |
|---|---|---|---|---|---|
| Date | Account Debited | Invoice Number | PR | Accounts Receivable Dr. Sales Cr. | Cost of Goods Sold Dr. Merchandise Inventory Cr. |
|  |  |  |  |  |  |
|  |  |  |  |  |  |
|  |  |  |  |  |  |
|  |  |  |  |  |  |
|  |  |  |  |  |  |
|  |  |  |  |  |  |
|  |  |  |  |  |  |
|  |  |  |  |  |  |

| Cash Receipts Journal | | | | | | | | | Page 3 |
|---|---|---|---|---|---|---|---|---|---|
| Date | Account Credited | PR | Explanation | Cash Dr. | Sales Disc. Dr. | Accts. Rec. Cr. | Sales Cr. | Other Accts. Cr. | COGS Dr. Merch. Inv. Cr. |
|  |  |  |  |  |  |  |  |  |  |
|  |  |  |  |  |  |  |  |  |  |
|  |  |  |  |  |  |  |  |  |  |
|  |  |  |  |  |  |  |  |  |  |
|  |  |  |  |  |  |  |  |  |  |
|  |  |  |  |  |  |  |  |  |  |
|  |  |  |  |  |  |  |  |  |  |

| Purchases Journal | | | | | | | | Page 3 |
|---|---|---|---|---|---|---|---|---|
| Date | Account | Date of Invoice | Terms | PR | Accounts Payable Cr. | Merch. Inventory Dr. | Office Supplies Dr. | Other Accounts Dr. |
|  |  |  |  |  |  |  |  |  |
|  |  |  |  |  |  |  |  |  |
|  |  |  |  |  |  |  |  |  |
|  |  |  |  |  |  |  |  |  |
|  |  |  |  |  |  |  |  |  |
|  |  |  |  |  |  |  |  |  |

| Cash Disbursements Journal | | | | | | | | Page 3 |
|---|---|---|---|---|---|---|---|---|
| Date | Ch. No. | Payee | Account Debited | PR | Cash Cr. | Merch. Inventory Cr. | Other Accounts Dr. | Accounts Payable Dr. |
|  |  |  |  |  |  |  |  |  |
|  |  |  |  |  |  |  |  |  |
|  |  |  |  |  |  |  |  |  |
|  |  |  |  |  |  |  |  |  |
|  |  |  |  |  |  |  |  |  |
|  |  |  |  |  |  |  |  |  |
|  |  |  |  |  |  |  |  |  |

## Problem AII-2A (concl'd.)

### GENERAL JOURNAL

Page____

| Date | Account Titles and Explanation | PR | Debit | Credit |
|------|-------------------------------|----|-------|--------|
|  |  |  |  |  |
|  |  |  |  |  |
|  |  |  |  |  |
|  |  |  |  |  |
|  |  |  |  |  |
|  |  |  |  |  |
|  |  |  |  |  |
|  |  |  |  |  |
|  |  |  |  |  |

## Problem AII-3A    Part 1

### ACCOUNTS RECEIVABLE SUBLEDGER

**Paul Abrams**                                                    ACCOUNT NO. 106-1

| DATE | EXPLANATION | PR | DEBIT | CREDIT | BALANCE |
|------|-------------|----|-------|--------|---------|
|  |  |  |  |  |  |
|  |  |  |  |  |  |
|  |  |  |  |  |  |
|  |  |  |  |  |  |

**Linda Hobart**                                                   ACCOUNT NO. 106-2

| DATE | EXPLANATION | PR | DEBIT | CREDIT | BALANCE |
|------|-------------|----|-------|--------|---------|
|  |  |  |  |  |  |
|  |  |  |  |  |  |
|  |  |  |  |  |  |
|  |  |  |  |  |  |
|  |  |  |  |  |  |

**Kelly Schaefer**                                                 ACCOUNT NO. 106-3

| DATE | EXPLANATION | PR | DEBIT | CREDIT | BALANCE |
|------|-------------|----|-------|--------|---------|
|  |  |  |  |  |  |
|  |  |  |  |  |  |
|  |  |  |  |  |  |
|  |  |  |  |  |  |

## Problem AII-3A (cont'd.)

**Part 2**                    **ACCOUNTS PAYABLE SUBLEDGER**

**Frank's Supply**                                   **ACCOUNT NO. 201-1**

| DATE | EXPLANATION | PR | DEBIT | CREDIT | BALANCE |
|------|-------------|----|-------|--------|---------|
|      |             |    |       |        |         |
|      |             |    |       |        |         |
|      |             |    |       |        |         |

**Baskin Company**                                   **ACCOUNT NO. 201-2**

| DATE | EXPLANATION | PR | DEBIT | CREDIT | BALANCE |
|------|-------------|----|-------|--------|---------|
|      |             |    |       |        |         |
|      |             |    |       |        |         |
|      |             |    |       |        |         |
|      |             |    |       |        |         |

**Sprocket Company**                                 **ACCOUNT NO. 201-3**

| DATE | EXPLANATION | PR | DEBIT | CREDIT | BALANCE |
|------|-------------|----|-------|--------|---------|
|      |             |    |       |        |         |
|      |             |    |       |        |         |
|      |             |    |       |        |         |
|      |             |    |       |        |         |

**Eau Claire Inc.**                                  **ACCOUNT NO. 201-4**

| DATE | EXPLANATION | PR | DEBIT | CREDIT | BALANCE |
|------|-------------|----|-------|--------|---------|
|      |             |    |       |        |         |
|      |             |    |       |        |         |

Part 3

| | Sales Journal | | | | Page 3 |
|---|---|---|---|---|---|
| Date | Account Debited | Invoice Number | PR | Accounts Receivable Dr. Sales Cr. | Cost of Goods Sold Dr. Merchandise Inventory Cr. |
| | | | | | |
| | | | | | |
| | | | | | |
| | | | | | |
| | | | | | |
| | | | | | |
| | | | | | |
| | | | | | |
| | | | | | |
| | | | | | |
| | | | | | |
| | | | | | |
| | | | | | |

| | Cash Receipts Journal | | | | | | | | Page 3 |
|---|---|---|---|---|---|---|---|---|---|
| Date | Accounts Credited | PR | Explanation | Cash Dr. | Sales Disc. Dr. | Accts. Rec. Cr. | Sales Cr. | Other Accts. Cr. | COGS Dr. Merch. Inv. Cr. |
| | | | | | | | | | |
| | | | | | | | | | |
| | | | | | | | | | |
| | | | | | | | | | |
| | | | | | | | | | |
| | | | | | | | | | |
| | | | | | | | | | |
| | | | | | | | | | |
| | | | | | | | | | |
| | | | | | | | | | |
| | | | | | | | | | |
| | | | | | | | | | |
| | | | | | | | | | |
| | | | | | | | | | |

## Problem AII-3A (concl'd.)

| | | | | | Purchases Journal | | | | Page 3 |
|---|---|---|---|---|---|---|---|---|---|
| Date | Account Credited | Date of Invoice | Terms | PR | Accounts Payable Cr. | Merch. Inventory Dr. | Office Supplies Dr. | Other Accounts Dr. | |
| | | | | | | | | | |
| | | | | | | | | | |
| | | | | | | | | | |
| | | | | | | | | | |
| | | | | | | | | | |
| | | | | | | | | | |
| | | | | | | | | | |
| | | | | | | | | | |
| | | | | | | | | | |
| | | | | | | | | | |
| | | | | | | | | | |
| | | | | | | | | | |

| | | | | | Cash Disbursements Journal | | | | Page 3 |
|---|---|---|---|---|---|---|---|---|---|
| Date | Ch. No. | Payee | Account Debited | PR | Cash Cr. | Merch. Inventory Cr. | Other Accounts Dr. | Accounts Payable Dr. | |
| | | | | | | | | | |
| | | | | | | | | | |
| | | | | | | | | | |
| | | | | | | | | | |
| | | | | | | | | | |
| | | | | | | | | | |
| | | | | | | | | | |
| | | | | | | | | | |
| | | | | | | | | | |
| | | | | | | | | | |
| | | | | | | | | | |

## GENERAL JOURNAL                              Page____

| Date | | Account Titles and Explanation | PR | Debit | Credit |
|---|---|---|---|---|---|
| | | | | | |
| | | | | | |
| | | | | | |
| | | | | | |
| | | | | | |
| | | | | | |
| | | | | | |
| | | | | | |
| | | | | | |
| | | | | | |

## Problem AII-4A  Parts 1,4

### GENERAL LEDGER

#### Cash                                                          ACCOUNT NO. 101

| DATE | EXPLANATION | PR | DEBIT | CREDIT | BALANCE |
|------|-------------|----|-------|--------|---------|
| 2017 | | | | | |
| Mar. 31 | Balance brought forward | | | | 167,000 |
| | | | | | |
| | | | | | |

#### Accounts Receivable                                          ACCOUNT NO. 106

| DATE | EXPLANATION | PR | DEBIT | CREDIT | BALANCE |
|------|-------------|----|-------|--------|---------|
| | | | | | |
| | | | | | |

#### Merchandise Inventory                                        ACCOUNT NO. 119

| DATE | EXPLANATION | PR | DEBIT | CREDIT | BALANCE |
|------|-------------|----|-------|--------|---------|
| 2017 | | | | | |
| Mar. 31 | Balance brought forward | | | | 105,000 |
| | | | | | |
| | | | | | |
| | | | | | |
| | | | | | |

#### Office Supplies                                              ACCOUNT NO. 124

| DATE | EXPLANATION | PR | DEBIT | CREDIT | BALANCE |
|------|-------------|----|-------|--------|---------|
| | | | | | |
| | | | | | |
| | | | | | |

#### Store Supplies                                               ACCOUNT NO. 125

| DATE | EXPLANATION | PR | DEBIT | CREDIT | BALANCE |
|------|-------------|----|-------|--------|---------|
| | | | | | |
| | | | | | |

#### Store Equipment                                              ACCOUNT NO. 165

| DATE | EXPLANATION | PR | DEBIT | CREDIT | BALANCE |
|------|-------------|----|-------|--------|---------|
| | | | | | |
| | | | | | |

**Problem AII-4A (cont'd)**

### Accounts Payable                              ACCOUNT NO. 201

| DATE | EXPLANATION | PR | DEBIT | CREDIT | BALANCE |
|------|-------------|----|-------|--------|---------|
|      |             |    |       |        |         |
|      |             |    |       |        |         |
|      |             |    |       |        |         |
|      |             |    |       |        |         |
|      |             |    |       |        |         |

### Long-Term Notes Payable                        ACCOUNT NO. 251

| DATE | EXPLANATION | PR | DEBIT | CREDIT | BALANCE |
|------|-------------|----|-------|--------|---------|
| 2017 |             |    |       |        |         |
| Mar. 31 | Balance brought forward |  |    |        | 167,000 |
|      |             |    |       |        |         |

### Jeff Newton, Capital                           ACCOUNT NO. 301

| DATE | EXPLANATION | PR | DEBIT | CREDIT | BALANCE |
|------|-------------|----|-------|--------|---------|
| 2017 |             |    |       |        |         |
| Mar. 31 | Balance brought forward |  |    |        | 105,000 |
|      |             |    |       |        |         |

### Sales                                          ACCOUNT NO. 413

| DATE | EXPLANATION | PR | DEBIT | CREDIT | BALANCE |
|------|-------------|----|-------|--------|---------|
|      |             |    |       |        |         |
|      |             |    |       |        |         |
|      |             |    |       |        |         |

### Sales Discounts                                ACCOUNT NO. 415

| DATE | EXPLANATION | PR | DEBIT | CREDIT | BALANCE |
|------|-------------|----|-------|--------|---------|
|      |             |    |       |        |         |
|      |             |    |       |        |         |
|      |             |    |       |        |         |

### Cost of Goods Sold                             ACCOUNT NO. 502

| DATE | EXPLANATION | PR | DEBIT | CREDIT | BALANCE |
|------|-------------|----|-------|--------|---------|
|      |             |    |       |        |         |
|      |             |    |       |        |         |
|      |             |    |       |        |         |

### Sales Salaries Expense                         ACCOUNT NO. 621

| DATE | EXPLANATION | PR | DEBIT | CREDIT | BALANCE |
|------|-------------|----|-------|--------|---------|
|      |             |    |       |        |         |
|      |             |    |       |        |         |
|      |             |    |       |        |         |

### Problem AII-4A (cont'd)

**Advertising Expense**                                      **ACCOUNT NO. 655**

| DATE | EXPLANATION | PR | DEBIT | CREDIT | BALANCE |
|------|-------------|----|-------|--------|---------|
|      |             |    |       |        |         |
|      |             |    |       |        |         |
|      |             |    |       |        |         |

*NOTE: For Parts 2 and 3, journalizing and posting, continue journalizing the transactions in the journals provided in Problem AII-3A.*

### Part 5

**Trial Balance**

|  | Debit | Credit |
|--|-------|--------|
|  |       |        |
|  |       |        |
|  |       |        |
|  |       |        |
|  |       |        |
|  |       |        |
|  |       |        |
|  |       |        |
|  |       |        |
|  |       |        |
|  |       |        |
|  |       |        |
|  |       |        |
|  |       |        |
|  |       |        |
|  |       |        |
|  |       |        |
|  |       |        |
|  |       |        |
|  |       |        |
|  |       |        |
|  |       |        |
|  |       |        |
|  |       |        |

Name:_____

**Problem AII-4A (concl'd.)**

## Schedule of Accounts Receivable

| | | |
|---|---|---|
| | | |
| | | |
| | | |
| | | |
| | | |
| | | |

## Schedule of Accounts Payable

| | | |
|---|---|---|
| | | |
| | | |
| | | |
| | | |
| | | |
| | | |

*Analysis component:*

_____
_____
_____
_____
_____
_____
_____
_____
_____
_____
_____

## Problem AII-5A

### Parts 1, 2, 3

| | | | | Sales Journal | Page 3 |
|---|---|---|---|---|---|
| Date | Account Debited | Invoice Number | PR | Accounts Receivable Dr. Sales Cr. | Cost of Goods Sold Dr. Merchandise Inventory Cr. |
| 2017 | | | | | |
| Oct. 6 | M. Craig | 913 | √ | 3,300 | 1,600 |
| 12 | V. Foresman | 914 | √ | 3,650 | 1,900 |
| 15 | A. Ihrig | 915 | √ | 3,100 | 1,700 |
| | | | | | |
| | | | | | |
| | | | | | |
| | | | | | |
| | | | | | |

| | | | | | Purchases Journal | | | Page 2 |
|---|---|---|---|---|---|---|---|---|
| Date | Account | Date of Invoice | Terms | PR | Accounts Payable Cr. | Merch. Inventory Dr. | Office Supplies Dr. | Other Accounts Dr. |
| 2017 | | | | | | | | |
| Oct. 2 | Shore Co. | Oct. 2 | 2/10,n/60 | √ | 3,200 | 3,200 | | |
| 5 | Brown Sup. | Oct. 3 | n/10,EOM | √ | 1,300 | 1,300 | | |
| 15 | Shore Co. | Oct. 15 | 2/10,n/60 | √ | 3,990 | 3,990 | | |
| 15 | Sunshine Co | Oct. 15 | 2/10,n/60 | √ | 2,650 | 2,650 | | |
| | | | | | | | | |
| | | | | | | | | |
| | | | | | | | | |
| | | | | | | | | |
| | | | | | | | | |
| | | | | | | | | |
| | | | | | | | | |

| Cash Receipts Journal | | | | | | | | | Page 3 |
|---|---|---|---|---|---|---|---|---|---|
| Date | Account Credited | PR | Explanation | Cash Dr. | Sales Disc. Dr. | Accts. Rec. Cr. | Sales Cr. | Other Accts. Cr. | COGS Dr. Merch. Inv. Cr. |
| 2017 | | | | | | | | | |
| Oct. 2 | B. Grigsby | √ | Inv. 09/23 | 4,116 | 84 | 4,200 | | | |
| 15 | Sales | | Cash sales | 38,830 | | | 38,830 | | 21,400 |
| 15 | M. Craig | √ | Inv. 10/6 | 2,401 | 49 | 2,450 | | | |
| | | | | | | | | | |
| | | | | | | | | | |
| | | | | | | | | | |
| | | | | | | | | | |
| | | | | | | | | | |
| | | | | | | | | | |
| | | | | | | | | | |
| | | | | | | | | | |
| | | | | | | | | | |
| | | | | | | | | | |

| Cash Disbursements Journal | | | | | | | | Page 4 |
|---|---|---|---|---|---|---|---|---|
| Date | Ch. No. | Payee | Account Debited | PR | Cash Cr. | Merch. Inventory Cr. | Other Accounts Dr. | Accounts Payable Dr. |
| 2017 | | | | | | | | |
| Oct. 2 | 619 | Omni Realty | Rent Exp. | 640 | 2,250 | | 2,250 | |
| 6 | 620 | Fireside Co. | Fireside Co. | √ | 3,724 | 76 | | 3,800 |
| 12 | 621 | Shore Co. | Shore Co. | √ | 3,136 | 64 | | 3,200 |
| 15 | 622 | Jamie Green | Sales Sal. Exp. | 621 | 2,020 | | 2,020 | |
| | | | | | | | | |
| | | | | | | | | |
| | | | | | | | | |
| | | | | | | | | |
| | | | | | | | | |
| | | | | | | | | |
| | | | | | | | | |
| | | | | | | | | |
| | | | | | | | | |
| | | | | | | | | |

**Problem AII-5A (cont'd.)**

## GENERAL JOURNAL

| Date | | | Account Titles and Explanation | PR | Debit | Credit |
|---|---|---|---|---|---|---|
| 2017 | | | | | | |
| Oct. | 4 | | Accounts Payable—Fireside Company | 201/√ | 460 | |
| | | |    Merchandise Inventory | 119 | | 460 |
| | | |    *Received a credit memo for returns.* | | | |
| | | | | | | |
| | 9 | | Sales Returns and Allowances | 414 | 850 | |
| | | |    Accounts Receivable—Marge Craig | 106/√ | | 850 |
| | | |    *Issued a credit memorandum.* | | | |
| | | | | | | |
| | 9 | | Merchandise Inventory | 119 | 430 | |
| | | |    Cost of Goods Sold | 502 | | 430 |
| | | |    *Merchandise returned to inventory.* | | | |
| | | | | | | |
| | | | | | | |
| | | | | | | |
| | | | | | | |
| | | | | | | |
| | | | | | | |
| | | | | | | |
| | | | | | | |
| | | | | | | |
| | | | | | | |
| | | | | | | |

## ACCOUNTS RECEIVABLE SUBLEDGER

### Marge Craig

| DATE | | EXPLANATION | PR | DEBIT | CREDIT | BALANCE |
|---|---|---|---|---|---|---|
| 2017 | | | | | | |
| Oct. | 6 | | S3 | 3,300 | | 3,300 |
| | 9 | | G2 | | 8,50 | 2,450 |
| | 15 | | CR3 | | 2,450 | -0- |
| | | | | | | |

### Vickie Foresman

| DATE | | EXPLANATION | PR | DEBIT | CREDIT | BALANCE |
|---|---|---|---|---|---|---|
| 2017 | | | | | | |
| Oct. | 12 | | S3 | 3,650 | | 3,650 |
| | | | | | | |
| | | | | | | |

## Problem AII-5A (cont'd.)

### Parts 2 and 3

#### Bill Grigsby

| DATE | | EXPLANATION | PR | DEBIT | CREDIT | BALANCE |
|---|---|---|---|---|---|---|
| 2017 | | | | | | |
| Sept. | 23 | | S2 | 4,200 | | 4,200 |
| Oct. | 2 | | CR3 | | 4,200 | -0- |
| | | | | | | |

#### Amy Ihrig

| DATE | | EXPLANATION | PR | DEBIT | CREDIT | BALANCE |
|---|---|---|---|---|---|---|
| 2017 | | | | | | |
| Oct. | 15 | | S3 | 3,100 | | 3,100 |
| | | | | | | |
| | | | | | | |

### ACCOUNTS PAYABLE SUBLEDGER

#### Fireside Company

| DATE | | EXPLANATION | PR | DEBIT | CREDIT | BALANCE |
|---|---|---|---|---|---|---|
| 2017 | | | | | | |
| Sept. | 28 | | P1 | | 4,260 | 4,260 |
| Oct. | 4 | | G2 | 460 | | 3,800 |
| | 6 | | CD4 | 3,800 | | -0- |
| | | | | | | |

#### Brown Supply Company

| DATE | | EXPLANATION | PR | DEBIT | CREDIT | BALANCE |
|---|---|---|---|---|---|---|
| 2017 | | | | | | |
| Oct. | 5 | | P2 | | 1,300 | 1,300 |
| | | | | | | |
| | | | | | | |
| | | | | | | |

#### Sunshine Company

| DATE | | EXPLANATION | PR | DEBIT | CREDIT | BALANCE |
|---|---|---|---|---|---|---|
| 2017 | | | | | | |
| Oct. | 15 | | P2 | | 2,650 | 2,650 |
| | | | | | | |
| | | | | | | |

**Problem AII-5A (cont'd.)**

**Parts 2 and 3   (Cont'd.)**

### Shore Company

| DATE | EXPLANATION | PR | DEBIT | CREDIT | BALANCE |
|---|---|---|---|---|---|
| 2017 | | | | | |
| Oct.   2 | | P2 | | 3,200 | 3,200 |
| 12 | | CD4 | 3,200 | | -0- |
| 15 | | P2 | | 3,990 | 3,990 |
| | | | | | |
| | | | | | |

**Parts 2 and 3**                    **GENERAL LEDGER**

### Cash                                ACCOUNT NO. 101

| DATE | EXPLANATION | PR | DEBIT | CREDIT | BALANCE |
|---|---|---|---|---|---|
| 2017 | | | | | |
| Sept.  30 | Balance | | | | 5,361 |
| | | | | | |
| | | | | | |
| | | | | | |

### Accounts Receivable              ACCOUNT NO. 106

| DATE | EXPLANATION | PR | DEBIT | CREDIT | BALANCE |
|---|---|---|---|---|---|
| 2017 | | | | | |
| Sept.  30 | Balance | | | | 4,200 |
| Oct.   9 | | G2 | | 850 | 3,350 |
| | | | | | |
| | | | | | |
| | | | | | |

### Merchandise Inventory            ACCOUNT NO. 119

| DATE | EXPLANATION | PR | DEBIT | CREDIT | BALANCE |
|---|---|---|---|---|---|
| 2017 | | | | | |
| Sept.  30 | Balance | | | | 66,970 |
| Oct.   4 | | G2 | | 460 | 66,510 |
| 9 | | G2 | 430 | | 66,940 |
| | | | | | |
| | | | | | |
| | | | | | |
| | | | | | |
| | | | | | |
| | | | | | |

Name:_____

## Problem AII-5A (cont'd.)

### Office Supplies — ACCOUNT NO. 124

| DATE | EXPLANATION | PR | DEBIT | CREDIT | BALANCE |
|---|---|---|---|---|---|
| 2017 | | | | | |
| Sept. 30 | Balance | | | | 607 |
| | | | | | |
| | | | | | |
| | | | | | |

### Store Supplies — ACCOUNT NO. 125

| DATE | EXPLANATION | PR | DEBIT | CREDIT | BALANCE |
|---|---|---|---|---|---|
| 2017 | | | | | |
| Sept. 30 | Balance | | | | 346 |
| | | | | | |

### Store Equipment — ACCOUNT NO. 165

| DATE | EXPLANATION | PR | DEBIT | CREDIT | BALANCE |
|---|---|---|---|---|---|
| 2017 | | | | | |
| Sept. 30 | Balance | | | | 42,129 |
| | | | | | |

### Accumulated Depreciation, Store Equipment — ACCOUNT NO. 166

| DATE | EXPLANATION | PR | DEBIT | CREDIT | BALANCE |
|---|---|---|---|---|---|
| 2017 | | | | | |
| Sept. 30 | Balance | | | | 9,153 |
| | | | | | |

### Accounts Payable — ACCOUNT NO. 201

| DATE | EXPLANATION | PR | DEBIT | CREDIT | BALANCE |
|---|---|---|---|---|---|
| 2017 | | | | | |
| Sept. 30 | Balance | | | | 4,260 |
| Oct. 4 | | G2 | 460 | | 3,800 |
| | | | | | |
| | | | | | |
| | | | | | |
| | | | | | |

### Ken Shaw, Capital — ACCOUNT NO. 301

| DATE | EXPLANATION | PR | DEBIT | CREDIT | BALANCE |
|---|---|---|---|---|---|
| 2017 | | | | | |
| Sept. 30 | Balance | | | | 106,200 |
| | | | | | |

## Problem AII-5A (cont'd.)

### Ken Shaw, Withdrawals                                                    ACCOUNT NO. 302

| DATE | EXPLANATION | PR | DEBIT | CREDIT | BALANCE |
|------|-------------|----|-------|--------|---------|
| 2017 | | | | | |
| | | | | | |
| | | | | | |
| | | | | | |

### Sales                                                    ACCOUNT NO. 413

| DATE | EXPLANATION | PR | DEBIT | CREDIT | BALANCE |
|------|-------------|----|-------|--------|---------|
| 2017 | | | | | |
| | | | | | |
| | | | | | |
| | | | | | |

### Sales Returns and Allowances                                                    ACCOUNT NO. 414

| DATE | EXPLANATION | PR | DEBIT | CREDIT | BALANCE |
|------|-------------|----|-------|--------|---------|
| 2017 | | | | | |
| Oct.   9 | | G2 | 850 | | 850 |
| | | | | | |

### Sales Discounts                                                    ACCOUNT NO. 415

| DATE | EXPLANATION | PR | DEBIT | CREDIT | BALANCE |
|------|-------------|----|-------|--------|---------|
| 2017 | | | | | |
| | | | | | |

### Cost of Goods Sold                                                    ACCOUNT NO. 502

| DATE | EXPLANATION | PR | DEBIT | CREDIT | BALANCE |
|------|-------------|----|-------|--------|---------|
| 2017 | | | | | |
| Oct.   9 | | G2 | | 430 | (430) |
| | | | | | |
| | | | | | |

### Sales Salaries Expense                                                    ACCOUNT NO. 621

| DATE | EXPLANATION | PR | DEBIT | CREDIT | BALANCE |
|------|-------------|----|-------|--------|---------|
| 2017 | | | | | |
| Oct. 15 | | CD4 | 2,020 | | 2,020 |
| | | | | | |

### Rent Expense                                                    ACCOUNT NO. 640

| DATE | EXPLANATION | PR | DEBIT | CREDIT | BALANCE |
|------|-------------|----|-------|--------|---------|
| 2017 | | | | | |
| Oct.   2 | | CD4 | 2,250 | | 2,250 |
| | | | | | |

**Problem AII-5A (cont'd.)**

| | Utilities Expense | | | | ACCOUNT NO. 690 |
|---|---|---|---|---|---|
| DATE | EXPLANATION | PR | DEBIT | CREDIT | BALANCE |
| 2017 | | | | | |
| | | | | | |

**Part 4**

**SASKAN ENTERPRISES**
**Trial Balance**
**October 31, 2017**

| | | |
|---|---|---|
| | | |
| | | |
| | | |
| | | |
| | | |
| | | |
| | | |
| | | |
| | | |
| | | |
| | | |
| | | |
| | | |
| | | |
| | | |
| | | |
| | | |
| | | |
| | | |
| | | |
| | | |
| | | |
| | | |
| | | |
| | | |
| | | |
| | | |
| | | |
| | | |
| | | |

**Problem AII-5A (concl'd.)**

**Part 4**

<table>
<tr><td colspan="3" align="center">SASKAN ENTERPRISES</td></tr>
<tr><td colspan="3" align="center">Schedule of Accounts Receivable</td></tr>
<tr><td colspan="3" align="center">October 31, 2017</td></tr>
<tr><td></td><td></td><td></td></tr>
<tr><td></td><td></td><td></td></tr>
<tr><td></td><td></td><td></td></tr>
<tr><td></td><td></td><td></td></tr>
<tr><td></td><td></td><td></td></tr>
<tr><td></td><td></td><td></td></tr>
<tr><td></td><td></td><td></td></tr>
</table>

<table>
<tr><td colspan="3" align="center">SASKAN ENTERPRISES</td></tr>
<tr><td colspan="3" align="center">Schedule of Accounts Payable</td></tr>
<tr><td colspan="3" align="center">October 31, 2017</td></tr>
<tr><td></td><td></td><td></td></tr>
<tr><td></td><td></td><td></td></tr>
<tr><td></td><td></td><td></td></tr>
<tr><td></td><td></td><td></td></tr>
<tr><td></td><td></td><td></td></tr>
<tr><td></td><td></td><td></td></tr>
<tr><td></td><td></td><td></td></tr>
</table>

**Problem AII-6A**

| | | | | Sales Journal | | Page |
|---|---|---|---|---|---|---|
| Date | Account Debited | Invoice Number | PR | Accounts Receivable Dr. Sales Cr. | PR | Cost of Goods Sold Dr. Merch. Inventory Cr. |
| | | | | | | |
| | | | | | | |
| | | | | | | |
| | | | | | | |
| | | | | | | |
| | | | | | | |

| | | | | | Purchases Journal | | | | Page |
|---|---|---|---|---|---|---|---|---|---|
| Date | Account Credited | Date of Invoice | Terms | PR | Accts. Payable Cr. | PR | Merch. Inventory Dr. | Office Supplies Dr. | Other Accounts Dr. |
| | | | | | | | | | |
| | | | | | | | | | |
| | | | | | | | | | |
| | | | | | | | | | |

*NOTE: An additional PR column has been added to both journals to facilitate the referencing of inventory entries into the inventory subsidiary ledger.*

Name:_____

## Problem AII-6A (concl'd.)

### Inventory Subledger Record – FIFO Perpetual

| Date | PR | Purchases | Sales (at cost) | Inventory Balance |
|------|-----|-----------|-----------------|-------------------|
|      |     |           |                 |                   |
|      |     |           |                 |                   |
|      |     |           |                 |                   |
|      |     |           |                 |                   |
|      |     |           |                 |                   |
|      |     |           |                 |                   |
|      |     |           |                 |                   |
|      |     |           |                 |                   |
|      |     |           |                 |                   |
|      |     |           |                 |                   |
|      |     |           |                 |                   |
|      |     |           |                 |                   |
|      |     |           |                 |                   |
|      |     |           |                 |                   |
|      |     |           |                 |                   |
|      |     |           |                 |                   |
|      |     |           |                 |                   |
|      |     |           |                 |                   |
|      |     |           |                 |                   |
|      |     |           |                 |                   |

*Note: An additional PR column has been added to the Inventory Subledger Record to facilitate referencing of inventory entries.*

## *Problem AII-7A

### Part 1        ACCOUNTS RECEIVABLE SUBLEDGER

Paul Abrams        **ACCOUNT NO. 106-1**

| DATE | EXPLANATION | PR | DEBIT | CREDIT | BALANCE |
|------|-------------|-----|-------|--------|---------|
|      |             |     |       |        |         |
|      |             |     |       |        |         |
|      |             |     |       |        |         |
|      |             |     |       |        |         |

## *Problem AII-7A (cont'd.)

| | Linda Hobart | | | | ACCOUNT NO. 106-2 |
|---|---|---|---|---|---|
| DATE | EXPLANATION | PR | DEBIT | CREDIT | BALANCE |
| | | | | | |
| | | | | | |
| | | | | | |
| | | | | | |
| | | | | | |

| | Kelly Schaefer | | | | ACCOUNT NO. 106-3 |
|---|---|---|---|---|---|
| DATE | EXPLANATION | PR | DEBIT | CREDIT | BALANCE |
| | | | | | |
| | | | | | |
| | | | | | |

**Part 2**                          **ACCOUNTS PAYABLE SUBLEDGER**

| | Frank's Supply | | | | ACCOUNT NO. 201-1 |
|---|---|---|---|---|---|
| DATE | EXPLANATION | PR | DEBIT | CREDIT | BALANCE |
| | | | | | |
| | | | | | |
| | | | | | |
| | | | | | |

| | Baskin Company | | | | ACCOUNT NO. 201-2 |
|---|---|---|---|---|---|
| DATE | EXPLANATION | PR | DEBIT | CREDIT | BALANCE |
| | | | | | |
| | | | | | |
| | | | | | |
| | | | | | |
| | | | | | |

| | Sprocket Company | | | | ACCOUNT NO. 201-3 |
|---|---|---|---|---|---|
| DATE | EXPLANATION | PR | DEBIT | CREDIT | BALANCE |
| | | | | | |
| | | | | | |
| | | | | | |
| | | | | | |
| | | | | | |

**\*Problem AII-7A (cont'd.)**

| | Eau Claire Inc. | | | | ACCOUNT NO. 201-4 |
|---|---|---|---|---|---|
| **DATE** | **EXPLANATION** | **PR** | **DEBIT** | **CREDIT** | **BALANCE** |
| | | | | | |
| | | | | | |
| | | | | | |
| | | | | | |

**Part 3**

| | Sales Journal | | | Page |
|---|---|---|---|---|
| **Date** | **Account Debited** | **Invoice No.** | **PR** | **Accounts Receivable Dr. Sales Cr.** |
| | | | | |
| | | | | |
| | | | | |
| | | | | |
| | | | | |
| | | | | |
| | | | | |
| | | | | |
| | | | | |
| | | | | |

| | Cash Receipts Journal | | | | | | | Page |
|---|---|---|---|---|---|---|---|---|
| **Date** | **Account Credited** | **PR** | **Explanation** | **Cash Dr.** | **Sales Disc. Dr.** | **Accts. Rec. Cr.** | **Sales Cr.** | **Other Accts. Cr.** |
| | | | | | | | | |
| | | | | | | | | |
| | | | | | | | | |
| | | | | | | | | |
| | | | | | | | | |
| | | | | | | | | |
| | | | | | | | | |
| | | | | | | | | |
| | | | | | | | | |
| | | | | | | | | |

Name:_____

## *Problem AII-7A (concl'd.)

| | | | | | Purchases Journal | | | Page | |
|---|---|---|---|---|---|---|---|---|---|
| Date | Account Credited | Date of Invoice | Terms | PR | Accts. Payable Cr. | Purchases Dr. | Office Supplies Dr. | Other Accts. Dr. |
| | | | | | | | | |
| | | | | | | | | |
| | | | | | | | | |
| | | | | | | | | |
| | | | | | | | | |
| | | | | | | | | |
| | | | | | | | | |
| | | | | | | | | |
| | | | | | | | | |

| | | | | | Cash Disbursements Journal | | | Page | |
|---|---|---|---|---|---|---|---|---|---|
| Date | Ch. No. | Payee | Account Debited | PR | Cash Cr. | Purch. Disc. Cr. | Other Accounts Dr. | Accts. Payable Dr. |
| | | | | | | | | |
| | | | | | | | | |
| | | | | | | | | |
| | | | | | | | | |
| | | | | | | | | |
| | | | | | | | | |
| | | | | | | | | |
| | | | | | | | | |
| | | | | | | | | |

### GENERAL JOURNAL

Page_____

| Date | Account Titles and Explanation | PR | Debit | Credit |
|---|---|---|---|---|
| | | | | |
| | | | | |
| | | | | |
| | | | | |
| | | | | |
| | | | | |
| | | | | |
| | | | | |
| | | | | |
| | | | | |
| | | | | |
| | | | | |
| | | | | |

# Appendix II

Name:_____

## *Problem AII-8A

Parts 1 and 4

### GENERAL LEDGER

#### Cash                                                                                          ACCOUNT NO. 101

| DATE | EXPLANATION | PR | DEBIT | CREDIT | BALANCE |
|---|---|---|---|---|---|
| 2017 | | | | | |
| Mar. 31 | | | | | 167,000 |
| | | | | | |
| | | | | | |

#### Accounts Receivable                                                          ACCOUNT NO. 106

| DATE | EXPLANATION | PR | DEBIT | CREDIT | BALANCE |
|---|---|---|---|---|---|
| | | | | | |
| | | | | | |
| | | | | | |

#### Merchandise Inventory                                                    ACCOUNT NO. 119

| DATE | EXPLANATION | PR | DEBIT | CREDIT | BALANCE |
|---|---|---|---|---|---|
| 2017 | | | | | |
| Mar. 31 | | | | | 105,000 |
| | | | | | |

#### Office Supplies                                                                    ACCOUNT NO. 124

| DATE | EXPLANATION | PR | DEBIT | CREDIT | BALANCE |
|---|---|---|---|---|---|
| | | | | | |
| | | | | | |
| | | | | | |

#### Store Supplies                                                                    ACCOUNT NO. 125

| DATE | EXPLANATION | PR | DEBIT | CREDIT | BALANCE |
|---|---|---|---|---|---|
| | | | | | |
| | | | | | |
| | | | | | |

#### Store Equipment                                                              ACCOUNT NO. 165

| DATE | EXPLANATION | PR | DEBIT | CREDIT | BALANCE |
|---|---|---|---|---|---|
| | | | | | |
| | | | | | |
| | | | | | |

#### Accounts Payable                                                            ACCOUNT NO. 201

| DATE | EXPLANATION | PR | DEBIT | CREDIT | BALANCE |
|---|---|---|---|---|---|
| | | | | | |
| | | | | | |
| | | | | | |
| | | | | | |

**\*Problem AII-8A (cont'd)**

### Long-Term Notes Payable — ACCOUNT NO. 251

| DATE | EXPLANATION | PR | DEBIT | CREDIT | BALANCE |
|------|-------------|----|-------|--------|---------|
| 2017 | | | | | |
| Mar. 31 | | | | | 167,000 |
| | | | | | |

### Jeff Newton, Capital — ACCOUNT NO. 301

| DATE | EXPLANATION | PR | DEBIT | CREDIT | BALANCE |
|------|-------------|----|-------|--------|---------|
| 2017 | | | | | |
| Mar. 31 | | | | | 105,000 |
| | | | | | |

### Sales — ACCOUNT NO. 413

| DATE | EXPLANATION | PR | DEBIT | CREDIT | BALANCE |
|------|-------------|----|-------|--------|---------|
| | | | | | |
| | | | | | |
| | | | | | |

### Sales Discounts — ACCOUNT NO. 415

| DATE | EXPLANATION | PR | DEBIT | CREDIT | BALANCE |
|------|-------------|----|-------|--------|---------|
| | | | | | |
| | | | | | |
| | | | | | |

### Purchases — ACCOUNT NO. 505

| DATE | EXPLANATION | PR | DEBIT | CREDIT | BALANCE |
|------|-------------|----|-------|--------|---------|
| | | | | | |
| | | | | | |
| | | | | | |

### Purchases Discounts — ACCOUNT NO. 506

| DATE | EXPLANATION | PR | DEBIT | CREDIT | BALANCE |
|------|-------------|----|-------|--------|---------|
| | | | | | |
| | | | | | |
| | | | | | |

### Purchases Returns and Allowances — ACCOUNT NO. 507

| DATE | EXPLANATION | PR | DEBIT | CREDIT | BALANCE |
|------|-------------|----|-------|--------|---------|
| | | | | | |
| | | | | | |
| | | | | | |

**\*Problem AII-8A (cont'd)**

### Sales Salaries Expense                    ACCOUNT NO. 621

| DATE | EXPLANATION | PR | DEBIT | CREDIT | BALANCE |
|------|-------------|----|----|----|----|
|  |  |  |  |  |  |
|  |  |  |  |  |  |
|  |  |  |  |  |  |

### Advertising Expense                    ACCOUNT NO. 655

| DATE | EXPLANATION | PR | DEBIT | CREDIT | BALANCE |
|------|-------------|----|----|----|----|
|  |  |  |  |  |  |
|  |  |  |  |  |  |
|  |  |  |  |  |  |

**NOTE:** For Parts 2 and 3, journalizing and posting, continue journalizing the transactions in the journals provided in \*Problem AII-7A.

## Trial Balance

| | Debit | Credit |
|---|---|---|
| | | |
| | | |
| | | |
| | | |
| | | |
| | | |
| | | |
| | | |
| | | |
| | | |
| | | |
| | | |
| | | |
| | | |
| | | |
| | | |
| | | |
| | | |
| | | |
| | | |
| | | |
| | | |

**\*Problem AII-8A (concl'd.)**

### Schedule of Accounts Receivable

|  |  |  |
|---|---|---|
|  |  |  |
|  |  |  |
|  |  |  |
|  |  |  |

### Schedule of Accounts Payable

|  |  |  |
|---|---|---|
|  |  |  |
|  |  |  |
|  |  |  |

**Problem AII-1B**

| | Special Journal | | | Subledger | |
|---|---|---|---|---|---|
| | Sales.................................... | S | | Accounts Receivable ....... | AR |
| | Purchases......................... | P | | Accounts Payable ............. | AP |
| | Cash Receipts ................. | CR | | Merchandise Inventory ... | MI |
| | Cash Disbursements...... | CD | | No Effect ........................... | NE |
| | General Journal .............. | G | | | |

| Date | Transaction | Special Journal | Subledger |
|---|---|---|---|
| May 1 | The owner invested an automobile into the business. | | |
| 2 | Sold merchandise and received cash. | | |
| 3 | Purchased merchandise inventory on credit; terms 1/5, n30. | | |
| 4 | Sold merchandise on credit. | | |
| 5 | The customer of May 4 returned defective merchandise; the merchandise was scrapped. | | |
| 6 | Regarding the May 3 purchase, received a credit memorandum from the supplier granting an allowance. | | |
| 15 | Paid mid-month salaries. | | |
| 17 | Purchased office supplies on credit; terms n/30. | | |
| 19 | Paid for the balance owing on the May 3 purchase. | | |
| 22 | Received payment on the May 4 sale. | | |
| 25 | Borrowed money from bank. | | |
| 29 | Purchased merchandise inventory; paid cash. | | |
| 30 | Accrued interest revenue. | | |
| 30 | Closed all revenue accounts to the Income Summary account. | | |

### Sales Journal — Page S1

| Date | Account Debited | Invoice Number | PR | Accounts Receivable Dr. Sales Cr. | Cost of Goods Sold Dr. Merchandise Inventory Cr. |
|------|-----------------|----------------|-----|-----------------------------------|--------------------------------------------------|
|  |  |  |  |  |  |
|  |  |  |  |  |  |
|  |  |  |  |  |  |
|  |  |  |  |  |  |
|  |  |  |  |  |  |
|  |  |  |  |  |  |

### Cash Receipts Journal — Page CR1

| Date | Accounts Credited | PR | Explanation | Cash Dr. | Sales Disc. Dr. | Accts. Rec. Cr. | Sales Cr. | Other Accts. Cr. | COGS Dr. Merch. Inv. Cr. |
|------|-------------------|-----|-------------|----------|-----------------|-----------------|-----------|------------------|--------------------------|
|  |  |  |  |  |  |  |  |  |  |
|  |  |  |  |  |  |  |  |  |  |
|  |  |  |  |  |  |  |  |  |  |
|  |  |  |  |  |  |  |  |  |  |
|  |  |  |  |  |  |  |  |  |  |

### Purchases Journal — Page P1

| Date | Account Credited | Date of Invoice | Terms | PR | Accounts Payable Cr. | Merch. Inventory Dr. | Office Supplies Dr. | Other Accounts Dr. |
|------|------------------|-----------------|-------|-----|----------------------|----------------------|---------------------|--------------------|
|  |  |  |  |  |  |  |  |  |
|  |  |  |  |  |  |  |  |  |
|  |  |  |  |  |  |  |  |  |
|  |  |  |  |  |  |  |  |  |
|  |  |  |  |  |  |  |  |  |

### Cash Disbursements Journal — Page CD1

| Date | Ch. No. | Payee | Account Debited | PR | Cash Cr. | Merch. Inventory Cr. | Other Accounts Dr. | Accounts Payable Dr. |
|------|---------|-------|-----------------|-----|----------|----------------------|--------------------|----------------------|
|  |  |  |  |  |  |  |  |  |
|  |  |  |  |  |  |  |  |  |
|  |  |  |  |  |  |  |  |  |
|  |  |  |  |  |  |  |  |  |
|  |  |  |  |  |  |  |  |  |
|  |  |  |  |  |  |  |  |  |

**Problem AII-2B (concl'd.)**

## GENERAL JOURNAL                                    Page_____

| Date | Account Titles and Explanation | PR | Debit | Credit |
|------|-------------------------------|----|-------|--------|
|      |                               |    |       |        |
|      |                               |    |       |        |
|      |                               |    |       |        |
|      |                               |    |       |        |
|      |                               |    |       |        |
|      |                               |    |       |        |
|      |                               |    |       |        |
|      |                               |    |       |        |
|      |                               |    |       |        |
|      |                               |    |       |        |
|      |                               |    |       |        |
|      |                               |    |       |        |
|      |                               |    |       |        |

**Problem AII-3B    Parts 2, 3, 5**

**Part 1**                             **ACCOUNTS RECEIVABLE SUBLEDGER**

**Kelly Grody**                                    ACCOUNT NO. 106-1

| DATE | EXPLANATION | PR | DEBIT | CREDIT | BALANCE |
|------|-------------|----|-------|--------|---------|
|      |             |    |       |        |         |
|      |             |    |       |        |         |
|      |             |    |       |        |         |
|      |             |    |       |        |         |

**Karen Harden**                                    ACCOUNT NO. 106-2

| DATE | EXPLANATION | PR | DEBIT | CREDIT | BALANCE |
|------|-------------|----|-------|--------|---------|
|      |             |    |       |        |         |
|      |             |    |       |        |         |
|      |             |    |       |        |         |
|      |             |    |       |        |         |

**Paul Kane**                                    ACCOUNT NO. 106-3

| DATE | EXPLANATION | PR | DEBIT | CREDIT | BALANCE |
|------|-------------|----|-------|--------|---------|
|      |             |    |       |        |         |
|      |             |    |       |        |         |
|      |             |    |       |        |         |
|      |             |    |       |        |         |

**Problem AII-3B (cont'd.)**

**Part 2**

### ACCOUNTS PAYABLE SUBLEDGER

**Beech Company**                                    ACCOUNT NO. 201-1

| DATE | EXPLANATION | PR | DEBIT | CREDIT | BALANCE |
|------|-------------|----|-------|--------|---------|
|      |             |    |       |        |         |
|      |             |    |       |        |         |
|      |             |    |       |        |         |
|      |             |    |       |        |         |
|      |             |    |       |        |         |

**Blackwater Inc.**                                    ACCOUNT NO. 201-2

| DATE | EXPLANATION | PR | DEBIT | CREDIT | BALANCE |
|------|-------------|----|-------|--------|---------|
|      |             |    |       |        |         |
|      |             |    |       |        |         |
|      |             |    |       |        |         |

**Poppe's Supply**                                    ACCOUNT NO. 201-3

| DATE | EXPLANATION | PR | DEBIT | CREDIT | BALANCE |
|------|-------------|----|-------|--------|---------|
|      |             |    |       |        |         |
|      |             |    |       |        |         |
|      |             |    |       |        |         |
|      |             |    |       |        |         |

**Sprague Company**                                    ACCOUNT NO. 201-4

| DATE | EXPLANATION | PR | DEBIT | CREDIT | BALANCE |
|------|-------------|----|-------|--------|---------|
|      |             |    |       |        |         |
|      |             |    |       |        |         |
|      |             |    |       |        |         |
|      |             |    |       |        |         |

**Part 3**

| Sales Journal | | | | | Page 3 |
|------|-------------------|-------------------|----|------------------------------------|----------------------------------------------------|
| Date | Account Debited | Invoice Number | PR | Accounts Receivable Dr. Sales Cr. | Cost of Goods Sold Dr. Merchandise Inventory Cr. |
|      |                   |                   |    |                                    |                                                    |
|      |                   |                   |    |                                    |                                                    |
|      |                   |                   |    |                                    |                                                    |
|      |                   |                   |    |                                    |                                                    |
|      |                   |                   |    |                                    |                                                    |
|      |                   |                   |    |                                    |                                                    |
|      |                   |                   |    |                                    |                                                    |
|      |                   |                   |    |                                    |                                                    |

## Problem AII-3B (cont'd.)

| Cash Receipts Journal | | | | | | | | | Page 3 |
|---|---|---|---|---|---|---|---|---|---|
| Date | Account Credited | PR | Explanation | Cash Dr. | Sales Disc. Dr. | Accts. Rec. Cr. | Sales Cr. | Other Accts. Cr. | COGS Dr. Merch. Inv. Cr. |
| | | | | | | | | | |
| | | | | | | | | | |
| | | | | | | | | | |
| | | | | | | | | | |
| | | | | | | | | | |
| | | | | | | | | | |
| | | | | | | | | | |
| | | | | | | | | | |
| | | | | | | | | | |
| | | | | | | | | | |

| Purchases Journal | | | | | | | | Page 3 |
|---|---|---|---|---|---|---|---|---|
| Date | Account Credited | Date of Invoice | Terms | PR | Accounts Payable Cr. | Merch. Inventory Dr. | Office Supplies Dr. | Other Accounts Dr. |
| | | | | | | | | |
| | | | | | | | | |
| | | | | | | | | |
| | | | | | | | | |
| | | | | | | | | |
| | | | | | | | | |
| | | | | | | | | |
| | | | | | | | | |
| | | | | | | | | |
| | | | | | | | | |

| Cash Disbursements Journal | | | | | | | | Page 3 |
|---|---|---|---|---|---|---|---|---|
| Date | Ch. No. | Payee | Account Debited | PR | Cash Cr. | Merch. Inventory Cr. | Other Accounts Dr. | Accounts Payable Dr. |
| | | | | | | | | |
| | | | | | | | | |
| | | | | | | | | |
| | | | | | | | | |
| | | | | | | | | |
| | | | | | | | | |
| | | | | | | | | |
| | | | | | | | | |
| | | | | | | | | |
| | | | | | | | | |

**Problem AII-3B (concl'd.)**

### GENERAL JOURNAL

Page____

| Date | | Account Titles and Explanation | PR | Debit | Credit |
|---|---|---|---|---|---|
| | | | | | |
| | | | | | |
| | | | | | |
| | | | | | |
| | | | | | |
| | | | | | |
| | | | | | |
| | | | | | |
| | | | | | |
| | | | | | |
| | | | | | |
| | | | | | |
| | | | | | |
| | | | | | |

**Problem AII-4B**

**Part 1, 4**

### GENERAL LEDGER

Cash                                                    ACCOUNT NO. 101

| DATE | EXPLANATION | PR | DEBIT | CREDIT | BALANCE |
|---|---|---|---|---|---|
| 2017 | | | | | |
| Jun. 30 | Balance brought forward | | | | 190,000 |
| | | | | | |
| | | | | | |

Accounts Receivable                                ACCOUNT NO. 106

| DATE | EXPLANATION | PR | DEBIT | CREDIT | BALANCE |
|---|---|---|---|---|---|
| | | | | | |
| | | | | | |
| | | | | | |

Merchandise Inventory                             ACCOUNT NO. 119

| DATE | EXPLANATION | PR | DEBIT | CREDIT | BALANCE |
|---|---|---|---|---|---|
| 2017 | | | | | |
| Jun. 30 | Balance brought forward | | | | 334,000 |
| | | | | | |
| | | | | | |
| | | | | | |
| | | | | | |
| | | | | | |

**Problem AII-4B (cont'd.)**

### Office Supplies — ACCOUNT NO. 124

| DATE | EXPLANATION | PR | DEBIT | CREDIT | BALANCE |
|------|-------------|----|-------|--------|---------|
|      |             |    |       |        |         |
|      |             |    |       |        |         |
|      |             |    |       |        |         |

### Store Supplies — ACCOUNT NO. 125

| DATE | EXPLANATION | PR | DEBIT | CREDIT | BALANCE |
|------|-------------|----|-------|--------|---------|
|      |             |    |       |        |         |
|      |             |    |       |        |         |
|      |             |    |       |        |         |

### Store Equipment — ACCOUNT NO. 165

| DATE | EXPLANATION | PR | DEBIT | CREDIT | BALANCE |
|------|-------------|----|-------|--------|---------|
|      |             |    |       |        |         |
|      |             |    |       |        |         |
|      |             |    |       |        |         |

### Accounts Payable — ACCOUNT NO. 201

| DATE | EXPLANATION | PR | DEBIT | CREDIT | BALANCE |
|------|-------------|----|-------|--------|---------|
|      |             |    |       |        |         |
|      |             |    |       |        |         |
|      |             |    |       |        |         |
|      |             |    |       |        |         |
|      |             |    |       |        |         |

### Long-Term Notes Payable — ACCOUNT NO. 251

| DATE | EXPLANATION | PR | DEBIT | CREDIT | BALANCE |
|------|-------------|----|-------|--------|---------|
| 2017 |             |    |       |        |         |
| Jun. 30 | Balance brought forward |  |  |  | 334,000 |
|      |             |    |       |        |         |

### Gene Duncan, Capital — ACCOUNT NO. 301

| DATE | EXPLANATION | PR | DEBIT | CREDIT | BALANCE |
|------|-------------|----|-------|--------|---------|
| 2017 |             |    |       |        |         |
| Jun. 30 | Balance brought forward |  |  |  | 190,000 |
|      |             |    |       |        |         |

**Problem AII-4B (cont'd.)**

Sales ACCOUNT NO. 413

| DATE | EXPLANATION | PR | DEBIT | CREDIT | BALANCE |
|---|---|---|---|---|---|
| | | | | | |
| | | | | | |
| | | | | | |

Sales Discounts ACCOUNT NO. 415

| DATE | EXPLANATION | PR | DEBIT | CREDIT | BALANCE |
|---|---|---|---|---|---|
| | | | | | |
| | | | | | |
| | | | | | |

Cost of Goods Sold ACCOUNT NO. 502

| DATE | EXPLANATION | PR | DEBIT | CREDIT | BALANCE |
|---|---|---|---|---|---|
| | | | | | |
| | | | | | |
| | | | | | |

Sales Salaries Expense ACCOUNT NO. 621

| DATE | EXPLANATION | PR | DEBIT | CREDIT | BALANCE |
|---|---|---|---|---|---|
| | | | | | |
| | | | | | |
| | | | | | |

Advertising Expense ACCOUNT NO. 655

| DATE | EXPLANATION | PR | DEBIT | CREDIT | BALANCE |
|---|---|---|---|---|---|
| | | | | | |
| | | | | | |
| | | | | | |

*NOTE: For Parts 2, 3, and 4, journalizing and posting, continue journalizing the transactions in the accounts provided in Problem AII-3A.*

**Problem AII-4B (cont'd.)**

**Part 5**

**DUNCAN INDUSTRIES**

**Trial Balance**

**July 31, 2017**

| | Debit | Credit |
|---|---|---|
| | | |
| | | |
| | | |
| | | |
| | | |
| | | |
| | | |
| | | |
| | | |
| | | |
| | | |
| | | |
| | | |
| | | |
| | | |
| | | |
| | | |
| | | |
| | | |

**DUNCAN INDUSTRIES**

**Schedule of Accounts Receivable**

**July 31, 2017**

| | | |
|---|---|---|
| | | |
| | | |
| | | |
| | | |
| | | |
| | | |

**DUNCAN INDUSTRIES**

**Schedule of Accounts Payable**

**July 31, 2017**

| | | |
|---|---|---|
| | | |
| | | |
| | | |
| | | |
| | | |
| | | |

## Problem AII-4B (concl'd.)

### Analysis component:

_____
_____
_____
_____
_____
_____
_____
_____
_____

## Problem AII-5B

### Part 1

| | | | | Sales Journal | Page 3 |
|---|---|---|---|---|---|
| Date | Account Debited | Invoice Number | PR | Accounts Receivable Dr. Sales Cr. | Cost of Goods Sold Dr. Merchandise Inventory Cr. |
| 2017 | | | | | |
| Oct. 6 | M. Craig | 913 | √ | 6,600 | 3,600 |
| 12 | H. Flatt | 914 | √ | 7,300 | 4,000 |
| 15 | A. Izon | 915 | √ | 6,200 | 3,400 |
| | | | | | |
| | | | | | |
| | | | | | |
| | | | | | |

| | | | Cash Receipts Journal | | | | | | Page 3 |
|---|---|---|---|---|---|---|---|---|---|
| Date | Account Credited | PR | Explanation | Cash Dr. | Sales Disc. Dr. | Accts. Rec. Cr. | Sales Cr. | Other Accts. Cr. | COGS Dr. Merch. Inv. Cr. |
| 2017 | | | | | | | | | |
| Oct. 2 | J. Wildman | √ | Inv. 09/23 | 8,232 | 168 | 8,400 | | | |
| 15 | Sales | | Cash sales | 77,660 | | | 77,660 | | 42,800 |
| 15 | M. Craig | √ | Inv. 10/6 | 4,802 | 98 | 4,900 | | | |
| | | | | | | | | | |
| | | | | | | | | | |
| | | | | | | | | | |
| | | | | | | | | | |
| | | | | | | | | | |
| | | | | | | | | | |

## Problem AII-5B (cont'd.)

| Purchases Journal | | | | | | | | Page 2 |
|---|---|---|---|---|---|---|---|---|
| Date | Account Credited | Date of Invoice | Terms | PR | Accounts Payable Cr. | Merch. Inventory Dr. | Office Supplies Dr. | Other Accounts Dr. |
| 2017 | | | | | | | | |
| Oct. 2 | Walters Co. | 10/2 | 2/10,n/60 | √ | 6,400 | 6,400 | | |
| 5 | Green Supply | 10/3 | n/10,EOM | √ | 2,600 | 2,600 | | |
| 15 | Walters Co. | 10/15 | 2/10,n/60 | √ | 7,980 | 7,980 | | |
| 15 | Sunshine Co. | 10/15 | 2/10,n/60 | √ | 5,300 | 5,300 | | |
| | | | | | | | | |
| | | | | | | | | |
| | | | | | | | | |
| | | | | | | | | |
| | | | | | | | | |

| Cash Disbursements Journal | | | | | | | | Page 4 |
|---|---|---|---|---|---|---|---|---|
| Date | Ch. No. | Payee | Account Debited | PR | Cash Cr. | Merch. Inventory Cr. | Other Accounts Dr. | Accounts Payable Dr. |
| 2017 | | | | | | | | |
| Oct. 2 | 619 | Omni Realty | Rent Exp. | 640 | 4,500 | | 4,500 | |
| 6 | 620 | Fireside Co. | Fireside Co. | √ | 7,448 | 152 | | 7,600 |
| 12 | 621 | Walters Co. | Walters Co. | √ | 6,272 | 128 | | 6,400 |
| 15 | 622 | Jamie Ford | Sales Sal. Exp. | 621 | 5,240 | | 5,240 | |
| | | | | | | | | |
| | | | | | | | | |
| | | | | | | | | |
| | | | | | | | | |
| | | | | | | | | |
| | | | | | | | | |
| | | | | | | | | |
| | | | | | | | | |

**Problem AII-5B (cont'd.)**

### GENERAL JOURNAL

| Date | | Account Titles and Explanation | PR | Debit | Credit |
|------|---|------------------------------|-----|-------|--------|
| 2017 | | | | | |
| Oct. | 4 | Accounts Payable—Fireside Company | 201/√ | 920 | |
| | | Merchandise Inventory | 119 | | 920 |
| | | *Received a credit memo for returns.* | | | |
| | | | | | |
| | 9 | Sales Returns and Allowances | 414 | 1,700 | |
| | | Accounts Receivable—Marge Craig | 106/√ | | 1,700 |
| | | *Issued a credit memorandum.* | | | |
| | | | | | |
| | | | | | |
| | | | | | |
| | | | | | |
| | | | | | |
| | | | | | |
| | | | | | |
| | | | | | |
| | | | | | |
| | | | | | |
| | | | | | |
| | | | | | |
| | | | | | |

### ACCOUNTS RECEIVABLE SUBLEDGER

**Marge Craig**

| DATE | | EXPLANATION | PR | DEBIT | CREDIT | BALANCE |
|------|---|------------|-----|-------|--------|---------|
| 2017 | | | | | | |
| Oct. | 6 | | S3 | 6,600 | | 6,600 |
| | 9 | | G2 | | 1,700 | 4,900 |
| | 15 | | CR3 | | 4,900 | -0- |
| | | | | | | |

**Heather Flatt**

| DATE | | EXPLANATION | PR | DEBIT | CREDIT | BALANCE |
|------|---|------------|-----|-------|--------|---------|
| 2017 | | | | | | |
| Oct. | 12 | | S3 | 7,300 | | 7,300 |
| | | | | | | |
| | | | | | | |

## Problem AII-5B (cont'd.)

### Amy Izon

| DATE | | EXPLANATION | PR | DEBIT | CREDIT | BALANCE |
|---|---|---|---|---|---|---|
| 2017 | | | | | | |
| Oct. | 15 | | S3 | 6,200 | | 6,200 |
| | | | | | | |
| | | | | | | |

### Jan Wildman

| DATE | | EXPLANATION | PR | DEBIT | CREDIT | BALANCE |
|---|---|---|---|---|---|---|
| 2017 | | | | | | |
| Sept. | 23 | | S2 | 8,400 | | 8,400 |
| Oct. | 2 | | CR3 | | 8,400 | -0- |
| | | | | | | |

### ACCOUNTS PAYABLE SUBLEDGER

### Fireside Company

| DATE | | EXPLANATION | PR | DEBIT | CREDIT | BALANCE |
|---|---|---|---|---|---|---|
| 2017 | | | | | | |
| Sept. | 28 | | P1 | | 8,520 | 8,520 |
| Oct. | 4 | | G2 | 920 | | 7,600 |
| | 6 | | CD4 | 7,600 | | -0- |
| | | | | | | |

### Green Supply Company

| DATE | | EXPLANATION | PR | DEBIT | CREDIT | BALANCE |
|---|---|---|---|---|---|---|
| 2017 | | | | | | |
| Oct. | 5 | | P2 | | 2,600 | 2,600 |
| | | | | | | |
| | | | | | | |
| | | | | | | |

### Sunshine Company

| DATE | | EXPLANATION | PR | DEBIT | CREDIT | BALANCE |
|---|---|---|---|---|---|---|
| 2017 | | | | | | |
| Oct. | 15 | | P2 | | 5,300 | 5,300 |
| | | | | | | |
| | | | | | | |

## Problem AII-5B (cont'd.)

### Walters Company

| DATE | | EXPLANATION | PR | DEBIT | CREDIT | BALANCE |
|---|---|---|---|---|---|---|
| 2017 | | | | | | |
| Oct. | 2 | | P2 | | 6,400 | 6,400 |
| | 12 | | CD4 | 6,400 | | -0- |
| | 15 | | P2 | | 7,980 | 7,980 |
| | | | | | | |
| | | | | | | |
| | | | | | | |

**Parts 2 and 3**

## GENERAL LEDGER

### Cash                                                    ACCOUNT NO. 101

| DATE | | EXPLANATION | PR | DEBIT | CREDIT | BALANCE |
|---|---|---|---|---|---|---|
| 2017 | | | | | | |
| Sept. | 30 | Balance | | | | 10,722 |
| | | | | | | |
| | | | | | | |

### Accounts Receivable                          ACCOUNT NO. 106

| DATE | | EXPLANATION | PR | DEBIT | CREDIT | BALANCE |
|---|---|---|---|---|---|---|
| 2017 | | | | | | |
| Sept. | 30 | Balance | | | | 8,400 |
| Oct. | 9 | | G2 | | 1,700 | 6,700 |
| | | | | | | |
| | | | | | | |
| | | | | | | |

### Merchandise Inventory                        ACCOUNT NO. 119

| DATE | | EXPLANATION | PR | DEBIT | CREDIT | BALANCE |
|---|---|---|---|---|---|---|
| 2017 | | | | | | |
| Sept. | 30 | Balance | | | | 133,940 |
| Oct. | 4 | | G2 | | 920 | 133,020 |
| | | | | | | |
| | | | | | | |
| | | | | | | |
| | | | | | | |

## Problem AII-5B (cont'd.)

### Office Supplies                                    ACCOUNT NO. 124

| DATE | | EXPLANATION | PR | DEBIT | CREDIT | BALANCE |
|---|---|---|---|---|---|---|
| 2017 | | | | | | |
| Sept. | 30 | Balance | | | | 1,214 |
| | | | | | | |
| | | | | | | |

### Store Supplies                                    ACCOUNT NO. 125

| DATE | | EXPLANATION | PR | DEBIT | CREDIT | BALANCE |
|---|---|---|---|---|---|---|
| 2017 | | | | | | |
| Sept. | 30 | Balance | | | | 692 |
| | | | | | | |
| | | | | | | |

### Store Equipment                                   ACCOUNT NO. 165

| DATE | | EXPLANATION | PR | DEBIT | CREDIT | BALANCE |
|---|---|---|---|---|---|---|
| 2017 | | | | | | |
| Sept. | 30 | Balance | | | | 84,258 |
| | | | | | | |
| | | | | | | |

### Accumulated Depreciation, Store Equipment         ACCOUNT NO. 166

| DATE | | EXPLANATION | PR | DEBIT | CREDIT | BALANCE |
|---|---|---|---|---|---|---|
| 2017 | | | | | | |
| Sept. | 30 | Balance | | | | 18,306 |
| | | | | | | |

### Accounts Payable                                  ACCOUNT NO. 201

| DATE | | EXPLANATION | PR | DEBIT | CREDIT | BALANCE |
|---|---|---|---|---|---|---|
| 2017 | | | | | | |
| Sept. | 30 | Balance | | | | 8,520 |
| Oct. | 4 | | G2 | 920 | | 7,600 |
| | | | | | | |
| | | | | | | |
| | | | | | | |
| | | | | | | |

## Problem AII-5B (cont'd.)

### Marlee Levin, Capital — ACCOUNT NO. 301

| DATE | EXPLANATION | PR | DEBIT | CREDIT | BALANCE |
|------|-------------|----|-------|--------|---------|
| 2017 | | | | | |
| Sept. 30 | Balance | | | | 212,400 |
| | | | | | |

### Marlee Levin, Withdrawals — ACCOUNT NO. 302

| DATE | EXPLANATION | PR | DEBIT | CREDIT | BALANCE |
|------|-------------|----|-------|--------|---------|
| 2017 | | | | | |
| | | | | | |
| | | | | | |

### Sales — ACCOUNT NO. 413

| DATE | EXPLANATION | PR | DEBIT | CREDIT | BALANCE |
|------|-------------|----|-------|--------|---------|
| 2017 | | | | | |
| | | | | | |
| | | | | | |

### Sales Returns and Allowances — ACCOUNT NO. 414

| DATE | EXPLANATION | PR | DEBIT | CREDIT | BALANCE |
|------|-------------|----|-------|--------|---------|
| 2017 | | | | | |
| Oct. 9 | | G2 | 1,700 | | 1,700 |
| | | | | | |

### Sales Discounts — ACCOUNT NO. 415

| DATE | EXPLANATION | PR | DEBIT | CREDIT | BALANCE |
|------|-------------|----|-------|--------|---------|
| 2017 | | | | | |
| | | | | | |
| | | | | | |

### Cost of Goods Sold — ACCOUNT NO. 502

| DATE | EXPLANATION | PR | DEBIT | CREDIT | BALANCE |
|------|-------------|----|-------|--------|---------|
| 2017 | | | | | |
| | | | | | |
| | | | | | |

### Sales Salaries Expense — ACCOUNT NO. 621

| DATE | EXPLANATION | PR | DEBIT | CREDIT | BALANCE |
|------|-------------|----|-------|--------|---------|
| 2017 | | | | | |
| Oct. 15 | | CD4 | 5,240 | | 5,240 |
| | | | | | |

## Problem AII-5B (cont'd.)

**Rent Expense**                                                    ACCOUNT NO. 640

| DATE | EXPLANATION | PR | DEBIT | CREDIT | BALANCE |
|------|-------------|----|-------|--------|---------|
| 2017 | | | | | |
| Oct.  2 | | CD4 | 4,500 | | 4,500 |
| | | | | | |

**Utilities Expense**                                              ACCOUNT NO. 690

| DATE | EXPLANATION | PR | DEBIT | CREDIT | BALANCE |
|------|-------------|----|-------|--------|---------|
| 2017 | | | | | |
| | | | | | |
| | | | | | |

## Part 4

### CHINA MOON PRODUCTS
### Trial Balance
### October 31, 2017

| | Debit | Credit |
|---|-------|--------|
| | | |
| | | |
| | | |
| | | |
| | | |
| | | |
| | | |
| | | |
| | | |
| | | |
| | | |
| | | |
| | | |
| | | |
| | | |
| | | |
| | | |
| | | |
| | | |
| | | |
| | | |
| | | |
| | | |
| | | |

**Problem AII-5B (concl'd.)**

### CHINA MOON PRODUCTS
#### Schedule of Accounts Receivable
#### October 31, 2017

| | | |
|---|---|---|
| | | |
| | | |
| | | |
| | | |
| | | |

### CHINA MOON PRODUCTS
#### Schedule of Accounts Payable
#### October 31, 2017

| | | |
|---|---|---|
| | | |
| | | |
| | | |
| | | |
| | | |
| | | |

**Problem AII-6B**

| | | | | Sales Journal | | Page 1 |
|---|---|---|---|---|---|---|
| Date | Account Debited | Invoice Number | PR | Accounts Receivable Dr. Sales Cr. | PR | Cost of Goods Sold Dr. Merch. Inventory Cr. |
| | | | | | | |
| | | | | | | |
| | | | | | | |
| | | | | | | |
| | | | | | | |
| | | | | | | |

| | | | | | Purchases Journal | | | | Page 1 |
|---|---|---|---|---|---|---|---|---|---|
| Date | Account Credited | Date of Invoice | Terms | PR | Accts. Payable Cr. | PR | Merch. Inventory Dr. | Office Supplies Dr. | Other Accounts Dr. |
| | | | | | | | | | |
| | | | | | | | | | |
| | | | | | | | | | |
| | | | | | | | | | |

*NOTE: An additional PR column has been added to both journals to facilitate the referencing of inventory entries into the inventory subledger.*

Name:_____

### Problem AII-6B (concl'd.)

**Inventory Subledger Record – Weighted Average Perpetual**

| Date | PR | Purchases | Sales (at cost) | Inventory Balance |
|------|----|-----------|-----------------|-------------------|
|      |    |           |                 |                   |

*Note: An additional PR column has been added to the Inventory Subledger Record to facilitate referencing of inventory entries.*

### *Problem AII-7B
Part 1        ACCOUNTS RECEIVABLE SUBLEDGER

**Kelly Grody**        ACCOUNT NO. 106-1

| DATE | EXPLANATION | PR | DEBIT | CREDIT | BALANCE |
|------|-------------|----|-------|--------|---------|
|      |             |    |       |        |         |
|      |             |    |       |        |         |
|      |             |    |       |        |         |
|      |             |    |       |        |         |

**Karen Harden**        ACCOUNT NO. 106-2

| DATE | EXPLANATION | PR | DEBIT | CREDIT | BALANCE |
|------|-------------|----|-------|--------|---------|
|      |             |    |       |        |         |
|      |             |    |       |        |         |
|      |             |    |       |        |         |
|      |             |    |       |        |         |

**\*Problem AII-7B (cont'd.)**

Paul Kane

ACCOUNT NO. 106-3

| DATE | EXPLANATION | PR | DEBIT | CREDIT | BALANCE |
|------|-------------|----|-------|--------|---------|
|      |             |    |       |        |         |
|      |             |    |       |        |         |
|      |             |    |       |        |         |

**Part 2**                    **ACCOUNTS PAYABLE SUBLEDGER**

Beech Company

ACCOUNT NO. 201-1

| DATE | EXPLANATION | PR | DEBIT | CREDIT | BALANCE |
|------|-------------|----|-------|--------|---------|
|      |             |    |       |        |         |
|      |             |    |       |        |         |
|      |             |    |       |        |         |
|      |             |    |       |        |         |

Blackwater Inc.

ACCOUNT NO. 201-2

| DATE | EXPLANATION | PR | DEBIT | CREDIT | BALANCE |
|------|-------------|----|-------|--------|---------|
|      |             |    |       |        |         |
|      |             |    |       |        |         |
|      |             |    |       |        |         |

Poppe's Supply

ACCOUNT NO. 201-3

| DATE | EXPLANATION | PR | DEBIT | CREDIT | BALANCE |
|------|-------------|----|-------|--------|---------|
|      |             |    |       |        |         |
|      |             |    |       |        |         |
|      |             |    |       |        |         |

Sprague Company

ACCOUNT NO. 201-4

| DATE | EXPLANATION | PR | DEBIT | CREDIT | BALANCE |
|------|-------------|----|-------|--------|---------|
|      |             |    |       |        |         |
|      |             |    |       |        |         |
|      |             |    |       |        |         |

**\*Problem AII-7B (cont'd.)**

**Part 3**

| Sales Journal | | | | Page 3 |
|---|---|---|---|---|
| Date | Account Debited | Invoice No. | PR | Accounts Receivable Dr. Sales Cr. |
|  |  |  |  |  |
|  |  |  |  |  |
|  |  |  |  |  |
|  |  |  |  |  |
|  |  |  |  |  |
|  |  |  |  |  |
|  |  |  |  |  |
|  |  |  |  |  |
|  |  |  |  |  |

| Cash Receipts Journal | | | | | | | | Page 3 |
|---|---|---|---|---|---|---|---|---|
| Date | Account Credited | PR | Explanation | Cash Dr. | Sales Disc. Dr. | Accts. Rec. Cr. | Sales Cr. | Other Accts. Cr. |
|  |  |  |  |  |  |  |  |  |
|  |  |  |  |  |  |  |  |  |
|  |  |  |  |  |  |  |  |  |
|  |  |  |  |  |  |  |  |  |
|  |  |  |  |  |  |  |  |  |
|  |  |  |  |  |  |  |  |  |
|  |  |  |  |  |  |  |  |  |
|  |  |  |  |  |  |  |  |  |
|  |  |  |  |  |  |  |  |  |
|  |  |  |  |  |  |  |  |  |

| Purchases Journal | | | | | | | | Page 3 |
|---|---|---|---|---|---|---|---|---|
| Date | Account Credited | Date of Invoice | Terms | PR | Accts. Payable Cr. | Purchases Dr. | Office Supplies Dr. | Other Accts. Dr. |
|  |  |  |  |  |  |  |  |  |
|  |  |  |  |  |  |  |  |  |
|  |  |  |  |  |  |  |  |  |
|  |  |  |  |  |  |  |  |  |
|  |  |  |  |  |  |  |  |  |
|  |  |  |  |  |  |  |  |  |
|  |  |  |  |  |  |  |  |  |
|  |  |  |  |  |  |  |  |  |
|  |  |  |  |  |  |  |  |  |

## *Problem AII-7B (concl'd.)

| Cash Disbursements Journal | | | | | | | | | Page 3 |
|---|---|---|---|---|---|---|---|---|---|
| Date | Ch. No. | Payee | Account Debited | PR | Cash Cr. | Purch. Disc. Cr. | Other Accounts Dr. | Accts. Payable Dr. |
|  |  |  |  |  |  |  |  |  |
|  |  |  |  |  |  |  |  |  |
|  |  |  |  |  |  |  |  |  |
|  |  |  |  |  |  |  |  |  |
|  |  |  |  |  |  |  |  |  |
|  |  |  |  |  |  |  |  |  |
|  |  |  |  |  |  |  |  |  |
|  |  |  |  |  |  |  |  |  |
|  |  |  |  |  |  |  |  |  |

### GENERAL JOURNAL                                    Page____

| Date | Account Titles and Explanation | PR | Debit | Credit |
|---|---|---|---|---|
|  |  |  |  |  |
|  |  |  |  |  |
|  |  |  |  |  |
|  |  |  |  |  |
|  |  |  |  |  |
|  |  |  |  |  |
|  |  |  |  |  |
|  |  |  |  |  |
|  |  |  |  |  |
|  |  |  |  |  |
|  |  |  |  |  |

## *Problem AII-8B

**Part 1**                                    GENERAL LEDGER

Cash                                    ACCOUNT NO. 101

| DATE | EXPLANATION | PR | DEBIT | CREDIT | BALANCE |
|---|---|---|---|---|---|
| 2017 |  |  |  |  |  |
| Jun. 30 | Balance brought forward |  |  |  | 190,000 |
|  |  |  |  |  |  |
|  |  |  |  |  |  |

Accounts Receivable                                    ACCOUNT NO. 106

| DATE | EXPLANATION | PR | DEBIT | CREDIT | BALANCE |
|---|---|---|---|---|---|
|  |  |  |  |  |  |
|  |  |  |  |  |  |
|  |  |  |  |  |  |

**\*Problem AII-8B (cont'd.)**

## Merchandise Inventory                    ACCOUNT NO. 119

| DATE | EXPLANATION | PR | DEBIT | CREDIT | BALANCE |
|------|-------------|----|----|----|----|
| 2017 | | | | | |
| Jun. 30 | Balance brought forward | | | | 334,000 |
| | | | | | |
| | | | | | |
| | | | | | |
| | | | | | |
| | | | | | |

## Office Supplies                         ACCOUNT NO. 124

| DATE | EXPLANATION | PR | DEBIT | CREDIT | BALANCE |
|------|-------------|----|----|----|----|
| | | | | | |
| | | | | | |
| | | | | | |

## Store Supplies                          ACCOUNT NO. 125

| DATE | EXPLANATION | PR | DEBIT | CREDIT | BALANCE |
|------|-------------|----|----|----|----|
| | | | | | |
| | | | | | |
| | | | | | |

## Store Equipment                         ACCOUNT NO. 165

| DATE | EXPLANATION | PR | DEBIT | CREDIT | BALANCE |
|------|-------------|----|----|----|----|
| | | | | | |
| | | | | | |
| | | | | | |

## Accounts Payable                        ACCOUNT NO. 201

| DATE | EXPLANATION | PR | DEBIT | CREDIT | BALANCE |
|------|-------------|----|----|----|----|
| | | | | | |
| | | | | | |
| | | | | | |
| | | | | | |
| | | | | | |
| | | | | | |

## Long-Term Notes Payable                 ACCOUNT NO. 251

| DATE | EXPLANATION | PR | DEBIT | CREDIT | BALANCE |
|------|-------------|----|----|----|----|
| 2017 | | | | | |
| Jun. 30 | Balance brought forward | | | | 334,000 |
| | | | | | |

**\*Problem All-8B (cont'd.)**

### Gene Duncan, Capital      ACCOUNT NO. 301

| DATE | EXPLANATION | PR | DEBIT | CREDIT | BALANCE |
|---|---|---|---|---|---|
| 2017 | | | | | |
| Jun. 30 | Balance brought forward | | | | 190,000 |
| | | | | | |

### Sales      ACCOUNT NO. 413

| DATE | EXPLANATION | PR | DEBIT | CREDIT | BALANCE |
|---|---|---|---|---|---|
| | | | | | |
| | | | | | |
| | | | | | |

### Sales Discounts      ACCOUNT NO. 415

| DATE | EXPLANATION | PR | DEBIT | CREDIT | BALANCE |
|---|---|---|---|---|---|
| | | | | | |
| | | | | | |
| | | | | | |

### Purchases      ACCOUNT NO. 505

| DATE | EXPLANATION | PR | DEBIT | CREDIT | BALANCE |
|---|---|---|---|---|---|
| | | | | | |
| | | | | | |
| | | | | | |

### Purchase Discounts      ACCOUNT NO. 506

| DATE | EXPLANATION | PR | DEBIT | CREDIT | BALANCE |
|---|---|---|---|---|---|
| | | | | | |
| | | | | | |
| | | | | | |

### Purchase Returns and Allowances      ACCOUNT NO. 507

| DATE | EXPLANATION | PR | DEBIT | CREDIT | BALANCE |
|---|---|---|---|---|---|
| | | | | | |
| | | | | | |
| | | | | | |

**\*Problem AII-8B (cont'd.)**

**Sales Salaries Expense**                                 **ACCOUNT NO. 621**

| DATE | EXPLANATION | PR | DEBIT | CREDIT | BALANCE |
|------|-------------|----|-------|--------|---------|
|      |             |    |       |        |         |
|      |             |    |       |        |         |
|      |             |    |       |        |         |

**Advertising Expense**                                    **ACCOUNT NO. 655**

| DATE | EXPLANATION | PR | DEBIT | CREDIT | BALANCE |
|------|-------------|----|-------|--------|---------|
|      |             |    |       |        |         |
|      |             |    |       |        |         |
|      |             |    |       |        |         |

*NOTE:  For Parts 2 and 3, journalizing and posting, continue journalizing the transactions in the accounts provided in \*Problem AII-7B.*

**Part 5**

**DUNCAN INDUSTRIES**

**Trial Balance**

**July 31, 2017**

|  | Debit | Credit |
|--|-------|--------|
|  |       |        |
|  |       |        |
|  |       |        |
|  |       |        |
|  |       |        |
|  |       |        |
|  |       |        |
|  |       |        |
|  |       |        |
|  |       |        |
|  |       |        |
|  |       |        |
|  |       |        |
|  |       |        |
|  |       |        |
|  |       |        |
|  |       |        |
|  |       |        |
|  |       |        |
|  |       |        |
|  |       |        |
|  |       |        |

Name:_____

**\*Problem AII-8B (concl'd.)**

### DUNCAN INDUSTRIES
#### Schedule of Accounts Receivable
#### July 31, 2017

| | | |
|---|---|---|
| | | |
| | | |
| | | |
| | | |
| | | |
| | | |
| | | |

### DUNCAN INDUSTRIES
#### Schedule of Accounts Payable
#### July 31, 2017

| | | |
|---|---|---|
| | | |
| | | |
| | | |
| | | |
| | | |
| | | |

## Comprehensive Problem

## Alpine Company - Perpetual

| | | | | Sales Journal | | Page 2 |
|---|---|---|---|---|---|---|
| Date | Account Debited | Invoice Number | PR | Accounts Receivable Dr. Sales Cr. | | Cost of Goods Sold Dr. Merchandise Inventory Cr. |
| | | | | | | |
| | | | | | | |
| | | | | | | |
| | | | | | | |
| | | | | | | |
| | | | | | | |
| | | | | | | |
| | | | | | | |

| | | | | | Purchases Journal | | | Page 2 |
|---|---|---|---|---|---|---|---|---|
| Date | Account Credited | Date of Invoice | Terms | PR | Accounts Payable Cr. | Merch. Inventory Dr. | Office Supplies Dr. | Other Accounts Dr. |
| | | | | | | | | |
| | | | | | | | | |
| | | | | | | | | |
| | | | | | | | | |
| | | | | | | | | |
| | | | | | | | | |
| | | | | | | | | |
| | | | | | | | | |
| | | | | | | | | |
| | | | | | | | | |

| | | | | | | Cash Receipts Journal | | | | Page 2 |
|---|---|---|---|---|---|---|---|---|---|---|
| Date | Account Credited | PR | Explanation | Cash Dr. | Sales Disc. Dr. | Accts. Rec. Cr. | Sales Cr. | Other Accts. Cr. | COGS Dr. Merch. Inv. Cr. |
| | | | | | | | | | |
| | | | | | | | | | |
| | | | | | | | | | |
| | | | | | | | | | |
| | | | | | | | | | |
| | | | | | | | | | |
| | | | | | | | | | |
| | | | | | | | | | |
| | | | | | | | | | |
| | | | | | | | | | |
| | | | | | | | | | |

## Comprehensive Problem

### Alpine Company - Perpetual (Continued)

| | | | | | | Cash Disbursements Journal | | | Page 2 |
|---|---|---|---|---|---|---|---|---|---|
| Date | Ch. No. | Payee | Account Debited | PR | Cash Cr. | Merch. Inventory Cr. | Other Accounts Dr. | Accounts Payable Dr. |
| | | | | | | | | | |
| | | | | | | | | | |
| | | | | | | | | | |
| | | | | | | | | | |
| | | | | | | | | | |
| | | | | | | | | | |
| | | | | | | | | | |
| | | | | | | | | | |
| | | | | | | | | | |
| | | | | | | | | | |
| | | | | | | | | | |
| | | | | | | | | | |
| | | | | | | | | | |
| | | | | | | | | | |
| | | | | | | | | | |

### GENERAL JOURNAL                    Page 3

| Date | Account Titles and Explanation | PR | Debit | Credit |
|---|---|---|---|---|
| | | | | |
| | | | | |
| | | | | |
| | | | | |
| | | | | |
| | | | | |
| | | | | |
| | | | | |
| | | | | |
| | | | | |
| | | | | |
| | | | | |
| | | | | |
| | | | | |
| | | | | |
| | | | | |
| | | | | |
| | | | | |
| | | | | |

Name:_____

**Comprehensive Problem**

**Alpine Company - Perpetual (Continued)**

| | GENERAL JOURNAL | | | Page 3 |
|---|---|---|---|---|

| Date | Account Titles and Explanation | PR | Debit | Credit |
|---|---|---|---|---|
| | | | | |
| | | | | |
| | | | | |
| | | | | |
| | | | | |
| | | | | |
| | | | | |
| | | | | |
| | | | | |
| | | | | |
| | | | | |
| | | | | |
| | | | | |
| | | | | |
| | | | | |
| | | | | |
| | | | | |
| | | | | |
| | | | | |
| | | | | |
| | | | | |
| | | | | |
| | | | | |
| | | | | |
| | | | | |
| | | | | |
| | | | | |
| | | | | |
| | | | | |
| | | | | |
| | | | | |
| | | | | |
| | | | | |
| | | | | |
| | | | | |
| | | | | |
| | | | | |
| | | | | |

## Comprehensive Problem

### Alpine Company - Perpetual (Continued)

| Date | Account Titles and Explanation | PR | Debit | Credit |
|------|-------------------------------|-----|-------|--------|
|      |                               |     |       |        |
|      |                               |     |       |        |
|      |                               |     |       |        |
|      |                               |     |       |        |
|      |                               |     |       |        |
|      |                               |     |       |        |
|      |                               |     |       |        |
|      |                               |     |       |        |
|      |                               |     |       |        |
|      |                               |     |       |        |
|      |                               |     |       |        |
|      |                               |     |       |        |
|      |                               |     |       |        |
|      |                               |     |       |        |
|      |                               |     |       |        |
|      |                               |     |       |        |
|      |                               |     |       |        |
|      |                               |     |       |        |
|      |                               |     |       |        |
|      |                               |     |       |        |
|      |                               |     |       |        |
|      |                               |     |       |        |
|      |                               |     |       |        |
|      |                               |     |       |        |
|      |                               |     |       |        |
|      |                               |     |       |        |
|      |                               |     |       |        |
|      |                               |     |       |        |
|      |                               |     |       |        |
|      |                               |     |       |        |
|      |                               |     |       |        |
|      |                               |     |       |        |
|      |                               |     |       |        |
|      |                               |     |       |        |
|      |                               |     |       |        |
|      |                               |     |       |        |
|      |                               |     |       |        |
|      |                               |     |       |        |
|      |                               |     |       |        |
|      |                               |     |       |        |
|      |                               |     |       |        |
|      |                               |     |       |        |

## Comprehensive Problem

### Alpine Company - Perpetual (Continued)

**Cash**  **ACCOUNT NO. 101**

| DATE | | EXPLANATION | PR | DEBIT | CREDIT | BALANCE |
|---|---|---|---|---|---|---|
| 2017 | | | | | | |
| Apr. | 30 | Balance | | | | 50,247 |
| | | | | | | |
| | | | | | | |
| | | | | | | |

**Accounts Receivable**  **ACCOUNT NO. 106**

| DATE | | EXPLANATION | PR | DEBIT | CREDIT | BALANCE |
|---|---|---|---|---|---|---|
| 2017 | | | | | | |
| Apr. | 30 | Balance | | | | 4,730 |
| | | | | | | |
| | | | | | | |
| | | | | | | |

**Merchandise Inventory**  **ACCOUNT NO. 119**

| DATE | | EXPLANATION | PR | DEBIT | CREDIT | BALANCE |
|---|---|---|---|---|---|---|
| 2017 | | | | | | |
| Apr. | 30 | Balance | | | | 220,080 |
| | | | | | | |
| | | | | | | |
| | | | | | | |
| | | | | | | |

**Office Supplies**  **ACCOUNT NO. 124**

| DATE | | EXPLANATION | PR | DEBIT | CREDIT | BALANCE |
|---|---|---|---|---|---|---|
| 2017 | | | | | | |
| Apr. | 30 | Balance | | | | 430 |
| | | | | | | |
| | | | | | | |

**Store Supplies**  **ACCOUNT NO. 125**

| DATE | | EXPLANATION | PR | DEBIT | CREDIT | BALANCE |
|---|---|---|---|---|---|---|
| 2017 | | | | | | |
| Apr. | 30 | Balance | | | | 2,447 |
| | | | | | | |
| | | | | | | |
| | | | | | | |

*Fundamental Accounting Principles,* **15ce,** Working Papers

**Comprehensive Problem**

**Alpine Company - Perpetual (Continued)**

### Prepaid Insurance — ACCOUNT NO. 128

| DATE | EXPLANATION | PR | DEBIT | CREDIT | BALANCE |
|------|-------------|----|-------|--------|---------|
| 2017 | | | | | |
| Apr. 30 | Balance | | | | 3,318 |
| | | | | | |
| | | | | | |
| | | | | | |

### Office Equipment — ACCOUNT NO. 163

| DATE | EXPLANATION | PR | DEBIT | CREDIT | BALANCE |
|------|-------------|----|-------|--------|---------|
| 2017 | | | | | |
| Apr. 30 | Balance | | | | 22,470 |
| | | | | | |
| | | | | | |
| | | | | | |
| | | | | | |

### Accumulated Depreciation, Office Equipment — ACCOUNT NO. 164

| DATE | EXPLANATION | PR | DEBIT | CREDIT | BALANCE |
|------|-------------|----|-------|--------|---------|
| 2017 | | | | | |
| Apr. 30 | Balance | | | | 9,898 |
| | | | | | |
| | | | | | |
| | | | | | |

### Store Equipment — ACCOUNT NO. 165

| DATE | EXPLANATION | PR | DEBIT | CREDIT | BALANCE |
|------|-------------|----|-------|--------|---------|
| 2017 | | | | | |
| Apr. 30 | Balance | | | | 38,920 |
| | | | | | |
| | | | | | |

### Accumulated Depreciation, Store Equipment — ACCOUNT NO. 166

| DATE | EXPLANATION | PR | DEBIT | CREDIT | BALANCE |
|------|-------------|----|-------|--------|---------|
| 2017 | | | | | |
| Apr. 30 | Balance | | | | 17,556 |
| | | | | | |
| | | | | | |
| | | | | | |

**Comprehensive Problem**

**Alpine Company - Perpetual (Continued)**

### Accounts Payable                    ACCOUNT NO. 201

| DATE | EXPLANATION | PR | DEBIT | CREDIT | BALANCE |
|------|-------------|----|-------|--------|---------|
| 2017 | | | | | |
| Apr. 30 | Balance | | | | 7,100 |
| | | | | | |
| | | | | | |
| | | | | | |
| | | | | | |
| | | | | | |
| | | | | | |

### Clint Barry, Capital                    ACCOUNT NO. 301

| DATE | EXPLANATION | PR | DEBIT | CREDIT | BALANCE |
|------|-------------|----|-------|--------|---------|
| 2017 | | | | | |
| Apr. 30 | Balance | | | | 308,088 |
| | | | | | |
| | | | | | |
| | | | | | |

### Clint Barry, Withdrawals                    ACCOUNT NO. 302

| DATE | EXPLANATION | PR | DEBIT | CREDIT | BALANCE |
|------|-------------|----|-------|--------|---------|
| 2017 | | | | | |
| | | | | | |
| | | | | | |
| | | | | | |

### Sales                    ACCOUNT NO. 413

| DATE | EXPLANATION | PR | DEBIT | CREDIT | BALANCE |
|------|-------------|----|-------|--------|---------|
| | | | | | |
| | | | | | |
| | | | | | |
| | | | | | |
| | | | | | |

### Sales Discounts                    ACCOUNT NO. 414

| DATE | EXPLANATION | PR | DEBIT | CREDIT | BALANCE |
|------|-------------|----|-------|--------|---------|
| | | | | | |
| | | | | | |
| | | | | | |
| | | | | | |

**Comprehensive Problem**

**Alpine Company - Perpetual (Continued)**

### Sales Returns and Allowances — ACCOUNT NO. 415

| DATE | EXPLANATION | PR | DEBIT | CREDIT | BALANCE |
|------|-------------|----|----|----|----|
|  |  |  |  |  |  |
|  |  |  |  |  |  |
|  |  |  |  |  |  |
|  |  |  |  |  |  |

### Cost of Goods Sold — ACCOUNT NO. 502

| DATE | EXPLANATION | PR | DEBIT | CREDIT | BALANCE |
|------|-------------|----|----|----|----|
|  |  |  |  |  |  |
|  |  |  |  |  |  |
|  |  |  |  |  |  |
|  |  |  |  |  |  |
|  |  |  |  |  |  |
|  |  |  |  |  |  |

### Depreciation Expense, Office Equipment — ACCOUNT NO. 612

| DATE | EXPLANATION | PR | DEBIT | CREDIT | BALANCE |
|------|-------------|----|----|----|----|
|  |  |  |  |  |  |
|  |  |  |  |  |  |
|  |  |  |  |  |  |
|  |  |  |  |  |  |

### Depreciation Expense, Store Equipment — ACCOUNT NO. 613

| DATE | EXPLANATION | PR | DEBIT | CREDIT | BALANCE |
|------|-------------|----|----|----|----|
|  |  |  |  |  |  |
|  |  |  |  |  |  |
|  |  |  |  |  |  |
|  |  |  |  |  |  |

### Office Salaries Expense — ACCOUNT NO. 620

| DATE | EXPLANATION | PR | DEBIT | CREDIT | BALANCE |
|------|-------------|----|----|----|----|
|  |  |  |  |  |  |
|  |  |  |  |  |  |
|  |  |  |  |  |  |
|  |  |  |  |  |  |
|  |  |  |  |  |  |

**Comprehensive Problem**

**Alpine Company - Perpetual (Continued)**

### Sales Salaries Expense — ACCOUNT NO. 621

| DATE | EXPLANATION | PR | DEBIT | CREDIT | BALANCE |
|------|-------------|----|-------|--------|---------|
|      |             |    |       |        |         |
|      |             |    |       |        |         |
|      |             |    |       |        |         |
|      |             |    |       |        |         |
|      |             |    |       |        |         |

### Insurance Expense — ACCOUNT NO. 637

| DATE | EXPLANATION | PR | DEBIT | CREDIT | BALANCE |
|------|-------------|----|-------|--------|---------|
|      |             |    |       |        |         |
|      |             |    |       |        |         |
|      |             |    |       |        |         |
|      |             |    |       |        |         |

### Rent Expense, Office Space — ACCOUNT NO. 641

| DATE | EXPLANATION | PR | DEBIT | CREDIT | BALANCE |
|------|-------------|----|-------|--------|---------|
|      |             |    |       |        |         |
|      |             |    |       |        |         |
|      |             |    |       |        |         |
|      |             |    |       |        |         |

### Rent Expense, Selling Space — ACCOUNT NO. 642

| DATE | EXPLANATION | PR | DEBIT | CREDIT | BALANCE |
|------|-------------|----|-------|--------|---------|
|      |             |    |       |        |         |
|      |             |    |       |        |         |
|      |             |    |       |        |         |
|      |             |    |       |        |         |

### Office Supplies Expense — ACCOUNT NO. 650

| DATE | EXPLANATION | PR | DEBIT | CREDIT | BALANCE |
|------|-------------|----|-------|--------|---------|
|      |             |    |       |        |         |
|      |             |    |       |        |         |
|      |             |    |       |        |         |
|      |             |    |       |        |         |

## Comprehensive Problem

### Alpine Company - Perpetual (Continued)

**Store Supplies Expense**                                    ACCOUNT NO. 651

| DATE | EXPLANATION | PR | DEBIT | CREDIT | BALANCE |
|------|-------------|----|----|----|----|
| 2017 | | | | | |
| | | | | | |
| | | | | | |

**Utilities Expense**                                    ACCOUNT NO. 690

| DATE | EXPLANATION | PR | DEBIT | CREDIT | BALANCE |
|------|-------------|----|----|----|----|
| 2017 | | | | | |
| | | | | | |
| | | | | | |

**Income Summary**                                    ACCOUNT NO. 901

| DATE | EXPLANATION | PR | DEBIT | CREDIT | BALANCE |
|------|-------------|----|----|----|----|
| | | | | | |
| | | | | | |
| | | | | | |
| | | | | | |

### ACCOUNTS RECEIVABLE LEDGER

**NAME**        Deaver Corp.

| DATE | EXPLANATION | PR | DEBIT | CREDIT | BALANCE |
|------|-------------|----|----|----|----|
| | | | | | |
| | | | | | |
| | | | | | |

**NAME**        Essex Company

| DATE | EXPLANATION | PR | DEBIT | CREDIT | BALANCE |
|------|-------------|----|----|----|----|
| | | | | | |
| | | | | | |
| | | | | | |
| | | | | | |

**NAME**        Nabors, Inc.

| DATE | EXPLANATION | PR | DEBIT | CREDIT | BALANCE |
|------|-------------|----|----|----|----|
| 2017 | | | | | |
| Apr. 28 | | S2 | 4,730 | | 4,730 |
| | | | | | |
| | | | | | |

## Comprehensive Problem

### Alpine Company - Perpetual (Continued)

NAME      Oscar Services.

| DATE | EXPLANATION | PR | DEBIT | CREDIT | BALANCE |
|------|-------------|----|-------|--------|---------|
| 2017 | | | | | |
| | | | | | |
| | | | | | |

### ACCOUNTS PAYABLE LEDGER

NAME      Chandler Corp.

| DATE | EXPLANATION | PR | DEBIT | CREDIT | BALANCE |
|------|-------------|----|-------|--------|---------|
| 2017 | | | | | |
| | | | | | |
| | | | | | |

NAME      Gale, Inc.

| DATE | EXPLANATION | PR | DEBIT | CREDIT | BALANCE |
|------|-------------|----|-------|--------|---------|
| 2017 | | | | | |
| | | | | | |
| | | | | | |

NAME      Parkay Products

| DATE | EXPLANATION | PR | DEBIT | CREDIT | BALANCE |
|------|-------------|----|-------|--------|---------|
| 2017 | | | | | |
| Apr. 29 | | P2 | | 7,100 | 7,100 |
| | | | | | |
| | | | | | |
| | | | | | |

NAME      Thompson Supply Co.

| DATE | EXPLANATION | PR | DEBIT | CREDIT | BALANCE |
|------|-------------|----|-------|--------|---------|
| | | | | | |
| | | | | | |
| | | | | | |
| | | | | | |
| | | | | | |

**Comprehensive Problem**

**Alpine Company - Perpetual (Continued)**

Alpine Company
Work Sheet
For Month Ended May 31, 2017

| Account Titles | Trial Balance | | Adjustments | | Income Statement | | Balance Sheet and Statement of Changes in Equity | |
|---|---|---|---|---|---|---|---|---|
| | Debit | Credit | Debit | Credit | Debit | Credit | Debit | Credit |
| | | | | | | | | |
| | | | | | | | | |
| | | | | | | | | |
| | | | | | | | | |
| | | | | | | | | |
| | | | | | | | | |
| | | | | | | | | |
| | | | | | | | | |
| | | | | | | | | |
| | | | | | | | | |
| | | | | | | | | |
| | | | | | | | | |
| | | | | | | | | |
| | | | | | | | | |
| | | | | | | | | |
| | | | | | | | | |
| | | | | | | | | |
| | | | | | | | | |
| | | | | | | | | |

**Comprehensive Problem**

**Alpine Company - Perpetual (Continued)**

| Alpine Company | | | |
|---|---|---|---|
| Income Statement | | | |
| For Month Ended May 31, 2017 | | | |
| | | | |
| | | | |
| | | | |
| | | | |
| | | | |
| | | | |
| | | | |
| | | | |
| | | | |
| | | | |
| | | | |
| | | | |
| | | | |
| | | | |
| | | | |
| | | | |
| | | | |
| | | | |
| | | | |
| | | | |
| | | | |
| | | | |
| | | | |
| | | | |
| | | | |
| | | | |
| | | | |
| | | | |
| | | | |
| | | | |

**Comprehensive Problem**

**Alpine Company - Perpetual (Continued)**

Name:_____

**Alpine Company**

**Statement of Changes in Equity**

**For Month Ended May 31, 2017**

| | | | |
|---|---|---|---|
| | | | |
| | | | |
| | | | |
| | | | |
| | | | |
| | | | |
| | | | |

**Alpine Company**

**Balance Sheet**

**May 31, 2017**

| | | | |
|---|---|---|---|
| | | | |
| | | | |
| | | | |
| | | | |
| | | | |
| | | | |
| | | | |
| | | | |
| | | | |
| | | | |
| | | | |
| | | | |
| | | | |
| | | | |
| | | | |
| | | | |
| | | | |
| | | | |
| | | | |
| | | | |
| | | | |
| | | | |

**Comprehensive Problem**

**Alpine Company - Perpetual (Concluded)**

### Alpine Company
### Post-Closing Trial Balance
### May 31, 2017

| | Debit | Credit |
|---|---|---|
| | | |
| | | |
| | | |
| | | |
| | | |
| | | |
| | | |
| | | |
| | | |
| | | |
| | | |
| | | |
| | | |
| | | |
| | | |
| | | |
| | | |
| | | |

### Alpine Company
### Schedule of Accounts Receivable
### May 31, 2017

| | | |
|---|---|---|
| | | |
| | | |
| | | |
| | | |

### Alpine Company
### Schedule of Accounts Payable
### May 31, 2017

| | | |
|---|---|---|
| | | |
| | | |
| | | |
| | | |
| | | |

**Comprehensive Problem**

Alpine Company - Periodic

| | Sales Journal | | | Page 2 |
|---|---|---|---|---|
| **Date** | **Account Debited** | **Invoice Number** | **PR** | **Accts. Receivable Dr. Sales Cr.** |
| | | | | |
| | | | | |
| | | | | |
| | | | | |
| | | | | |
| | | | | |
| | | | | |

| | | | | Purchases Journal | | | Page 2 | |
|---|---|---|---|---|---|---|---|---|
| **Date** | **Account Credited** | **Date of Inv.** | **Terms** | **PR** | **Accts. Pay. Cr.** | **Purchases Dr.** | **Office Supplies Dr.** | **Other Accts. Dr.** |
| | | | | | | | | |
| | | | | | | | | |
| | | | | | | | | |
| | | | | | | | | |
| | | | | | | | | |
| | | | | | | | | |
| | | | | | | | | |
| | | | | | | | | |
| | | | | | | | | |
| | | | | | | | | |

| | | | Cash Receipts Journal | | | | Page 2 | |
|---|---|---|---|---|---|---|---|---|
| **Date** | **Accounts Credited** | **Explanation** | **PR** | **Cash Dr.** | **Sales Disc. Dr.** | **Accts. Rec. Cr.** | **Sales Cr.** | **Other Accts. Cr.** |
| | | | | | | | | |
| | | | | | | | | |
| | | | | | | | | |
| | | | | | | | | |
| | | | | | | | | |
| | | | | | | | | |
| | | | | | | | | |
| | | | | | | | | |
| | | | | | | | | |

## Comprehensive Problem

### Alpine Company - Periodic (Continued)

| | | | Cash Disbursements Journal | | | | Page 2 | |
|---|---|---|---|---|---|---|---|---|
| Date | Ch. No. | Payee | Account Debited | PR | Cash Cr. | Purch. Disc. Cr. | Other Accts. Dr. | Accts. Payable Dr. |
| | | | | | | | | |
| | | | | | | | | |
| | | | | | | | | |
| | | | | | | | | |
| | | | | | | | | |
| | | | | | | | | |
| | | | | | | | | |
| | | | | | | | | |
| | | | | | | | | |
| | | | | | | | | |
| | | | | | | | | |
| | | | | | | | | |
| | | | | | | | | |
| | | | | | | | | |

### GENERAL JOURNAL                                    Page 3

| Date | Account Titles and Explanation | PR | Debit | Credit |
|---|---|---|---|---|
| | | | | |
| | | | | |
| | | | | |
| | | | | |
| | | | | |
| | | | | |
| | | | | |
| | | | | |
| | | | | |
| | | | | |
| | | | | |
| | | | | |
| | | | | |
| | | | | |
| | | | | |
| | | | | |
| | | | | |
| | | | | |
| | | | | |
| | | | | |
| | | | | |
| | | | | |
| | | | | |

**Comprehensive Problem**

Alpine Company - Periodic (Continued)

| | GENERAL JOURNAL | | | Page 3 |

| Date | Account Titles and Explanation | PR | Debit | Credit |
|------|-------------------------------|----|----|----|
| | | | | |
| | | | | |
| | | | | |
| | | | | |
| | | | | |
| | | | | |
| | | | | |
| | | | | |
| | | | | |
| | | | | |
| | | | | |
| | | | | |
| | | | | |
| | | | | |
| | | | | |
| | | | | |
| | | | | |
| | | | | |
| | | | | |
| | | | | |
| | | | | |
| | | | | |
| | | | | |
| | | | | |
| | | | | |
| | | | | |
| | | | | |
| | | | | |
| | | | | |
| | | | | |
| | | | | |
| | | | | |
| | | | | |
| | | | | |
| | | | | |
| | | | | |
| | | | | |
| | | | | |
| | | | | |

**Comprehensive Problem**

**Alpine Company - Periodic (Continued)**

## GENERAL LEDGER

### Cash                                                                ACCOUNT NO. 101

| DATE | EXPLANATION | PR | DEBIT | CREDIT | BALANCE |
|------|-------------|----|-------|--------|---------|
| 2017 | | | | | |
| Apr. 30 | Balance | | | | 50,247 |
| | | | | | |
| | | | | | |

### Accounts Receivable                                          ACCOUNT NO. 106

| DATE | EXPLANATION | PR | DEBIT | CREDIT | BALANCE |
|------|-------------|----|-------|--------|---------|
| 2017 | | | | | |
| Apr. 30 | Balance | | | | 4,730 |
| | | | | | |
| | | | | | |
| | | | | | |

### Merchandise Inventory                                       ACCOUNT NO. 119

| DATE | EXPLANATION | PR | DEBIT | CREDIT | BALANCE |
|------|-------------|----|-------|--------|---------|
| 2017 | | | | | |
| Apr. 30 | Balance | | | | 220,080 |
| | | | | | |
| | | | | | |
| | | | | | |

### Office Supplies                                                  ACCOUNT NO. 124

| DATE | EXPLANATION | PR | DEBIT | CREDIT | BALANCE |
|------|-------------|----|-------|--------|---------|
| 2017 | | | | | |
| Apr. 30 | Balance | | | | 430 |
| | | | | | |
| | | | | | |
| | | | | | |

### Store Supplies                                                    ACCOUNT NO. 125

| DATE | EXPLANATION | PR | DEBIT | CREDIT | BALANCE |
|------|-------------|----|-------|--------|---------|
| 2017 | | | | | |
| Apr. 30 | Balance | | | | 2,447 |
| | | | | | |
| | | | | | |
| | | | | | |

**Comprehensive Problem**

**Alpine Company - Periodic (Continued)**

### Prepaid Insurance      ACCOUNT NO. 128

| DATE | EXPLANATION | PR | DEBIT | CREDIT | BALANCE |
|------|-------------|----|-------|--------|---------|
| 2017 | | | | | |
| Apr. 30 | Balance | | | | 3,318 |
| | | | | | |
| | | | | | |
| | | | | | |

### Office Equipment      ACCOUNT NO. 163

| DATE | EXPLANATION | PR | DEBIT | CREDIT | BALANCE |
|------|-------------|----|-------|--------|---------|
| 2017 | | | | | |
| Apr. 30 | Balance | | | | 22,470 |
| | | | | | |
| | | | | | |
| | | | | | |

### Accumulated Depreciation, Office Equipment      ACCOUNT NO. 164

| DATE | EXPLANATION | PR | DEBIT | CREDIT | BALANCE |
|------|-------------|----|-------|--------|---------|
| 2017 | | | | | |
| Apr. 30 | Balance | | | | 9,898 |
| | | | | | |
| | | | | | |

### Store Equipment      ACCOUNT NO. 165

| DATE | EXPLANATION | PR | DEBIT | CREDIT | BALANCE |
|------|-------------|----|-------|--------|---------|
| 2017 | | | | | |
| Apr. 30 | Balance | | | | 38,920 |
| | | | | | |
| | | | | | |

### Accumulated Depreciation, Store Equipment      ACCOUNT NO. 166

| DATE | EXPLANATION | PR | DEBIT | CREDIT | BALANCE |
|------|-------------|----|-------|--------|---------|
| 2017 | | | | | |
| Apr. 30 | Balance | | | | 17,556 |
| | | | | | |
| | | | | | |

**Comprehensive Problem**

**Alpine Company - Periodic (Continued)**

### Accounts Payable                                          ACCOUNT NO. 201

| DATE | EXPLANATION | PR | DEBIT | CREDIT | BALANCE |
|------|-------------|----|-------|--------|---------|
| 20171 | | | | | |
| Apr.  30 | Balance | | | | 7,100 |
| | | | | | |
| | | | | | |
| | | | | | |
| | | | | | |

### Clint Barry, Capital                                       ACCOUNT NO. 301

| DATE | EXPLANATION | PR | DEBIT | CREDIT | BALANCE |
|------|-------------|----|-------|--------|---------|
| 2017 | | | | | |
| Apr.  30 | Balance | | | | 308,088 |
| | | | | | |
| | | | | | |

### Clint Barry, Withdrawals                                   ACCOUNT NO. 302

| DATE | EXPLANATION | PR | DEBIT | CREDIT | BALANCE |
|------|-------------|----|-------|--------|---------|
| 2017 | | | | | |
| | | | | | |
| | | | | | |
| | | | | | |

### Sales                                                      ACCOUNT NO. 413

| DATE | EXPLANATION | PR | DEBIT | CREDIT | BALANCE |
|------|-------------|----|-------|--------|---------|
| | | | | | |
| | | | | | |
| | | | | | |
| | | | | | |

### Sales Discounts                                            ACCOUNT NO. 414

| DATE | EXPLANATION | PR | DEBIT | CREDIT | BALANCE |
|------|-------------|----|-------|--------|---------|
| | | | | | |
| | | | | | |
| | | | | | |

### Sales Returns and Allowances                               ACCOUNT NO. 415

| DATE | EXPLANATION | PR | DEBIT | CREDIT | BALANCE |
|------|-------------|----|-------|--------|---------|
| | | | | | |
| | | | | | |
| | | | | | |

Name:_____

## Comprehensive Problem

### Alpine Company - Periodic (Continued)

**Purchases**          **ACCOUNT NO. 505**

| DATE | EXPLANATION | PR | DEBIT | CREDIT | BALANCE |
|------|-------------|----|-------|--------|---------|
|      |             |    |       |        |         |
|      |             |    |       |        |         |
|      |             |    |       |        |         |

**Purchases Discounts**          **ACCOUNT NO. 506**

| DATE | EXPLANATION | PR | DEBIT | CREDIT | BALANCE |
|------|-------------|----|-------|--------|---------|
|      |             |    |       |        |         |
|      |             |    |       |        |         |
|      |             |    |       |        |         |

**Purchases Returns and Allowances**      **ACCOUNT NO. 507**

| DATE | EXPLANATION | PR | DEBIT | CREDIT | BALANCE |
|------|-------------|----|-------|--------|---------|
|      |             |    |       |        |         |
|      |             |    |       |        |         |
|      |             |    |       |        |         |

**Depreciation Expense, Office Equipment**      **ACCOUNT NO. 612**

| DATE | EXPLANATION | PR | DEBIT | CREDIT | BALANCE |
|------|-------------|----|-------|--------|---------|
|      |             |    |       |        |         |
|      |             |    |       |        |         |
|      |             |    |       |        |         |

**Depreciation Expense, Store Equipment**      **ACCOUNT NO. 613**

| DATE | EXPLANATION | PR | DEBIT | CREDIT | BALANCE |
|------|-------------|----|-------|--------|---------|
|      |             |    |       |        |         |
|      |             |    |       |        |         |
|      |             |    |       |        |         |
|      |             |    |       |        |         |

**Office Salaries Expense**          **ACCOUNT NO. 620**

| DATE | EXPLANATION | PR | DEBIT | CREDIT | BALANCE |
|------|-------------|----|-------|--------|---------|
|      |             |    |       |        |         |
|      |             |    |       |        |         |
|      |             |    |       |        |         |
|      |             |    |       |        |         |

**Comprehensive Problem**

**Alpine Company - Periodic (Continued)**

### Sales Salaries Expense — ACCOUNT NO. 621

| DATE | EXPLANATION | PR | DEBIT | CREDIT | BALANCE |
|------|-------------|----|-------|--------|---------|
|  |  |  |  |  |  |
|  |  |  |  |  |  |
|  |  |  |  |  |  |
|  |  |  |  |  |  |
|  |  |  |  |  |  |

### Insurance Expense — ACCOUNT NO. 637

| DATE | EXPLANATION | PR | DEBIT | CREDIT | BALANCE |
|------|-------------|----|-------|--------|---------|
|  |  |  |  |  |  |
|  |  |  |  |  |  |
|  |  |  |  |  |  |
|  |  |  |  |  |  |

### Rent Expense, Office Space — ACCOUNT NO. 641

| DATE | EXPLANATION | PR | DEBIT | CREDIT | BALANCE |
|------|-------------|----|-------|--------|---------|
|  |  |  |  |  |  |
|  |  |  |  |  |  |
|  |  |  |  |  |  |
|  |  |  |  |  |  |

### Rent Expense, Selling Space — ACCOUNT NO. 642

| DATE | EXPLANATION | PR | DEBIT | CREDIT | BALANCE |
|------|-------------|----|-------|--------|---------|
|  |  |  |  |  |  |
|  |  |  |  |  |  |
|  |  |  |  |  |  |
|  |  |  |  |  |  |

### Office Supplies Expense — ACCOUNT NO. 650

| DATE | EXPLANATION | PR | DEBIT | CREDIT | BALANCE |
|------|-------------|----|-------|--------|---------|
|  |  |  |  |  |  |
|  |  |  |  |  |  |
|  |  |  |  |  |  |
|  |  |  |  |  |  |

Name:_____

## Comprehensive Problem

### Alpine Company - Periodic (Continued)

Store Supplies Expense          **ACCOUNT NO. 651**

| DATE | EXPLANATION | PR | DEBIT | CREDIT | BALANCE |
|------|-------------|----|-------|--------|---------|
| 2017 | | | | | |
| | | | | | |
| | | | | | |

Utilities Expense          **ACCOUNT NO. 690**

| DATE | EXPLANATION | PR | DEBIT | CREDIT | BALANCE |
|------|-------------|----|-------|--------|---------|
| 2017 | | | | | |
| | | | | | |
| | | | | | |

Income Summary          **ACCOUNT NO. 901**

| DATE | EXPLANATION | PR | DEBIT | CREDIT | BALANCE |
|------|-------------|----|-------|--------|---------|
| | | | | | |
| | | | | | |
| | | | | | |
| | | | | | |

### ACCOUNTS RECEIVABLE LEDGER

**NAME**     Deaver Corp.

| DATE | EXPLANATION | PR | DEBIT | CREDIT | BALANCE |
|------|-------------|----|-------|--------|---------|
| | | | | | |
| | | | | | |
| | | | | | |

**NAME**     Essex Company

| DATE | EXPLANATION | PR | DEBIT | CREDIT | BALANCE |
|------|-------------|----|-------|--------|---------|
| | | | | | |
| | | | | | |
| | | | | | |
| | | | | | |

**NAME**     Nabors, Inc.

| DATE | EXPLANATION | PR | DEBIT | CREDIT | BALANCE |
|------|-------------|----|-------|--------|---------|
| 2017 | | | | | |
| Apr. 28 | | S2 | 4,730 | | 4,730 |
| | | | | | |
| | | | | | |

## Comprehensive Problem

## Alpine Company - Periodic (Continued)

NAME          Oscar Services.

| DATE | EXPLANATION | PR | DEBIT | CREDIT | BALANCE |
|------|-------------|----|-------|--------|---------|
| 2017 |             |    |       |        |         |
|      |             |    |       |        |         |
|      |             |    |       |        |         |

## ACCOUNTS PAYABLE LEDGER

NAME          Chandler Corp.

| DATE | EXPLANATION | PR | DEBIT | CREDIT | BALANCE |
|------|-------------|----|-------|--------|---------|
| 2017 |             |    |       |        |         |
|      |             |    |       |        |         |

NAME          Gale, Inc.

| DATE | EXPLANATION | PR | DEBIT | CREDIT | BALANCE |
|------|-------------|----|-------|--------|---------|
| 2017 |             |    |       |        |         |
|      |             |    |       |        |         |
|      |             |    |       |        |         |

NAME          Parkay Products

| DATE | EXPLANATION | PR | DEBIT | CREDIT | BALANCE |
|---------|-------------|----|-------|--------|---------|
| 2017    |             |    |       |        |         |
| Apr.  29 |            | P2 |       | 7,100  | 7,100   |
|         |             |    |       |        |         |
|         |             |    |       |        |         |
|         |             |    |       |        |         |

NAME          Thompson Supply Co.

| DATE | EXPLANATION | PR | DEBIT | CREDIT | BALANCE |
|------|-------------|----|-------|--------|---------|
|      |             |    |       |        |         |
|      |             |    |       |        |         |
|      |             |    |       |        |         |
|      |             |    |       |        |         |
|      |             |    |       |        |         |

**Comprehensive Problem**

Alpine Company - Periodic (Continued)

**Alpine Company**
**Work Sheet**
**For Month Ended May 31, 2017**

| Account Titles | Trial Balance | | Adjustments | | Income Statement | | Balance Sheet and Statement of Changes in Equity | |
|---|---|---|---|---|---|---|---|---|
| | Debit | Credit | Debit | Credit | Debit | Credit | Debit | Credit |
| | | | | | | | | |
| | | | | | | | | |
| | | | | | | | | |
| | | | | | | | | |
| | | | | | | | | |
| | | | | | | | | |
| | | | | | | | | |
| | | | | | | | | |
| | | | | | | | | |
| | | | | | | | | |
| | | | | | | | | |
| | | | | | | | | |
| | | | | | | | | |
| | | | | | | | | |
| | | | | | | | | |
| | | | | | | | | |
| | | | | | | | | |
| | | | | | | | | |
| | | | | | | | | |
| | | | | | | | | |

**Comprehensive Problem**

Alpine Company - Periodic (Continued)

**Alpine Company**

**Income Statement**

**For Month Ended May 31, 2017**

| | | | | |
|---|---|---|---|---|
| | | | | |
| | | | | |
| | | | | |
| | | | | |
| | | | | |
| | | | | |
| | | | | |
| | | | | |
| | | | | |
| | | | | |
| | | | | |
| | | | | |
| | | | | |
| | | | | |
| | | | | |
| | | | | |
| | | | | |
| | | | | |
| | | | | |
| | | | | |
| | | | | |
| | | | | |
| | | | | |
| | | | | |
| | | | | |
| | | | | |
| | | | | |
| | | | | |
| | | | | |
| | | | | |
| | | | | |
| | | | | |
| | | | | |
| | | | | |
| | | | | |
| | | | | |
| | | | | |
| | | | | |

**Comprehensive Problem**

Alpine Company - Periodic (Continued)

### Alpine Company
### Statement of Changes in Equity
### For Month Ended May 31, 2017

|  |  |  |
|---|---|---|
|  |  |  |
|  |  |  |
|  |  |  |
|  |  |  |
|  |  |  |
|  |  |  |

### Alpine Company
### Balance Sheet
### May 31, 2017

|  |  |  |  |
|---|---|---|---|
|  |  |  |  |
|  |  |  |  |
|  |  |  |  |
|  |  |  |  |
|  |  |  |  |
|  |  |  |  |
|  |  |  |  |
|  |  |  |  |
|  |  |  |  |
|  |  |  |  |
|  |  |  |  |
|  |  |  |  |
|  |  |  |  |
|  |  |  |  |
|  |  |  |  |
|  |  |  |  |
|  |  |  |  |
|  |  |  |  |
|  |  |  |  |
|  |  |  |  |
|  |  |  |  |
|  |  |  |  |
|  |  |  |  |
|  |  |  |  |
|  |  |  |  |
|  |  |  |  |

**Comprehensive Problem**

**Alpine Company - Periodic (Concluded)**

**Alpine Company**
**Post-Closing Trial Balance**
**May 31, 2017**

|  | Debit | Credit |
|---|---|---|
|  |  |  |
|  |  |  |
|  |  |  |
|  |  |  |
|  |  |  |
|  |  |  |
|  |  |  |
|  |  |  |
|  |  |  |
|  |  |  |
|  |  |  |
|  |  |  |
|  |  |  |
|  |  |  |
|  |  |  |
|  |  |  |
|  |  |  |
|  |  |  |
|  |  |  |
|  |  |  |

**Alpine Company**
**Schedule of Accounts Receivable**
**May 31, 2017**

|  |  |  |
|---|---|---|
|  |  |  |
|  |  |  |
|  |  |  |
|  |  |  |

**Alpine Company**
**Schedule of Accounts Payable**
**May 31, 2017**

|  |  |  |
|---|---|---|
|  |  |  |
|  |  |  |
|  |  |  |
|  |  |  |